Glencoe Marketing Series

marketingseries.glencoe.com

FASHION MARKETING

DESIGNERS

STYLE

In partnership with

Gigi Ekstrom
Margaret Justiss

Glencoe

New York, New York   Columbus, Ohio   Chicago, Illinois   Peoria, Illinois   Woodland Hills, California

About the Authors

GIGI GANO EKSTROM served as the teacher/coordinator for the award-winning Marketing Education and Academy of Travel and Tourism programs at Thomas Jefferson High School in Dallas, Texas. She was selected as the Teacher of the Year by the Rotary Club of Dallas for 1998, the Region IV ACTE Outstanding New Career and Technical Education Teacher for 2000, and the National ACTE Outstanding New Career and Technical Education Teacher for 2001. She holds a Bachelor of Business Administration from the University of Texas at Arlington and a Master of International Management from The American Graduate School of International Management.

MARGARET JUSTISS began her teaching career after 17 years in the fashion industry. She rose from buyer to assistant controller with a major department store before managing a women's specialty store. She then served as a training sponsor to career and technical education students for several years. She also launched a nationally recognized Academy of Travel and Tourism program, providing a wealth of real-world experiences to her students. A frequent presenter at business and educational conferences, Justiss is an active volunteer with local programs, serving on several local boards and committees. She received a Bachelor of Science degree in Clothing and Textiles from the University of North Texas.

Gigi Gano Ekstrom and **Margaret Justiss** are partners and owners of Career Education Resources, an educational consulting firm. They have coauthored several competitive events for national DECA, as well as Curriculum Guides and Independent Study Guides for the state of Texas, including one for fashion marketing.

Glencoe

The McGraw-Hill Companies

Printed in the United States of America.

Send all inquiries to:
Glencoe/McGraw-Hill
21600 Oxnard Street, Suite 500
Woodland Hills, CA 91367

ISBN 0-07-868295-9 (Student Edition)
ISBN 0-07-868809-4 (Teacher Annotated Edition)

3 4 5 6 7 8 9   079   10 09 08 07 06

Advisory Board

To best research and address the needs of today's workplace, Glencoe/McGraw-Hill assembled an advisory board of educators. These educators lent their expertise and experience to establish the foundation for this innovative, real-world, marketing education program. Glencoe/McGraw-Hill would like to acknowledge the following individuals for their support and commitment to this project:

KEVA BOUGHNER
Frisco High School
Frisco, Texas

CASSANDRA JONES
Allen High School
Allen, Texas

CATHY MASON
South Pasadena High School
South Pasadena, California

ATKINS D. "TREY" MICHAEL, III
Marketing Education consultant
Raleigh, North Carolina

GORDON NICHOLSON
West High School
Manchester, New Hampshire

Consulting Editors

PRISCILLA R. McCALLA
Professional and Program Development Director
DECA
Reston, Virginia

MARLENE MORBITT-DUNN
Department Chair
Merchandise Marketing
Merchandise Product Development
Graphic Design, Website Design
The Fashion Institute of Design & Merchandising
Los Angeles, California

Exploring the World of Fashion

As part of the Glencoe Marketing Series, this first edition of *Fashion Marketing* focuses on the real-world business perspective by using examples from the fashion world to illustrate features, concepts, and activities. Information on featured designers, companies, organizations, their products, and services is included for educational purposes only and does not represent or imply endorsement of the Glencoe marketing programs. The following are a few of the companies that appear in features and throughout the text:

Table of Contents

Table of Contents

Table of Contents

Table of Contents

Table of Contents

Welcome to
Fashion Marketing

Welcome to *Fashion Marketing*, part of the Glencoe Marketing Series. Get ready to learn about one of the most exciting—and competitive—businesses in the world. Fashion marketing is a subject that you can relate to and make your own. After all, fashion is all around us. We find signs of it everywhere—not just in malls and shopping centers, but on street corners, on television and radio, in catalogs, and on the Internet.

Understanding the Unit

The units introduce you to the scope of the fashion business, in which marketing plays a vital role. Each unit opens with a preview and concludes with application activities featuring a reading activity from *BusinessWeek* magazine and a fashion-marketing simulation. The 14 chapters in *Fashion Marketing* are divided into four units:

UNIT 1: The World of Fashion

UNIT 2: Producing Fashion

UNIT 3: Fashion Marketing and Merchandising

UNIT 4: Exploring Careers in Fashion Marketing

Previewing the Unit

Each unit opener focuses on the content of the upcoming unit.

Unit Opener Photo

The unit opener photo illustrates a concept that is relevant to the upcoming unit. Ask yourself, "How does the photo relate to the content of the unit?"

Unit Overview

The *Unit Overview* provides a brief road map of the unit chapters.

In This Unit...

The titles of the unit chapters are listed on the left-hand side of the unit opener spread. Think about what you can learn in each chapter. A quotation helps you focus on what is to come.

Unit Lab Preview

The *Unit Lab Preview* prepares you for *House of Style,* the unit's culminating real-world simulation and hands-on activity.

The Marketing Wheel

This visual representation of the National Marketing Education Standards highlights the two main parts of marketing—the foundations and the functions. The functions of marketing relate to how marketing is applied in the fashion world: Distribution, Financing, Marketing-Information Management, Pricing, Product/Service Management, Promotion, and Selling. The functions or foundations addressed in each unit are listed on this page.

Closing the Unit

UNIT 1 ACTIVITIES

BusinessWeek News

NIKE'S NEW ADVICE? JUST STRUT IT

When Mindy F. Grossman took the helm of Nike Inc.'s apparel division three years ago, it was staggering along like a winded sprinter. The New York fashion veteran wasted no time whipping things into shape: slashing costs, consolidating global sourcing, and centralizing design. Her efforts have paid off. While sales at the core footwear business grew just 5.4 percent to $5.9 billion for the fiscal year [2003], apparel sales climbed 11.7 percent to $3.1 billion.

But this race isn't anywhere near done. With a host of collections set to hit stores next spring, Grossman wants to move the sneaker giant well beyond clothes for serious jocks and into the market for sporty street apparel. For now, she's targeting women, many of whom are as likely to wear yoga pants as jeans when they head to the mall. By combining Nike's high-tech athletic materials with casual fashion, she hopes to gain an edge over other apparel makers in creating "must-have outfits."

So are a lot of other companies, ranging from Gap and Tommy Hilfiger to rivals like Adidas. While Nike has a strong brand in athletic apparel, getting it right in the faddish casual-wear market is notoriously difficult.

Street Cred

If anyone can pull it off, say industry watchers, it's Grossman. They credit her with rebuilding Polo Ralph Lauren Corp.'s jeans business in the 1990s by focusing on what people wanted, from fit and styling to price. By the time she left the company in 2000, Polo Jeans was generating $450 million a year in sales, up from virtually zero.

Despite her reputation, Grossman has had to prove herself amid Nike's male-dominated sports culture. But her success turning around the struggling apparel unit won her the "street cred" [street credibility] to push Nike into broader markets. Grossman wants people to wear Nike clothes at the coffee shop, mall, and disco. Nike's Sun Tech line will combine trendy beach-inspired styles with Nike materials designed to keep people cool and dry. To turn more women into customers, Nike opened a half-dozen NIKEgoddess boutiques. They carry a range of crossover apparel for women.

Will Grossman make the Nike brand synonymous with casual fashion? Sneaker makers have tried and failed before. The company is betting that Grossman's business sense and fashion instincts will help it sprint into the fashion arena.

By Stanley Holmes

Excerpted by permission. November 3, 2003. Copyright 2000–2004, by The McGraw-Hill Companies, Inc. All rights reserved.

TO GO FAR, GO FAST.

CREATIVE JOURNAL

In your journal, write your responses:

CRITICAL THINKING
1. What type of fashion apparel is Nike making and [...]ing? What challenges does the company face wit[...] of fashion?

APPLICATION
2. Describe a new fashion apparel product that Ni[...] make and sell and why you think it would be s[...] Also describe the target market for this produc[...]

Go to businessweek.com for current *BusinessWe[...]*

88 Unit 1 The World of Fashion

UNIT LAB

House of Style

At the end of each unit, the unit lab simulation *House of Style* will take you on an exciting journey through the world of fashion marketing and merchandising.

BusinessWeek NEWS

A reading and writing exercise entitled *BusinessWeek News* concludes each unit. A relevant excerpt from a real *BusinessWeek* article caps the unit content.

UNIT LAB   UNIT 1 ACTIVITIES

House of Style

You've just entered the real world of fashion. The House of Style assists fashion businesses and individuals to conceive, plan, produce, and sell the latest and most popular fashion products. Acting as the owner, manager, or employee of the House of Style, you will have the opportunity to work on different projects to promote the success of this fashion business.

What's Old Is New Again—Do the Research

SITUATION You are a researcher for a well-known fashion clothing manufacturer. The clothing produced by the company is designed to appeal to the teen and early 20s age groups. Your job is to research fashion trends and looks to inspire your company's designers. You have observed that one of the current trends is "retro" styles, or styles from the past, for fabric selections and designs. You have also observed that the fabric and design styles are not necessarily related. For example, a fabric that has a look and feel of the 1960s would not necessarily be used for a style that was influenced by the 1960s. You believe this fashion trend will probably continue into the next two or three seasons.

ASSIGNMENT Complete these tasks:
- Determine three fashion influences from the past that your designers can adapt for designs in an upcoming season.
- Research the influences of fashions from the recent and distant past.
- Make a report to your designers.

TOOLS AND RESOURCES To complete the assignment, you will need to:
- Conduct research at the library, on the Internet, or by talking to local fashion retailers.
- Ask a local fashion retailer about current best-selling fashion looks.
- Have word-processing, spreadsheet, and presentation software.

RESEARCH Do your research:
- Research the demographics and psychographics of the company's target customer.
- Determine looks from the past that would offer inspiration for the designers' adaptations.
- Determine the possibility of the designs' success with your target market.

REPORT Prepare a written report using the following tools, if available:
- *Word-processing program:* Prepare a written report listing the demographic and psychographic characteristics of the company's target-market customer.
- *Spreadsheet program:* Prepare a chart comparing your fashion looks from the past with those that are current bestsellers.
- *Presentation program:* Prepare a ten-slide visual presentation with key points, photos of each proposed retro design, and descriptive text.

PRESENTATION AND EVALUATION You will present your report to your designers and head researcher. You will be evaluated on the basis of:
- Your knowledge of the company's target market and the proposed design looks
- Continuity of presentation
- Voice quality
- Eye contact

PORTFOLIO
Add this report to your career portfolio.

Unit 1 The World of Fashion **89**

Understanding the Chapter

Each unit of *Fashion Marketing* includes two to four chapters. Each chapter focuses on one specific area of fashion, such as design or promotion.

Previewing the Chapter

The chapter opener resources are designed to capture your interest and set a purpose for reading.

Chapter Opener Photo

The chapter opener photo focuses on the chapter topic. You might ask yourself, "How does this photo relate to the chapter title?"

Chapter Objectives

The objectives help you identify exactly what you should know upon completion of the chapter.

Case Study

Each chapter opens with the Case Study, Part 1, which presents a real-world fashion industry situation. Critical-thinking questions help focus content. Part 2 continues within the chapter.

Using the Sections

Each chapter of *Fashion Marketing* is divided into two sections. By using the activities and resources in each section, you can maximize learning.

AS YOU READ . . .

You Will Learn lists the knowledge you can expect to learn.

Why It's Important explains how the chapter concepts relate to the real world of fashion.

Key Terms list major terms presented in each section.

Photographs and Figures

Photographs, illustrations, charts, and graphs reinforce content. Captions with questions guide you.

Quick Check

The section-ending *Quick Check* helps you to review and respond to what you have read.

Understanding the Features

Special features in each chapter are designed to interest and promote your understanding of the chapter content. Features incorporate activities and critical-thinking questions to help you integrate what you have learned.

World Market presents interesting highlights from the global world of fashion marketing.

Hot Property

Hot Property profiles successful or creative fashion businesses, both large and small. To close the feature, two critical-thinking questions focus on chapter topics.

Profiles in Fashion

Profiles in Fashion provides insight through personal interviews of successful or noteworthy individuals working in fashion-related careers. A chapter-related, critical-thinking question follows the feature. The "Career Data" column provides education, skills, outlook, and career-path information for this career.

THE Electronic CHANNEL

The Electronic Channel links chapter content to the expanding world of e-commerce and communication in the fashion industry.

Style Point

Style Point presents brief, memorable facts to illustrate fashion industry issues and trends.

ETHICS & ISSUES

Ethics & Issues links chapter content to current ethical issues in the fashion industry, as well as legal, community-service, and character-education issues and practices.

Math Check

Math Check provides a math problem related to chapter discussions.

TECH NOTES

Technology is today's number-one marketing trend. *Tech Notes* highlights the wide range of technological applications enhancing the fashion industry today. An exercise directs you to the book's Web site at **marketingseries.glencoe.com**.

Worksheets and Portfolio Works

At the end of each chapter's text, before the review section, special write-on worksheet pages provide review and skill-building activities related to chapter content.

Chapter Worksheets

Two one-page worksheets give you the opportunity to complete an activity or exercise and apply the chapter content in a variety of interesting formats.

Portfolio Works

The *Portfolio Works* worksheet at the end of each chapter guides you through the development of an employability portfolio. The portfolio is developed throughout the course. You can assess, reflect on, and plan for your career. Record what you have learned and how you would demonstrate those necessary values, skills, personal qualities, and knowledge. These activities provide the foundation for a career development portfolio. Save these pages for a prospective employer to demonstrate your combination of knowledge and workplace skills needed to succeed in a fashion-related career.

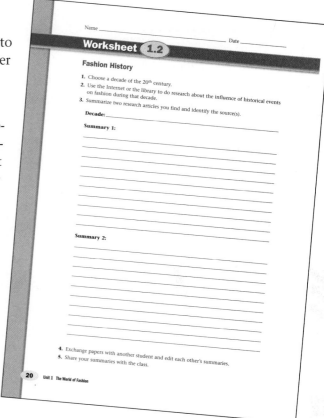

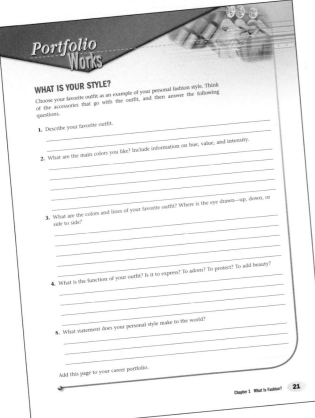

You can also include in your portfolio various documents that demonstrate your marketing competencies, employability skills, career goals, service and leadership activities. Recommendation letters, a résumé, and a job application form are also valuable additions.

Building an employability portfolio helps you relate what you learn in school to the skills you will need for success on the job. When you have completed the project, you will have an expanded résumé to use in your job search.

Understanding Assessments

At the end of each chapter, *Chapter Review and Activities* presents a chapter summary with key terms, recall and critical-thinking questions, and a variety of activities to help develop and apply your academic and workplace skills.

Chapter Summary

The *Chapter Summary* is a bulleted list of the main points developed within each section and related to the chapter objectives. The key terms are listed with page references alongside the summary points.

Cross-Curriculum Skills

These skill-building exercises are divided into two categories: work-based learning and school-based learning. *Work-Based Learning* activities are hands-on projects that help you develop foundation skills and workplace competencies. *School-Based Learning* activities ask you to apply academic skills, such as math, science, and literacy skills, to real-life scenarios related to the world of fashion.

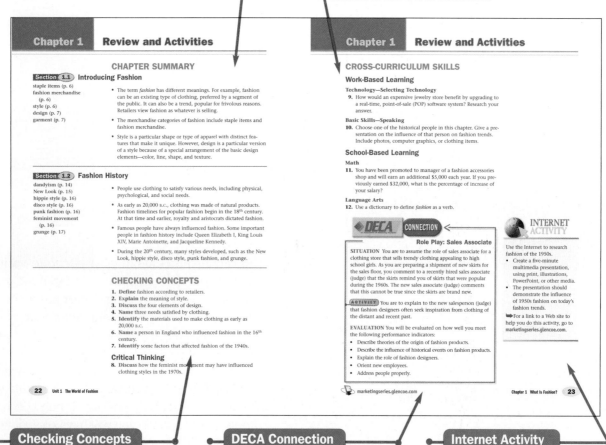

Checking Concepts

Seven review exercises help you check your understanding of the text by defining terms, describing processes, and explaining concepts. The eighth exercise focuses on your critical-thinking skills.

DECA Connection

In every chapter-review section, the *DECA Connection* offers specially created, DECA-approved role-play activities. These activities provide opportunities to practice for DECA's events that relate to fashion marketing—and they are based on a real DECA role-play situation.

Internet Activity

In every chapter-review section, the *Internet Activity* provides a Web-based research activity. Resources for each exercise can be found through the book's Web site at **marketingseries.glencoe.com**.

The DECA Connection

DECA is an association of marketing students that sponsors skill-building events. It is a co-curricular club with chapters in more than 6,000 high schools. The membership includes representation from all 50 states, four U.S. territories, the District of Columbia, and two Canadian provinces. All DECA activities further student development in one or more of the following areas: leadership development, social intelligence, vocational understanding, and civic consciousness. Through individual and group DECA activities with the marketing education instructional program, students develop skills to become future leaders in the areas of marketing and management.

DECA Builds Leadership Skills

The structure of a DECA chapter encourages leadership development for student members. Each chapter elects officers who, with the membership, choose an annual program of work. Committee chairpersons may organize and execute the activities in the program. Local activities encourage every member to act responsibly as a leader or member of a group. Chapter activities focus on the advantages of participating in a free enterprise system, marketing research, and an individual's civic responsibility.

National DECA provides opportunities for local chapter officers and members to receive additional training. Annual Regional Conferences are held in the fall each year. In the spring, students may attend the Leadership Development Academy at the Career Development Conference (CDC). During the summer, students can attend a State Officer Leadership Institute. The skills and leadership qualities gained are shared with all members of the chapter. The recognition received by individuals and teams within a DECA chapter serve as a showcase of your marketing program to your local school and community.

The following is a listing of the individual DECA competitive event areas:

- Apparel and Accessories Marketing Series
- Business Services Marketing Series
- Food Marketing Series
- Full-Service Restaurant Management Series
- Marketing Management Series
- Quick-Serve Restaurant Management Series
- Retail Merchandising Series
- Vehicles and Petroleum Marketing Series

The *Fashion Marketing* Web Site

The *Fashion Marketing* Web site draws on the vast resources of the Internet to extend your exploration of career topics.

The student site provides many resources, including the following:

- Chapter Objectives
- Interactive Practice Tests for each chapter with automatic scoring
- *Math Check* solution tips
- E-flashcard games
- Web links for doing feature exercises from *Tech Notes, The Electronic Channel,* and *Internet Activities*
- DECA Competitive Events practice
- RRA test preparation information
- Disability Support Links

At the *Career Clusters* Web site, you can explore career options with print and .pdf resources as well as links to job-search tips, external career planning sites, and educational resources.

Reading Strategies

How can you get the most from your reading? Effective readers are active readers. Become actively involved with the text. Think of your textbook as a tool to help you learn more about the world around you. It is a form of nonfiction writing—it describes real-life ideas, people, events, and places. Use the reading strategies in the *Power Read* box at the beginning of each chapter, followed by more strategies in the margins throughout the chapter to help you read actively.

PREDICT Make educated guesses about what the section is about by combining clues in the text with what you already know. Predicting helps you anticipate questions and stay alert to new information.

Ask yourself:
- What does this section heading mean?
- What is this section about?
- How does this section tie in with what I have read so far?
- Why is this information important in understanding the subject?

CONNECT Draw parallels between what you are reading and the events and circumstances in your own life.

Ask yourself:
- What do I know about the topic?
- How do my experiences compare to the information in the text?
- How could I apply this information in my own life?
- Why is this information important for understanding the subject?

QUESTION Ask yourself questions to help you clarify meaning as you read.

Ask yourself:
- Do I understand what I have read so far?
- What is this section about?
- What does this mean?
- Why is this information important for understanding the subject?

RESPOND React to what you are reading. Form opinions and make judgments about the section while you are reading—not just after you've finished.

Ask yourself:
- Does this information make sense?
- What can I learn from this section?
- How can I use this information to start planning for my future?
- Why is this information important for understanding the subject?

More Reading Strategies
Use this menu for more reading strategies to get the most from your reading.

BEFORE YOU READ ...

SET A PURPOSE
- Why are you reading the textbook?
- How does the subject relate to your life?
- How might you be able to use what you learn in your own life?

PREVIEW
- Read the chapter title to preview the topic.
- Read the subtitles to see what you will learn about the topic.
- Skim the photos, charts, graphs, or maps. How do they support the topic?
- Look for key terms that are boldfaced. How are they defined?

DRAW FROM YOUR BACKGROUND
- What have you read or heard concerning new information on the topic?
- How is the new information different from what you already know?
- How will the information that you already know help you understand the new information?

AS YOU READ ...

PREDICT
- Predict events or outcomes by using clues and information that you already know.
- Change your predictions as you read and gather new information.

CONNECT
- Think about people, places, and events in your own life. Are there any similarities with those in your textbook?
- Can you relate the textbook information to other areas of your life?

QUESTION
- What is the main idea?
- How do the photos, charts, graphs, and maps support the main idea?

VISUALIZE
- Pay careful attention to details and descriptions.
- Create graphic organizers to show relationships that you find in the information.

NOTICE COMPARE AND CONTRAST SENTENCES
- Look for clue words and phrases that signal comparison, such as *similarly, just as, both, in common, also,* and *too.*
- Look for clue words and phrases that signal contrast, such as *on the other hand, in contrast to, however, different, instead of, rather than, but,* and *unlike.*

NOTICE CAUSE-AND-EFFECT SENTENCES
- Look for clue words and phrases, such as *because, as a result, therefore, that is why, since, so, for this reason,* and *consequently.*

NOTICE CHRONOLOGICAL SENTENCES
- Look for clue words and phrases, such as *after, before, first, next, last, during, finally, earlier, later, since,* and *then.*

AFTER YOU READ ...

SUMMARIZE
- Describe the main idea and how the details support it.
- Use your own words to explain what you have read.

ASSESS
- What was the main idea?
- Did the text clearly support the main idea?

- Did you learn anything new from the material?
- Can you use this new information in other school subjects or at home?
- What other sources could you use to find more information about the topic?

UNIT 1
THE WORLD OF FASHION

> **"** Fashion is a kind of communication. It is language without words. Fashion is about attitude, not hemlines. **"**
>
> —Helmut Lang
> Austrian fashion designer

UNIT OVERVIEW

Fashion marketing is one of the most exciting businesses in the world, representing billions of dollars in sales to those involved in the industry. The fashion business continues to grow rapidly in the United States and around the world with new opportunities.

We begin by focusing on the world of fashion in Chapter 1, discovering the components of fashion and why fashion has been important throughout history. Chapter 2 explores the basics of marketing fashion products. Chapter 3 examines the wide variety of fashion businesses and why they play an important role in domestic and global economies. In Chapter 4, you will learn about fashion design centers and buying centers and how fashion travels around the world.

■ UNIT LAB Preview

House of Style

Think about all of the different places where you go to learn about fashion. Where do designers get ideas? What is the source of their inspiration?

Functions of Marketing

- Marketing-Information Management
- Financing
- Pricing
- Promotion
- Product/Service Management
- Distribution
- Selling

Foundations
- Professional Development
- Economics
- Business, Management, Entrepreneurship
- Communication, Interpersonal Skills

Academic Concepts • Technology

These functions are highlighted in this unit:
- Marketing-Information Management
- Products/Service Management
- Financing
- Promotion
- Distribution

Chapter **1**

What Is Fashion?

Chapter Objectives

- Explain the different definitions of fashion.
- Identify the merchandise categories of fashion.
- Explain the difference between style and design.
- Identify the needs satisfied by clothing.
- Discuss the early history of clothing.
- Name some influential people in fashion history.
- Identify specific styles in the 20th century.

DESIGNER LEGACY: CHANEL

Gabrielle "Coco" Chanel, the founder of the House of Chanel, once remarked, "Fashion that doesn't reach the streets is not a fashion." Beginning in 1912, Chanel brought her designs to the "streets," revolutionizing the way most women dress. At a time when women were laced up in corsets, Chanel introduced trousers, box coats, and short skirts. Inspired by men's clothing, she created a casual style that gave women the ease of movement to match their growing social freedom. Chanel built a fashion empire on the simple elegance of a little black dress, the tweed suit, two-tone shoes—and her name.

When Chanel died in 1971, the company lost the designer behind the name. Marie-Louise de Clermont-Tonnerre became Chanel's managing director for international public relations after Chanel's death. According to her, doing business was difficult without a designer. All the company could do was recycle Chanel's established designs. The future of the House of Chanel depended upon finding a way to continue Chanel's legacy without Coco Chanel.

ANALYZE AND WRITE

1. How did Chanel change fashion? Write a paragraph explaining your ideas.
2. List pros and cons of tying a designer's name to products.

Case Study Part 2 on page 15

POWER READ

Be an active reader and use these reading strategies:

PREDICT what the section will be about.

CONNECT what you read with your life.

QUESTION as you read to make sure you understand the content.

RESPOND to what you've read.

Introducing Fashion

AS YOU READ ...

YOU WILL LEARN

- To explain the different definitions of fashion.
- To identify the merchandise categories of fashion.
- To explain the difference between style and design.

WHY IT'S IMPORTANT

Fashion is an exciting industry that generates billions of dollars. Understanding the industry and basic terms is necessary for marketing success.

KEY TERMS

- staple items
- fashion merchandise
- style
- design
- garment

PREDICT

What products could be called *fashion*?

staple items basic merchandise items that customers purchase on a regular basis

fashion merchandise goods that are popular at a particular time

style a particular shape or type of apparel item identified by the distinct features that make it unique

Fashion Defined

Few words in any language have as many different meanings as the word *fashion*. In the apparel industry, fashion is the existing type of clothing that is preferred by a large segment of the public at a given time. A fashion can be a current trend that is popular for frivolous reasons. To many people, fashion means a precise style of dress or behavior that may be acceptable in one year but not in another. Retailers view fashion as whatever is currently selling. However, sociologists believe fashion represents a way of social interaction and status seeking. No matter what fashion means to various groups, it represents billions of dollars in sales to businesses involved with the design, production, distribution, and marketing of fashion merchandise.

Merchandise Categories

Fashion retailers group merchandise into categories—basic merchandise and fashion merchandise. **Staple items** are basic merchandise items that customers purchase on a regular basis, such as men's socks or children's sleepwear. Retailers know customers' purchasing habits of these items and keep the merchandise in stock at all times.

Fashion merchandise, however, includes goods that are popular at a particular time. Customers may see merchandise advertised in print and through the Internet or displayed in stores, and then purchase it. Keeping fashion merchandise in the stores is sometimes a difficult task for retailers. Sales vary based on the styles customers want at different times.

Fashion Basics

To be successful in the fashion industry, designers, producers, marketers, and retailers must have an understanding of basic fashion terms, such as *style* and *design*.

Style

Style is a particular shape or type of apparel item, such as a mini-skirt or Capri pants, identified by the distinct features that make it unique. A style becomes a fashion when it becomes popular. It remains a fashion as long as it is accepted. While fashion constantly changes, *style* remains constant. A style such as the mini-skirt may gain and lose popularity, but it maintains its identification as a particular style. Many external factors can influence style, including social, technological, regulatory, competitive, and economic factors.

Design

Though the terms *style* and *design* are sometimes used interchangeably, they have different meanings. **Design** is a particular or unique version of a style because of a specific arrangement of the basic design elements. The four basic elements of design are color, line, shape, and texture. (See **Figure 1.1**.) Design is an important part of the development of fashion because it establishes the appearance of the finished product. For example, a V-neck sweater is a specific style, but its design can vary based on the color and texture of the fabric or sleeve length.

COLOR Color is a critical element of design and may be the most important. A retail customer may select a garment based on its color. A **garment** is any article of clothing, such as a dress, suit, coat, or sweater. The three dimensions of color are:

- **Hue**—the quality of the color

- **Value**—the lightness or darkness of a color

- **Intensity**—the brightness or dullness of a color

LINE Line is an element of design that directs the path of eye movement. A line is a distinct, elongated mark that directs the eye up and down, side to side, or around an object. Construction details of a garment, such as the seams and darts, create lines. The popularity of these structural and decorative lines changes with fashion trends.

SHAPE Shape, or silhouette, is the overall form or outline of a garment. Shape is often the key design feature that occupies the minds of the designers, manufacturers, and retailers. The shape, or silhouette, is the three-dimensional form of clothing, accessories, or shoes. There are three basic shapes in fashion: *straight,* or tubular; *bell-shaped,* or bouffant; and *bustle shaped,* or back full.

design a particular or unique version of a style because of a specific arrangement of the basic design elements

garment any article of clothing, such as a dress, suit, coat, or sweater

Figure 1.1

Design Elements

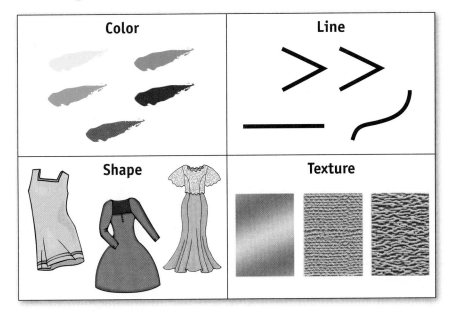

Color

Line

Shape

Texture

THE BASICS OF DESIGN AND STYLE These simple design elements can be used in various combinations to create your favorite look in apparel. *Think of an outfit you've seen at a store, in a magazine, online, or on TV and identify its color, line, shape, and texture.*

CONNECT
Do you consider color or
line when you buy clothing?

TEXTURE Texture is how the surface of a material, or fabric, feels and looks. Fibers, yarns, and the method of fabric construction can determine texture. Different terms can describe texture: *smooth, rough, dull, shiny, delicate, fine, shaggy,* or *flat.* Texture can affect the appearance of shape, giving a bulky or slender look, depending on the roughness or smoothness of the materials. Texture can also influence the drape, or how a garment falls. Clingy or flowing fabrics make good choices for soft styles, while firm or bulky fabrics are more suitable for tailored garments.

FUNCTION Function is a fifth design element that refers to the intended use or purpose of an object. Fashion is expected to function in various ways, including to beautify, to adorn, to express, to identify, to protect, and even to provide therapy.

What Are Fashion Products?

Fashion is anything that has strong customer appeal at a given time. It is usually determined by personal taste. Taste refers to the current opinion of what is attractive and appropriate for an individual and occasion. Jeans might be suitable for a day at the mall but not for the school prom. Fashion products can be many things besides clothing, including accessories and home furnishings.

Hot Property

Accessorizing With UGG® Boots

 According to Irish fashion writer Julie Shackleton, "This footwear is *du jour* [popular] in New York, L.A., and London." An Australian surfer who wanted to keep his feet warm when coming out of the water created the sheepskin boot. Sheepskin boots have been popular with surfers in Australia and New Zealand since then. It took marketing strategy for them to become fashionable in the rest of the world.

In 1978, a young Australian surfer named Brian Smith came to the United States to sell the boots, using his UGG® Australia brand name. Brian's first stop was New York City. No one there seemed to want his boots, but Brian did not give up. He traveled to California.

While surfing in California, Brian met other surfers on the beach. Some of them had been to Australia and New Zealand. Surfers who had traveled to these countries had seen craftspeople sitting on the beach stitching together the sheepskin boots. UGG® Australia boots became a hit with the California surfers.

Then the celebrity crowd put UGG® boots and Smith's company, UGG® Australia, on the map. Celebrities such as Rachel Hunter of MTV's *Cribs* showed off her boots. Cat Deely, a British television star, wore her UGG® boots with a mini-skirt. The boots became a must-have by the famous and not so famous around the globe.

UGG® Australia is a registered TM of UGG Holdings, Inc.

1. Why do you think UGG® boots became so popular after international celebrities were seen wearing them?
2. Why is it wise for fashion marketers to pay attention to what celebrities are wearing?

Clothing

Clothing is a garment used to cover the body. Garment refers to any article of wearing apparel. Women's, men's, and children's wear are all classified as garments.

Accessories

Also considered fashion, accessories are additional articles that complete or enhance outfits. They help achieve a complete fashion look. Examples of accessories are shoes, handbags, leather goods, jewelry, scarves/neckwear, underwear/lingerie, eyeglasses, and fragrances.

Home Furnishings

Home furnishings include window treatments (curtains, draperies, valences, shades, or vertical blinds), furniture coverings (slipcovers and upholstery), and miscellaneous decorative home accessories (throw pillows, lampshades, artificial flowers, and wall hangings). These items are also influenced by fashion trends.

The Importance of Fashion

Economic and political trends, current events, and social issues are often reflected in fashion. Changes in fashion reflect shifts in the economy and the makeup of the population. Fashion serves as a historical record of culture and lifestyle, and it can be an indicator of what is occurring in a society at a particular time.

QUESTION
Can a garment be an accessory? Why or why not?

Math Check

SMART DECISION?
Cammie plans to spend $3,000 to buy clothes for her vintage shop. She marks up merchandise by one-third. If she sells everything, what will be her profit?

➡ For tips on finding the solution, go to **marketingseries.glencoe.com**.

HIGH FASHION SPIRITS Style during the 1960s and 1970s reflected less conservative attitudes of the time. *Do you think current fashions are influenced by fashions of past decades such as the 60s and 70s? Why or why not?*

Importance to People

Throughout history, fashion and clothing have played important roles in personal appearance. Appearance can identify social position. It can also reflect a person's self-image. At every level of society, people care about appearance as it affects self-esteem and their interactions with others.

Economic Importance

As one of the largest industries in the world, fashion affects global and local economies. Many types of fashion businesses benefit from the fashion industry in cities such as New York, Los Angeles, Chicago, San Francisco as well as Paris, Milan, London, and Tokyo. For example, the fashion industry in New York City has a sales volume of over $14 billion per year. Besides creating revenue from fashion businesses, such as textile, manufacturing, and apparel retailers, fashion generates indirect income from other sources, such as transportation, hotels, restaurants, and other non-fashion businesses.

In addition, fashion can be a reflection of the economic environment. When people are unable to satisfy their basic needs for food and shelter, style becomes less important. For example, in an era of war or difficult economic times, clothing styles take on a more austere, conservative image. In better economic times, when spirits are high, styles are more fun and adventurous. Historic clothing examined in Section 1.2 illustrates how economic and political conditions have always had an impact on fashion.

Quick Check ✓

RESPOND to what you've read by answering these questions.

1. What is the difference between style and design? _____
_____
_____
_____

2. What are the four basic elements of design? _____
_____
_____
_____

3. How do economic conditions affect fashion? _____
_____
_____
_____

Fashion History

Earliest Clothing

The earliest clothing dates from about 20,000 B.C., as evidenced by the discovery of sewing needles made of bone and ivory. People probably wore clothes made of natural products, such as fur, animal skin, leaves, and grass. The earliest clothes were developed primarily for protection from the weather and environment.

Why People Wear Clothes

Clothing has always held a prominent place in human history. Besides satisfying basic physical needs, the use of clothing satisfies psychological and social needs. Physically, clothing protects people from weather and other environmental factors. Psychologically, it provides a means of adornment and identification. The particular culture determines the types of adornment. Clothing can identify a person or the position he or she holds. For example, uniforms, badges, colors, and special jewelry may represent occupations or personalities. Clothing can identify a position in society or rank. People also satisfy social needs by wearing clothing and identifying with a peer group. Society also dictates a code of decency through wearing clothing. The basic reasons for wearing clothing have remained constant throughout the years. Today people may also experience pleasure from their apparel, while fulfilling the three basic needs. (See **Figure 1.2** on page 12.)

Physical Needs: Protection and Safety

Physical needs dictate the use of clothing for protection and safety. For example, people in cold climates usually wear heavy clothing, while people in warmer climates may wear hats and sunglasses for physical protection. Garments also shield people from the environment. Imagine walking or running on rocky, hard, and hot surfaces without the proper footwear. A variety of professions require people to wear protective garments, such as gloves or masks, for sanitation and safety purposes. In the construction industry, workers are required to wear hard hats and safety goggles. Athletes, from football players to skateboarders, use protective garments such as helmets and pads. It is vital for people in law enforcement and the military to use protective apparel.

Psychological Needs: Appearance Enhancement

Psychological needs are fulfilled through adornment, or attractive decoration, and self-identification. By simply adding or changing jewelry, accessories, or hairstyles, people feel they are enhancing their appearance. Adornment is also associated with cultural influences. In some cultures, body tattooing and piercing are symbols of adornment. In India, for example, the practice of henna tattooing on hands and feet is an example of this type of appearance enhancement.

People may establish identity by what they wear. Clothing can identify individuals in various jobs, professions, or religious organizations, and positions in society. Individuals, such as firefighters and police personnel, working in the area of security wear safety-wear uniforms. This sets them apart and identifies their positions of authority. Some people seek to identify themselves with different social classes by wearing expensive garments with designer labels.

Social Needs: Affiliation and Standards

Related to psychological needs, social needs are defined by affiliation and standards. Each decade seems to have a representation of social *affiliation*. From the hippie era of the 1960s–1970s to the Gothic look of the 1990s, people have chosen clothes so they will fit into groups. This affiliation with a specific group is also evident in sports when fans dress like team members.

Society maintains certain social *standards* that are represented by clothing. Modesty, which is the covering of a person's body according to society's code of decency, often dictates the styles of clothing that people wear. For example, during the 1800s, it was unacceptable for a woman's ankle to be visible. However, with each decade through the 20th century, skirts became shorter and more of the body was visible.

As you study fashion marketing, you will become aware that physical, psychological, and social needs have important influences on the clothes that people wear and how they are marketed. The combination of these needs with other factors—such as personal values, the need of conformity, and individual expression—keeps the fashion industry constantly changing and thriving.

Figure 1.2

Reasons for Clothing

NOT JUST TO COVER UP The reasons for wearing clothing can be simple or complex. Clothing makers study these reasons to make products that meet all the needs of their customers. *What item of clothing would you buy to satisfy only physical needs?*

Physical Needs
• protection
• safety

Why Clothing?

Psychological Needs
• identity
• adornment
• cultural identity

Social Needs
• affiliation/fitting in
• standards

Sources of Clothing History

Clothing tells us a great deal about social values at certain times in history. The evolution of dress can represent a visual history of a culture. Costume history serves as a source of creative ideas that designers use to create new looks.

While there are various sources of fashion history, each has its limitations. Actual garments are one source of clothing history, although few samples exist that pre-date the 18th century. Old paintings and other works of art can be helpful for research, but they can be limited in visual detail, particularly before the 14th century. Fashion publications came into existence for the first time in the 17th century, yet many items in these fashion "magazines" were never seen by the average consumer and are rare. Photographs are a source after the 1850s. Written descriptions in personal letters, diaries, novels, and other sources are also valuable sources of clothing history.

Fashion Through the Ages

Centuries ago, people dressed according to what society allowed for the social classes. Rare and expensive apparel became a status symbol and reflected the economic class of the wearer. Fashion timelines for popular fashion begin in the late 18th century, but even before this time, the wealthy classes dictated fashion. They often mimicked costumes worn by royalty. During the 18th century, the influence of the upper class diminished with the American Revolutionary War and the French Revolution. The resulting political and social shifts contributed to the growth and influence of the middle or working class.

The industrial revolution of the 1800s fostered new inventions. Garments once produced by artists and tailors began being mass produced with the invention of the sewing machine. During this same era, the invention of photography would also greatly influence the spread of styles to the middle-class population. *Vogue* magazine was first published in 1892, allowing the public more exposure to fashion styles. Paintings had been the main source of documenting styles, but with a printed magazine, many people could view the latest fashions.

Historical Trendsetters

Throughout history, famous people have always influenced the development and acceptance of fashion. From royalty to celebrities, famous people make fashion famous. Those in the public eye influence the changing face of fashion. In western cultures, there have been numerous historical trendsetters:

- **Elizabeth I** reigned as Queen of England from 1558 to 1603. Clothing during this period reflected the social status of the wearer and was an indication of wealth. Women of the aristocracy in the mid-16th century did not seem to mind the stiff look worn by Queen Elizabeth. This look consisted of Tudor ruffs (large, round collar), epaulets (shoulder ornaments), jeweled wigs, plucked forehead and brows, rib-crushing corsets, and the farthingale, or skirt hoop.

OLD-FASHIONED ELEGANCE Queen Elizabeth I was a trendsetter among her peers in the 16th century, but her style was unaffordable for the average person. *Are some fashions and designs of today too expensive for most people?*

MARKETING SERIES *Online*

Remember to check out this book's Web site for fashion history information and more great resources at **marketingseries.glencoe.com**.

dandyism during the 1800s, a style of dress for men and a lifestyle that celebrated elegance and refinement

---

- **Louis XIV,** the King of France from 1643 to 1715, sent life-sized fashion dolls to every European court, so that all of Europe would know about Paris fashions. The exquisite dolls were dressed in the latest styles. Tailors copied the clothes, footwear, hats, and accessories on the dolls for nobility in other countries.

- **Marie Antoinette,** the Queen of France from 1775 to 1793, was a trendsetter for ornate styles of the late 18th century. She used papier-mâché paste to whiten and stiffen her hair to extreme heights. Her excessive fashion included high headdresses, plumes, and voluminous dresses.

- **George Bryan "Beau" Brummell** led the trend in the early 1800s for men to wear understated but beautifully tailored clothing and elaborate neckwear. He claimed to take five hours to get dressed and recommended that men's boots should be polished with champagne. His style was known as dandyism. **Dandyism**, during the 1800s, was a style of dress for men and a lifestyle that celebrated elegance and refinement. Straight posture, well-fitting clothes, and accessories such as a top hat, tailcoat, and white gloves, were all characteristics of a "dandy" such as Brummell, who was a companion of British royalty.

- **Jacqueline Kennedy Onassis** brought her understated elegance to fashion of the early 1960s as First Lady of the United States. While her trademark pillbox hat and her suits with three-quarter sleeves were famous, she had a sense of style for any type of attire. Today some of her wardrobe is conserved at the John F. Kennedy Library and Museum in Boston, Massachusetts.

- **The Beatles** came to America in 1964 as the famous trendsetting British band, wearing "mop-top" hairstyles. This fashion from the working classes challenged the shorthaired, conservative look of the crew cut. While longer hairstyles became standard for men by the 1970s, they were extreme in the early 1960s.

Fashion: 20th Century to the Present

By the end of the Victorian era of the 1800s, women were wearing corsets to shape their bodies into an unnatural "S-bend" to create a more feminine silhouette. They wore slim-fitting skirts, long sleeves, and high collars for a look that was feminine but stiff. The death of England's Queen Victoria in 1901 marked a fashion milestone and the beginning of economic, social, and technological changes.

The Early 1900s

In 1909, the American fashion magazine *Vogue* featured a fashionable young woman on the cover who wore a new, loose-fitting style of dress. By 1915, styles had continued to soften. Corsets were disappearing. Women wore full skirts with a slightly shorter length. The invention of the first manufactured fiber *rayon,* or artificial silk, led to clothing that was more functional for women who were entering the work force at a time when men left to fight in World War I.

The 1920s

The fashion legend Gabrielle "Coco" Chanel (1883–1971) was one of the first designers to introduce sportswear garments for everyday wear—as well as trousers for women that would influence fashion for years to come. The silhouettes of her clothing designs epitomize 1920s styles as well as timeless classics. She promoted the styles we associate with *flappers,* who were young, independent-minded, and free-spirited women known for wearing shorter hemlines and hairstyles. Chanel was also the originator of "the little black dress," a fashion staple.

Simpler styles in the 1920s meant that women could get dressed faster and more easily—and could home-sew their clothing. In 1926, the Women's Fashion Institute designed the "one-hour dress," which could be sewn in only one hour.

The 1930s–1950s

In the 1930s and 1940s, movie stars set the fashion trends in hair, makeup, and clothes, as Hollywood brought its glamorous fashions to America and the world. The chemical company DuPont also changed the fashion world with the invention of nylon, which was less expensive than silk for making hosiery. Women enjoyed nylon stockings with the look of silk at cheaper prices and with greater durability.

With World War II in the 1940s came fabric shortages, which resulted in shorter skirt hemlines and the increased use of synthetic rayon. The U.S. fashion industry had less access to French designers, and so American designers became important fashion innovators.

During the Second World War, austere clothing mirrored the economic atmosphere. Simple styles became representative of patriotism. The trend toward simplicity was also influenced by wartime rationing of cloth and textiles, especially wool, as it was used to make military uniforms. Women's apparel also reflected women's roles as workers in military product factories.

After the war, women returned to their primary roles as homemakers and mothers. Styles moved toward a more traditionally feminine look. People also wanted luxury after the years of sacrifice during the war.

To meet this demand and to reestablish the French fashion industry, the French designer Christian Dior launched his new fashion style in 1947. *Life* magazine called it the **New Look**, which was a style of the 1940s and 1950s that featured long hemlines, narrow shoulders, and tightly fitted bodices with long, full, or narrow skirts. The New Look remained fashionable for about ten years until the late 1950s.

Case Study | PART 2

DESIGNER LEGACY: CHANEL
Continued from Part 1 on page 5

Chanel's managing director Marie-Louise de Clermont-Tonnerre stated that the decision to hire a designer who did not carry the name of the design house (Chanel) was revolutionary. When designer Karl Lagerfeld became Artistic Director of Chanel, Inc. Fashion in 1983, the business started to grow again. Lagerfeld's designs skillfully combined the Chanel legacy with his contemporary fashions by using the interlocking "C" symbol of *Chanel Couture* on his clothes and accessories. This branding took advantage of the 1980s consumer love of status symbols. It also helped revitalize the House of Chanel. Chanel executive Richard Collasse says the company's continued success is due to the fact that "while we stay in touch with our roots, reaching back some 100 years, we have always been striving for modernity."

ANALYZE AND WRITE

1. What revolutionary move did Chanel, Inc. make in 1983?
2. How did Chanel extend its lines to fashion items other than clothing? Write a paragraph giving examples.

New Look a style of the 1940s and 1950s that featured long hemlines, narrow shoulders, and tightly fitted bodices with long, full, or narrow skirts

hippie style of the 1960s, a fashion consisting of clothing from the Middle and Far East, bright colors, peasant embroidery, cheesecloth, and safari jackets

disco style of the 1970s, a fashion consisting of gold lamé, leopard print, stretch halter jumpsuits, and white clothing that glowed under ultraviolet lighting

punk fashion of the 1970s, a style featuring intentionally torn clothing worn by young people with limited income, such as students and the unemployed

feminist movement of the 1970s, the organized effort to establish equal social, economic, and political rights and opportunities for women; influenced women's fashion with shorter hemlines and the pantsuit for the workplace

QUESTION

What style of women's wear for the office developed in the 1970s?

The 1960s

Social changes, the Vietnam War, art, film, and music all influenced the fashion of the 1960s youth movement. New fabrics developed as huge production plants for synthetic fibers sprang up around the world. The **hippie style** of the 1960s was fashion consisting of clothing from the Middle and Far East and the use of bright colors, peasant embroidery, cheesecloth, and safari jackets.

The 1970s

By the 1970s, the disco dance scene was popular as dance clubs provided an arena for a new kind of clothing made with stretchable and light-reflecting fabrics. The **disco style** of the 1970s was fashion consisting of gold lamé, leopard print, stretch halter jumpsuits, and white clothing that glowed under ultraviolet lighting. The film *Saturday Night Fever* highlighted the flared trousers, pastel-colored jackets, and platform shoes popular during the disco era.

Another fashion called **punk fashion** was a style featuring intentionally torn clothing worn by young people with limited incomes, such as students and the unemployed. Frayed trousers and Doc Martens, which are heavy, functional work shoes, were punk style. Pieces of fabric were held together with safety pins and chains. While torn clothing, frayed edges, and damaged print fabrics are not unusual styles in the 21st century, during the 1970s, the look shocked people.

Feminism also marked the 1970s. The **feminist movement** was the organized effort to establish equal social, economic, and political rights and opportunities for women. It influenced women's styles, such as shorter skirts and the pantsuit for the workplace.

This decade that began with polyester double-knit would end on a different fashion note. Environmentally conscious Americans returned to the use of natural fibers in their clothing designs.

The 1980s

During the 1980s, various trends caused fashion to move in many new directions. Millions of professional women moved up in the workplace, adopting "the power look," which was a uniform style of suits and blazers with shoulder pads. A more casual style of dress for men in the office developed, and business-casual attire began replacing suits and ties.

At the same time, values regarding fashion began to change. People no longer felt that high price determined high fashion. Manufacturers began to produce more quality products at moderate prices.

Many people became fitness conscious in the 1980s. Synthetic fabrics, with their easy care, durability, and stretch properties, were the ideal choice for most athletic wear. These fabrics could be dyed in the bright colors that were popular at the time.

The 1990s

In the 1990s, Americans began dressing down, or less formally, with an appreciation of streamlined styles. Many people liked the comfort of sports clothes, and athletic clothing became a wardrobe staple.

STARTING OUT

Rebecca Jarrell
Freelance Stylist

What is your job?
"I am a freelance fashion stylist and designer."

What do you do in your job?
"I choose and gather together the clothes and accessories that models wear for photo shoots done for advertisements or other print media. I find outfits by shopping, going to showrooms, and getting clothes on loan from vendors."

What kind of training did you have?
"I earned a master's degree in theater at Indiana University and moved to New York to really get started in the fashion world."

What advice would you give students?
"You have to get out there and do it. You can move to a big market like New York and make it, but it takes time, money, and effort. You have to be willing to make some sacrifices and be willing to put yourself out there."

What's your key to success?
"I do a lot of work for free to build up my book, which is a portfolio of samples of my work. It's the catch-22 of fashion: You won't get hired without a portfolio, and it's hard to build a portfolio without getting hired. But I'm building mine up, doing the ground work, networking, meeting people, and taking any opportunity to work. I'm having a great time doing what I love to do, and I know it will pay off down the road."

What strategies could a beginning stylist use to market him- or herself to potential employers?

Career Data: Freelance Stylist

Education and Training Associate degree, bachelor's degree in liberal arts, theater, or fashion, and apprenticeship

Skills and Abilities Visual styling, fitting, budgeting, networking, scheduling, organizational, and communication skills

Career Outlook Average growth through 2012

Career Path Intern, fashion or production assistant, fashion stylist to fashion editor

---

Grunge is a style started by the youth culture in the Pacific Northwest region of the United States in the early 1990s; it is messy, uncombed, and disheveled, as if not too much effort has been made. Though grunge died out quickly, the fashion term sometimes describes unappealing styles or unkempt individuals.

By the mid-1990s, fashion designers, apparel makers, and retailers began to lose their traditional ability to dictate trends. As fashion designer Oscar de la Renta noted in the *New York Times Magazine*, "Today, there is no fashion, really. There are just . . . choices. Women dress today to reveal their personalities. They used to reveal the designer's personality. Until the 70s, women listened to designers. Now women want to do it their own way. There are no boundaries."

grunge a style started by the youth culture in the Pacific Northwest region of the United States in the early 1990s; it is messy, uncombed, and disheveled

Wild-West Style

The Stetson hat was once called the "Boss of the Plains." It was the hat of choice for the Texas Rangers. They found the hat had many purposes. Rangers could drink from the hat, or use it to fan a campfire, to blindfold a nervous horse, to move a steer, and to smother Texas grass fires. The hats became a characteristic of cowboys, both real ones and those in popular fiction.

John B. Stetson designed Stetson hats. In the mid-1800s, Mr. Stetson left Philadelphia to go west because of his health. He made a hat to protect himself from the sun and weather.

Later he returned to his native Philadelphia and opened a hat factory to manufacture his designs.

Stetson hats are still big business and big fashion. Today the Stetson Hat Company's factory—one of the largest in the country—is located in St. Joseph, Missouri. Hats are sold worldwide in stores and through the Internet.

Why do you think the Stetson hat first became popular and remains popular today?

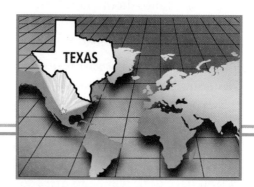

Fashion Today

Today consumers make well-informed choices about what to wear, where to shop, and how much to spend on products. More than ever, fashion makers and marketers must be better informed and aware of consumers' wants and needs.

Quick Check

RESPOND to what you've read by answering these questions.

1. What three basic needs are satisfied by the use of clothing?_____
_____
_____

2. How did World War II affect the fashion industry?_____
_____
_____

3. What fashion trends emerged in the 1980s?_____
_____
_____

Worksheet 1.1

Fashion Inventory

1. Visit three different types of fashion stores in your community.

2. Make a list of the merchandise you find in each store.

3. Identify each store's merchandise as mainly staple items or fashion merchandise.

Store 1:

Name of store: _____

Merchandise: _____   _____

_____   _____

Category of merchandise: _____

Store 2:

Name of store: _____

Merchandise: _____   _____

_____   _____

Category of merchandise: _____

Store 3:

Name of store: _____

Merchandise: _____   _____

_____   _____

Category of merchandise: _____

Store 4:

Name of store: _____

Merchandise: _____   _____

_____   _____

Category of merchandise: _____

Worksheet 1.2

Fashion History

1. Choose a decade of the 20th century.
2. Use the Internet or the library to do research about the influence of historical events on fashion during that decade.
3. Summarize two research articles you find and identify the source(s).

Decade: _____

Summary 1:

_____
_____
_____
_____
_____
_____
_____
_____

Summary 2:

_____
_____
_____
_____
_____
_____
_____
_____

4. Exchange papers with another student and edit each other's summaries.
5. Share your summaries with the class.

Portfolio Works

WHAT IS YOUR STYLE?

Choose your favorite outfit as an example of your personal fashion style. Think of the accessories that go with the outfit, and then answer the following questions.

1. Describe your favorite outfit.

_____

_____

2. What are the main colors you like? Include information on hue, value, and intensity.

_____

_____

_____

_____

3. What are the colors and lines of your favorite outfit? Where is the eye drawn—up, down, or side to side?

_____

_____

_____

_____

4. What is the function of your outfit? Is it to express? To adorn? To protect? To add beauty?

_____

_____

_____

5. What statement does your personal style make to the world?

_____

_____

_____

Add this page to your career portfolio.

CHAPTER SUMMARY

Section 1.1 Introducing Fashion

staple items (p. 6)
fashion merchandise
   (p. 6)
style (p. 6)
design (p. 7)
garment (p. 7)

- The term *fashion* has different meanings. For example, fashion can be an existing type of clothing, preferred by a segment of the public. It can also be a trend, popular for frivolous reasons. Retailers view fashion as whatever is selling.

- The merchandise categories of fashion include staple items and fashion merchandise.

- Style is a particular shape or type of apparel with distinct features that make it unique. However, design is a particular version of a style because of a special arrangement of the basic design elements—color, line, shape, and texture.

Section 1.2 Fashion History

dandyism (p. 14)
New Look (p. 15)
hippie style (p. 16)
disco style (p. 16)
punk fashion (p. 16)
feminist movement
   (p. 16)
grunge (p. 17)

- People use clothing to satisfy various needs, including physical, psychological, and social needs.

- As early as 20,000 B.C., clothing was made of natural products. Fashion timelines for popular fashion begin in the 18th century. At that time and earlier, royalty and aristocrats dictated fashion.

- Famous people have always influenced fashion. Some important people in fashion history include Queen Elizabeth I, King Louis XIV, Marie Antoinette, and Jacqueline Kennedy.

- During the 20th century, many styles developed, such as the New Look, hippie style, disco style, punk fashion, and grunge.

CHECKING CONCEPTS

1. **Define** fashion according to retailers.
2. **Explain** the meaning of style.
3. **Discuss** the four elements of design.
4. **Name** three needs satisfied by clothing.
5. **Identify** the materials used to make clothing as early as 20,000 B.C.
6. **Name** a person in England who influenced fashion in the 16th century.
7. **Identify** some factors that affected fashion of the 1940s.

Critical Thinking

8. **Discuss** how the feminist movement may have influenced clothing styles in the 1970s.

CROSS-CURRICULUM SKILLS

Work-Based Learning

Technology—Selecting Technology

9. How would an expensive jewelry store benefit by upgrading to a real-time, point-of-sale (POP) software system? Research your answer.

Basic Skills—Speaking

10. Choose one of the historical people in this chapter. Give a presentation on the influence of that person on fashion trends. Include photos, computer graphics, or clothing items.

School-Based Learning

Math

11. You have been promoted to manager of a fashion accessories shop and will earn an additional $5,000 each year. If you previously earned $32,000, what is the percentage of increase of your salary?

Language Arts

12. Use a dictionary to define *fashion* as a verb.

Role Play: Sales Associate

SITUATION You are to assume the role of sales associate for a clothing store that sells trendy clothing appealing to high school girls. As you are preparing a shipment of new skirts for the sales floor, you comment to a recently hired sales associate (judge) that the skirts remind you of skirts that were popular during the 1960s. The new sales associate (judge) comments that this cannot be true since the skirts are brand new.

(ACTIVITY) You are to explain to the new salesperson (judge) that fashion designers often seek inspiration from clothing of the distant and recent past.

EVALUATION You will be evaluated on how well you meet the following performance indicators:

- Describe theories of the origin of fashion products.
- Describe the influence of historical events on fashion products.
- Explain the role of fashion designers.
- Orient new employees.
- Address people properly.

Use the Internet to research fashion of the 1950s.
- Create a five-minute multimedia presentation, using print, illustrations, PowerPoint, or other media.
- The presentation should demonstrate the influence of 1950s fashion on today's fashion trends.

➡ For a link to a Web site to help you do this activity, go to **marketingseries.glencoe.com**.

Chapter 2

Fashion and Marketing

Section 2.1
Fashion Marketing Basics

Section 2.2
Marketing Strategies

Chapter Objectives

- Define the term *marketing*.
- Explain types of customer characteristics used to define a target market.
- Explain fashion merchandising.
- Describe the four components of the marketing mix.
- Identify the four types of promotion.
- Identify the seven functions of marketing.

CLOSING THE GAP?

Since 1969, Gap, Inc., has opened stores in malls across the United States. The popular retail clothing chain experienced the economic boom of the 1990s, as sales almost tripled from $5.3 billion in 1996 to $14 billion in 2001. The company continued to open new stores, construct a new corporate headquarters, and pour money into distribution centers.

Gap was banking on the continued success of its products. That success, however, never completely materialized. There were too many stores, and Gap's customers did not like the new, edgier designs and unfamiliar clothing lines. By the end of 2001, Gap, Inc., showed a loss of $8 million.

In October 2003, Gap hired Paul Pressler from The Walt Disney Company to revive Gap, Inc. As chief executive of Gap, Inc., Pressler's first step was to insist that the company "listen to customers." But was this approach successful?

ANALYZE AND WRITE

1. Why did Gap's expansion result in losses? List two reasons.
2. How important is understanding the needs and wants of the consumer for fashion businesses? Discuss your answer in one paragraph.

Case Study Part 2 on page 35

POWER READ

Be an active reader and use these reading strategies:

PREDICT what the section will be about.

CONNECT what you read with your life.

QUESTION as you read to make sure you understand the content.

RESPOND to what you've read.

Fashion Marketing Basics

AS YOU READ...

YOU WILL LEARN

- To define the term *marketing*.
- To explain types of customer characteristics used to define a target market.
- To explain fashion merchandising.

WHY IT'S IMPORTANT

Understanding basic marketing terms and principles helps fashion marketers develop strategies.

KEY TERMS

- marketing
- marketing concept
- target market
- market segmentation
- demographics
- psychographics
- geographics
- behavioristics
- fashion merchandising

PREDICT

Describe a target market in your own words.

marketing is the process of developing, promoting, and distributing products to satisfy customers' needs and wants

marketing concept the idea that businesses must satisfy customer needs and wants in order to make a profit

How Fashion Is Marketed

Marketing is a term used in just about every industry, including the fashion industry. It is probably one of the most important aspects of any business. **Marketing** is the process of developing, promoting, and distributing products to satisfy customers' needs and wants. Marketing starts at the very beginning of the product development and continues after a consumer purchases that product. It is a series of activities that fashion businesses undertake so that customers will buy products from them instead of their competitors.

The Marketing Concept

To market effectively, fashion marketers follow the principles of the **marketing concept**, which is the idea that businesses must satisfy customers' needs and wants in order to make a profit. Businesses identify the customers, determine the products they want, and make the products available at a price the customers are willing to pay. Businesses must also be able to communicate this information effectively to their customers. Fashion products are presented in a way that makes the customer want to buy the merchandise. Fashion marketers must offer the right product to their customers at the right time and at the right price. In addition, they must develop strategies to tell their selected market about these products.

In addition, retailers, or store owners, must consider the location, atmosphere, and image of the store. The products they offer must match style, quality, and price to their customers. The goal is to accomplish these tasks and make a profit. Fashion businesses must be marketing oriented at all levels of the business by planning all activities around satisfying customer needs and wants.

Target Market

Successful fashion marketers will identify specific segments of the market to which they will target all of their marketing efforts. A **target market** is the specific group of people that a business is trying to reach.

Businesses identify a target market through research and by the shared characteristics of the specific group of people. Identifying a group of consumers, or target market, is achieved through **market segmentation**, which is a way of analyzing a market by categorizing specific characteristics. Marketers divide the people into groups of possible consumers based on various shared characteristics.

This allows fashion marketers to concentrate on meeting the needs of certain types of buyers rather than the needs of all shoppers. Specific customer characteristics that are expressed as statistics include:

- Demographic
- Psychographic
- Geographic
- Behavioristic

Demographics

Demographics are statistics that describe a population in terms of personal characteristics such as age, gender, income, ethnic background, education, religion, occupation, and lifestyle. A retailer such as PacSun targets a teen or young adult customer.

Psychographics

Psychographics are studies of consumers based on social and psychological characteristics such as attitudes, interests, and opinions. **Figure 2.1** provides examples of some current psychographic trends. Consumers' attitudes and values are often represented by how they choose to spend their time and money. In the example of PacSun, many of the customers may be interested in surfing or skateboarding.

target market the specific group of people that a business is trying to reach

market segmentation a way of analyzing a market by categorizing specific characteristics

demographics statistics that describe a population in terms of personal characteristics such as age, gender, income, ethnic background, education, religion, occupation, and lifestyle

psychographics studies of consumers based on social and psychological characteristics such as attitudes, interests, and opinions

Figure 2.1

Psychographic Trends

Women in the workforce

Urban population

Home and family activities

Travel

Work at home

Home computer use

Casual dress for home and office

Value of time over money

Larger clothing sizes

CHANGING LIFESTYLES Manufacturers and marketers consider these psychographic trends when planning products and identifying target customers for the products. *Choose two of the trends in this figure and describe how clothing fashion might be influenced by these trends.*

Geographics

geographics statistics about where people live

Geographics are statistics about where people live. Typical geographic breakdowns could include the region of the country, size of the city or county, the density of the population (urban, suburban, or rural), or even the climate. The location of where people live has a tremendous influence on their buying patterns. Fashion marketers located in the northern part of the United States will offer more warm clothing such as coats, whereas stores in Florida may carry lightweight apparel. PacSun tends to focus its marketing campaigns in warmer and coastal regions rather than in the colder climates.

Behavioristics

behavioristics statistics about consumers based on their knowledge, attitudes, use, or response to a product

Behavioristics are statistics about consumers based on their knowledge, attitudes, use, or response to a product. Behavioristic segmentation is a way of analyzing a market by those classifications and placing consumers into product-related groups. Marketers may look at the purchase occasion for a product, the product benefits sought by consumers, or usage level and commitment towards a product:

Hot Property

Eco-Friendly Silk

Ahimsa Peace Silk

In India the organization People for Animals found a compassionate way to make silk—and the idea is catching on. The country's largest organization for the humane treatment of animals founded the Ahimsa Peace Silk division to produce silk without destroying the silkworm—or the quality of the fabric.

Traditionally, silk is made from cocoons of silkworm larvae. Approximately 3,000 silkworms are steamed in the early stage of development to produce each pound of silk. Instead of destroying the silkworm at that stage, Ahimsa Peace Silk uses the cocoons after the silkworms have become adult moths and have left the cocoons. Silk yarn is spun from these empty cocoons found in the jungles of India. Forests that were once stripped of vegetation in remote regions of India are now being restored so the trees can host the silkworms.

SILK WORKERS

The livelihoods of the people who live there are dependent on the host trees and Ahimsa Peace Silk. Tribal weavers produce the line of Ahimsa Peace Silk products, which include shawls, jackets, bags, scarves, shoes, and even home furnishings. Hand-woven designs and motifs on the garments and fabrics are adapted from traditional arts-and-crafts designs.

The organization markets the products worldwide. It targets consumers who believe in eco-friendly production processes. Designers adapt the garments to current fashion trends to interest and maintain customers. The company spokesperson says, "All consumers who respect the right of life for living beings and care for the environment can wear this product with a clear conscience and enjoy the soft and luxurious feel of spun silk."

1. Who is the target market for Ahimsa Peace Silk products?
2. Is the organization targeting the right market for their products? Why?

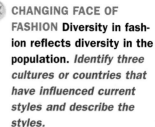

CHANGING FACE OF FASHION **Diversity in fashion reflects diversity in the population.** *Identify three cultures or countries that have influenced current styles and describe the styles.*

- **Purchase occasion**—This identifies the instance when a consumer might use a product. For example, apparel can be classified by categories such as "after-five," casual, or work attire.

- **Product benefits**—This segmentation allows marketers to study the benefits that consumers desire in a fashion product or service, such as stain-resistance or wrinkle-resistance.

- **Usage level and commitment**—This segmentation category is a common identification. Consumers can be identified by how often they use a product and their loyalty to purchasing it.

Diverse and Changing Markets

The fashion market is too large and too diverse to reach with a single marketing approach. Some fashion marketers will try to attract several different market segments at once. For example, Gap offers merchandise for women, men, and children. Within these groups they also offer dressy and casual wear.

Consumer buying habits do not always remain the same. A mistake that some fashion marketers make is to take a market for granted. Changes in economic or social conditions can affect the consumer's choices. Businesses must know about competitors that offer new products and develop strategies that affect their diverse customer bases. Businesses constantly evaluate products and pricing due to the changing market influences.

CONNECT

Name a special occasion for which you have purchased an outfit.

QUESTION

What mistake do some retailers make?

THE Electronic CHANNEL

Fashion Online

Walking past attractively displayed fashions in store windows can easily lure you into a store to shop. However, it's not as easy to draw customers online. Research indicates that 99 percent of pop-up or banner ads do not get clicked. One solution is linking through Web sites that already attract an established demographic.

➡ Find and visit the online edition of *Seventeen* and list the products being advertised as sponsored links through **marketingseries.glencoe.com**.

fashion merchandising the planning, buying, and selling of fashion apparel and accessories to offer the right merchandise blend to meet consumer demand

Fashion Merchandising

After fashion marketers have identified their target customers and desired products, they must develop plans to have the products available. **Fashion merchandising** is the planning, buying, and selling of fashion apparel and accessories to offer the right merchandise blend to meet consumer demand.

Retailers and Fashion Merchandising

Merchandising is the main function of apparel retailing. Retailers buy large quantities of finished garments and other fashion products at wholesale prices and sell them at retail prices as single items or smaller quantities of goods. Retailers not only focus on styles and fashion merchandising, they also conduct business at their stores. Other retail responsibilities focus on store operations, financial control, personnel, and sales promotion.

Merchandising Market Factors

As we examine the planning phase of merchandising, it is important to understand internal factors that can be controlled and external factors that are not so easily controlled. Economic issues can influence customer buying habits and can cause customers to spend less during times of hardship. Also, new technology developed by a competitor might allow that competitor to produce similar merchandise at less cost. Those factors are not always predictable and can affect a business's marketing plans. However, the basic marketing principles found in the marketing mix, discussed in Section 2.2, are a controllable part of planning marketing strategies.

Quick Check ✓

RESPOND to what you've read by answering these questions.

1. What is a target market?_____

_____

_____

2. What customer characteristics are used to segment markets? _____

_____

_____

_____

3. What is fashion merchandising?_____

_____

_____

_____

Marketing Strategies

The Marketing Mix and Fashion

To successfully sell a fashion product to target customers, businesses must apply the marketing mix. The **marketing mix** consists of four basic marketing strategies known as the four Ps of marketing—product, place, price, and promotion. The marketing mix refers to how the basic elements are combined to meet consumer needs and wants. It is a blend of features that satisfies a chosen market.

Product

Product refers to what a company is offering for sale to customers to satisfy their needs and wants. Products include goods and/or services. Fashion marketers develop strategies that include producing, packaging, and naming a product. How a product is perceived by consumers is also a consideration. Examples of products are goods such as jeans, sweaters, jewelry, cosmetics, and shoes, and services such as hairstyling and makeup services.

Place

Place refers to the way products are distributed and their systems of delivery. Distribution means getting the product to the consumer, and it includes all the steps of distribution, from getting the raw material for fabric and manufacturing textiles to making a garment available to a customer. Important place decisions include how and where a product will be distributed, where the customer will purchase the item, and when the product is distributed. For a retailer, place (or location of the store) is a critical consideration. For example, a store owner who is selling trendy hip-hop merchandise might not want to position the store in a small rural community because customers there may not want or need that type of merchandise.

Price

Price is the amount of money consumers will pay for a product. Fashion marketers must determine how much consumers are willing to pay. The price of a fashion product depends on the cost of producing the item, the markup, and customer demand. Although customer preference plays an important role in establishing the price of an item, businesses must make a profit.

Promotion

Promotion is any form of communication that a business or organization uses to inform, persuade, or remind people to buy its product.

AS YOU READ...

YOU WILL LEARN
- To describe the four components of the marketing mix.
- To identify the four types of promotion.
- To identify the seven functions of marketing.

WHY IT'S IMPORTANT

Businesses must have a full understanding of the marketing mix, marketing strategies, and the functions of marketing in order to effectively reach consumers and make profits.

KEY TERMS
- marketing mix
- channel of distribution
- functions of marketing

marketing mix four basic marketing strategies, known as the four Ps of marketing—product, place, price, and promotion

PREDICT

Why are marketing strategies important for selling products?

LABELS OF THE PAST
Before the 1960s, American clothing was usually labeled with store names. After 1960, apparel firms and American designers began to tag their creations with their own names. They also launched advertising campaigns to promote the designer labels.

PRINT ADVERTISEMENT
Fashion marketers spend millions of dollars on eye-catching print ads in magazines and on billboards because they are effective marketing tools for boosting sales. *What might be the difference between advertising and publicity in the promotional mix?*

Promotional activities can inform the customer about the features of the product and persuade the customer to make a purchase. There are four types of promotion that all businesses use and combine in a *promotional mix:* sales promotion, public relations and publicity, advertising, and personal selling.

SALES PROMOTION Fashion retailers use special contests, displayed merchandise in windows, or special coupons as forms of *sales promotion*. The purpose of sales promotional activities is to increase customer traffic in a store so people will buy products. The three types of promotional activities—contests, displays, and coupons—do not require any direct contact with the customer.

PUBLIC RELATIONS AND PUBLICITY Businesses that attempt to create a demand for their products by securing news in newspapers or on radio or television use public relations and publicity. *Public relations* are activities that promote the image and communications a company has with employees, customers, and the public. *Publicity* is usually an unpaid mention of a business, its employees, or its merchandise in the media. Retail stores that sponsor charitable events are using the events for public relations and publicity.

COVERGIRL

Vintage denim, surf and sand...
It's color from where the ocean meets land!
stonewashed
The look starts with Fresh Complexion
Pocket Powder Foundation and Undereye Concealer.
Get your Stonewashed look—
join My CoverGirl now! www.covergirl.com
easy breezy beautiful COVERGIRL

COVERGIRL MOLLY SIMS

Figure 2.2

Promotional Mix at the Mall

TYPE OF PROMOTION	EXAMPLE
Advertising	Announcement signs are placed at the entrances to the mall.
Sales Promotion	The staff working on the fashion show wears T-shirts imprinted with the name of the performer and the new line of clothing.
Publicity	The organizers of the event book the music star on a local television morning show.
Public Relations	In the evening a prominent TV newscaster mentions the fashion show and comments on the performer's involvement in charitable organizations.
Personal Selling	On the day of the fashion show, thousands of fans attend the fashion show. After the show they approach salespeople to buy the performer's clothing line.

EVENTFUL PROMOTION
A fashion show is planned by a retail store promoting a new line of clothing created by a teen music star. *Give an example of a promotional event that you have seen advertised or have attended.*

ADVERTISING *Advertising* is a paid message that a business sends to the public about the product. These messages appear in magazines, newspapers, brochures, television commercials, and outdoor signage. Fashion merchandisers use print ads in fashion magazines targeted to specific consumers. Users of the Internet receive advertising messages from fashion stores through e-mail.

PERSONAL SELLING The fourth type of promotion is *personal selling*. It is different because personal selling requires personal communication and contact with customers by the sales personnel.

APPLYING THE PROMOTIONAL MIX Fashion businesses might utilize all or one of these methods. Chapter 12 discusses fashion promotion further. **Figure 2.2** provides an example of a real-world promotional mix.

Marketing Strategies

The combination of an effective merchandising plan and sound marketing strategies results in higher profits. There are three strategies that fashion marketers use to increase their business:

1. Increase the number of customers.
2. Increase the average transaction.
3. Increase the frequency of repurchase.

TECH
NOTES

Body Scanning = Better Fit

According to surveys conducted by a consulting firm, many consumers are still searching for that perfect fit. With this idea in mind, Brooks Brothers introduced digital tailoring in 2001. After a customer steps into a booth and stands perfectly still, his or her body is scanned by a white light. A computer program then creates a 3-D image of the customer, which ensures expert tailoring.

➡ Describe how this technology benefits the consumer. The retailer? The manufacturer? Learn more about it at **marketingseries.glencoe.com**.

channel of distribution the path a product takes from the producer to the consumer

Increasing the Number of Customers

Promotion plays a key part in this strategy. Customers must be aware of the retail location and the products offered. Businesses cannot rely on the same customers. They need to seek new ones to increase profits.

Increasing the Average Transaction

How many times have you gone to a store to purchase a pair of jeans and bought other items as well? You may have seen in-store displays of jeans and tops. A sales associate may have showed you merchandise to coordinate with the jeans. Stores like the Gap sell perfume at the register area to entice customers to make additional purchases at point of sale (or POS). The strategies used in these examples can increase sales.

Increasing the Frequency of Repurchase

It is a common practice among retailers, particularly specialty stores, to send special mailings offering discounts and coupons to their customers. Some stores host fashion events targeted to their existing customers so there is a reason to return and shop more often.

Channels of Distribution

Merchandise undertakes quite a journey before it arrives at its final destination, the consumer. This journey is the **channel of distribution**, or the path a product takes from the producer to the consumer. This path can also represent *place* in the marketing mix. Fashion marketers must determine the best ways to get the products to potential customers.

A *direct channel of distribution* is a path of distribution in which products are sold by the producer directly to the customer. An *indirect channel of distribution* is a path of distribution of products that involves one or more steps, or intermediaries. For example, a product moves from the manufacturer, to the wholesaler, to the retailer, and then to the consumer.

Fashion and Distribution

For apparel and home furnishings, the movement through the channels of distribution is called the *soft-goods chain*. This chain includes three specific segments:

1. **Textile segment**—The soft-goods chain begins with the textile segment, which includes fiber, yarn, and fabric production.

2. **Apparel segment**—The apparel segment is responsible for producing the finished garments and accessories. The apparel is designed, produced by manufacturers, and sold to retailers.

3. **Retail segment**—The retail segment includes stores or outlets that sell the products to customers. Consumers are the end users who buy and/or use the fashion products.

The Functions of Marketing

To sell and market products, all businesses conduct marketing activities that can be classified into seven basic functions. These seven **functions of marketing** are the activities that include:

- Product/service management
- Distribution
- Financing
- Pricing
- Marketing-information management
- Promotion
- Selling

Performing these functions, which correspond to the marketing mix, is the responsibility of fashion marketers. In order to have a successful fashion business, business owners follow the principles outlined in these functions.

Product/Service Management Function

Because consumers are continually seeking new fashions from the fashion industry, businesses must exercise efficient *product/service management*. They must develop, maintain, and improve their products in response to customer demands. Fashion producers must look for new ways to use existing items or produce new ones that will continue to interest the consumer. For example, one of the current textiles used in apparel is spandex, a lightweight, yet extremely strong, synthetic fiber. Although this material had been in existence for years, its popularity increased when designers began using it for women's and men's active-wear fashions.

Distribution Function

In order for merchandise to get to the customer on a timely basis, marketers must consider the *distribution* of the goods. This includes the methods of physically moving and storing goods. Distribution technology allows businesses to track and monitor merchandise all the way from the manufacturer to the retail outlet to the customer. Retailers use computer systems that instantly record sales and can determine what merchandise is available in their stores. If an item such as a spandex top is selling better than expected, the retailer can communicate this information to the manufacturer. The manufacturer can then ship goods quickly to restock the store's supply.

Case Study   PART 2

CLOSING THE GAP?

Continued from Part 1 on page 25

In 2003, Paul Pressler began to steer Gap, Inc., out of financial difficulty by listening to customers. Pressler focused on selling products with proven appeal. In addition, he expanded marketing efforts and online and international business. Pressler developed a mix of "basic, on-trend, and emerging" fashion products. Gap wanted to keep core customers while introducing new merchandise. Learning from past mistakes, the company now uses strict research-based marketing and development methods. The strategies seem to be working. By the end of 2003, sales had increased by 94 percent.

ANALYZE AND WRITE

1. Write two sentences about how Gap has tried to find a balance between giving customers what they want and introducing new products.
2. What is the importance of having a marketing strategy for fashion businesses? Write a paragraph to explain your answer.

functions of marketing the activities that include product/service management, distribution, financing, pricing, marketing-information management, promotion, and selling

MARKETING SERIES Online

Remember to check out this book's Web site for fashion marketing information and more great resources at **marketingseries.glencoe.com**.

COMPLETE OUTFITTING

Ann Crump
Clothing Boutique Owner
Franklin and Main

What is your job?

"I own a store that is a women's apparel and accessory boutique. We attract a lot of pedestrian traffic from tourists walking to the waterfalls in town and customers who want a one-stop shop. We can provide an entire outfit from the dress to undergarments, shoes, and jewelry. This service is very popular in the spring when many customers come in for wedding, graduation, or prom outfits."

What do you do in your job?

"I do all the buying for the store as well as the management. This includes handling advertising, employees, payroll, stock, store location, and service to the customers."

What kind of training did you have?

"I graduated from Ohio University with a liberal arts degree, but I had wanted to run a boutique since I was a little girl. When I got married and moved to Chagrin Falls, Ohio, I saw there was a boutique for sale, so I bought it. I learned a lot through experience those first couple of years. I came to know my clientele, and I learned the importance of the quality of the merchandise and service."

What advice would you give students?

"Work in a store before owning one. You will learn a lot through trial and error. Also, you have to be people oriented to offer good service. Keep up with trends and your clientele."

What's your key to success?

"Buy what you like, because it's easier to sell. But make a budget and stick to it. It's very easy to spend too much money at the big shows on great clothes."

What does it mean to "know your clientele"?

Career Data: Boutique Owner

Education and Training High school diploma, associate degree, or bachelor's degree

Skills and Abilities Management, organizational, computer, and communication skills

Career Outlook As fast as average growth through 2012

Career Path Sales associate, store owner to franchise owner; other possible paths

CONNECT

Have you ever made a financial plan for yourself? If so, why?

Financing Function

Any type of business requires *financing*, or the means of getting the money to pay for the operation of a business. Careful planning is important. Financial planning can include many factors, such as production costs of the product, product pricing for the customer, and everyday expenses such as rent, supplies, and payroll.

Pricing Function

A primary goal of any business is to make a profit. A key factor in achieving this goal is to price a product accurately. *Pricing* includes how much to charge for goods and services in order to maximize profits. Although companies price their merchandise based on what the customer is willing to pay, they must be careful not to set prices so low that the business does not make a profit.

Marketing-Information Management Function

The world of fashion is ever-changing. It is a real challenge for fashion businesses to stay on top of these changes. Gathering information is critical. Information is obtained primarily through marketing research, which helps fashion businesses determine their customers' preferences and how to better market products. Businesses are able to effectively use the information through *marketing-information management* systems. The five main elements in an information system are:

1. **Input**—reports, past records, or surveys
2. **Storage**—placing information on a disk or hard drive of a computer
3. **Analysis**—the study of the information gathered so that decisions can be made
4. **Output**—reports of the analysis and conclusions drawn from the information
5. **Decision making**—the final result of the first four elements

For example, the manufacturer produces women's expensive sportswear and plans to introduce new items. To gather marketing information, the company might conduct research by hosting a focus group. A focus group would include people from the company's target market. The members of the group would be the same age and share the same income level of customers who purchase this type of sportswear. Using the information obtained from the survey questions concerning styles, fabrics, and prices, the manufacturer produces a report. Marketers can then draw conclusions about their customers' needs and wants and make decisions about producing new fashion items.

Promotion Function

When new or existing products are developed, fashion marketers must promote their products to make sales. *Promotion* is the communication technique a business uses, such as advertising and other promotional methods, to interest customers in buying the products. Manufacturers also promote their merchandise to retailers through catalog and Internet methods.

Selling Function

The *selling* function involves the direct personal contact that businesses have with their customers. Developing good selling skills is especially important for selling more expensive apparel and designer fashions. Sales personnel must be able to communicate the benefits and features of the items so that customers are willing to pay higher prices.

ETHICS & ISSUES

Designing for You?

According to an article in *Observer* magazine titled "Fashion's Power 30," the esoteric and noncommercial designs of Junya Watanabe influence other designers. "What may look like an unintelligible silhouette from Watanabe in one season is sure to have altered the way we think about clothes by the next." Designers are creative people who depict their vision of fashion, sometimes ahead of the market. However, if their designs do not have commercial appeal, designers lose customers and sales. *Is it more important for a designer to create clothes with commercial appeal or clothes that are true to a personal vision of fashion? Why?*

QUESTION

What are the elements of a marketing-information management system?

World Market

Global Outlets

In the 1990s, manufacturers' outlet malls ranked as the fastest-growing segment of the retail industry. These outlet malls represented a $12.2 billion industry with more than 300 centers in the United States. By 2004, sales grew to $15 billion.

Outlet malls exist around the world in places such as Austria, Canada, the Czech Republic, France, Guam, Israel, Italy, Netherlands, Singapore, Spain, Switzerland, the United Kingdom—and Japan.

Many of the same fashion stores in American outlets can be found in the malls of other countries. In the Gotemba Premium Outlets of Tokyo,

Japanese consumers shop at Brooks Brothers, Eddie Bauer, and the Gap as well as Tasaki, a jewelry store, and Muji, a clothing store. "Where Style Meets Value" is the marketing slogan of Premium Outlets. In Japan, as in the United States, it's just what thrifty-minded consumers ordered.

How would marketing a fashion outlet mall differ from promotion for an upscale fashion mall?

Marketing the Fashion Product

Fashion marketers must focus on marketing strategies to get a particular product in the hands of the consumer. By focusing on a specific segment of the market, or group of customers, and tailoring products and promotional messages to this segment, marketers can reach their target customers and increase sales. Successful fashion marketers combine the marketing mix and functions of marketing to develop, distribute, and promote their fashion products.

Quick Check

RESPOND to what you've read by answering these questions.

1. What are the four Ps of marketing?_____

2. What three marketing strategies are used to increase retail business?_____

3. What are the seven functions of marketing?_____

Worksheet 2.1

Studying Customer Characteristics

1. Visit two types of clothing stores in your area. For example, choose one store where you shop regularly. Choose another store where an adult might shop.

2. Answer the following questions about each store:
   - **Demographics:** What demographic segment is this store trying to reach?
   - **Psychographics:** What psychographic segment is this store trying to reach?
   - **Geographics:** How do geographics affect the selection of merchandise?
   - **Behavioristics:** Do you think the store's marketers considered purchase occasion, product benefits, or usage level and commitment in choosing merchandise? Explain.

Store 1:

Demographics

_____
_____
_____

Psychographics

_____
_____
_____

Geographics

_____
_____
_____

Behavioristics

_____
_____
_____
_____

Store 2:

Demographics

_____
_____
_____

Psychographics

_____
_____
_____

Geographics

_____
_____
_____

Behavioristics

_____
_____
_____
_____

Worksheet 2.2

The Promotional Mix for a Store

Select a fashion retailer that does a lot of promotion. Over the next month, watch newspapers and look at magazines, television, and the Internet to find pieces about the store and its merchandise. Visit the store at least two times. Then write a summary about the promotional methods used by the fashion retailer.

_____

_____

_____

_____

_____

_____

_____

_____

_____

_____

_____

_____

_____

_____

_____

_____

_____

_____

_____

_____

_____

_____

_____

_____

_____

Portfolio Works

THE BEST PROMOTION

Read the two case studies below, and then decide on the best marketing strategy for each store. Name the strategy, and then suggest a marketing promotion that might be used. Write your answers on the lines provided.

Example:

Monica's is a high-end specialty store that carries evening dresses, wraps, and accessories for women. Named after the owner, the store has a loyal clientele who shop there. Monica would like to increase her sales. What should she do?

The best strategy for Monica's is to increase the frequency of repurchase with her loyal client base. Monica could host a fashion event. She could send a special mailing to her customers to invite them to a trunk sale that will show off new merchandise.

Case 1:

Josh opened an athletic shoe store in 2000. Recently sales have been dropping. To make money, Josh needs to sell at least 45 pairs of shoes daily. What is the best marketing strategy for Josh?

_____

_____

_____

_____

_____

Case 2:

Adrien is an assistant marketing manager for a new clothing store in the mall. The store's target market is young people between the ages of 15 to 25. His supervisor has asked Adrien to come up with a way to increase sales.

_____

_____

_____

_____

_____

Add this page to your career portfolio.

CHAPTER SUMMARY

Section 2.1 Fashion Marketing Basics

marketing (p. 26)
marketing concept
(p. 26)
target market (p. 27)
market segmentation
(p. 27)
demographics (p. 27)
psychographics (p. 27)
geographics (p. 28)
behavioristics (p. 28)
fashion merchandising
(p. 30)

- Marketing is the process of developing, promoting, and distributing products to satisfy customers' needs and wants.

- Marketers use different customer characteristics to identify a target market that a business wants to reach. The characteristics include demographic, psychographic, geographic, and behavioristic characteristics.

- Fashion merchandising is the planning, buying, and selling of fashion apparel and accessories to offer the right merchandise blend to meet consumer demand.

Section 2.2 Marketing Strategies

marketing mix (p. 31)
channel of distribution
(p. 34)
functions of marketing
(p. 35)

- The marketing mix includes four basic marketing strategies or four components, which are also called the four Ps of marketing—product, place, price, and promotion.

- One component of the marketing mix is promotion, which includes four types of promotion—sales promotion, publicity and public relations, advertising, and personal selling.

- The seven functions of marketing are the activities that include product/service management, distribution, financing, pricing, marketing-information management, promotion, and selling.

CHECKING CONCEPTS

1. **Explain** the term *marketing*.
2. **List** four types of customer characteristics used to identify a target market.
3. **Describe** fashion merchandising.
4. **Name** the components of the marketing mix.
5. **List** the different methods of promotion.
6. **Explain** the different channels of distribution.
7. **Identify** the activities associated with the functions of marketing.

Critical Thinking

8. **Compare** the marketing mix with the functions of marketing.

CROSS-CURRICULUM SKILLS

Work-Based Learning

Interpersonal Skills—Working With Diversity

9. Collect five ads about the same type of merchandise. Prepare a short oral presentation about the diversity shown or not shown in the promotion of the same type of merchandise.

Personal Qualities—Integrity and Honesty

10. Work with a group of three other students. Discuss the question: Can promotion and advertising cross a line and become unethical? What is that line? Present a summary to the class.

School-Based Learning

History

11. Use the Internet or contact a fashion merchant to learn the history of the company and its marketing strategies. Write a summary of the strategies used in the past and today.

Language Arts

12. Write a one-page essay on why fashion retailers such as PacSun, Abercrombie & Fitch, and the Gap target young customers?

Role Play: Assistant Manager

SITUATION You are to assume the role of assistant manager of a children's clothing store. The store's owner (judge) has decided to open a new store. The owner wants the new store to build on the success of the existing store but plans to carry a different merchandise line. The new store will carry clothing for young women. The store's owner (judge) wants the new store to have its own identity.

(ACTIVITY) The store's owner (judge) has asked you to create a few marketing ideas for the new store. Your ideas should consider the four Ps of marketing.

EVALUATION You will be evaluated on how well you meet the following performance indicators:

- Explain the nature of marketing plans.
- Develop a marketing plan.
- Explain the concept of marketing strategies.
- Select a target market.
- Make oral presentations.

Fashion retail merchants such as PacSun, Abercrombie & Fitch, and the Gap appeal to high school students and young adults. Work with a partner to do this activity.

- Use the Internet to research PacSun, Abercrombie & Fitch, or the Gap.
- Using presentation software, create a three- to four-minute presentation about the company.
- Highlight some of the best-selling clothes.

➡️ For a link to a Web site to help you do this activity, go to **marketingseries.glencoe.com**.

Chapter 3

The Fashion Business

Section 3.1

Types of Businesses

Section 3.2

Fashion and Economics

Chapter Objectives

- Explain the three main market segments of the fashion industry.
- Describe the primary forms of business ownership.
- Identify the key risks faced by fashion businesses.
- Explain how globalization has affected the fashion industry.
- Describe the impact of the fashion industry on the U.S. and world economies.
- Explain the relationship between supply and demand.

44

TEEN-STAR FASHIONS

A number of celebrities are aware of the connection between fame and fashion. They have developed their own lines of clothing, believing they will have a built-in customer base—their fans. With TV, film, and music success already on her résumé, teen-star Hilary Duff did just that in 2003 by starting an international fashion company called Stuff by Hilary Duff. Her fashions, including clothing and accessories, are designed for her fans—girls in their "tweens," ages 6 to 12 years old. Casual T-shirts, skirts, pants, jewelry, and backpacks are offered in hopes of making Stuff a brand name in fashion.

However, pop stardom does not always guarantee success in the fashion industry. Teen fashion is a specific segment of the fashion industry and is risky because styles go in and out of favor quickly. In addition, the teen fashion market is flooded with popular brands such as Abercrombie & Fitch. So how can Stuff by Hilary Duff compete in the world of teen fashion?

ANALYZE AND WRITE

1. Would you classify Stuff by Hilary Duff as a producer or retailer of fashion? Write one sentence in response.
2. Is Stuff by Hilary Duff a corporation or a small business? Explain your answer.

Case Study Part 2 on page 59

POWER READ

Be an active reader and use these reading strategies:

PREDICT what the section will be about.

CONNECT what you read with your life.

QUESTION as you read to make sure you understand the content.

RESPOND to what you've read.

Types of Businesses

AS YOU READ ...

YOU WILL LEARN

- To explain the three main market segments of the fashion industry.
- To describe the primary forms of business ownership.
- To identify the key risks faced by fashion businesses.

WHY IT'S IMPORTANT

The fashion industry is made up of interrelated and interdependent segments. Understanding the structure and organization of the fashion industry as well as the risks involved can help fashion businesses be successful.

KEY TERMS

- primary market
- secondary market
- tertiary market
- retailing
- sole proprietorship
- partnership
- corporation
- risk
- risk management

PREDICT

What key term(s) do you think relates to types of fashion businesses?

Fashion Businesses

A series of events must take place for a business to have a fashion product that consumers will accept and buy. Textiles are produced; ideas are transformed into designing and creating a new product; and the product is produced and marketed. In order to fully understand the marketing of fashion, it is important to understand the various businesses that comprise the fashion industry.

Fashion Industry Segments

There are three main segments in the fashion industry. Each segment includes specific businesses. The first is the **primary market**, which is the industry segment that includes businesses that grow and produce the raw materials that become fashion apparel or accessories. The raw materials then move into the **secondary market**, which is the industry segment that includes businesses that transform the raw materials into fashion in the merchandise production phase. These businesses serve as the link to the retail world. The third segment, or **tertiary market**, is the industry segment that includes retail businesses such as stores.

People who work in each of the segments must have knowledge of the other segments of the industry. For example, the creator of fibers must understand how fabrics will translate into finished garments.

Primary Market

The primary market plays a key role in the development of fashion. Because this phase involves technical research and planning as well as complex production processes, these businesses must be aware of current consumer needs and fashion trends. The production schedule for the primary market is ahead of schedules in other industry segments. The businesses in this market generate the products used in the production of the final products.

TEXTILES The textile industry is the largest segment of the primary market. *Textiles* is a broad term referring to any material that can be made into fabric by any method. This industry produces the fiber, fabric, leather, fur, plastic, metal, paper, and any other substance involved in production. Besides production for apparel, the textile industry also develops and produces products for other industries. Home furnishings and interior decorating businesses also use textiles. The textile market is the foundation in the building process of fashions.

Secondary Market

Businesses in the secondary market produce garments by transforming textiles to the finished product, or wearing apparel. Producers are responsible for designing, producing, and selling the goods to retailers.

The work of divisions within the businesses in the secondary market is interrelated and interdependent. For example, a design division creates new styles while keeping in mind the customer's needs. If a company specializes in large-sized clothing, designers concentrate on styles that will suit that figure type. The sales staff works with retailers that purchase the finished apparel. Production takes place based on the needs of the retailers. The producer supplies the garments to the retailer in the sizes and fabrics ordered.

The main types of producers in the secondary market include *manufacturers, wholesalers, contractors,* and *product development teams.*

MANUFACTURERS The producers who are manufacturers handle all operations such as buying the fabric, designing or buying designs, making garments, and selling and delivering the finished garments.

WHOLESALERS Producers who are wholesalers are similar to manufacturers but do not actually make the clothing. They have design staffs who produce the designs. Wholesalers purchase textiles or other raw materials necessary for the designs and then plan the cutting of the materials. They also coordinate the selling and delivery processes. Many of the industry's top fashion design companies are classified as wholesalers.

primary market the industry segment that includes businesses that grow and produce the raw materials that become fashion apparel or accessories

secondary market the industry segment that includes businesses that transform raw materials into fashion in the merchandise production phase

tertiary market the industry segment that includes retail businesses such as stores

THE SECONDARY MARKET
In the secondary market, many contracting companies successfully make and market clothing to well-established stores that tag the clothing with store names. *Do you think a young designer would have an advantage if his or her designs were labeled with a store name, or private label? Why or why not?*

CONTRACTORS These producers are different from wholesalers. They may be responsible for many aspects of production—from sewing and sometimes cutting to the delivery of goods. Contractors may produce designs for merchandise that carries a store's label, or *private label*. Many large department stores sell private-label fashion. Contractors incorporate certain fabrics or treatments in the garments and make samples for retailers. Their products are tested in particular stores to forecast selling potential of the garment designs. If customer response is good, more garments are made for other stores.

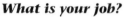

Profiles in Fashion

THE BUSINESS OF CREATIVITY

Jessica Fields
Jewelry Designer
Jessica Fields Designs

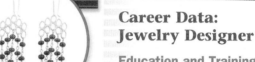

© 2004 Jessica Fields

What is your job?
"I am a jewelry designer."

What do you do in your job?
"I do design, construction, and polishing as well as purchasing of gems and materials. I also do all the administration that comes with running a small business. I sell my jewelry in boutiques and in shows and open studios. I have set up a Web site as an online portfolio of my designs."

What kind of training did you have?
"I started taking classes in metalwork when I was in high school. When I went to college, I majored in English, but I took art classes. After college I enrolled in the Fashion Institute of Technology in New York to learn jewelry design and production. I didn't like the program at first, so I decided to pursue my interest in English, but I missed the creativity of design. So I re-enrolled at FIT. I knew exactly which skills I wanted to learn so I could create my own jewelry."

What advice would you give students?
"You need skills such as goldsmithing so you can build jewelry. A thick skin also helps, particularly for women breaking into a historically male-dominated industry. However, once you find vendors you trust, they help you build your network."

What's your key to success?
"I try to be open-minded about the different directions in which the business can go. Never be afraid to take opportunities that may be unplanned."

What different segments of the fashion industry can contribute to a jewelry business? Explain.

Career Data: Jewelry Designer

Education and Training
Associate degree or bachelor's degree

Skills and Abilities
Goldsmithing, drawing and design rendering, business administration, and marketing skills

Career Outlook As fast as average growth through 2012

Career Path Independent designer distributing through boutiques, distributing through department stores to establishing own store and employing other designers

PRODUCT DEVELOPMENT TEAMS In most cases today, retailers may have their own product development teams. These teams design, merchandise, and outsource work to contractors in the United States or outside of the country.

Tertiary Market

The final segment, or tertiary market, is the retail industry. **Retailing** is the selling of products to customers. Selling can be either direct selling or the exchange of merchandise in return for money or credit. The different types of retail operations include department stores, specialty stores, discount department stores, variety stores, off-price stores, warehouse stores, outlet stores, and nonstore retailers. Retail operations distribute directly to the consumers who buy and/or use the products. This is the link between the consumer and the manufacturer. However, retailers cannot be everything to everyone. They generally direct their purchasing and marketing efforts to their target customers' needs and desires.

Support Industries

There are numerous business opportunities in the fashion industry, because each segment of the industry has other support industries. For example, businesses do not always have their own in-house advertising departments and must rely upon other companies that specialize in advertising and public-relations services. Accounting and financial companies can provide specialized services as well. Due to the ever-changing nature of technology, many new companies have emerged that specialize in product development and market research. These companies offer their services to segments of the fashion industry. Support industries may help lower operation costs and allow fashion companies to focus on fashion.

Types of Fashion Business Organization

The fashion industry and other industries are comprised of businesses that have one of the three most common types of business organization: *sole proprietorship, partnership,* or *corporation.* New fashion companies must decide which form of business entity to establish. Each form of business is affected by specific regulations regarding taxes, management, liability of the owner, and distribution of profits. A business owned by one person is a sole proprietorship. A partnership is owned by two or more people under a legal agreement. A corporation is a separate legal entity formed according to state laws.

Sole Proprietorship

Probably one of the most common forms of business is the **sole proprietorship**, which is a business owned and operated by one person. It is one of the oldest forms of business ownership. A sole proprietorship may require some licensing from local authorities; however, it is not controlled by federal government regulations. The business does not exist apart from the owner.

MARKETING SERIES *Online*

Remember to check out this book's Web site for fashion business information and more great resources at marketingseries.glencoe.com.

retailing the selling of products to customers

CONNECT

In a popular magazine, find a fashion ad that might have been created by an ad agency.

sole proprietorship a business owned and operated by one person

RISKS The owner takes responsibility for all assets owned, whether used in the business or personally owned. In a sole proprietorship, the owner (sole proprietor) is personally liable for the company and, thus, places all of his or her personal assets at risk.

TAXES The business profit is taxed as personal income tax at a rate less than the rate imposed on corporations. The owner includes the income and expenses of the business on his or her personal tax return.

PROS AND CONS One of the most compelling reasons for having this type of ownership is that the owner has the freedom to operate as he or she feels is necessary. The owner can sell the business. The sole proprietorship remains in existence for as long as the owner is willing or able to stay in business. However, because the financial management and liability is the responsibility of the owner, operating a sole proprietorship can be an awesome task for one person. Most family-owned-and-operated retail stores are sole proprietorships.

Hot Property

The Luck of Aran

For hundreds of years, the men and women of Inis Mór, Ireland, have been designers, manufacturers, wholesalers, and retailers of the traditional Aran sweater. Well known for their high-quality wool, the Aran sweaters are quickly becoming a staple in wardrobes around the world.

Located on the largest of the Aran Islands on the west coast of Ireland, the Aran Sweater Market has grown from humble beginnings. It is now one of the most successful fashion craft businesses in the world. The company is a cornerstone of the small island's economy, employing islanders in every phase of the business.

SYMBOLS OF TRADITION
Artisans knit the wool sweaters in the tradition of the island's ancestors. From generation to generation, fishermen and farmers have passed down the combination of stitches that represent each family's, or *clan's*, identity. A cable stitch depicts the fisherman's ropes and represents a wish for a fruitful day at sea. A diamond stitch symbolizes the small fields of the island. The Irish-moss stitch represents the seaweed that fertilizes barren fields and produces a good harvest. If knitted inside the diamond stitch, the Irish-moss stitch wishes the wearer success and wealth.

MODERN METHODS
Traditionally, the sweaters were hand knit. Each sweater, made up of approximately 100,000 stitches, could take a knitter up to 60 days to complete. Today the demand and potential for profit have necessitated machine production of the sweaters.

With each stitch, the sweaters have traveled far beyond their humble origins on a wind-swept island off the west coast of Ireland to become part of today's global market.

1. Which type of business organization do you think is best for this company—sole proprietorship, partnership, or corporation? Why?
2. What natural risks might this company face?

Partnership

A **partnership** is a business created through a legal agreement between two or more people who are jointly responsible for the success or failure of the business. The agreement includes arrangements for the contribution of each partner and the division of profits, and it states the authority of each partner. Each partner contributes money, property, labor, or skill, and expects to share in the profits and losses of the business. Many apparel manufacturers are partnerships.

TAXES A partnership has fewer regulations than a corporation, and each partner is taxed separately on individual tax returns. A partnership must file an annual information return to report income, expenses, deductions, profits, and losses from its operations. However, it does not pay any income tax. Profits and losses are included on each partner's personal tax return.

PERSONAL LIABILITY Each partner is personally liable for debts of the partnership. For example, if the assets of a partnership are not enough to pay its creditors' claims, the personal assets of the partners can be used. A partnership ends upon the death or withdrawal of one of the partners, but most partnership agreements make provisions for these types of events.

Corporation

Many of the larger businesses in the fashion industry are corporations. A **corporation** is a business that is chartered by a state and legally operates apart from the owner or owners. State governments require that this type of ownership be chartered. A charter is a legal document that grants certain rights and privileges to the company by the state. Corporations exist throughout the fashion industry. One of the most prominent examples in the retail industry is Wal-Mart, the number-one retail corporation in the world.

STOCKS AND SHAREHOLDERS A corporation also has the right to issue stock. Corporations are traded on the stock exchange, and their ownership is divided into shares of stock that can be owned by a large number of stockholders, or owners. It is a more complicated form of business than the sole proprietorship and the partnership. In forming a corporation, prospective shareholders transfer money, property, or both, for the corporation's capital stock.

TAXES The profit of a corporation is taxed to both the corporation and to the shareholders when the profit is distributed as dividends. A corporation may be allowed to take special deductions. However, shareholders are not allowed to deduct any losses of the corporation. Policy decisions and management of a corporation are handled by its board of directors.

In a partnership, the death of an owner could be grounds for termination of the partnership. However, in a corporation, the business continues to exist even after the death of one of the owners, or shareholders.

THE Electronic CHANNEL

Web Power

For emerging designers wanting to sell their products, the choice is between clicks or bricks—online retail versus traditional in-store retail. Online stores are a great way to start a business without the overhead of renting retail space. However, building an online store means reaching customers and providing them with a secure way to pay for and receive their purchases. To do this, many entrepreneurs team up with established e-tailers such as Yahoo, eBay, and Amazon. Known as an online auction site, eBay also sponsors online fashion stores.

➡ Make a list of the online fashion stores partnered with eBay through **marketingseries.glencoe.com**.

partnership a business created through a legal agreement between two or more people who are jointly responsible for the success or failure of the business

corporation a business that is chartered by a state and legally operates apart from the owner or owners

Fashion Risks

Fashion businesses must constantly respond to consumers' demand for change. They develop new products and services with the hope of generating a profit. As with all businesses, there is a chance for success and a chance for failure. **Risk** is the possibility that a loss can occur as the result of a business decision or activity. Fashion business owners take risks when they start businesses. For example, in the case of sole proprietorships and partnerships, owners take risks when they invest their own money. Corporations invest money from their shareholders to operate, and there is risk that stock values will decrease. For designers, there is the risk that someone will copy their designs and produce apparel faster or less expensively.

risk the possibility that a loss can occur as the result of a business decision or activity

Risk Management

There are no methods to completely safeguard a business from risk. However, there are ways risk can be reduced and managed. **Risk management** is a strategy to offset business risks. According to the American Risk and Insurance Association, risk management is a systematic process of managing an organization's risk exposure to achieve objectives in a manner consistent with public interest, human safety, environmental factors, and the law. Business owners who use marketing information, consider opportunities for avoiding losses, and make good decisions can effectively manage risk.

risk management a strategy to offset business risks

Figure 3.1

Sources of Inventory Shortages

HUMAN ERRORS The latest fashionable apparel is often a target of shoplifting and pilfering by employees. *How might designer boutiques manage this type of human risk?*

- 48% Employee theft
- 32% Shoplifting
- 15% Administrative and paper error
- 5% Vendor fraud

SOURCE: Richard C. Hollinger and Jason L Davis, *2002 National Retail Security Survey Final Report,* University of Florida

Types of Risks

There are three types of risks that businesses usually face. These are *economic, human,* and *natural risks:*

- **Economic risks** are risks that occur from changes in overall business conditions. When many people are without jobs, they spend less money on fashion goods. Therefore, the fashion industry has the risk of not selling merchandise.

- **Human risks** are risks caused by human mistakes as well as by the unpredictability of customers, employees, or the work environment. A customer tripping on a carpet in a store is an example of this type of risk. A safe environment helps to attract and keep customers and employees coming back to a store. Businesses must also consider the loss of merchandise, money, and other company assets as risk. These losses can also be caused by problems such as errors in financial records or customer and employee theft. (See **Figure 3.1** for examples.)

- **Natural risks** are risks that result from natural causes such as the weather. Even an unexpected change in climate can prove to be a risk for fashion retailers. A store that is located in a ski resort area where the weather is unusually warm during a skiing season may face the risk of fewer sales of coats.

Other Categories of Risks

Identifying, categorizing, and addressing potential risks can reduce negative impact. Besides the basic types of risks, other categories of risks are pure, speculative, controllable, uncontrollable, insurable, and uninsurable risks:

- **Pure risks** are risks that occur when there is a possibility of a loss, but no chance to gain from the event. For example, if you ride a motorcycle, you are taking a risk of having an accident. You could be hurt from the accident. But if you choose not to ride, there is no particular opportunity for gain.

- **Speculative risks** are risks that occur when gains or losses are possible. A designer who believes that a new style is going to be very popular might decide to produce large quantities. The designer is taking the risk that the customer will accept or reject the new merchandise.

- **Controllable risks** are risks that can be prevented or reduced in frequency. For example, a retailer might have very expensive jewelry in a store. To control the risk of theft, the store owner would place the jewelry in a locked display case.

- **Uncontrollable risks** are events that a fashion business cannot prevent from occurring, such as the weather. For example, one of the largest producers of raw materials for textiles is the cotton farming industry. The chance of bad weather ruining a crop is a risk these business owners take.

QUESTION

What are three risks that could reduce the profits of a clothing store?

- **Insurable risks** are pure risks that could exist for a large number of businesses, including those for which the probability and amount of loss is predictable. For example, business owners purchase insurance to cover the possibility of loss due to fire or accidents. Retailers must also consider accidents involving employees and customers.

- **Uninsurable risks** are risks that occur when the chances of risk cannot be predicted or when the amount of loss cannot be estimated, as in the case of the designer's speculative risk. That designer cannot insure against the customer choosing not to buy the new styles.

Managing Potential Risk

Businesses can handle risk by different methods. Purchasing insurance is necessary for any business owner. Prevention methods can include employee training. Retailers can transfer risk back to the manufacturer through product warranties. Paying attention to the various types of risks can save fashion businesses valuable time as well as money. Risk is one important factor affecting the overall economics of all types of fashion businesses.

Quick Check ✓

RESPOND to what you've read by answering these questions.

1. What are the three main market segments of the fashion industry?_____

_____

_____

_____

_____

2. What are the three types of fashion business ownership?_____

_____

_____

_____

_____

3. How can fashion businesses minimize risk?_____

_____

_____

_____

_____

Fashion and Economics

Impact on Global Economy

For centuries, ships have carried goods from exotic ports of call, bringing their cargo to the world. Since the 18th century, the international trade of textiles and apparel has contributed to worldwide economic activity. In the 20th century, changes in government policies and new trends in international trade have caused the market for fashion goods to increase.

Globalization and Fashion

Globalization is the increasing integration of the world economy. Countries are no longer limited by their own borders. Citizens of most countries are able to shop for and enjoy products from around the world. **Figure 3.2** on page 56 illustrates how shoppers around the world spend money on clothing. Technological advances have made the world a much smaller place. For example, improved worldwide communication systems, such as the Internet, and the ease of world travel have opened the doors to other countries.

Global Competition

This globalization has created increased competition between countries in the manufacturing sector of fashion. Labor is a major component of the cost of production for fashion products. Thus, countries with lower wages have an advantage over countries with higher wages, such as the United States. As a result, many garments are manufactured outside the United States, which has caused the loss of some manufacturing jobs in the United States. Many foreign governments offer incentives, such as favored status and tax exemptions, that make their countries appealing. Producers in the United States must deal with safety regulations, minimum-wage requirements, and mandatory payment of benefits for workers. Those cost factors may not be present in other countries.

The Balance of Trade

Because of their importance to the U.S. economy, textiles and apparel have been major issues in U.S. trade arrangements with a number of countries and regions. Trade involves imports, exports, and exchanges of money. **Imports** are goods that come into a country from foreign sources or goods that a country buys from other countries. The United States is the largest consumer market of apparel goods in the world. **Exports** are goods that a country sends to a foreign source or goods that a country sells to other countries.

Figure 3.2

Apparel Shopping

GLOBAL SHOPPING SPREE
No matter what languages they speak, people around the world understand the appeal of shopping for clothing.
Check the label of the shirt or top you are wearing to see where it was made.

Country		Shopping Trips/ Year	Average Spent/ Year (U.S.$)
U.S.A.		22	$1,044
U.K.		18	$1,144
Germany		16	$1,312
Hong Kong		16	$1,260
Korea		15	$520
Taiwan		11	$1,000
France		11	$856
Italy		11	$852
Japan		8	$884
Brazil		7	$776

SOURCE: Lifestyle Monitor™ and Global Lifestyle Monitor™.
© 2004 Cotton Inc. All rights reserved.

exports goods that a country sends to a foreign source or goods that a country sells to other countries

balance of trade the relationship between a country's imports and exports

Math Check

TEXTILE TRADE
If Singapore exports $18 million of textiles and imports $2 million, what is the trade deficit or surplus?

➡For tips on finding the solution, go to **marketingseries.glencoe.com.**

The **balance of trade** is the relationship between a country's imports and exports, and it affects the economic health of a country. A *trade deficit* occurs when a country imports more goods than it exports. The United States has a large trade deficit, which includes many textile and apparel products that are imported into the country. A *trade surplus* occurs when a country sells more goods to other countries than it buys. Japan is one country that has a trade surplus.

Trade Agreements and Restrictions

Free trade exists when a government allows products to move freely across its borders. The United States has formed many trade agreements to improve the flow of goods with its trading partners.

 marketingseries.glencoe.com

NAFTA and WTO

The North American Free Trade Agreement (NAFTA) between the United States, Mexico, and Canada is an example of a free-trade agreement. The goal of NAFTA is to enable all countries to experience free trade by eliminating or reducing tariffs, or fees, for trading goods. To resolve conflicts, international agreements restrict the quantities of textiles and apparel traded.

The World Trade Organization (WTO) is an international organization that promotes and enforces trade laws and regulations. Formed in 1995, the WTO now has more than 145 member countries from around the world. Various WTO agreements also reduce barriers to trade. Disputes have resulted because some provisions for removing quotas, or limits on amounts, previously protected the U.S. textile and apparel manufacturers.

Globalization and America

The globalization of the fashion industry is evident in the United States. International stores line Fifth Avenue in New York City and other retail locations in America. Givenchy of France has stores in New York City, Europe, the Middle East, and Asia. Companies such as Escada of Germany have shops in Las Vegas, Nevada. Benetton of Italy has stores in the United States and India. Gap stores are in the United States, Canada, France, Japan, and Germany. Fashion encompasses the entire globe.

Style Point

SHOPPING FOR PLEASURE?

The Global Lifestyle Monitor™ surveyed apparel consumers in ten countries. About 66 percent of consumers in eight countries either "love" or "like" shopping for clothing. However, people in Hong Kong have indifferent attitudes. American women "love" shopping for fashion, but American men tend to "hate" it.

CONNECT

Think of two foreign clothing labels you might find in a department store.

World Market

Batik—the Art of Textile

In the terraced rice fields and lush jungles of Bali, Indonesia, high fashion is being created with batik—a textile that is also an art form. Village artists twist different blends and bundles of yarn together with plastic ties and die the yarn before it is woven. Once dried, the dyed yarn is woven into designs that are passed down in the artists' family.

Another form of batik is wax writing. Part of a plain fabric is covered with wax, and then the fabric is dyed. The waxed area keeps its original color. When the wax is removed, a pattern appears from the dyed and undyed areas of the fabric.

Throughout the islands of Indonesia, batik fabric and garments are sold in the modern malls of the cities and in the villages where artists work with the designs of their ancestors. Village shops bargain with visitors over price. By saying the Bahasa words *mahal-mahal*—which mean "too expensive"—a merchant just might give you an extra 30 percent off the price.

Do you think textile imports to the United States will increase from Indonesia with the removal of quotas and trade restrictions? Could this help the American fashion industry?

INDONESIA

International Fashions

Advances in technology have increased communication around the world. Many companies place their orders via the Internet instead of in person or by telephone. The fashion business is truly international, as producers, designers, and retail buyers cover the globe in search of new products and ideas.

The international influence in today's world of fashion is unlimited. For example, a garment in a boutique on Rodeo Drive in Beverly Hills, California, might have exciting international origins:

- Produced in China with fabric from India and buttons from Bali
- Designed by a designer in France
- Modeled on the runways in Milan, Italy, and Paris, France
- Purchased by a customer in New York City to wear at a trendy party

Impact on Domestic Economy

The fashion industry impacts the economy of the United States every time consumers spend money on products. According to the American Textile Manufacturers Institute (ATMI), U.S. consumers spend $275 billion every year on apparel. This includes purchases of 3 billion slacks or pants, 5.7 billion shirts or blouses, and 370 million sweaters. In 2002, Americans also spent approximately $320 billion on home fashion products, including 560 million sheets and pillowcases and 1.8 billion towels and washcloths.

Textile Industry Impact

As a major contributor to the U.S. economy, the textile industry includes textile mills, textile producers, apparel, fibers, and machinery. It is third among basic manufacturing industries. Approximately 1 million employees work in the U.S. textile segment, representing 6 percent of all U.S. manufacturing industries. These industries support 2.75 million jobs in the textile industry.

MEETING DEMAND Textile workers are integral to the process of making fashion and to the U.S. economy. *How have textile businesses adapted to increasing global competition?*

marketingseries.glencoe.com

Textile Industry Issues

Issues surrounding the textile industry have dramatic impact on the economy. For example, the use of cotton by U.S. textile mills has declined substantially since the increase of imported cotton products devastated the industry during the 1990s. This decline in the demand for raw cotton directly affects the financial condition of all areas of the U.S. cotton industry. The U.S. textile industry and U.S. cotton growers share an economic interest in having solid textile and apparel industries.

Because of the rise in global competition, the U.S. textile and apparel industries have become more competitive. New equipment and techniques have produced higher-quality products at lower costs to meet consumer demand.

Supply and Demand

The law of supply and demand affects pricing in the fashion industry as in other industries. The relationship of these two factors results in the prices people are willing to pay for various products producers are willing to make. **Supply** is the quantity of product offered for sale at all possible prices. **Demand** is the consumer's willingness and ability to buy and/or use products. If a number of stores have an item, then consumers can shop for the lowest price for the item, which may cause the price to drop further. Retailers that have unsold products have to reduce the price of those items in order to stimulate demand. According to economic theory, if the price is low enough, the demand for a product will probably increase. For example, there will be a much greater demand for a new athletic shoe priced at $29 and featured in fashion magazines than for a similar shoe priced at $150. In addition to price and availability, consumers' needs and wants also stimulate demand.

The interaction of supply and demand creates the conditions of *surplus, shortage,* or *equilibrium.* These conditions often determine whether prices will go up, down, or stay the same. For example, surplus can occur with fad items. Producers identify a particular style as being very popular. They make many items, saturating the market until everyone has purchased the items. Consumer demand then decreases while there is still an abundance of the item, which causes the price to decrease. On the other hand, merchandise such as fur apparel, produced in limited quantities due to scarcity of material, may have higher prices.

Case Study | PART 2

TEEN-STAR FASHIONS
Continued from Part 1 on page 45

With many popular brands of teen fashion on the market, Hilary Duff's designs face stiff competition. So, Duff chose to design for her established target market, tweens, offering striped velour skirts, lace-front T-shirts, and preppy-punk jeans. In addition, the Texas-born star promoted her clothing and accessories in the United States as well as Canada. Stuff by Hilary Duff struck a deal with America's Target stores, where her fashions are priced to fit the budgets of "tweenage" girls and their families. The Canadian chain Zellers also picked up her fashions. Zellers' president and COO Thomas Haig explained, "The Stuff by Hilary Duff collection is sure to be a hit with our younger customers, not to mention parents looking for good value."

With the right target market, designs, pricing, and international retailers, Duff's fashions were wildly successful just a year after hitting the stores.

ANALYZE AND WRITE
1. Explain how Stuff by Hilary Duff has contributed to the globalization of fashion.
2. Explain how the principles of supply and demand apply to how Stuff is priced.

supply the quantity of product offered for sale at all possible prices

demand the consumer's willingness and ability to buy and/or use products

QUESTION

What three conditions related to supply and demand determine price levels?

ETHICS & ISSUES

profit the money a business makes after all costs and expenses are paid

trade quotas restrictions on the quantity of a particular good or service that a country is allowed to sell or trade

Profit

Profit, which is the money a business makes after all costs and expenses are paid, is the motivation to do business. As a result, profit dictates the supply of goods available for sale. When the demand for an item is high and the supply of an item is low, the price will be high, causing the producer to manufacture more. Companies exist to make a profit, and consumers are limited in the amount of money they can spend. Because of this, price influences the quantity of a garment to be produced and sold.

Other factors that influence supply include governmental laws or regulations, such as subsidies, bad publicity or consumer action such as boycotts because of child labor violations, and promotion such as advertising.

Employment in the Fashion Industry

The most obvious impact the fashion industry has on the domestic economy is in the area of employment, because producing fashion products requires so much labor. Apparel businesses in the United States employ over 1.3 million people. The textile industry is one of the largest segments of the manufacturing industry. For the past 30 years until 2004, the United States has regulated the amount of imported textiles, by setting **trade quotas**, or restrictions on the amount of a particular good or service that a country is allowed to sell or trade. This regulation ended at the close of 2004. For businesses to survive, they must be able to compete without quotas.

Global Employment

Studies show that skilled labor, such as the designing and marketing segments of the industry, remain in the United States. Manual labor, or the actual construction of garments, is being outsourced, or sent to other countries to be done. However, studies also indicate that the textile and apparel industries will continue to be a major provider of a variety of jobs as the fashion business continues to grow.

Quick Check ✓

RESPOND to what you've read by answering these questions.

1. How has globalization impacted the fashion industry?_____

_____

_____

2. What is the difference between supply and demand?_____

_____

_____

3. Describe the state of employment in the U.S. fashion industry. _____

_____

_____

Worksheet 3.1

Private Labels

Contractors produce private-label garments for many large department stores. By phone, mail, or the Internet, contact a major department store in your community to learn the name of its private label brand(s) for clothing, accessories, and home furnishings. The name may be the same as the store name, or it may be different. Then visit the store and make a list of items you find under its private label.

Clothing	Accessories	Home Furnishings

Name _____ Date _____

Worksheet 3.2

Employment in the Fashion Industry

Apparel businesses in the United States employ more than 1.3 million people. Trade magazines and Internet Web sites such as 24 Seven help job seekers find jobs in the fashion industry. Do the following exercise and write your findings on the lines below.

1. Find a trade magazine or log on to 24 Seven or a similar Web site.
2. Choose three jobs you find under the job category "fashion merchandising."
3. Then use the *Occupational Outlook Handbook* at the U.S. Department of Labor Bureau of Labor Statistics Web site to learn more about these jobs, including their future outlooks.

Job 1:

_____

_____

_____

_____

_____

Job 2:

_____

_____

_____

_____

_____

Job 3:

_____

_____

_____

_____

_____

UNDERSTANDING FASHION PRODUCERS

On a separate sheet of paper, design a graphic organizer that helps you understand the types of fashion producers: manufacturers, wholesalers, contractors, and product development teams. Include the following information:

Manufacturers

- Buy the fabric
- Design or buy designs
- Make the garments
- Sell the garments
- Deliver the garments

Wholesalers

- Do not make the garments
- Have a design staff which produces designs
- Purchase textiles or materials needed for design and cutting
- Coordinate the selling and delivery process
- Include industry's top fashion design companies

Contractors

- May be responsible for many aspects of production, from cutting and sewing to delivery of goods
- May incorporate certain fabrics or treatments
- May produce for a store under private label

Product Development Teams

- Design garments
- Merchandise the garments
- Source out work to contractors in and out of the country

Add this page to your career portfolio.

CHAPTER SUMMARY

Section 3.1 Types of Businesses

primary market (p. 47)
secondary market (p. 47)
tertiary market (p. 47)
retailing (p. 49)
sole proprietorship
   (p. 49)
partnership (p. 50)
corporation (p. 51)
risk (p. 52)
risk management (p. 52)

- The fashion industry is made up of various businesses that are divided into three segments: the primary market that produces raw material, the secondary market that uses raw material to make products, and the tertiary market that includes retail businesses that sell products.

- The three primary forms of business ownership for fashion businesses and other businesses are sole proprietorship, partnership, and corporation.

- Key risks for fashion businesses include economic, human, and natural risks.

Section 3.2 Fashion and Economics

globalization (p. 55)
imports (p. 55)
exports (p. 56)
balance of trade (p. 56)
supply (p. 59)
demand (p. 59)
profit (p. 60)
trade quotas (p. 60)

- Globalization in the fashion industry has allowed people in most countries to have access to products from around the world. It has also caused increased competition between countries in the manufacturing sector of fashion.

- The fashion industry is a major contributor to the U.S. economy. Americans spend $275 billion per year on apparel. The textile industry is third among manufacturing industries. American fashion businesses have presences around the world.

- The relationship of supply and demand results in the prices people are willing to pay for products.

CHECKING CONCEPTS

1. **Name** the three segments of the fashion industry.
2. **Identify** common forms of business organization in the fashion industry.
3. **List** risks experienced by fashion businesses.
4. **Define** globalization.
5. **Explain** how globalization has affected the fashion industry in the U.S. and around the world.
6. **Define** supply and demand.
7. **Describe** economic conditions that result from the interaction of supply and demand.

Critical Thinking

8. **Discuss** the impact of NAFTA on the fashion industry.

CROSS-CURRICULUM SKILLS

Work-Based Learning

Information—Organizing and Maintaining Information

9. Design a chart describing the three types of fashion business ownership. Include at least three facts about each type of ownership in your chart.

Interpersonal Skills—Teaching Others

10. Prepare a report on fashion risks and risk management. Present the report as a lesson to a group of your classmates. Include the types of risks and ways businesses can minimize risks.

School-Based Learning

Language Arts

11. Do you think free-trade agreements are a benefit or hindrance to the fashion industry? Write an essay defending your position.

Arts

12. Draw a political cartoon that illustrates your position on ending the regulation of textile imports into the United States.

 CONNECTION

Role Play: Fashion Marketing Student

SITUATION You are to assume the role of a student in a fashion marketing class. You have been assigned to research jobs in the fashion industry. You are to focus your research on jobs that represent the great variety of jobs available in the fashion industry and the impact of those jobs on the economy of the United States and the global economy. Your report will become part of a presentation that you will make to a civic organization in your town.

(ACTIVITY) You are to prepare an outline of your presentation to discuss with your marketing teacher (judge).

EVALUATION You will be evaluated on how well you meet the following performance indicators:

- Discuss career opportunities in the field of apparel and accessories.
- Explain the effect of international trade on retailing.
- Explain marketing and its importance in a global economy.
- Explain the principles of supply and demand.
- Prepare simple written reports.

 INTERNET ACTIVITY

With globalization, jobs in textile manufacturing are changing in the United States. Use the Internet to research the outlook for textile jobs.

- Search the *Occupational Outlook Handbook* at the U.S. Department of Labor Bureau of Labor Statistics Web site.
- Click OOH Search/A-Z Index.
- Type *fashion*. Click Search.
- Click Textile, Apparel, and Furnishings Occupations.
- Summarize the main points.
- Post summaries in class.

➡️For a link to the *Occupational Outlook Handbook*, go to **marketingseries.glencoe.com**.

Chapter 4

Fashion Centers

Chapter Objectives

- Describe a fashion design center.
- Define a buying center.
- Explain how design and buying centers impact local economies.
- Identify the most important design and buying centers.
- Explain the importance of global sourcing in the fashion industry.
- Describe how cultural influences affect mainstream fashion.

BUILDING A FASHION CENTER IN INDIA

India has been an important source of textile and garment production for many years. Textiles make up about 14 percent of India's industrial production. Cotton from India comprises 15 percent of the world's total cotton crop. The country is also a major producer of silk and jute. India boasts a well-established design industry, garment workers with traditional skills, and a culture that embraces color and pattern.

Despite these advantages, India has struggled to be recognized as an international fashion center. Lack of sponsorship, media attention, and international interest have hindered India's development as a fashion center. Thus, the Fashion Design Council of India was formed in 2001. The Council hired the International Management Group (IMG) to produce India Fashion Week, a series of shows highlighting the best of Indian fashion. The fifth biannual Lakme India Fashion Week took place in New Delhi in April 2004. Have these events put India on the international fashion map?

ANALYZE AND WRITE

1. What has hindered India's development as a fashion center? List three factors.
2. Write a paragraph on how fashion shows promote a country's fashion industry.

Case Study Part 2 on page 75

POWER READ

Be an active reader and use these reading strategies:

PREDICT what the section will be about.

CONNECT what you read with your life.

QUESTION as you read to make sure you understand the content.

RESPOND to what you've read.

Design and Buying Centers

AS YOU READ ...

YOU WILL LEARN

- To describe a fashion design center.
- To define a buying center.
- To explain how design and buying centers impact local economies.
- To identify the most important design and buying centers.

WHY IT'S IMPORTANT

Becoming familiar with international and domestic design and buying centers allows you to know how and where fashions are developed and marketed.

KEY TERMS

- design center
- fashion weeks
- haute couture
- couturiers
- buying center
- market weeks
- mart

PREDICT

What is the difference between a design center and a buying center?

design center a district in a city where fashion design and production firms are clustered together

What Is a Design Center?

A **design center** is a district in a city where fashion design and production firms are clustered together. Designers join together to make their city and country important in the fashion world. The influences of other designers serve as inspiration for new creations. Design centers host important fashion shows during **fashion weeks**, which are periods during each year when fashion designers present new designs or collections. The most important collection shows are held twice a year, featuring spring-summer and fall-winter lines.

Impact of Design Centers

Local governments often support design centers through favorable regulations. Some cities have organizations established to help promote the fashion industry during fashion weeks. The industry has a great economic impact on cities. In addition to the direct revenue from the fashion business, cities also benefit indirectly from income generated by other businesses, such as hotels and restaurants.

International Design Centers

The fashion industry is truly international. Its presence is found in cities around the world, including cities that are the major design centers: Paris, France; Milan, Italy; and New York City in the United States. Designers in these cities set the tone for fashions that people wear all around the world. Other international design centers, such as London, England, and Tokyo, Japan, also influence the world of fashion.

Design Center: Paris

Since the 1700s, the city of Paris has remained the center of the fashion world. Paris is synonymous with **haute couture**, a French term for high fashion, which is expensive, trend-setting, custom-made apparel. The city has been the home to **couturiers**, professional fashion designers involved in designing, making, and selling high-fashion. Coco Chanel and Yves St. Laurent are examples of couturiers.

PARIS FASHION SHOWS From the late 1600s to early 1700s, King Louis XIV of France used dolls to display the latest fashions. Today designers in Paris showcase their latest high-fashion creations in extravagant fashion shows. The average consumer would probably not wear this expensive clothing. The people who attend these shows range from fashion writers, editors, and celebrities to apparel manufacturers, retail buyers, and patternmakers from around the world.

FASHION IDEAS FOR SALE The attendees acquire ideas to take back to their companies and then translate the ideas into fashions that their target customers will purchase and wear. These professionals pay fees to attend the fashion shows. In fact, they pay a considerable amount because they are paying for the right to copy the designs. These copied designs are modified versions of the originals, and retailers sell them at all prices around the world.

THE IMPORTANCE OF FASHION IN PARIS Because of high exposure and global reputation, Paris is often the first choice of top designers from other countries as a place to show collections. The design business is important to the city of Paris because it is one of France's top-three export industries. It is also one of the top employers in that country. The French government has been a longtime supporter of the industry. Many promotion agencies and fashion trade associations have offices located in Paris, because of its designation as a design center. In addition, the city is home to several design schools where aspiring designers learn and improve their craft.

Design Center: Milan

The Italians show their creations during fashion fairs. The Italian and French fashion shows take place at different times so that attendees can cover both markets. *Alta moda,* the Italian term for high fashion, is centered in the city of Rome, but designers in Milan concentrate primarily on ready-to-wear garments. Italian fashion is known for its beautiful fabrics and sophisticated prints.

The Milan fashion industry began with making leather goods, and the Milan fashion center is still the leader in the production of leather accessories, such as shoes and handbags. In the 1940s, garment design and production were limited to men's wear but later expanded to include others types of clothing.

Many of the Italian fashion houses are family businesses that pass the craft of designing on from generation to generation. Besides shoes, clothing is one of the most exported products of Italy. Next to tourism, the fashion industry is the second largest industry in Italy.

Design Center: New York City

During World War II, the American fashion industry was isolated, unable to receive much European design influence. Fashion producers in the United States had to rely on themselves for new ideas. New York City emerged as the main fashion design center, primarily because of the concentration of supplies and labor there.

Today New York City is still considered to be the center of U.S. fashion. Almost two-thirds of U.S. fashion manufacturing is located in New York. New York also has eight schools dedicated to fashion.

As Paris and Milan host fashion shows to highlight their latest creations, New York designers present their creations during designated fashion weeks. The shows in New York follow the French collection showings in Paris.

fashion weeks periods during each year when fashion designers present new designs or collections

haute couture French term for high fashion, which is expensive, trend-setting, custom-made apparel

couturiers professional fashion designers involved in designing, making, and selling high fashion

TECH
NOTES

Television's Global Influence

As new technology makes hundreds of channels available, television is narrowing its focus. Cable channels now seek viewers with specific interests. In 1997, Fashion TV (FTV) became the first international television channel devoted to fashion, beauty, and style. Broadcasted via 32 satellites, FTV brings new ideas about fashion to millions of viewers around the world.

How has television influenced India's emerging fashion industry? Answer this question after reading an article at **marketingseries.glencoe.com.**

GLOBAL CENTER New York City is a hub of fashion where fashion shows are exciting events attended by celebrities and professionals. *Why do you think fashion shows are so popular among celebrities and the public?*

CONNECT

What type of clothing or style reminds you of English styles?

Design Center: London

London is known as a design center, but it has not always made the same impact on the world of fashion as Paris or Milan. Originally noted for men's business-suit classic styles, London fashion now focuses on high-quality, ready-to-wear garments. The youth-oriented styles in the 1960s, including the Mod designs of Mary Quant and the popular look of Twiggy, brought London immediate attention. During the 1980s to the 1990s, Princess Diana promoted the style of many British designers. There are about ten design centers throughout the United Kingdom, primarily located where there are clusters of textile and clothing companies.

Design Center: Tokyo

After World War II, Japanese women became interested in adopting western styles primarily from Paris. Japanese designers emerged on the fashion scene in the 1960s. Designers from Japan continue to influence western fashion with their colors, asymmetrical balance, unusual shapes, and use of fibers. The largest city in Japan, Tokyo, has quickly become one of the leading fashion design centers. Fashion companies in Tokyo not only produce Japanese designs but also have licenses to produce European and American apparel products.

U.S. Design Centers

There are numerous cities within the United States that serve as design centers for the American market. Los Angeles, California, and Dallas, Texas, are important design centers. New York City is an international design center as well as a U.S. design center.

U.S. Design Center: New York City

New York City remains an important center of garment production and wholesale business. New York's apparel factories produce 18 percent of women's outerwear (dresses, coats, suits, and sportswear) and 28 percent of all dresses made in the United States. Fashion Week shows are held twice a year at Bryant Park in Manhattan. Over 50 spectacular shows are staged, showcasing the current designs for buyers. Celebrities often sit in the front rows of the exhibitions, along with fashion reporters, buyers, and other industry professionals.

U.S. Design Center: Los Angeles

Located in the heart of downtown, the design center of Los Angeles houses the largest concentration of fashion-related businesses in the western United States. Professionals have long considered Los Angeles as one of the key fashion centers in the United States. Designers, wholesalers, retailers, sewing contractors, patternmakers, manufacturers, market centers, and apparel marts all exist in an 82-block business district known as the city's fashion district. In fact, the fashion and apparel industry has become one of California's leading employers.

MARKETING SERIES *Online*

Remember to check out this book's Web site for information on fashion centers and more great resources at **marketingseries.glencoe.com.**

Hot Property

Fashion Meets Technology

 Combining fashion and technology is hot, and Nautica sizzles when it comes to the marriage of high-tech fabrics with stylish classic designs. David Chu, founder and fashion designer of the company, says that "Nautica is as much about technology as it is about fashion." Technological innovation in fabric is at the core of Nautica's strategies. Founded in 1983, the company is a global fashion icon with products for men, women, children, and the home.

DESIGNED WITH NEW FABRICS

Technology has enabled fashion textiles to repel oils and spills while keeping the fabrics soft, breathable, and comfortable.

Chu studied the classic knit shirt for ways to make it better. The answer was to make the shirt in a stain-resistant fabric. Nautica introduced the Performance Classics knit shirt for men in such a fabric. "The pique knit is one of the most versatile pieces in a man's wardrobe," he states. Worn casually on weekends, the shirt also coordinates well with a blazer for business-casual attire. The shirts are available in a wide range of colors at fine department stores and specialty stores in fashion centers and other cities nationwide.

Nautica designs are marketed to fitness-conscious, fashion-savvy teens as well as urban professionals. Nautica combines high-quality European fabrics and design details to create clothes for an active lifestyle.

In 2003, Nautica Enterprises, Inc., merged with VF Corporation. VF Corporation is the world's largest apparel company and a leader in jeans, intimate apparel, sportswear, playwear, work wear, and daypacks. The merger increased Nautica's global possibilities.

1. How has Nautica used technology in its designs?
2. In which U.S. or international buying centers would you expect to find Nautica clothes? Explain your answer.

buying center a central district in a city where fashion businesses sell products to retail buyers

market weeks the major times scheduled by fashion producers to show fashions to buyers

FOCUS ON WOMEN'S FASHION Women's apparel is the main component of this industry, with a focus on young women's moderately priced sportswear. Designers in Los Angeles are known for innovative styling in sportswear, surfwear, and Hollywood-style evening wear. Active wear is also a specialty of Los Angeles designers. The clothing is distinct from garments made in the eastern United States. Los Angeles also hosts one of the major textile shows in the country that presents more than 11,000 textile designers.

U.S. Design Center: Dallas

Though Dallas, Texas, is more notable as a buying center, the city has developed a reputation as a design center, producing moderately priced apparel lines. Men's and boys' clothes—shirts, trousers, jeans, and neckties—account for 36 percent of apparel manufacturing in Texas.

What Is a Buying Center?

A **buying center** is a central district in a city where fashion businesses sell products to retail buyers. Centers may be the garment districts of cities or regional marts located in areas around the United States. These buying centers are concentrated in geographic areas where manufacturers promote their newest lines or a group of styles and designs. Manufacturers produce new selections based on orders placed by retailers who buy products for resale in their stores. The manufacturers have showrooms where retail buyers preview the lines and place orders for the upcoming seasons.

The Importance of Buying Centers

Most cities have not-for-profit corporations that help promote a particular city's apparel industry. Recognizing the importance of the industry to the city's economy, many buying centers have made enormous renovations in their buying districts by updating and increasing showroom capacity. These fashion corporations are directly involved in the promotion of fashion weeks. Each year thousands of out-of-town apparel buyers generate millions of dollars in revenue for the hotels, restaurants, transportation services, and other non-apparel businesses located in these cities.

U.S. Buying Centers

Retail buyers can order merchandise from manufacturers on a continuous basis. There are specific times when manufacturers present their new product lines to buyers. Thousands of buyers visit buying-center cities at these times. Buyers attend showings during **market weeks**, which are the major times scheduled by fashion producers to show fashions to buyers. The apparel industry designates particular weeks to present different components of fashion. For example, shoes and accessories, men's wear, women's wear, or children's wear showings are each scheduled during different weeks.

 marketingseries.glencoe.com

Figure 4.1

The Garment District of New York

FASHION MANHATTAN STYLE Like most garment districts in major cities, New York's district covers many city blocks with buildings that house a variety of businesses and services related to fashion. *Why do you think these businesses are clustered together?*

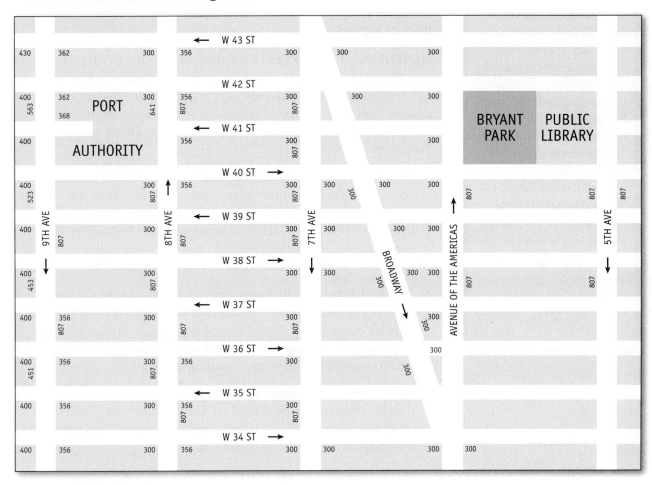

Characteristics of U.S. buying centers vary, based on the physical layout of a district and the specific merchandise presented for sale. The renovation of district areas in New York City, Los Angeles, Dallas, Chicago, Atlanta, and Miami emphasizes the importance of the fashion industry to these cities. New York City's Garment District, illustrated in **Figure 4.1**, is the primary buying center in the country.

However, many retailers avoid New York and use regional buying centers in cities such as Los Angeles, Dallas, Chicago, Atlanta, or Miami. These cities have fashion buying centers that include marts. A **mart** is a building that houses thousands of showrooms for specific merchandise categories. The larger regional centers may have several building clusters, or marts, that are devoted to specific apparel or accessory groups, such as women's, men's, or children's marts. These facilities are more convenient for buyers because they can visit all of the manufacturers without ever leaving the building.

mart a building that houses thousands of showrooms for a specific merchandise category

Buying Center: New York City

New York City remains the nation's leading buying center, with over 5,000 fashion showrooms. The city's fashion industry reports sales of $14 billion annually, including $12 billion in wholesale apparel sales. The New York buying center is comprised of manufacturers housed in various buildings within a designated *district* in the city known as the Garment Center. Retail buyers go from building to building, visiting offices or showrooms to consider different lines of apparel.

BUSINESS IMPROVEMENT The Fashion Center Business Improvement District is a not-for-profit corporation established in 1993 to promote New York City's apparel industry. The purpose of this organization is to improve the quality of life and strengthen the economic status of Manhattan's garment district. Other programs and features include:

- **New York Fashion International**—This program was formed to address the needs of companies interested in exporting goods. It is a cooperative effort with Fashion Exports/New York and the U.S. Department of Commerce. The program assists businesses in exploring foreign markets and developing export strategies. It also promotes the New York design market internationally.

- **The Fashion Walk of Fame**—This commemorative sidewalk on Seventh Avenue celebrates the fashion designers who established New York City as a world fashion capital. Plaques on the sidewalks honor current and historic designers, giving the district a historical reference point and creating a tourist attraction.

- **Fashion Center Banners**—Festive banners bearing the garment district's button logo are draped on district lampposts to increase unity and pride within the community. The banners also enhance the neighborhood's visual appearance.

Through special events, marketing programs, information services, and advertising opportunities, The Fashion Center increases the district's visibility to the public and to apparel buyers nationally and internationally.

Buying Center: Los Angeles

The Los Angeles Fashion District (formerly known as The Garment District) has the largest concentration of fashion-related businesses in the western United States. It is the home of the California Market Center, a facility with more than 1,800 showrooms featuring apparel and accessory manufacturers. This is the hub of the southern California apparel industry. Generating over $8 billion in business, the Los Angeles Fashion District rivals New York's garment district in size and reputation for premiering trend-setting fashions.

BUSINESS IMPROVEMENT The district in Los Angeles attracts millions of wholesale and retail buyers every year. The diversity of fashion businesses cover every stage of apparel production.

The district is an ideal place for small to mid-sized businesses. The Los Angeles Fashion District is a business improvement district that is funded by property owners. It also provides maintenance, security, and marketing programs.

THE CALIFORNIA MARKET CENTER (CMC) This section of the Los Angeles Fashion District, formerly known as the California Mart, is a center for style industries in Los Angeles. About 1,800 showrooms and 10,000 product lines are housed in three 13-story buildings, which are interconnected on every floor. Wholesale buyers can find women's wear, men's wear, children's wear, fashion accessories, swimwear, footwear, gifts, toys, furniture and décor, textiles, garden accessories, flowers, stationery, intimate apparel, and personal care products in the CMC. Fashion markets in the spring and the fall run concurrently with Fashion Week runway shows. The center hosts various activities and events:

- Five major fashion markets

- Two textile markets

- The Los Angeles gift-and-home markets

- Market days

- Fashion weeks

- Educational events

- Seminars

THE NEW MART This mart is California's exclusive contemporary and young-designer apparel marketplace in the heart of the Los Angeles Fashion District. It features designers and manufacturers from California, New York, and Europe who focus on contemporary and young styles.

Buying Center: Dallas

Dallas is home to the Dallas Market Center, the world's largest wholesale merchandise resource with nearly 7 million square feet of available space. The Dallas Market Center offers hundreds of events and seminars geared toward helping retailers expand business and increase profits. As a result, more than $7.5 billion in estimated wholesale transactions occur annually within the Dallas Market Center complex.

Case Study PART 2

BUILDING A FASHION CENTER IN INDIA

Continued from Part 1 on page 67

To promote India as a fashion center, the Lakme India Fashion Week of April 2004 featured 57 designers in 35 shows and exhibitions. At least 30 international television crews and 350 media professionals attended, along with 400 buyers from 212 companies. IMG and the Fashion Design Council of India helped internationalize the event by moving the date of the show from August to April to coincide with international fashion seasons.

Increased Fashion Week sponsorship has also helped the India fashion industry. Some of the show's sponsors include international companies such as Hyundai, Foster's Beer, Sony Entertainment Television, and Dior Watches. According to Ravi Krishnan, Managing Director of IMG/TWI South Asia, "In a very bad market, we managed to increase sponsorship money. Through its global expertise in fashion, IMG has ensured that the event is organized to match international standards—and it is reflected in the amazing success and status it enjoys."

ANALYZE AND WRITE

1. List the strategies IMG used to make Fashion Week successful.

2. How might applying international standards to a fashion week help or hinder a developing fashion center? Write a paragraph explaining your answer.

QUESTION

How is the L.A. Fashion District financed?

FASHION FACILITY Recognized as one of the largest buying centers in the region, Dallas is the home to the new FashionCenterDallas. Opened in 2004, this facility is the 1-million square-foot home for apparel and accessories at Dallas Market Center. The state-of-the-art, wholesale facility offers retail buyers from around the world a modern, convenient marketplace on six floors of the World Trade Center at the Dallas Market Center. FashionCenterDallas houses 550 new permanent fashion showrooms, ranging in size from a few hundred square feet to more than 8,000 square feet. This represents the largest wholesale marketplace in the world.

DALLAS MARKET FOCUS Sportswear and western wear are prominent in the Dallas market, which includes everything from dresses and suits to fashion accessories and intimate apparel. Merchandise from other product segments, such as jewelry, gifts, and decorative accessories, are represented here. Dallas hosts more than 50 markets a year and draws more than 200,000 buyers annually.

Buying Center: Chicago

As a fashion buying center, Chicago is home to the Merchandise Mart and its sister building, the Chicago Apparel Center. The Merchandise Mart is a 1.5 million square-foot building housing wholesale apparel showrooms and office and retail space. Over 800,000 square feet are used for office space. The building also houses a conferencing facility and a 525-room business-class hotel.

The Apparel Center contains more than 300 wholesale showrooms for apparel and accessories. The center serves clothing retailers by hosting market events, fashion shows, seminars, and promotional programs designed to attract buyers. Women's and children's apparel, men's wear, and bridal fashions are some industries that use the Apparel Center.

Buying Center: Atlanta

AmericasMart in Atlanta consists of three buildings with exhibit space totaling 4.2 million square feet. Aerial walkways connect the buildings, making it convenient for buyers to visit the permanent showroom space, exhibit halls, and convention and meeting-room spaces. Although primarily known for its home-furnishings merchandise, AmericasMart also features better apparel and sportswear lines, which draw apparel buyers.

Buying Center: Miami

In Miami retailers go to the Miami International Merchandise Mart, Florida's only wholesale mart. Featuring more than 300 showrooms, the mart is adjacent to the Miami International Airport. This market is known for moderately priced sportswear, including cruise wear, swimwear and lightweight sportswear, and children's wear. The Miami market is important because of its geographical location. It is accessible to apparel production centers in Central America, South America, and the Caribbean.

CALIFORNIA MARKET CENTER Most buying centers across the country have state-of-the-art facilities such as the CMC in Los Angeles. CMC's sophisticated Web site provides information and schedules for the fashion industry. *What is the advantage of participating in fashion showings at a fashion mart?*

Heart of the Fashion Industry

Design centers and buying centers are different yet closely related. Together they form the heart of the fashion industry. Design centers represent the centers of creativity, while buying centers represent the centers of commerce. However, both centers are places where fashion, like art in a gallery, is on view for the industry as well as the public.

Quick Check ✔

RESPOND to what you've read by answering these questions.

1. What are three of the most important international design centers? _____

_____

_____

_____

2. What is the difference between a fashion design center and a buying center? _____

_____

_____

_____

_____

3. How do fashion design centers and buying centers benefit the cities in which they are located?

_____

_____

_____

_____

Global Impact of Fashion

AS YOU READ...

YOU WILL LEARN

- To explain the importance of global sourcing in the fashion industry.
- To describe how cultural influences affect mainstream fashion.

WHY IT'S IMPORTANT

Globalization is increasingly important to the fashion industry due to global sourcing and production. Diverse cultures influence the design and adaptation of fashions.

KEY TERMS

- global sourcing
- culture

PREDICT

Give your own definition of culture.

global sourcing the identifying and negotiating of supply chains in numerous world locations

How Fashion Travels

People around the world are more connected and interdepedent, resulting in globalization. As discussed in Chapter 3, globalization is the trend toward increasing integration of the world economy. With advances in transportation and communication technologies, goods and information move easily and quickly between countries, increasing international trade. The global chain of production must remain flexible to enable producers to respond to the latest fashion trends. This increase in globalization, combined with the need to reduce costs, time-to-market, and product lead times, requires more complex sourcing and production strategies.

Global Sourcing and Production

Fashion products are produced in more than one country. In the fashion industry, there is a continuous shift of the favored sources for supplies. To reduce costs and maximize profits, many textile and apparel manufacturers have begun **global sourcing**, or the identifying and negotiating of supply chains in numerous world locations. For example, some European countries have reduced their levels of local production due to high production costs. Many foreign countries do little or no manufacturing locally, choosing instead to use manufacturers in other countries. With the removal of trade restrictions in 2005, companies in the United States are changing their approach to sourcing and production. Supply companies that move away from their own manufacturing retain control over the sourcing cycle. They will source critical materials, such as fabric and yarn, and supply them to subcontractors who then make the finished merchandise.

Global Sourcing Risks

However, increased risks come with global sourcing. The lack of economic stability in developing nations creates many challenges for businesses. Economic and political factors around the world play a major role in establishing fashion businesses that succeed.

Global Production

Production of clothing is global. For example, a company based in the United States may buy cotton from many countries. Companies may take advantage of the skills of workers in specific regions.

Fashion businesses may produce their garments in other countries where workers earn lower wages. (See **Figure 4.2**.) In addition, companies choose factories in foreign countries where fashion products are made to suit the current demands of customers. In fact, changes in customer taste indirectly affect production jobs around the world.

CONNECT

How might tastes in clothing affect fashion jobs?

World Fashion

Today fashion is global with fashion centers in a variety of countries. Many countries are eager to export their fashions to other countries and host their own exhibits and trade fairs. Designers and apparel companies establish promotional offices in major fashion cities around the world where they show their collections. Retail buyers from around the world view the styles presented and then purchase merchandise to sell in their stores. The proximity, or closeness, of some markets, such as the Asia and California markets, helps to create trade patterns.

Figure 4.2

U.S. Import Activity

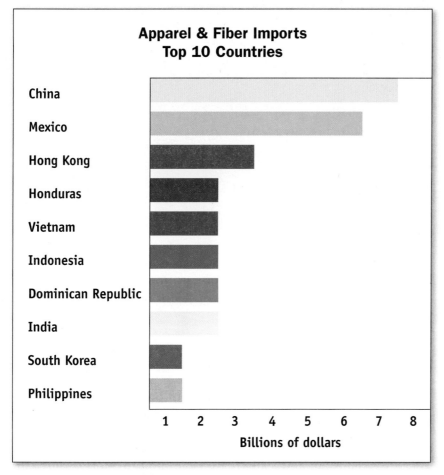

Apparel & Fiber Imports Top 10 Countries

Billions of dollars

COMING TO AMERICA Fashion companies in the United States rely on supplies of imported goods and materials made or produced in other countries. *Why do American companies import fashion goods from other countries? Give at least one reason.*

SOURCE: *Major Shippers Report* (April 2004). U.S. Department of Commerce, Office of Textile and Apparel.

ON TOP OF THE TRENDS

Amy Purshouse
Fashion Editor
Cosmopolitan, London

What is your job?
"I am an editor for a fashion magazine."

What do you do in your job?
"I attend shows and think of fashion story ideas. I try to imagine who the model is in the layout, and then come up with a scenario to dress him or her in particular fashions at a particular location. When I get a story approved, I put all the elements together, from the idea through production. I hire the models, photographers, and stylists. I choose the locations and clothes and oversee the page layouts for the magazine."

What kind of training did you have?
"I studied English at the University of Reading in England. While I was there, I started a fashion page for the school paper. This experience helped me get an internship at *Red* magazine, a British fashion and lifestyle magazine. In five years I worked from intern to fashion editor before moving to British *Cosmo*. I learned by doing the job, and I started to build a network of professionals with whom I work today."

What advice would you give students?
"Find ways to get experience. If you are starting out as a fashion editor, team up with aspiring photographers and models and put together samples of your work."

What's your key to success?
"Make a good impression on as many people as possible so that when an opportunity comes along, you can take it."

Why should you make a good impression as an intern?

Career Data: Fashion Magazine Editor

Education and Training
Bachelor's degree in English, communications, or fashion

Skills and Abilities
Communication, writing, organizational, budgeting, and management skills

Career Outlook As fast as average growth through 2012

Career Path Intern, fashion or production assistant, fashion stylist, fashion editor to fashion director

Culture and Fashion

The global nature of the fashion industry today requires cultural awareness and adaptability. **Culture** is the system of shared beliefs, values, customs, behaviors, and artifacts attributed to members of a specific society. Fashion trends may begin "on the street" and spread from a specific culture or ethnic group to a wider population. The influence of culture or ethnicity cycles in and out of fashion. Some ethnic styles also become classic, or standard.

culture the system of shared beliefs, values, customs, behaviors, and artifacts attributed to members of a specific society

Cultural Styles

Smart fashion marketers are aware of cultural influences on current fashion. Designers can travel around the world for ideas or find inspiration in their own diverse communities. It is not necessary for designers to leave their own cities for inspiring ideas. Designers may produce designs that reflect communities within their cities. For example, they may adapt style influences from cultures from the East or the West.

STYLES FROM THE EAST The impact of Asian fashion has been significant. During the 1970s, the Nehru jacket from India, a fashion specific to a culture, developed into a mainstream fashion. By 2003, Indian-henna skin art, while once considered exotic, became a popular fashion marketed by Avon the national cosmetics retailer. In addition, Indian sari styles of apparel were sold at upscale and mainstream retailers. Another example of Asian influence was evident when celebrity Madonna adopted a Japanese geisha style for several television appearances and magazine photo spreads. Examples of how cultures adapt a fashion are all around us.

WESTERN STYLES During the 1980s and at other times, the western or cowboy style of boots and denim moved from the wild West to the big city, as the "urban cowboy" style appeared in urban areas.

URBAN STYLES As of the late 1990s, the hip-hop look exerted influence, moving out of the African-American inner cities and around the world. Popular among suburban youth and international couturiers alike, this urban style has affected fashion in many countries.

PAINTED ACCESSORIES
Styles of adornment include body paint in many cultures. Native Americans painted their faces with colorful geometric patterns for protection in battle and from the weather. Japanese people created a style of body tattoos called *irezumi* during the 1600s and 1700s. A red powder spot on the forehead called *tilaka* is a sign of daily prayers for Hindus. *Mehndi* is the ancient Indian tradition of henna body painting. It is used to adorn brides. Recently, westerners adopted it as fashion.

QUESTION
What are three cultures that have influenced styles?

FASHION TRAVELS WELL
Diverse styles from Asia go in and out of fashion over the years. *What are some style features that distinguish Chinese or East Asian fashion?*

The Twins in Paris

Paris remains the most prominent design center in the world. Acceptance in the fashion world almost requires a Paris show. Paris designers began the tradition of the fashion show to showcase designer clothes. Now Paris also showcases ready-to-wear fashion designers. The spring/summer and fall/winter week-long shows bring together the best of the world's fashion statements.

In the best tradition of the haute-couture garments seen on the Paris runways, American celebrities Mary-Kate and Ashley Olsen unveiled their Mary-Kate and Ashley brand fashion collection at an annual show in the glamorous Hôtel d'Evreux of Paris. *Time* magazine voted the popular teenage twins the fourth most powerful women in the international fashion industry in 2004. The show featured logo T-shirts and denim mini-skirts. They have also impacted the global economy with their European-inspired floral dresses and cropped cargo pants in soft pastel colors. For the international public, designer names of Paris now include Mary-Kate and Ashley.

What impact is globalization having on Paris fashion shows?

World Fashion at Home

Consumers can buy an inexpensive outfit from a French e-tail store, order shirts from a London shirt maker's catalog, or go to the mall and find the latest fashions from around the world. The world of fashion is at the consumer's fingertips. Global production, fashion centers, catalogs, home shopping television, and the Internet continue to make fashion readily available to the consumer.

Quick Check

RESPOND to what you've read by answering these questions.

1. Why are fashion companies turning to global sourcing?_____

_____

2. How does culture impact current fashions?_____

_____

3. Describe a recent cultural influence that has moved into mainstream fashion._____

_____

Name _____ Date _____

Worksheet (4.1)

Buying Centers

Imagine you own a small specialty clothing and accessory shop. Do the following exercise:

- Choose men's or women's clothing and accessories as a specialty.

- Imagine that your local mall is the buying center, and the mall's retail stores are wholesale stores. Wholesale prices are 50 percent of the retail prices at the stores.

- Visit the mall stores, including department stores, and make a list of the "wholesale" items you want to purchase for your shop.

- Do not exceed your budget of $2,500.

Item	Wholesale cost	Number ordered	Total cost
TOTALS =			

Worksheet 4.2

Global Fashion

Visit a mall in your community. Read the labels on several different items of clothing and accessories. Determine the country in which the item was produced. Make a list of 20 different items. Then answer the question below.

Name of Item	Country
1.	
2.	
3.	
4.	
5.	
6.	
7.	
8.	
9.	
10.	
11.	
12.	
13.	
14.	
15.	
16.	
17.	
18.	
19.	
20.	

Question:

What conclusions can you draw from your research? _____

_____

_____

_____

Portfolio Works

RESEARCHING BUYING CENTERS

Choose one of the buying centers discussed in the chapter and research it on the Internet, in trade magazines, or at the library. Answer the following questions about the center.

1. In what city and state is the buying center located?

_____

2. What is the name of the buying center?

_____

3. What are five interesting facts about the buying center?

_____

_____

_____

_____

_____

_____

_____

_____

_____

_____

_____

4. Why did you choose this buying center?

_____

_____

_____

_____

_____

_____

_____

_____

_____

Add this page to your career portfolio.

CHAPTER SUMMARY

Section 4.1 **Design and Buying Centers**

design center (p. 68)
fashion weeks (p. 69)
haute couture (p. 69)
couturiers (p. 69)
buying center (p. 72)
market weeks (p. 72)
mart (p. 73)

- A fashion design center is a district in a city where fashion design and production firms are clustered together.

- A buying center is a central district in a city where fashion businesses sell products to retail buyers.

- Design and buying centers affect local economies by attracting business and revenue. Cities benefit directly from fashion business and benefit indirectly from other business generated by hotels, restaurants, and transportation services.

- The main international design centers are Paris, Milan, New York City, London, and Tokyo. The U.S. buying centers are New York City, Los Angeles, Dallas, Chicago, Atlanta, and Miami.

Section 4.2 **Global Impact of Fashion**

global sourcing (p. 78)
culture (p. 80)

- Global sourcing in the fashion industry is the identifying and negotiating of supply chains in numerous world locations. Many textile and apparel manufacturers use this strategy to reduce costs and increase profits because many European centers have reduced production.

- Diverse cultures influence designs and styles in fashion, especially with increased communication throughout the world today and exposure to international trends.

CHECKING CONCEPTS

1. **Describe** the concept of fashion weeks hosted by design centers.
2. **Explain** how local governments support design centers.
3. **Identify** the geographic areas where manufacturers promote their newest lines.
4. **Name** some businesses besides fashion businesses that benefit from design and buying centers.
5. **Identify** the major design centers of the world.
6. **Identify** the major buying centers of the United States.
7. **Describe** some risks of global sourcing.

Critical Thinking
8. **Identify** a culture that has significantly influenced fashion of the last two years and give examples of items of apparel.

CROSS-CURRICULUM SKILLS

Work-Based Learning

Thinking Skills—Reasoning

9. You have a line of high-fashion clothes made from sophisticated print fabrics. What two international shows would you choose for presentation?

Information—Acquiring and Evaluating Information

10. Choose a fashion show in a fashion center. Contact a travel agent or use the Internet to research flights, hotels, transportation, and restaurants. Write a travel expense report.

School-Based Learning

Social Science

11. Find a world map and copy it. Put a red mark on each international design center. Post your map in class.

Computer Technology

12. Write and present a one-page paper explaining how technology has increased the globalization of the fashion industry.

Role Play: Fashion Sales Associate

SITUATION You are to assume the role of experienced sales associate for a trendy women's fashion store. The store is located near several large office buildings. The store's buyer is preparing for a buying trip to New York City. You are helping to train a new sales associate (judge). The new sales associate (judge) asks why the buyer must travel to New York.

ACTIVITY You must explain to the new sales associate (judge) the importance of fashion centers and their role in the fashion business.

EVALUATION You will be evaluated on how well you meet the following performance indicators:

- Identify fashion market centers.
- Explain the role of fashion designers.
- Explain the nature of the buying process.
- Explain the nature and scope of distribution.
- Orient new employees.

The Miami International Merchandise Mart in Florida is important because centers in Central and South America and the Caribbean are near. Find the Web site for the Miami International Merchandise Mart and answer these questions:

- How many wholesale showrooms are featured?
- What is the square footage of the mart?
- How many floors are there in the mart?
- What major transportation center is next to the mart?

➡For a link to do this activity, go to **marketingseries.glencoe.com**.

BusinessWeek News

NIKE'S NEW ADVICE? JUST STRUT IT

When Mindy F. Grossman took the helm of Nike Inc.'s apparel division three years ago, it was staggering along like a winded sprinter. The New York fashion veteran wasted no time whipping things into shape: slashing costs, consolidating global sourcing, and centralizing design. Her efforts have paid off. While sales at the core footwear business grew just 5.4 percent to $5.9 billion for the fiscal year [2003], apparel sales climbed 11.7 percent to $3.1 billion.

But this race isn't anywhere near done. With a host of collections set to hit stores next spring, Grossman wants to move the sneaker giant well beyond clothes for serious jocks and into the market for sporty street apparel. For now, she's targeting women, many of whom are as likely to wear yoga pants as jeans when they head to the mall. By combining Nike's high-tech athletic materials with casual fashion, she hopes to gain an edge over other apparel makers in creating "must-have outfits."

So are a lot of other companies, ranging from Gap and Tommy Hilfiger to rivals like Adidas. While Nike has a strong brand in athletic apparel, getting it right in the faddish casual-wear market is notoriously difficult.

Street Cred

If anyone can pull it off, say industry watchers, it's Grossman. They credit her with rebuilding Polo Ralph Lauren Corp.'s jeans business in the 1990s by focusing on what people wanted, from fit and styling to price. By the time she left the company in 2000, Polo Jeans was generating $450 million a year in sales, up from virtually zero.

Despite her reputation, Grossman has had to prove herself amid Nike's male-dominated sports culture. But her success turning around the struggling apparel unit won her the "street cred" [street credibility] to push Nike into broader markets. Grossman wants people to wear Nike clothes at the coffee shop, mall, and disco. Nike's Sun Tech line will combine trendy beach-inspired styles with Nike materials designed to keep people cool and dry. To turn more women into customers, Nike opened a half-dozen NIKEgoddess boutiques. They carry a range of crossover apparel for women.

Will Grossman make the Nike brand synonymous with casual fashion? Sneaker makers have tried and failed before. The company is betting that Grossman's business sense and fashion instincts will help it sprint into the fashion arena.

By Stanley Holmes

TO GO FAR, GO FAST.

CREATIVE JOURNAL

In your journal, write your responses:

CRITICAL THINKING

1. What type of fashion apparel is Nike making and marketing? What challenges does the company face with this type of fashion?

APPLICATION

2. Describe a new fashion apparel product that Nike should make and sell and why you think it would be successful. Also describe the target market for this product.

 Go to **businessweek.com** for current *BusinessWeek* Online articles.

UNIT LAB

House of Style

You've just entered the real world of fashion. The House of Style assists fashion businesses and individuals to conceive, plan, produce, and sell the latest and most popular fashion products. Acting as the owner, manager, or employee of the House of Style, you will have the opportunity to work on different projects to promote the success of this fashion business.

What's Old Is New Again—Do the Research

SITUATION You are a researcher for a well-known fashion clothing manufacturer. The clothing produced by the company is designed to appeal to the teen and early 20s age groups. Your job is to research fashion trends and looks to inspire your company's designers. You have observed that one of the current trends is "retro" styles, or styles from the past, for fabric selections and designs. You have also observed that the fabric and design styles are not necessarily related. For example, a fabric that has a look and feel of the 1960s would not necessarily be used for a style that was influenced by the 1960s. You believe this fashion trend will probably continue into the next two or three seasons.

ASSIGNMENT Complete these tasks:
- Determine three fashion influences from the past that your designers can adapt for designs in an upcoming season.
- Research the influences of fashions from the recent and distant past.
- Make a report to your designers.

TOOLS AND RESOURCES To complete the assignment, you will need to:
- Conduct research at the library, on the Internet, or by talking to local fashion retailers.
- Ask a local fashion retailer about current best-selling fashion looks.
- Have word-processing, spreadsheet, and presentation software.

RESEARCH Do your research:
- Research the demographics and psychographics of the company's target customer.
- Determine looks from the past that would offer inspiration for the designers' adaptations.
- Determine the possibility of the designs' success with your target market.

REPORT Prepare a written report using the following tools, if available:
- *Word-processing program:* Prepare a written report listing the demographic and psychographic characteristics of the company's target-market customer.
- *Spreadsheet program:* Prepare a chart comparing your fashion looks from the past with those that are current bestsellers.
- *Presentation program:* Prepare a ten-slide visual presentation with key points, photos of each proposed retro design, and descriptive text.

PRESENTATION AND EVALUATION You will present your report to your designers and head researcher. You will be evaluated on the basis of:
- Your knowledge of the company's target market and the proposed design looks
- Continuity of presentation
- Voice quality
- Eye contact

PORTFOLIO
Add this report to your career portfolio.

UNIT 2
PRODUCING FASHION

"The artist is nothing without the gift, but the gift is nothing without work."

—Emile Zola
Author

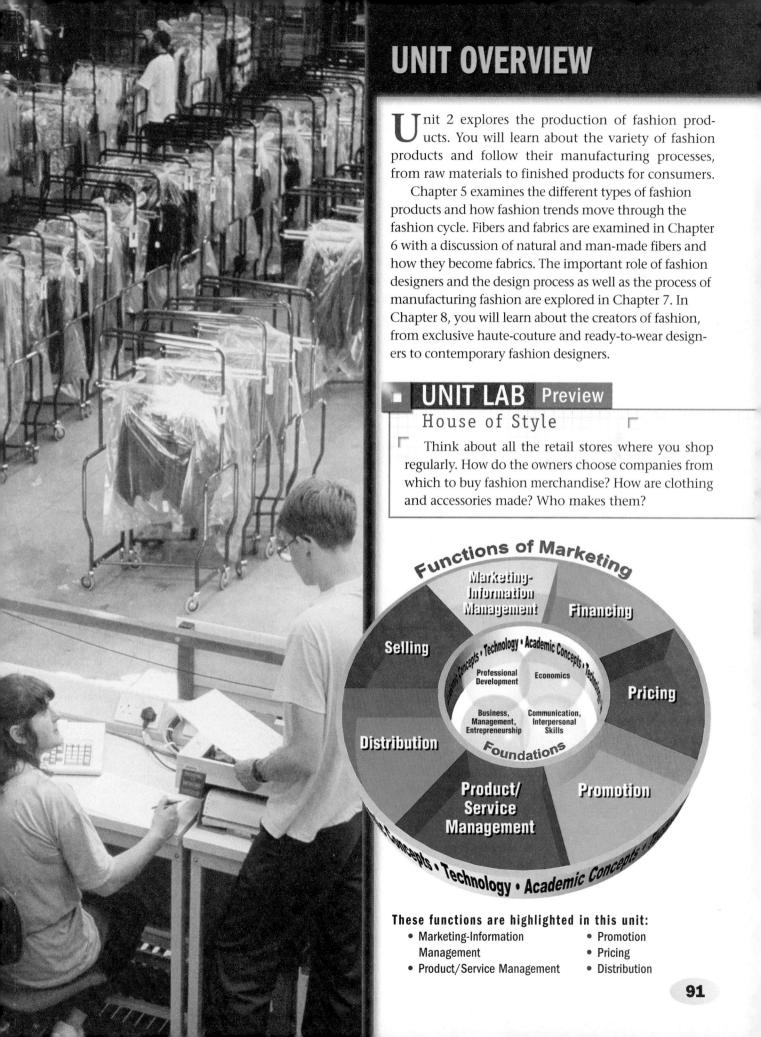

UNIT OVERVIEW

Unit 2 explores the production of fashion products. You will learn about the variety of fashion products and follow their manufacturing processes, from raw materials to finished products for consumers.

Chapter 5 examines the different types of fashion products and how fashion trends move through the fashion cycle. Fibers and fabrics are examined in Chapter 6 with a discussion of natural and man-made fibers and how they become fabrics. The important role of fashion designers and the design process as well as the process of manufacturing fashion are explored in Chapter 7. In Chapter 8, you will learn about the creators of fashion, from exclusive haute-couture and ready-to-wear designers to contemporary fashion designers.

UNIT LAB Preview

House of Style

Think about all the retail stores where you shop regularly. How do the owners choose companies from which to buy fashion merchandise? How are clothing and accessories made? Who makes them?

Functions of Marketing

- Marketing-Information Management
- Financing
- Selling
- Pricing
- Distribution
- Promotion
- Product/Service Management

Foundations
- Professional Development
- Economics
- Business, Management, Entrepreneurship
- Communication, Interpersonal Skills

Academic Concepts • Technology

These functions are highlighted in this unit:
- Marketing-Information Management
- Product/Service Management
- Promotion
- Pricing
- Distribution

91

Chapter 5

Types of Fashion and Trends

Chapter Objectives

- Identify the types of fashion products.
- Explain the main categories of fashion apparel.
- Identify the classifications of fashion apparel categories.
- Explain the fashion cycle.
- Discuss the role of fashion leaders.
- Identify the different theories of fashion movement.
- Discuss the difference between fashion trends and fads.

BRANDING BURBERRY

Burberry, the clothing company, was founded in 1856 by 21-year-old Thomas Burberry, an apprentice draper. Drapers made cloth and sold fabrics and dry goods. Burberry began making outdoor wear for local residents in rainy Basingstoke, England. In 1880, he invented a waterproof wool fabric called *gabardine*, which became one of the materials for Burberry's most famous creation—the trench coat. In 1920, Burberry registered a signature plaid pattern for wool, which would become the standard lining for the Burberry trench coat.

For the next 80 years, Burberry plaid was seen inside the trench coats of the English elite. The Burberry label came to represent old English fashion—and old ideas. By the 1990s, this image began to limit Burberry's appeal and market. So in 1997, a new marketing team, led by New Yorker Rose Marie Bravo, set out to revitalize the brand. By 2002, Burberry Group PLC became the United Kingdom's first publicly traded luxury-goods company. How did Burberry's marketing team transform Burberry from stuffy to chic?

ANALYZE AND WRITE

1. Write a paragraph about Burberry's type of fashion products.
2. Write a paragraph about why it is important for a product to be in style.

Case Study Part 2 on page 105

POWER READ

Be an active reader and use these reading strategies:

PREDICT what the section will be about.

CONNECT what you read with your life.

QUESTION as you read to make sure you understand the content.

RESPOND to what you've read.

Types of Fashion

AS YOU READ ...

YOU WILL LEARN

- To identify the types of fashion products.
- To explain the main categories of fashion apparel.
- To identify the classifications of fashion apparel categories.

WHY IT'S IMPORTANT

There are several categories and classifications of fashion products. Knowledge of these categories will help you understand how fashion products are manufactured, marketed, and sold.

KEY TERMS

- lines
- hardlines
- softlines
- apparel
- accessories
- home furnishings

PREDICT

What could be the definitions of the terms *hardlines* and *softlines*?

lines groups of styles and designs produced and sold as a set of related products for a given season

Types of Fashion Products

Fashion affects all areas of our lives, from the clothes and accessories we wear to the decorative furnishings we use in our homes. Manufacturers make a variety of product lines. **Lines** are groups of styles and designs produced and sold as a set of related products for a given season. The two main types of product lines are hardlines and softlines. **Hardlines** are lines of products that are non-textile, such as small and large appliances, home accessories, and items not made of fabric. **Softlines** are lines of products made from textiles that include apparel and household items such as towels, table linens, and bedding. Just as retailers target their merchandise to specific customer groups, manufacturers specialize in producing categories of fashion products for certain groups.

Types of Apparel

Apparel is the term used for clothing, as in personal attire or garments. Apparel is categorized by groups—women's wear, men's wear, and infants' and children's wear. Within these groups, there may be further divisions based on brands, age groups, sizes, prices, or styles offered.

Product Numbers

Apparel producers designate a certain number to represent each style of apparel so manufacturing and order fulfillment of the product is more efficient. Retailers use the same style numbers when ordering products, and then further divide those numbers into categories, such as colors, sizes, and classifications (e.g., tops or bottoms). This allows manufacturers and retailers to track sales of particular items and maintain accurate inventory records.

Types of Accessories

Accessories are fashion items that are added to complete or enhance outfits. These items may include footwear, handbags, headwear, scarves, neckties, jewelry, gloves, and hosiery. As discussed in Chapter 1, people use accessories as a form of adornment. Today accessories are a vital part of the fashion scene. They are one of the most exciting facets of the industry. Producers present accessories in two seasonal lines each year. Most accessories are softlines, such as scarves and ties, though some accessories, such as jewelry, are not made of textiles. All accessories are categorized with soft goods.

Varied Use of Accessories

Accessories can be used to create a new look or update a basic garment. This use of accessories is especially common if apparel styles are uninteresting. Accessory pieces can also transform a garment style from casual to formal.

Special Accessory Producers

Manufacturers specialize in producing each type of accessory. Although some items, such as shoes and belts, are more functional, designers and producers must stay on top of the trends in accessory fashion as well as in apparel fashion. Many of the top designers now produce their own lines of accessories, such as Liz Claiborne eyewear, Tommy Hilfiger belts, and Anne Klein handbags. Athletes and music celebrities have taken advantage of opportunities in the accessory business. Michael Jordan's Nike athletic shoes, Air Jordans, were very popular and were considered must-have items by many teenagers. Besides producing apparel, Sean "P. Diddy" Combs of music business fame also produces hats bearing his Sean John logo.

hardlines lines of products that are non-textile, such as small and large appliances, home accessories, and items not made of fabric

softlines lines of products made from textiles that include apparel and household items such as towels, table linens, and bedding

apparel term used for clothing, as in personal attire or garments

accessories fashion items that are added to complete or enhance outfits

Hot Property

Cool Shades

Because of his "raging distaste for mediocrity and a fierce devotion to innovation," scientist Jim Jannard created one of the world's hottest companies—Oakley. The company is best known for its popular line of sunglasses for the serious sports enthusiast as well as for the "in crowd" on the who's who list. Oakley is a technology company that creates art with innovative and functional designs. It supplies sports-minded individuals with high-performance apparel, footwear, wristwatches, and accessories. The company even has a line of ergonomically designed utility bags and backpacks—and eyewear cases called "durable metal vaults."

The worldwide company began in California when Jannard created a motocross handgrip with a unique "orbicular" (circular) design. Engineered to fit a closed hand, the handgrip was a hit. Today approximately 550 patents and 875 trademarks have been generated by Oakley.

X-TREME TESTING

After each new product is engineered and lab tested under stringent controls, a product is field tested by the world's top athletes. According to a company spokesperson, Oakley glasses are "welded by a kilowatt of ultra energy, and then the suspended exoskelton is fused to the subframe using ultrasonic energy. Sculpturally integrated hinges blend with wraparound contours that maximize peripheral clarity with patented XYZ Optics®." The unique design exceeds industrial standards for impact protection. All eyewear, including goggles, is available with prescription lenses.

Whether surfing, snow skiing, mountain biking, or playing a round of golf, the serious sports enthusiast—or just the person who wants to look good—wears Oakley.

1. Is Oakley's line of products hardline or softline?
2. What type of fashion products are Oakley sunglasses?

Math Check

REVENUE AND EXPENSES

The monthly revenue and expenses for Carl's Lamps include cash sales: $2,560; charge sales: $3,665; other: $215; employee salaries: $3,050; advertising: $960; rent: $800; and supplies: $240. What is the net income?

➡For tips on finding the solution, go to marketingseries.glencoe.com.

home furnishings the fashion product category that includes textiles used to furnish and decorate the home, such as towels, linens, and bedding

FASHION BY ANY NAME
Fashionable designs help create a wide variety of products, from apparel to furniture to cell phones. *How would these products be classified?*

Home Furnishings

Whether your vision is to create a Paris-style apartment, a modern mansion, a luxurious loft, or a comfortable college dorm room, you will find a variety of styles in today's home furnishings. **Home furnishings** is the fashion product category that includes textiles used to furnish and decorate the home, such as towels, linens, and bedding. Each year, consumers spend millions of dollars to redecorate homes. Many people give their homes fashion makeovers, by using new drapes, bedspreads, or carpeting. Fashion trends in the home furnishings industry move at a slower pace than those in the apparel industry. Many apparel designers also produce home furnishing lines, such as the lines by Ralph Lauren and Tommy Hilfiger.

Categories of Home Furnishings

Designers in the home furnishings industry create fashion through the use of colors, designs, and fabrics. Because household textiles are expected to last about ten years, performance is a main consideration in choosing textiles. Consumers want the fabrics in their homes to be strong and durable, colorfast (retains color over time), and stain resistant. The three main categories of home furnishings are *domestics* (bed linens, bathroom items, and table and kitchen linens), *home furnishings* (window treatments, upholstery furniture, and miscellaneous items such as throw pillows), and *floor coverings* (carpeting, area rugs, throw rugs, and non-fabric floor tiles). Non-textile merchandise includes all other home accessories such as pictures, lamps, and other decorative items.

Home Furnishings and the Economy

The economy can affect the success of home furnishing businesses and fashion apparel businesses. In times of hardship, people spend less money on home furnishings. When people experience high levels of employment and have extra money to spend, they tend to buy more of these products. New home sales also directly affect the purchase of home accessories.

 marketingseries.glencoe.com

Categories and Classifications in Apparel

The main categories of apparel are women's wear, men's wear, and infants' and children's wear. Each category has distinctive classifications that determine the manufacturing of merchandise.

Women's Wear

The women's wear category represents the largest share of the apparel industry. Fashion is continually moving and changing. Therefore, the women's apparel industry must stay in step with that movement by producing new merchandise. The industry manufactures new lines for five different seasons each year. The retail life of a line is approximately ten weeks. After that point, stores begin introducing new lines for their customers. Apparel manufacturers divide women's apparel into classifications based on the type of merchandise. These classifications include:

- Sportswear separates (tops, bottoms, sports attire for tennis, golf, etc.)

- Dresses (one- or two-piece, from casual to dressy)

- Evening and bridal (cocktail dresses, wedding gowns, other dressy/formal attire)

- Maternity

- Outerwear (coats, rainwear)

- Suits (indoor jackets with pants or skirts)

- Active wear (dancewear, jogging suits)

- Swimwear/beachwear

- Intimate apparel (foundations, lingerie, sleepwear, loungewear)

- Accessories (scarves, gloves, handbags, belts, hosiery, hats, jewelry, umbrellas)

- Footwear

- Miscellaneous apparel (uniforms, aprons, smocks, etc.)

  Women's wear is divided into size ranges that include:

- Misses

- Women's

- Petite

- Juniors

Misses represents regular sizes in even numbers from sizes 2 to 14. The women's size range includes plus sizes for larger women. Petite sizes are designed for women under 5 feet 4 inches tall, and junior sizes are designed for younger figures with odd-numbered sizes from sizes 1 to 13.

TECH
NOTES

Tech-cessories

With an ever-increasing assortment of decorative faceplates, musical ring-tones, and color screens, cell phones have become high-tech fashion accessories. A survey conducted by the Institute for Communication Research revealed that 60 percent of the college students in America own a cell phone. Statistics also show that cell-phone use by teenagers is on the rise, in spite of the fact that cell phones are banned on high school campuses.

➡️Is a cell phone a necessity or an accessory? Write a paragraph defending your opinion after reading the articles through **marketingseries.glencoe.com**.

CONNECT

Which women's wear classification might generate the most sales? Why?

Liberated Women's Wear

With the removal of apartheid, or racial segregation, in South Africa in the early 1990s, women of color changed their style of dress to reflect a new celebration of life. In modern South Africa, women began choosing bold, stylish clothes that reflected independence.

Leading the fashion revolution was one of South Africa's brightest actresses, Nkhen-sani Manganyi. Winner of the prestigious Vita theater award, Manganyi turned her theatrical flare into fashion with designs such as artful T-shirts that feature a photograph of a couple dancing. The man on the T-shirt wears a flamboyant 1940s-style zoot suit and hat as he throws his partner with swinging skirt into the air.

Manganyi also established her own clothing line Stoned Cherrie, which was chased by a host of other designers. These designers were young women making their marks in boutiques in South Africa's capital city, Johannesburg. Design houses such as Sun Goddess, Darkie, and Machere have followed in Manganyi's footsteps, as South Africa's women have stepped up to make a new fashion statement.

How did the removal of apartheid contribute to a new fashion trend for women in South Africa?

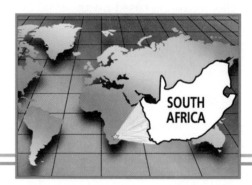

Men's Wear

Traditionally, men have not responded to fashion changes quickly. However, today men have become almost as fashion conscious as women. Fashion marketers present new lines twice a year. The fall/winter lines are the most important, followed by the spring/summer lines. The different seasons determine fabric weight. However, men wear suits year round, so many suit designs require light-weight, summer fabrics. The men's sportswear market has become style conscious, resulting in apparel makers showing new sportswear lines four times a year.

Men's wear producers specialize in categories, as do women's apparel makers. **Figure 5.1** illustrates examples of standard classifications of men's wear. The classifications include:

- Tailored apparel (suits, overcoats, sport coats, dress trousers)

- Furnishings (dress shirts, neckwear, underwear, hats, socks, sleepwear, robes)

- Sportswear (sports shirts, knot shirts, sweaters, shorts, slacks, exercise wear, swim trunks)

- Heavy outerwear (parkas, ski pants, jackets)

- Work clothing

- Footwear

- Miscellaneous apparel (rainwear, uniforms, caps)

QUESTION

What seasons are the most important for men's wear?

Figure 5.1

Men's Wear

CLASSIC MEN'S WEAR Items of clothing, such as suits and ties, have always been included in men's wardrobes. *What other kinds of men's wear do you think have become more popular in recent years?*

Men's wear in the United States is sized by chest, waist, and inseam measurements. Jacket lengths are designated as regular, long, or short. Dress shirts are sized by collar and sleeve measurements, while sportswear shirts are available in small, medium, large, and extra large.

Infants' and Children's Wear

Going back to school each year is not always the most anticipated event for children. However, for the children's wear industry, it is one of the most important events. Pre-fall is one of the three main production seasons for manufacturers. Marketers depend on parents buying new school clothes for their children each year. Children can be as fashion conscious as their parents. During this time fashion producers present new styles, fabrics, and colors. The other two seasons are the spring/summer season and the winter-holiday season.

TRENDS IN INFANTS' AND CHILDREN'S WEAR Styles designed for older age groups have begun to migrate to the children's market. Teen fashions are represented in the children's market.

Licensing of children's apparel has also become a big business. Children love to wear clothes bearing the images of their favorite cartoon or storybook characters. For decades Disney and Sesame Street® characters have appeared on children's apparel for all age groups.

Safety trends also affect the production of children's wear. Fabrics used in the children's apparel industry must meet flame-retardant standards. The clothing must not cause tripping or catch on objects.

Style Point

PLAY CLOTHES
Before the late 18th century, children were dressed as miniature adults in garments that limited physical freedom. The social revolution of the 18th century influenced beliefs that children should be happy and playful. In the late 18th and early 19th centuries, children's wear became distinct from adult clothing.

CLASSIFYING INFANTS' AND CHILDREN'S WEAR The classifications of children's clothing are organized by gender—boys or girls—and sizes that may also reflect age group:

- Infant

- Toddler

- Young children (sizes 2–6X)

- Girls (sizes 6–14)

- Boys (sizes 6–20)

Variety of Fashion

Fashion encompasses a broad range of products that include not only apparel for children, women, and men, but also textile products that include household items, such as towels, table linens, and bedding as well as non-textiles, such as small and large appliances, home accessories, and non-fabric items. Categories and classifications of these products allow producers and retailers to more efficiently make, market, and sell fashion to consumers.

Quick Check ✔

RESPOND to what you've read by answering these questions.

1. What are the three main merchandise categories of apparel? _____
_____
_____
_____
_____

2. What are the size classifications for women's clothing? _____
_____
_____
_____
_____

3. How is children's clothing classified? _____
_____
_____
_____
_____

The Fashion Cycle

Changing Fashions

The consumer dictates the fashions that are produced. Demand for certain goods can vary, and producers must be able to respond to the ever-changing movement of demand. It is a continuous process of consumers' needs and wants creating that demand for a product, producers responding to that demand, and consumers accepting the merchandise that is offered. Because of this movement, fashion changes.

The Fashion Cycle

As discussed in Chapter 1, fashion is the style that is most popular at a given time. The **fashion cycle** is the period of time or life span during which the fashion exists, moving through five stages, from introduction through obsolescence.

To better understand the different phases of the fashion cycle, it is important to understand style, acceptance, and timeliness of fashions. Style is a particular look, shape, or type of apparel item. When a customer purchases and wears a certain style, that style is considered accepted. This acceptance leads to the style becoming a fashion. Fashions do not always survive from year to year. Customers may become bored with a look and discard it for another one. The ability to gauge the timeliness, or occurrence at the right time, of a fashion is critical in the development and marketing of fashion products.

Stages of the Fashion Cycle

Fashion moves through different stages during its cycle of existence. Not only does a design go through phases, but special features, such as color, texture, and fabric, also go through fashion cycles. This fashion cycle may be illustrated by the shape of a bell or a hill. (See **Figure 5.2** on page 102.) Each section of the upward slope, to the top, and then downward, to the decline, represents different phases of acceptance—from acceptance by a few to acceptance by the majority. These stages include the introduction stage, rise stage, peak stage, decline stage, and obsolescence stage.

INTRODUCTION STAGE Designs first previewed during fashion weeks at the major design centers are in this stage. As the new styles, colors, or textures are first introduced, or begin the upward slope on the hill, a limited number of people accept them. Fashion leaders wear the styles, which are offered at high prices and produced in small quantities.

AS YOU READ . . .

YOU WILL LEARN
- To explain the fashion cycle.
- To discuss the role of fashion leaders.
- To identify the different theories of fashion movement.
- To discuss the difference between fashion trends and fads.

WHY IT'S IMPORTANT

Fashion is an economic force. To be successful in the industry, it is important to understand fashion cycles and fashion movement.

KEY TERMS
- fashion cycle
- fashion movement
- fashion leaders
- trickle-down theory
- trickle-up theory
- trickle-across theory
- fashion trend
- fad

PREDICT

Have you ever noticed a fashion product go in and out of style? What product?

fashion cycle the period of time or life span during which the fashion exists, moving through stages, from introduction through obsolescence

CONNECT

Have you ever purchased a style of clothing that you knew was out of style? Why?

RISE STAGE Manufacturers who copy new designer clothes will reproduce the styles as apparel that costs less by using less expensive fabrics or by minimizing details. In this stage, or the first incline up the hill, the fashions become accepted by more people because they can afford them. As consumer interest increases, additional manufacturers copy the fashions by adapting or changing some of the popular features. The climb up that first hill is very exciting, and fashion producers anticipate consumer excitement about a new product and purchase more merchandise. Mass production reduces the price of the fashion, and more sales result.

PEAK STAGE This stage is the top of the hill. The fashion is at its most popular and accepted stage in the fashion cycle. By this time, the merchandise is mass produced and distributed. The prices are not necessarily at the lowest levels. Because so many versions of the fashion have been offered, the prices may vary at this stage. Popularity of a fashion can determine how long it remains at this stage. It can survive longer if the fashion becomes a classic. Sometimes simple changes, such as updating or adding new details of design, color, or texture to the look can keep it in the peak stage.

DECLINE STAGE Consumers eventually grow tired of certain fashions and desire something new. At this stage of the fashion cycle, consumer demand is decreasing, or going down the slope. There are so many of the fashion items available that they have oversaturated, or flooded, the market. If consumers still want to buy the fashion, they probably do not want to pay a high price. During the decline stage, fashion retailers begin to mark down the price of the merchandise to make room for new designs.

OBSOLESCENCE STAGE This stage marks the end of the fashion cycle, or the bottom of the hill. Consumers are no longer interested in the fashion and find new looks, which signals the beginning of another fashion cycle. The price of the fashion product may be low at this point, but consumers will probably not buy the merchandise.

Figure 5.2

The Fashion Cycle

THE RISE AND FALL OF FASHION Every kind of product experiences a life cycle, but the life cycle of most fashion merchandise changes more frequently. *Name two fashion products that are currently in the peak stage of the fashion cycle.*

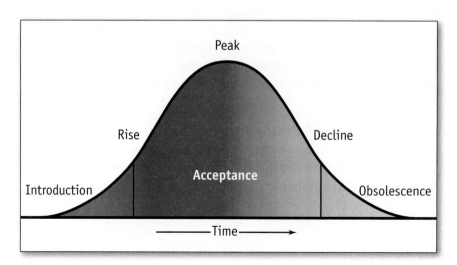

Fashion-Cycle Life Span

All fashions follow the life-cycle pattern, but the rate at which they move through the cycle varies with each fashion. It is difficult for fashion marketers to predict the life span of an item. The length of time that a particular fashion remains in any of the stages of the life cycle depends on the consumer's willingness to accept the fashion.

Fashion Movement

The only constant in the fashion world is that consumers look for new fashions and desire change. This is referred to as **fashion movement**, or the ongoing motion of fashions moving through the fashion cycle. There are many factors that can affect fashion movement. Economic and social factors can influence consumer interest in fashion. Introduction of new fibers and fabrics as well as advertising techniques can cause consumers to desire change in fashion. Designers and retailers appreciate consumer interest in new fashion because that interest keeps the fashion industry in business.

Old Is New Again

Some fashions never seem to fall to the decline or obsolescence stages of the fashion cycle—they just cycle around again. Jeans are a perfect example of this type of fashion movement. In the 1960s, jeans and denim-fabric clothing became very popular. The changes in silhouettes, such as boot-cut, baggy, and low-rise, have resulted in the life cycle lasting longer than usual. Today jeans continue to be one of the most popular apparel items.

Leading the Fashion Way

Every year fashion centers present new styles. These designs are not immediately worn by the majority of the population. Who decides what fashions will start the upward climb of the fashion cycle? **Fashion leaders** are the trendsetters, or individuals who are the first to wear new styles, after which the fashion is adopted by the general public. Fashion leaders may be high-profile people who get media attention. This exposure results in more people seeing the new designs and causes the general acceptance of a fashion.

These trendsetters used to be royalty or the very wealthy. In today's society, media celebrities often set the fashion cycles in motion. For example, during the 2003 Academy Awards, many of the female stars attending the televised ceremony wore chandelier-style earrings. This media exposure immediately caused that style of jewelry to be in demand.

VINTAGE FASHION EXPO 2004

Who'll be there?
Coco Chanel
Norman Norell
Pucci
Hermès
Pauline Trigère
Halston
Claire McCardell
Schiaparelli
Dior
Rudi Gernreich
Geoffrey Beene
James Galanos
Yves Saint Laurent
Valentino
Bonnie Cashin
Courrèges
Oscar de la Renta
Bill Blass and more.

RETRO CHIC Costume and retail apparel designers may search the racks of vintage clothing stores, movie wardrobe auctions, and garage sales to find the "newest" looks to recycle. *Do you think any current styles have been influenced by designs of the past? Explain your answer.*

fashion movement the ongoing motion of fashion moving through the fashion cycle

fashion leaders trendsetters, or individuals who are the first to wear new styles, after which the fashion is adopted by the general public

STAYING POWER

Betsey Johnson
Fashion Designer

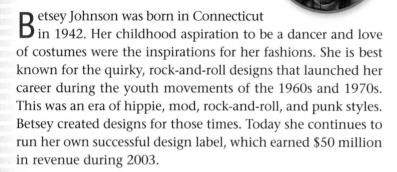

Betsey Johnson was born in Connecticut in 1942. Her childhood aspiration to be a dancer and love of costumes were the inspirations for her fashions. She is best known for the quirky, rock-and-roll designs that launched her career during the youth movements of the 1960s and 1970s. This was an era of hippie, mod, rock-and-roll, and punk styles. Betsey created designs for those times. Today she continues to run her own successful design label, which earned $50 million in revenue during 2003.

What kind of training did she have?

Betsey got her start in the fashion world by winning the *Mademoiselle* Magazine Guest Editor contest in 1964. A year later, she landed a job as top designer at Paraphernalia, a trendy clothing boutique. She learned by doing, staying on top of the trends, from the youth movement of the 1960s to the pop-art era of the 1970s. In 1978, she started her own clothing label and has been designing successfully ever since. In 2002, she celebrated her 60th birthday and the 24th anniversary of the label.

What does she like most about her job?

"Making clothes involves what I like—color, pattern, shape, and movement. I like the everyday process, the people, the pressure, and the surprise of seeing the work come alive, walking and dancing around on a stranger."

What is the key to her success?

The ability to change with the times while keeping her designs pure.

How can fashion professionals change with the times and still keep a personal design style?

Career Data: Designer

Education and Training Associate degree or bachelor's degree and apprenticeship

Skills and Abilities Design, construction, and management skills

Career Outlook Average growth through 2012

Career Path Internship, apprentice, assistant, designer, top designer to designing own label

QUESTION

What are fashion leaders?

Theories of Fashion Movement

Fashion leaders exist on all levels of society and affect fashion movement. The following three theories of fashion movement identify the starting point of a fashion trend:

- Trickle-Down Theory
- Trickle-Up Theory
- Trickle-Across Theory

A **fashion trend** is the direction of the movement of fashion that is accepted in the marketplace. Each theory focuses on a different set of fashion leaders. In one theory, fashion *trickles down* from a highly visible elite class. In another theory, it *trickles up* from the "street," once it is discovered by the fashion elite and introduced to mainstream consumers as an adapted version. If a fashion look is promoted by the media and manufactured quickly, the look can *trickle across* all levels of the market simultaneously.

TRICKLE-DOWN THEORY The **trickle-down theory** is a hypothesis that states the movement of fashion starts at the top with consumers of higher socioeconomic status and moves down to the general public. This is the oldest and most accepted theory of fashion change. Think of it as a ladder. According to this theory, people with lower incomes, at the bottom of the ladder, will only wear fashions that have become popular among consumers with higher incomes, at the top of the ladder. As more people begin to wear the fashions, those at the top become less interested in the fashion and begin looking for something new.

TRICKLE-UP THEORY The **trickle-up theory** is a hypothesis that states the movement of fashion starts with consumers on lower-income levels and then moves to consumers with higher incomes. Consumers on lower-income levels may also include younger consumers. It is essentially the opposite of the trickle-down theory. Examples of this theory include:

- **Athletic Apparel Style**—During the 1970s and 1980s, athletic apparel became widely accepted by the general population. High-fashion designers noticed its popularity and began to incorporate the athletic look into their designs. The look of fitness became chic, or fashionable. Today you can see athletic styles by the major designers in everything from footwear to apparel.

- **Hair Style**—The long-hair look of the Beatles music group during the 1960s is another example of how working-class fashion swept the public.

- **Punk Style**—Another look that moved from street fashion to the top end of the market was the punk look. Top designers decorated their apparel with large safety pins, and many fashion shops carried the torn and distressed clothing styles first popularized in the 1970s.

Case Study PART 2

BRANDING BURBERRY

Continued from Part 1 on page 93

To revive Burberry's sales and image, one of Rose Marie Bravo's first moves as head of Burberry's marketing was to brand Burberry's famous plaid. The pattern started to appear on everything from bikinis to dog jackets. Burberry marketed its brand using trendy models such as Kate Moss. More importantly, Burberry expanded its product lines to include hats, shoes, purses, and even motorcycle jackets. Bravo renegotiated licensing agreements for other companies to use the plaid—and dropped low-profile distributors such as tourist shops. These strategies increased Burberry's visibility and popularity among young adults and fashion followers.

In early 2000, Burberry's trench coat went from being the rainwear of choice for the Queen of England to the must-have accessory for fashion models and celebrities. When Burberry sold stock to the public in 2002, the company raised $414 million.

ANALYZE AND WRITE

1. Write a paragraph about how branding the Burberry plaid was a strategic marketing move?
2. Apply one theory of fashion movement to Burberry.

fashion trend the direction of the movement of fashion that is accepted in the marketplace

trickle-down theory a hypothesis that states the movement of fashion starts at the top with consumers of higher socioeconomic status

trickle-up theory a hypothesis that states the movement of fashion starts with consumers on lower-income levels and then moves to consumers with higher incomes

trickle-across theory a hypothesis stating that fashion acceptance begins among several socioeconomic classes at the same time

fad a fashion that is popular for a short period of time

TRICKLE–ACROSS THEORY In today's world of fashion, new designs are produced at all price levels at the same time. The merchandise quality and lines may vary, but new fashion exists for all groups. Who establishes acceptance of fashions in this situation? The **trickle-across theory** is a hypothesis stating that fashion acceptance begins among several socioeconomic classes at the same time, because there are fashion leaders in all groups. These leaders influence their groups to accept new styles. This theory is especially probable in the 21st century because technology allows designer fashions to be copied quickly and easily, making them available for all consumers.

Fashion Trends vs. Fads

Fashion is constantly moving. It is on its way in, on its way out, or is stable. A number of fashion trends can be present at any time. For example, fashion marketers identify trends according to the length of skirts as well as colors and fabrics.

A **fad** is a fashion that is popular for a short period of time. The merchandise may be produced and sold at lower prices and is relatively easy to copy. Therefore, it floods the market in a very short time. The item moves rapidly through the fashion cycle. A fad can be recognized by its sudden appearance and disappearance. Leg warmers in the 1980s are an example of a fad. However, a trend can be a fad that has stood the test of time. The fashion is present consistently, though its popularity might vary. Denim jeans and urban fashions are examples of trends.

Changing Fashions

Fashion and fashion products are constantly changing and going through movement known as the fashion cycle. Each new season challenges fashion producers, designers, and marketers to develop new approaches and ideas to meet consumer demand. The flux of consumer approval creates trends and fads—and keeps the fashion industry an exciting and dynamic business.

Quick Check

RESPOND to what you've read by answering these questions.

1. What are the five stages of the fashion cycle?_____

_____

2. What are three theories of how fashions become popular?_____

_____

3. What is the difference between a fashion trend and a fashion fad?_____

_____

Name _____ Date _____

Worksheet 5.1

Classifications of Apparel

Visit a local department store or mall. Describe two items under each classification of apparel that you find in the department store or the mall stores.

Women's Wear:

Sportswear

_____

_____

Footwear

_____

_____

Active wear

_____

_____

Dresses

_____

_____

Swimwear/beachwear

_____

_____

Intimate apparel

_____

_____

Evening and bridal

_____

_____

Accessories

_____

_____

Suits

_____

_____

Maternity

_____

_____

Swimwear/beachwear

_____

_____

Outerwear

_____

_____

Miscellaneous apparel

_____

_____

Men's Wear:

Sportswear

_____

_____

Work clothing

_____

_____

Furnishings

_____

_____

Footwear

_____

_____

Heavy outerwear

_____

_____

Miscellaneous apparel

_____

_____

Name _____ Date _____

Worksheet 5.2

Fashion Movement

Read the following statements. Each statement relates to one of the theories of fashion movement—trickle down, trickle up, or trickle across. Place the number of each statement in the appropriate category below.

1. As more people begin to wear certain fashions, those at the top become less interested in the fashions and begin looking for something new.

2. There are fashion leaders in all socioeconomic groups.

3. An example of this theory is that street fashion moved to the top end of the market.

4. As fashion becomes popular, it is accepted by people on the higher-income levels.

5. Fashion acceptance starts among several socioeconomic groups at the same time.

6. This is the oldest and most accepted theory of fashion change.

7. The movement of fashion starts at the top with a select few of higher social status, and then moves down to the general population.

8. Fashion is set by consumers on lower-income levels or the young.

9. Designer fashions can be copied quickly and easily, making them available for all socioeconomic groups.

Trickle Down:	Trickle Up:	Trickle Across:

Portfolio Works

FASHION TRENDS AND FADS

Look in your closet. Identify items of clothing that you think follow a fashion trend and items of clothing that are fashion fads. Then answer the questions below.

Fashion Trend Clothing:

_____

_____

_____

_____

_____

Fashion Fad Clothing:

_____

_____

_____

_____

_____

Questions:

1. Do you consider yourself a person who follows fashion trends or fashion fads? Explain your answer.

_____

_____

_____

2. If you had a very limited budget, would you buy clothes that are part of a fashion trend or fashion fad? Explain your answer.

_____

_____

_____

Add this page to your career portfolio.

Chapter 5 | Review and Activities

CHAPTER SUMMARY

Section 5.1 Types of Fashion

lines (p. 94)
hardlines (p. 95)
softlines (p. 95)
apparel (p. 95)
accessories (p. 95)
home furnishings (p. 96)

- Fashion products are grouped as lines: hardlines and softlines. Hardlines include non-textile products such as small and large appliances, home accessories, and non-fabric items. Softlines include apparel, and textiles such as towels, table linens, and bedding.

- Fashion apparel categories include women's wear, men's wear, and infants' and children's wear.

- Categories of fashion apparel have classifications, such as brand, age group, size, price, and style.

Section 5.2 The Fashion Cycle

fashion cycle (p. 101)
fashion movement
    (p. 103)
fashion leaders (p. 103)
fashion trend (p. 105)
trickle-down theory
    (p. 105)
trickle-up theory (p. 105)
trickle-across theory
    (p. 106)
fad (p. 106)

- The fashion cycle is the period of time or life span during which a fashion exists as it goes through five stages: introduction, rise, peak, decline, and obsolescence.

- Fashion leaders are trendsetters who are first to wear new styles, after which the general public follows and adopts the fashion.

- Three theories of fashion movement identify the starting point of a fashion trend. The theories include: the trickle-down theory, the trickle-up theory, and the trickle-across theory.

- A trend is the direction of the movement of fashion that is accepted in the marketplace. It tends to exist consistently, but a fad is a fashion that is popular for a short period of time.

CHECKING CONCEPTS

1. **Name** the main types of product lines.
2. **Identify** the categories of fashion apparel.
3. **Identify** how retailers designate each style of apparel.
4. **List** types of fashion accessories.
5. **Explain** the rise stage of the fashion cycle.
6. **Define** the term *fashion leaders*.
7. **Explain** the trickle-down theory of fashion movement.

Critical Thinking
8. **Discuss** how a fashion fad might become a fashion trend.

CROSS-CURRICULUM SKILLS

Work-Based Learning

Information—Organizing and Maintaining Information

9. Design a graphic organizer that will help you understand and remember the fashion cycle.

Interpersonal Skills—Serving Clients/Customers

10. The fashion designer of Teen Trends clothing company hires you to create a poster to show off his sports caps for boys and girls. Create and display the poster in class.

School-Based Learning

Science

11. Contact a jeweler and ask about the percentage of gold for these karats: 14, 18, 22, and 24. Create a chart.

History

12. Use the Internet or library to research the history of denim jeans, and then write a summary of your findings.

 DECA CONNECTION

Role Play: Sales Associate, Linens

SITUATION You are to assume the role of an experienced sales associate in the bath linens department of a suburban department store. Your department carries a wide selection of styles and colors of towels. The towel styles range from bath sheets to washcloths. You have been assigned to orient a new employee (judge). The employee (judge) asks why the store carries so many styles and colors of towels.

ACTIVITY You are to explain to the new employee (judge) that home furnishings, such as towels, follow fashion trends and must appeal to a broad range of customers.

EVALUATION You will be evaluated on how well you meet the following performance indicators:

- Explain the components of fashion (style, color, and functionality).
- Describe the principles of color in fashion.
- Explain the elements and principles of line and design.
- Explain fashion-brand images.
- Orient new employees.

 INTERNET ACTIVITY

Use the Internet to access a Web site on gems for information about gold used for jewelry.

- Read the information under What Is Gold?
- Write a fact sheet about the information.
- Write a short paragraph answering the following question: Why is gold jewelry so expensive?

➡️ For a link to a Web site to help you do this activity, go to **marketingseries.glencoe.com**.

Chapter 6

Textiles and Production

Chapter Objectives

- Discuss the fiber properties that determine appropriate use and quality of fabrics.
- Identify the main natural fibers.
- Identify the main manufactured fibers.
- Explain the importance of fabric in fashion.
- Discuss how synthetic fibers are produced.
- Identify the two primary methods for making fibers into fabrics.

SETTING STANDARDS: COTTON

Many people associate polyester with fashion and fabrics of the 1960s and 1970s. At that time, the use of new synthetic textiles, such as polyester and acetate, affected the cotton industry. In 1960, cotton made up 78 percent of the textile products sold at retail stores. However, by 1975, that share fell to an all-time low of 34 percent. In response, Congress passed the Cotton Research and Promotion Act in 1966, granting cotton growers money and resources for research and promotion. By 1970, Cotton Incorporated was formed with government support to formalize research and the marketing of cotton. This was a unique partnership between government and industry—but did it succeed in increasing consumer demand for cotton?

ANALYZE AND WRITE

1. How did the fashion market affect the cotton fabric industry in the 1970s? Write a paragraph explaining your answer.
2. Why do you think continued research into fabric uses is important to marketing fabrics? Write a paragraph explaining your answer.

Case Study Part 2 on page 119

POWER READ

Be an active reader and use these reading strategies:

PREDICT what the section will be about.

CONNECT what you read with your life.

QUESTION as you read to make sure you understand the content.

RESPOND to what you've read.

Textiles and Fashion

AS YOU READ ...

YOU WILL LEARN

- To discuss the fiber properties that determine appropriate use and quality of fabrics.
- To identify the main natural fibers.
- To identify the main manufactured fibers.
- To explain the importance of fabric in fashion.

WHY IT'S IMPORTANT

As a fashion marketer, it is important to be knowledgeable about fibers and understand their characteristics in order to provide the right products to the right target market.

KEY TERMS

- fabrics
- fibers
- yarns
- natural fibers
- filament
- manufactured fibers
- denier

PREDICT

What are some sources of the fibers that make fabrics?

fabrics long pieces of cloth

fibers thin, hairlike strands that are the basic units used to make fabrics and textile products

Fabrics and Fibers

Imagine an artist painting a picture without a canvas or some other medium with which to create his or her ideas. He or she would have wonderful and creative ideas that could never be enjoyed by other people. The same would be true of a fashion designer who did not have **fabrics**, or long pieces of cloth. Some designers work directly with fabric, draping and folding it into fashion creations. Others draw their ideas on paper and then transfer the designs to the fabric.

Characteristics of Fibers

The basic building blocks for all fabrics are fibers. Fashion marketers need to be knowledgeable about fibers in order to provide the right products to the right consumers, or target market. **Fibers** are thin, hairlike strands that are the basic units used to make fabrics and textile products. Different fibers have specific properties that affect the characteristics of fabric, such as:

- Appearance
- Strength
- Absorbency
- Warmth
- Shrinkage
- Price

The fiber's properties determine the appropriate use of the final fabric for certain items of apparel. Knowing how the fabric will perform and look as a finished garment is critical to having a successful fashion design.

Types of Fibers and Yarns

Fibers are spun into yarn, and the yarn is used to make fabric. **Yarns** are uninterrupted threads of textile fibers that are ready to be turned into fabrics. The different fibers can all be categorized as either natural or manufactured fibers. Leathers and furs are not fibers, but they are used in the apparel industry. Natural fibers can be *plant* or *animal* fibers. Manufactured fibers are either *synthetic* or *cellulosic* fibers. Synthetic fibers are composed of chemical compounds derived from petroleum or natural gas. Cellulosic fibers are made from plants combined with chemicals.

Natural Fibers

The use of natural fibers dates back 5,000 years when the Egyptians used fine linen for clothing. Today natural fibers are a main product in the fashion industry. **Natural fibers** are textile fibers made from plants or animals. There are two main groups of natural fibers: *cellulosic* and *protein* fibers. Cellulosic fibers are derived from the cell walls of certain plants. Examples of such fibers are cotton and linen (flax). Cellulose is also the major raw material component used in the production of certain manufactured fibers, such as acetate and rayon. Protein fibers come from animals and insects, and create fibers such as wool and silk.

Characteristics of Natural Fibers

When designers use fabrics made from natural fibers, they consider the characteristics that will affect the finished product. Natural fibers are usually more absorbent and cause a garment to be more comfortable or cooler to wear. These are characteristics of cotton. Many summer garments are made from cotton. However, they also tend to wrinkle more and shrink when washed. Another consideration is how the fibers are processed, which can affect price. Making linen fabric is more expensive than making cotton fabric because production requires more labor, and linen is often imported to the United States. The main natural fibers are cotton, linen, wool, and silk.

Cotton

Cotton is probably the most important textile fiber used by the fashion industry. It comes from the bolls, or seed pods, of cotton plants. Cotton is grown around the world, and the United States is one of its major producers. Cotton is also one of the main textile products of China and Mexico. It grows primarily in warm climates.

Advantages:	Disadvantages:
▪ Comfortable	▪ Shrinks in hot water
▪ Absorbent	▪ Wrinkles easily
▪ Good color retention	▪ Weakened by perspiration and sun
▪ Dyes and prints well	▪ Burns easily
▪ Washable	▪ Affected by mildew
▪ Strong	
▪ Drapes well	
▪ Easy to handle and sew	
▪ Inexpensive	

END USES Cotton is made into a wide range of wearing apparel, such as blouses, shirts, dresses, children's wear, separates, skirts, pants, underwear, socks, and outerwear. Cotton fabrics are also used for home furnishings, such as curtains, draperies, bedspreads, comforters, throws, sheets, towels, tablecloths, table mats, and napkins.

TECH
NOTES

Futuristic Fabric

Jeans that fight cellulite? Socks that always smell fresh? Thanks to microencapsulating technology, clothes can do more to help the wearer look and feel good. Tiny beads known as "microcapsules" form a chemical bond with fabric fibers. When the garment is worn, friction triggers the release of fragrance, moisturizers, and other substances contained within the microcapsules. Some companies claim that the fabric-enhancing ingredients can withstand up to 30 washings.

➡Use your imagination to create a futuristic fabric after learning more about micro-encapsulating technology at **marketingseries.glencoe.com**.

yarns uninterrupted threads of textile fibers that are ready to be turned into fabrics

natural fibers textile fibers made from plants or animals

Linens for Every Need

LINENS·N·THINGS

One of the nation's largest and fastest-growing retailers of textiles and home accessories also helps families save for college. Linens 'n Things gives a 5 percent rebate for college savings every time a Futuretrust™ member shops at the store. Futuretrust is a MasterCard®-linked college-savings program that automatically contributes to savings plans.

"It's a great benefit to give young people and their families a head start on college savings," says Norman Axelrod, Chairman and Chief Executive Officer of Linens 'n Things. Futuretrust Founder Rebecca Matthias notes that "saving for college is a huge financial undertaking these days. Spending for home accessories while saving for college is a great combination."

With more than 400 stores in the United States and Canada, Linens 'n Things has been a friend of young people since its beginning nearly three decades ago. Many of the 14,000 associates working in stores are students or recent graduates.

On college and university campuses across the country, Linens 'n Things actively recruits students through the company's Live on Campus! Program. Positions offered to students are in the management-development or assistant-buyer programs. The management-development program is a program that provides new employees with the basic tools needed for a successful transition into retail management. A college graduate hired for the assistant-buyer program enters the merchandising team as an assistant to a buyer.

1. What are different types of fabrics that you expect to find in a store such as Linens 'n Things? Explain why you chose these fabrics.
2. Why would you want to learn about different fabrics if you were planning to enter the Linens 'n Things assistant-buyer program?

See the Teacher Manual for answers.

EXTENDING THE LESSON

Ask the students to research the flax plant to find out where it grows, how it is harvested, and the process that is used to turn it into linen.

Linen (Flax)

Linen is a fabric made from fibers found inside the woody stem of the flax plant—a grass that has the appearance of a tall, slender reed. It is one of the oldest-known cellulosic fibers and dates back to the Stone Age, which ended about 5,000 years ago. Before it was used for apparel, linen was used for bedding. This is why towels, sheets, and tablecloths are called "linens."

Advantages:

- Strong
- Comfortable
- Hand-washable or dry-cleanable
- Absorbent
- Dyes and prints well
- Resists dirt and stains
- Durable
- Withstands high heat
- Lint-free

Disadvantages:

- Wrinkles easily
- Can be expensive
- Shrinks
- Burns easily
- Affected by mildew and perspiration
- Ravels
- Difficult to remove creases
- Shines if ironed

END USES Linen is used for apparel such as dresses, suits, skirts, jackets, blouses, shirts, and handkerchiefs. It is also used in manufacturing home furnishings, such as upholstery, draperies, table linens, sheets, and dish towels.

Wool

Wool fibers come from the sheared, or shaved, hair of sheep or lambs. Wool is the most commonly used animal fiber. Although many countries throughout the world raise sheep for wool, Australia is considered the main producer, with the United States as one of the major users. There is a high demand for wool products, and the supply cannot always meet the need. Therefore, in order to cut the cost of wool, recycled wool is used. Products must be labeled as either virgin (new wool) or recycled (reclaimed wool that has been used from used or unused woven goods). The term *wool* can also apply to all animal hair fibers, including the hair of the Cashmere or Angora goat or the specialty hair fibers of animals such as the camel, alpaca, llama, or vicuña.

Advantages:

- Warm
- Lightweight
- Wrinkle-resistant
- Absorbent
- Dyes well
- Comfortable
- Durable
- Creases well
- Easy to tailor
- Recyclable

Disadvantages:

- Affected by moths
- Shrinks with heat and moisture
- Needs special care, dry cleaning
- Absorbs odors
- Scratchy on skin
- Weakens when wet
- Harmed by bleach, perspiration

END USES Wool is used to make apparel such as sweaters, coats, suits, jackets, pants, skirts, socks, and scarves. It is also used for home furnishings such as carpets, draperies, upholstery, and blankets.

Silk

Silkworms spin *cocoons*, which are protective silk envelopes wrapped around the silkworm in its early stage of growth. Cocoons are used to make silk fiber, the only natural-filament fiber. A **filament** is a very long, fine, continuous thread. A silk cocoon can produce 600 to 2000 meters of continuous fiber. People who are silk harvesters unwind the filaments onto silk reels. This process requires many hours of labor, causing silk fabric to be very expensive. It can take as many as 500 cocoons to create the fabric to make one blouse.

Math Check

RETAIL MARKUP
Terri bought a bolt of Scottish tartan (plaid) wool for her shop. She paid $12 a yard. She added a $4 per yard markup. What is the retail price of a yard of the wool fabric?

➡️For tips on finding the solution, go to **marketingseries.glencoe.com.**

CONNECT
Why do you think wool is in great demand?

filament a very long, fine, continuous thread

The Wool Market

In 2004, a leading Australian agricultural business, Elders Ltd., sold the world's finest bale of wool. Bales are bundles of sheared, or cut, wool that is unprocessed. The large bale of 11.9-micron wool was the first in the world to break the 12-micron barrier, making it extremely high-quality wool.

The bale of wool sold for $675,000 dollars to Kathaytex, one of the top-ten industrialists in China. The company has a reputation for making quality men's suits and other garments. Buyers from Italy and Korea also competed for the bale of wool at the auction in Sydney, Australia. The purchase makes China a major player among wool-processing countries that value superior products. It is the first time high-quality wool has sold outside the traditional markets of Japan, Korea, and Italy.

Name two types of apparel and home fashions that might be made from this wool.

AUSTRALIA

Advantages:	Disadvantages:
▪ Soft	▪ Expensive
▪ Drapes well	▪ Needs special care, dry cleaning
▪ Dyes and prints well	▪ Stains with water
▪ Very strong	▪ Yellows with age
▪ Lightweight	▪ Weakened by perspiration, sun, soap
▪ Resists soil, mildew, and moths	▪ Attacked by insects, silverfish
▪ Comfortable	
▪ Absorbent	

END USES Apparel made from silk includes evening gowns, wedding gowns, lingerie, blouses, scarves, dresses, neckties, and suits for men or women. Silk is also used to make home furnishings such as curtains, draperies, upholstery, and decorative pillows.

Leather/Suede and Fur

Leather, a tough, flexible material, is made by preserving animal hides, or skins, through a process called tanning. The primary source of leather is cattle, or cows and steers, used in the meat-packing industry. Leather products produced from cattle hides are less expensive than leather from cattle that are raised only for leather. Other types of leather used for fashion products are sheep, goat, pig, and reptile.

SUEDE Leather that has a rough or "nappy" finish is *suede* leather. The surface is processed using special equipment that gives suede a rough appearance.

LEATHER AND SYNTHETICS Some leather producers are now blending synthetic fibers such as Lycra with leather to enhance its appearance and performance.

Advantages:	Disadvantages:
■ Durable	■ Scarce
■ Strong	■ Expensive
■ Flexible	
■ Comfortable	
■ Warm	

END USES Apparel made from leather includes coats, jackets, shoes, handbags, gloves, hats, and belts. It is also used in the manufacture of home furnishings, including upholstery and decorative accessories.

FUR *Fur* is the soft, hairy coat of an animal. The use of fur dates back to prehistoric times. Because of the scarcity of pelts or skins from fur-bearing animals, garments made from fur tend to be expensive. Many of the furs sold in the United States are imported.

A number of consumer groups advocate discontinuing the use of fur products, which has resulted in the production of faux, or imitation, fur. Some countries restrict or prohibit the commercial use of particular animals, such as seals and leopards.

Advantages:	Disadvantages:
■ Durable	■ Scarce
■ Soft	■ Expensive
■ Flexible	
■ Warm	

END USES Fur is used to make apparel such as coats, jackets, hats, belts, and coats. It is also used for home furnishings such as bed throws, rugs, and stuffed animals.

Case Study PART 2

SETTING STANDARDS: COTTON
Continued from Part 1 on page 113

Cotton has long been a major commodity in the United States. As early as 1907, international cotton growers were developing standards so that cotton would be priced and marketed consistently around the world. Later, the United States Department of Agriculture created a classification system for cotton. Classification helps growers market their crops and set a fair price. Cooperation between industry and government became vital as new textiles such as polyester threatened the cotton industry in the 1960s.

When Cotton Incorporated formed in 1970, the organization adopted a "push-pull" marketing strategy to promote cotton. They created pull to build consumer demand through advertising and promotion. Cotton Incorporated's efforts focused on building a recognizable identity. In 1973, the Seal of Cotton® was introduced to communicate comfort and quality to consumers. Ten years later, cotton's share of the market climbed to 39 percent. By 1987, cotton was once again on top, as its market share climbed to 49 percent. Then in 1989, Cotton Inc. launched THE FABRIC OF OUR LIVES® advertising campaign. Retail market share for cotton apparel and home products hit 60 percent in 1998. This was the first time since the mid-1960s that cotton surpassed synthetic fibers.

ANALYZE AND WRITE

1. What strategies did Cotton Incorporated use to improve cotton's market share? Make a list of strategies.
2. How does the fashion industry benefit from successfully marketing cotton fiber and fabric? Write a paragraph explaining your answer.

In 2001, the United States imported $1.9 billion in clothing and apparel from Pakistan. In the same year, 100 United States textile mills closed, and 63,200 textile workers were laid off. A struggling economy and competition from cheaper textile exporters, such as Pakistan, contributed to the decline in the United States textile industry. In 2002, in exchange for Pakistan's help with the war in Afghanistan, the United States government granted Pakistan special access to U.S. textile markets for three years. In return, Pakistan lowered taxes on their textile products exported to the United States. *Do you think it was appropriate for the United States government to grant Pakistan special access to the U.S. textile market while its own textile industry was struggling? Why or why not?*

manufactured fibers fibers created by a manufacturing process of any substance that is not a fiber

Manufactured Fibers

For thousands of years, apparel production was limited because of the characteristics of natural fibers. Then, in the late 19th century, the first manufactured fiber, rayon, was developed. **Manufactured fibers** are fibers created by a manufacturing process of any substance that is not a fiber. Made by chemical companies, there are two basic types of manufactured fibers: *cellulosic* (from the regenerated fibrous substance in plants) and *noncellulosic* or *synthetic* (from petrochemical products). The cost of these fibers is less than the cost of natural fibers. These fibers also tend to be stronger and more durable. Many designers use manufactured-fiber fabrics, such as polyester, to create beautiful designs.

When first introduced, manufactured fibers comprised about 1 percent of textiles. Manufactured fibers are now used in about three-quarters of American textile mills. There are numerous manufactured fibers, but some of the main fibers include rayon, acrylic, nylon, polyester, acetate, spandex, microfiber, and lyocell.

Rayon

As the original manufactured fiber, *rayon* was first manufactured in 1894. Commercial production of rayon began in 1910 by the American Viscose Company. The fiber was used during World War I for industrial products. It became popular in the 1920s when experimentation with rayon led to crepe, velvet, and satin fabrics. Rayon is composed of regenerated cellulose, which is derived from wood pulp, cotton linters, or other vegetable matter.

Advantages:	**Disadvantages:**
▪ Soft and comfortable	▪ Wrinkles easily unless treated
▪ Drapes well	▪ Low resiliency
▪ Durable	▪ Heat sensitive
▪ Highly absorbent	▪ Susceptible to mildew
▪ Dyes and prints well	▪ Stretches
▪ No static or pilling problems	▪ Weakens when wet
▪ Inexpensive	▪ Fabric shrinks if washed
▪ Colorfast	▪ May need dry cleaning
▪ May be washable	

END USES Rayon is used to make apparel such as blouses, dresses, jackets, lingerie, linings, slacks, sport shirts, sportswear, suits, and neckties. Home furnishings made with rayon include bedspreads, blankets, curtains, draperies, sheets, slipcovers, tablecloths, and upholstery.

Acetate

Acetate is another modern material developed in the early 20th century and first produced in 1924 by the Celanese Corporation. Acetate is a cellulosic fiber made from wood pulp or cotton linters. It is widely used by designers because of its luxurious feel and draping qualities. Acetate fabric is used for linings in coats and jackets. However, because of new fabric developments, many major designers now use acetate to make apparel.

Advantages:

- Luxurious appearance

- Crisp (texture) soft hand

- Wide range of colors; dyes and prints well

- Drapes well

- Resists shrinkage, moths, and mildew

- Low moisture absorbency, relatively fast drying

- No pilling, little static

Disadvantages:

- Requires dry cleaning

- Weak

- Heat sensitive

- Poor abrasion resistance

- Dissolved by nail polish remover (acetone)

END USES Apparel made with acetate includes blouses, dresses, linings, lingerie, special-occasion apparel, scarves, and shirts. Home furnishings made with acetate include items such as draperies, upholstery, curtains, and bedspreads.

Nylon

The invention of *nylon* in 1938 created a revolution in the fiber industry and opened the door to the production of more modern materials. Produced by E.I. du Pont de Nemours & Company (DuPont™), nylon was the first synthetic fiber. Rayon and acetate were derived from plant cellulose, but nylon was made completely from petrochemicals in an experimental laboratory.

Advantages:

- Lightweight

- Exceptional strength

- Abrasion resistant

- Easy to wash

- Resists shrinkage and wrinkles

- Resilient, pleat retentive

Disadvantages:

- Static and pilling

- Poor resistance to sunlight

- Low absorbency

- Picks up oils and dyes in wash

- Heat sensitive

Style Point !

STOCKING TRENDS

As a result of hemlines rising in 1915 through the 1920s, the color of silk stockings changed from black or white to flesh color. With the invention of nylon in the 1930s, nylon stockings began to appear but were not in demand. Then, during World War II, when the U.S. government took over nylon production for the military, nylon stockings became scarce. This seemed to boost their popularity when nylon became available after the war ended in 1945.

- Fast drying, low moisture absorbency

- Can be pre-colored or dyed in a wide range of colors

- Resists damage from oil and many chemicals

- Insulating properties

END USES Nylon is used to make apparel such as swimwear, intimate apparel, foundation garments, hosiery, blouses, dresses, sportswear, pants, jackets, skirts, raincoats, ski and snow apparel, and windbreakers. Home furnishings made with nylon include carpets, rugs, curtains, upholstery, draperies, and bedspreads. Nylon is also an excellent fabric for making other items such as luggage, backpacks, life vests, umbrellas, sleeping bags, and tents.

Acrylic

Acrylic fiber was first manufactured in the United States in 1950 by E. I. du Pont de Nemours & Company. Originally, *acrylic* was used for blankets and sweaters because it resembles wool. Today year-round sweaters and socks are made of acrylic. The fiber also blends well with polyester and rayon for other garments.

Advantages:

- Lightweight, soft, warm, wool-like hand

- Dyes to bright colors

- Machine washable, quick drying

- Resilient, retains shape, resists shrinkage and wrinkles

- Wool-like, cotton-like, or blended appearance

- Excellent pleat retention

- Resists moths, oil, chemicals

Disadvantages:

- Low absorbency

- Develops static

- Pilling

- Heat sensitive

- Weak

- Dissolved by nail polish remover (acetone)

END USES Apparel made from acrylic includes sweaters, socks, fleece, circular-knit apparel, sportswear, lingerie, scarves, and neckties. Home furnishings made with acrylic include blankets, throws, upholstery, awnings, outdoor furniture, and rugs, and other floor coverings.

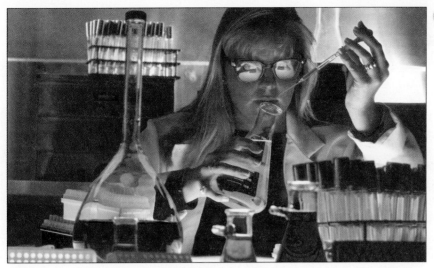

◄ SCIENTIFIC FABRICS
Synthetic fibers for fabrics that we wear every day, such as polyester and nylon, were invented in chemical laboratories before moving on to fashion designer showrooms. *Identify two advantages of polyester and nylon fibers.*

Polyester

Polyester is a synthetic fiber that was developed in the 1950s. The first commercial production of polyester fiber in the United States took place in 1953 at E. I. du Pont de Nemours & Company, Inc., innovators of other synthetic fibers. Polyester is the most widely sold synthetic fiber in the world. Because it is the best wash-and-wear fiber, it may be the most used in fashion production.

When polyester was first introduced, consumers could find it in almost every garment available. In fact, it was so overused that consumers grew tired of it. However, due to current developments, polyester has taken on a new life. When polyester is blended with other dry-clean-only fibers, such as wool, acetate, or rayon, the durability of the blended fabric improves. Thus, many fabrics become washable if they are blended with enough polyester.

Advantages:

- Strong

- Crisp, but soft hand

- Resists stretching and shrinkage

- Washable or dry-cleanable

- Quick drying

- Resilient, resists wrinkles

- Abrasion resistant

- Resistant to most chemicals

- Colorfast

- Strong, durable

- Dyes well

Disadvantages:

- Holds oily stains

- Low absorbency, difficult stain removal

- Static and pilling problems

DESIGN PHILOSOPHY

Jennifer Paige Barclay
Blue Fish Clothing

Jennifer Paige Barclay founded Blue Fish clothing in 1986 at the age of 18. By 1996, her business was worth $12 million. Her socially conscious design philosophy for Blue Fish is to create clothing made from "products that are sourced responsibly." Her artistic designs are made with low-impact dyes and pesticide-free cotton. Her creations are so valued that even pre-owned Blue Fish clothing can be found at eBay and other stores.

What kind of training did she have?
Jennifer was born in Bucks County, Pennsylvania. As a teen, she started making clothing in her parents' garage. She sold her creations at festivals and craft fairs. She attended Temple University and majored in art. With the help of her parents she set up a clothing factory in 1986 and began filling orders.

What is her key to success?
She spends little money on national advertising, choosing instead to develop a loyal customer base, which includes celebrities such as Oprah Winfrey. Due to the challenges that face a rapidly growing company, Blue Fish Clothing closed its doors in 2000. However, in response to people who missed her inspirational designs, Jennifer started her clothing company again in 2001, with stores in New Jersey and New Mexico. She gave the business a new name with the old spirit, Blue Fish at Barclay Studio—later to be changed to the original Blue Fish Clothing.

How can using particular fabrics be part of a design philosophy?

Career Data: Fashion Designer/ Manufacturer

Education and Training Associate degree or bachelor's degree and apprenticeship

Skills and Abilities Design, clothing-construction, and management skills

Career Outlook Average growth to 2012

Career Path Internship, apprentice, assistant, designer, top designer, to designer/owner of label

---

QUESTION

What are two unique advantages of polyester fibers?

END USES Polyester is used to make permanent-press fabrics, fiber-fill insulation, and apparel such as dresses, blouses, jackets, suits, shirts, pants, rainwear, lingerie, and children's wear. Home furnishings made from polyester include curtains, draperies, floor coverings, fiber-fill, upholstery, and bedding. Polyester is also used to make craft and gift-wrapping ribbons because of its strength and ability to prevent fraying and fading. Spun polyester thread is also valued for its strength and elasticity, making it suitable for sewing knits and synthetic fabrics. In addition, polyester manufacturing waste can be combined with recycled plastic soda bottles to produce fiber for fleece garments.

Spandex

When *spandex* was developed in 1959, chemists at DuPont were looking for a substitute for rubber. However, what they got was a synthetic fiber that dramatically changed the swimwear and foundations (underwear) industry. Spandex can stretch over 500 percent without breaking. The brand name for spandex fiber is Lycra®.

MARKETING SERIES *Online*

Remember to check out this book's Web site for textile information and more great resources at marketingseries.glencoe.com.

Advantages:

- Lightweight

- Retains original shape

- Abrasion resistant

- Stronger than rubber

- Soft, smooth, supple

- Resists body oils, perspiration, lotions, detergents

- No static or pilling

Disadvantages:

- Whites yellow with age

- Heat sensitive

- Harmed by chlorine beach

- Nonabsorbent

END USES Spandex is used to make apparel such as athletic apparel, bathing suits, foundation garments, ski pants, slacks, hosiery, socks, belts, support hose, and exercise and dance wear.

Microfibers

One of the new trends in fashion is the use of *microfibers*. This is the name given to ultra-fine manufactured fibers and also refers to the technology of developing these fibers. First developed in 1989 by DuPont, microfiber technology produces fibers that weigh less than 1.0 denier. **Denier** is a unit of measurement used to identify the thickness or diameter of a fiber.

The fabrics made from these extra-fine fibers provide a superior hand, a gentle drape, and incredible softness. Microfibers are two times finer than silk, three times finer than cotton, eight times finer than wool, and 100 times finer than a human hair. These fibers have the quality and appearance of expensive silk, making microfiber fabric popular. Microfiber can be woven tightly, creating a fabric that cannot be penetrated by wind, rain, or cold. For this reason, the raincoat industry depends on microfiber fabrics.

denier a unit of measurement used to identify the thickness or diameter of a fiber

Advantages:

- Extremely drapeable

- Very soft, luxurious hand

- Washable or dry cleanable

- Shrink-resistant

- Strong

- Insulates against wind, rain, and cold

Disadvantages:

- Heat sensitive

END USES Microfibers are used to make apparel such as hosiery, blouses, dresses, separates, sportswear, ties, scarves, menswear, intimate apparel, active wear, swimwear, outerwear, and rainwear. Home furnishings made with microfibers include curtains, draperies, upholstery, sheets, towels, and blankets.

Lyocell

Introduced in the mid-1990s by Courtaulds Fibers company, *lyocell* is the newest of the cellulosic manufactured fibers. A trade name for lyocell is Tencel®. The fiber is made with wood pulp from trees grown in managed and replanted forests. The chemicals used in production are recycled, and lyocell fiber is biodegradable. The production of lyocell is considered to be environmentally friendly with reduced chemical waste.

Advantages:

- Absorbent

- Biodegradable

- Strong

- Resists sunlight, aging, and abrasion

Disadvantages:

- Susceptible to mildew

END USES Lyocell is used to make items such as reusable nonwoven materials, fashion fabrics, soft denims, and apparel such as shirts.

Figure 6.1

Fabric Icons

SYMBOLS OF QUALITY During the mid-20th century, natural textile organizations began identifying and branding their fabrics with these recognizable logos. *Why do you think these groups began to use this marketing strategy?*

CERTIFICATION TRADE MARK

WOOLMARK

CERTIFICATION TRADE MARK

WOOLMARK
BLEND

NOTE: Woolmarks are reproduced with the kind permission of The Woolmark Company.

Fiber Trade Associations

With the development of synthetic fibers in the 20th century, natural fiber industries have had to compete to maintain their markets. Natural fiber trade associations have formed to provide information to consumers and fashion businesses while promoting and marketing natural fibers. (See **Figure 6.1** for natural fiber logos.) The leading natural fiber trade associations include:

- **Cotton Incorporated**—a marketing and and research organization

- **National Cotton Council**—the central organization of the cotton industry

- **Woolmark Americas, Inc.**—the U.S. subsidiary of The Woolmark Company Pty. Ltd., which promotes wool and wool-blend products as well as licensing the Woolmark trademarks.

- **Mohair Council of America**—the promotional organization for U.S. mohair producers

Fabric's Influence on Fashion

Historical records about apparel reveal that the cut and style of garments have always been determined by fiber and fabric. For example, cotton muslin, in existence since ancient Egyptian times, was a popular fabric used in women's clothing in the English Regency era of the early 1800s. This fabric was worn, even during bitter winters, because it clung to the body without bulkiness. Fabric will continue to influence fashion as availability and technology change.

Quick Check ✓

RESPOND to what you've read by answering these questions.

1. What are the four main natural fibers?_____

_____

_____

_____

2. What are the primary advantages and disadvantages of leather/suede?_____

_____

_____

_____

3. What are three manufactured fibers that are cellulosic?_____

_____

_____

_____

Making Textiles

AS YOU READ ...

YOU WILL LEARN

- To discuss how synthetic fibers are produced.
- To identify the two primary methods for making fibers into fabrics.

WHY IT'S IMPORTANT

A sound knowledge of fabrics is critical to turning fabric into fashion. The fashion industry responds to changes in consumer preferences by using a variety of textile products.

KEY TERMS

- extrusion
- finished fabric
- weaves
- knits

PREDICT

What might be the definition of a finished fabric?

extrusion a synthetic textile process in which solid raw materials are dissolved by chemicals or melted with heat to form a thick liquid that is extruded, or forced out, through the tiny holes of a device called a *spinneret* to create long fibers

Textile Processes: Past and Present

Textile manufacturing processes have progressed over the centuries. The first modern factories for natural fiber textiles were built during the Industrial Revolution of the 18th century in England. Inventions such as the cotton gin, by American Eli Whitney in 1793, mechanically removed cotton fibers from the seed pod and increased production. In 1801, French inventor Joseph Jacquard created a loom that automated the placement of threads in the weaving process. In the early 1800s, the newly developed steam engine powered more than 100,000 looms and 9 million spindles in Britain. In the 20th century, technological advances have enabled the invention of synthetic fibers and computerized textile processes.

Making Synthetic Fibers

Chemical companies manufacture fibers from raw materials and chemicals. Although the basic ingredients may vary among manufactured fibers, they are produced in the same basic way.

Extrusion Method

Most synthetic and cellulosic manufactured fibers are created by extrusion. **Extrusion** is a synthetic textile process in which solid raw materials are dissolved by chemicals or melted with heat to form a thick liquid (with the consistency of cold honey) that is extruded, or forced out, through the tiny holes of a device called a *spinneret* to create filaments. Think of a spinneret as a bathroom shower head that has from one to hundreds of holes. Each hole produces a continuous filament of a substance that is a semi-solid polymer. As the filaments come out of the holes of the spinneret, the polymer becomes rubbery and then solidifies into fibers. Sometimes these fibers are curled or cut into standard lengths to resemble natural fibers. Then the fibers are made into fabrics.

How Fibers Become Fabrics

How are natural and manufactured fibers transformed into the designer's canvas—fabric? *Weaving* and *knitting* are the two primary methods for making fibers into fabric. There are some fabrics that are made by pressing the yarn into fabric that is considered to be nonwoven. Examples of these fabrics are felt, net, and lace. A **finished fabric** is fabric that has gone through all the necessary finishing processes and is ready to be used for manufacturing garments.

Types of Weaves and Knits

The fashion industry is able to respond to changes in consumer preferences for apparel and accessories because of the variety of textile products available for use. A good knowledge of types of fabrics, such as weaves and knits, is key to turning fabric into fashion.

Weaves

Weaves, or woven fabrics, are composed of two sets of yarns with one set running the length and the other set running crosswise. The *warp* runs along the length of the fabric. The other set of yarns, the *fill* or *weft,* runs perpendicular to the warp. Woven fabrics are held together by weaving the warp and the fill yarns over and under each other. Weaving is the procedure of interlacing these two sets of yarns at right angles to each other. This is usually done on a loom. Large quantities of fabric are produced by industrial looms. There can be as many as 15,000 warp threads on one loom. In the apparel industry, clothing manufacturers need wide fabrics so that they can efficiently lay out patterns. The three basic weave types are *plain, twill,* and *satin.* (See **Figure 6.2** for illustrations.) They have different appearance and durability characteristics:

- **Plain weave** is a basic weave, utilizing a simple alternate interlacing of warp and filling yarns. Any type of yarn made from any type of fiber can be manufactured into a plain-weave fabric. Examples are gingham and calico fabrics.

- **Twill weave** is constructed by interlacing warp and filling yarns in a progressive alternation which creates a diagonal effect on the face, or right side, of the fabric. In some twill-weave fabrics, the diagonal effect may also be seen clearly on the back side of the fabric. Denim is a twill-weave fabric.

finished fabric fabric that has gone through all the necessary finishing processes and is ready to be used in the manufacturing of garments

weaves woven fabrics that are composed of two sets of yarns with one set running the length and the other set running crosswise

CONNECT

Which fabric type do you think is stronger—knits or weaves? Why?

Figure 6.2

Weaves and Knits

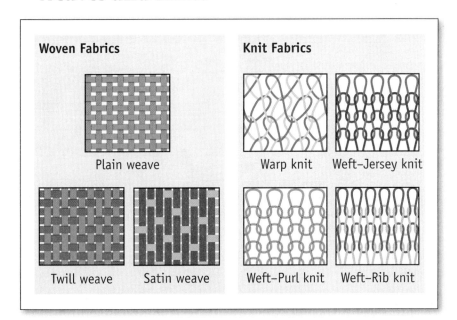

Woven Fabrics

Plain weave

Twill weave   Satin weave

Knit Fabrics

Warp knit   Weft–Jersey knit

Weft–Purl knit   Weft–Rib knit

FORMING A PATTERN These patterns form the basic weaves and knits of fabric used for most apparel. *What is one characteristic that distinguishes a knit from a weave?*

knits knitted fabrics made from only one set of yarns that runs in the same direction

QUESTION

What type of weave produces a diagonal appearance?

- **Satin weave** is characterized by long floats of yarn on the face of the fabric. The yarns are interlaced so there is no definite, visible pattern of interlacing. A smooth and shiny surface effect is achieved. The shiny surface effect is increased through the use of high-luster filament fibers in yarns that have a low amount of twist. A true satin-weave fabric has the warp yarns floating over filling yarns. Satin fabric is created with a satin weave.

Knits

Knits, or knitted fabrics, are made from only one set of yarns that runs in the same direction. Some knits have their yarns running along the length of the fabric, while others have their yarns running across the width of the fabric. Knit fabrics are held together by looping the yarns around each other. Knitting creates ridges in the fabric. *Wales* are the ridges that run lengthwise in the fabric; *courses* run crosswise. Knitted fabrics have natural flexibility and stretch built in by the knitting process. They shape comfortably and are versatile and wrinkle-resistant.

Textiles and Fashion Marketing

Yarns and fibers are transformed into fabrics through the magic of creativity and technology which play a major role in the characteristics and final designs of finished fabrics. Textiles, including fibers, yarns, and fabrics as well as fur and leather are the basic building blocks of all fashion products that are marketed to consumers.

Quick Check ✓

RESPOND to what you've read by answering these questions.

1. How are synthetic fabrics produced?_____

_____

_____

2. What are the two primary ways of turning fibers into fabric?_____

_____

_____

3. What are the three basic types of weave? _____

_____

Worksheet 6.1

Natural and Manufactured Fibers

Visit a local department store or mall. Read the labels on clothing and home furnishing items to learn about the fibers used in the items. Find as many different fibers as you can. Make a list of the items and name the fiber. Note an advantage and a disadvantage of each fiber. The first one is an example.

Item	Type of Fiber	Advantage	Disadvantage
1. shirt	cotton, natural	comfortable	shrinks in hot water

Name _____ Date _____

Worksheet 6.2

Different Types of Fabrics

Visit a local fabric store. Explain that you are doing a class assignment. Ask for a small sample (swatch) of four of the following fabrics:

- Felt
- Lace
- Net
- Plain woven cloth

- Twill
- Satin
- Knit
- Synthetic fabric

Glue your samples to this page. Name each sample and write two facts about each fabric under each fabric swatch.

FASHION AND FABRIC

Sketch an outfit you would like to wear. Then answer the questions below.

1. What fabrics would you choose for your outfit? Choose at least two.

_____

2. What are the characteristics of the fabrics?

_____

_____

3. Why did you choose these fabrics for this particular outfit?

_____

_____

_____

Add this page to your career portfolio.

CHAPTER SUMMARY

Section 6.1
Textiles and Fashion

fabrics (p. 114)
fibers (p. 114)
yarns (p. 115)
natural fibers (p. 115)
filament (p. 117)
manufactured fibers
(p. 120)
denier (p. 125)

- Different fibers have specific properties that affect the characteristics of fabric, such as appearance, strength, absorbency, warmth, shrinkage, and price. The fiber's properties determine the appropriate use of the final fabric for certain items of apparel.

- The main natural fibers include cotton, linen (flax), wool, silk, leather or suede, and fur.

- The main manufactured fibers are rayon, acrylic, nylon, polyester, acetate, spandex, microfibers, and lyocell.

- Throughout history, the cut and style of garments have been determined by fiber and fabric. Fabric will continue to influence fashion as availability and technology change.

Section 6.2
Making Textiles

extrusion (p. 128)
finished fabric (p. 128)
weaves (p. 129)
knits (p. 130)

- Synthetic and cellulosic manufactured fibers are created by extrusion, which is a process by which solid raw materials are dissolved by chemicals or melted with heat to form a thick liquid that is extruded, or forced out, through the tiny holes of a spinneret to create filaments. The rubbery filaments solidify into fibers. These fibers are curled or cut into standard lengths to resemble natural fibers.

- The two primary methods for transforming fibers into fabrics are knitting and weaving.

See the Teacher Manual for answers.

CHECKING CONCEPTS

1. **Name** the fiber characteristics that determine the appropriate use of fabric for specific fashion apparel.
2. **Define** the terms *fiber* and *yarns*.
3. **Identify** the main natural fibers used in fashion.
4. **Identify** the two groups of natural fibers.
5. **Describe** the different types of manufactured fibers.
6. **Discuss** the differences between natural and manufactured fibers.
7. **Explain** the difference between knits and weaves.

Critical Thinking

8. **Explain** how and why natural fiber associations promote their industry.

CROSS-CURRICULUM SKILLS

Work-Based Learning

Information—Organizing and Maintaining Information

9. Design a graphic organizer of the five fabrics in the chapter. Include advantages, disadvantages, and uses of each fabric.

Basic Skills—Listening/Writing

10. Interview a weaver by phone or e-mail. Ask about the yarn, the loom, and the final product. Write a question/answer article.

School-Based Learning

History/Social Science/Arts

11. Use the Internet or library to research the history of fibers. Use computer graphics or art supplies to make a colorful timeline.

Computer Technology

12. Use the Internet to research weavers' guilds. Write a report, comparing two guilds from different parts of the country.

Role Play: Assistant Manager, Men's Store

SITUATION You are to assume the role of assistant manager of a men's clothing store located in a small city. You are assisting a customer (judge) with the purchase of several shirts and trousers. The customer (judge) is confused about the fabrics and blends. The customer (judge) asks why it is necessary to have so many fabrics and blends from which to choose.

ACTIVITY You must explain to the customer (judge) the importance of the particular textile used to construct a garment, in terms of garment care and performance expectations.

EVALUATION You will be evaluated on how well you meet the following performance indicators:

- Analyze product information to identify product features and benefits.
- Use characteristics of fibers, yarns, fabrics, and materials to identify benefits.
- Use garment construction methods to identify benefits.
- Determine customer/client needs.
- Address the needs of individual personalities.

Use the Internet to access The Textile Museum Web site for information, and then answer the following questions:

- Where is The Textile Museum located?
- What is the textile of the month?
- Who is the founder of the museum?
- In what year was the museum founded?

➡️For a link to a Web site to help you do this activity, go to **marketingseries.glencoe.com**.

Chapter 7

Designing Fashion

Section 7.1
The Design Process

Section 7.2
Making Fashion

Chapter Objectives

- Explain the types of fashion designers.
- Identify the elements and principles of design used to create fashion.
- Name the steps of the fashion design process.
- Identify the steps in the garment production process.
- Compare haute-couture production and prêt-à-porter production.
- Explain how women's and men's apparel are sized.

FASHIONS BY KATE SPADE

In the early 1990s, Kate Spade was an accessories editor at *Mademoiselle* magazine. She noticed something missing in the accessories market. So she designed a functional handbag that would enhance an outfit in the same way a necklace or pin accessorizes. She created six designs that combined simple shapes with lively, colorful patterns. Then in 1993, she and her husband Andy Spade formed their company Kate Spade.

During the first two years in business, Spade made handbags in her New York apartment and marketed them at trade shows. Her first trade-show booth cost $2,500. She recalls, "We received a couple of small orders, though not enough to pay for the first booth. But the accounts were good, so we started building relationships." Opening stores in the fashionable SoHo district of New York City helped her handbags become must-have accessories. By 2000, the Kate Spade company was earning an estimated $60 million per year. However, after more than a decade of growth and success, Kate Spade products needed a new focus to avoid decline.

ANALYZE AND WRITE

1. Write a sentence about what inspired Kate Spade's designs.
2. Write a paragraph about the challenge(s) of keeping a design brand successful.

Case Study Part 2 on page 145

POWER READ

Be an active reader and use these reading strategies:

PREDICT what the section will be about.

CONNECT what you read with your life.

QUESTION as you read to make sure you understand the content.

RESPOND to what you've read.

The Design Process

AS YOU READ ...

YOU WILL LEARN

- To explain the types of fashion designers.
- To identify the elements and principles of design used to create fashion.
- To name the steps of the fashion design process.

WHY IT'S IMPORTANT

Successful designers of all types effectively use the elements and principles of design as guidelines to create fashion that sells.

KEY TERMS

- collection
- color
- silhouette
- line
- texture
- principles of design
- computer-aided design (CAD)

PREDICT

List some principles of design.

collection a group of clothes designed and produced for a specific season

The Role of the Fashion Designer

The designer uses fabric and other materials to transform unique and creative ideas into fashion. Designers keep fashion changing with the ultimate goal of creating new trends to increase consumer spending. From haute couture to ready-to-wear, designers on all levels must anticipate what their target market will buy. They must also produce finished garments or accessories at prices that customers will pay. For these reasons, the role of the designer goes beyond creating and conceptualizing fashion.

Designer Tasks

Besides creating the original designs, designers select the appropriate fabrics that will sell. They may monitor the process from pattern-making to sample production to manufacture of the completed line. Designers sometimes supervise assistants who carry out their ideas. Designers who run their own businesses may also devote time to developing new business contacts, examining equipment and space needs, and performing administrative tasks, such as reviewing catalogs and ordering samples. The use of up-to-date computer and communication systems is also an ongoing consideration for most designers.

Types of Designers

There are different levels or types of designers. No matter what degree of expertise they have, they keep their customers in mind to make sure their finished products will sell.

SELF-EMPLOYED DESIGNERS Some high-fashion designers are self-employed and create original garments as well as clothing that follows established fashion trends.

DESIGN-HOUSE DESIGNERS Couture designers work for design houses, such as Chanel, and may produce two major collections each year. A **collection** is a group of clothes designed and produced for a specific season.

DESIGNERS FOR MANUFACTURERS Most apparel industry designers employed in the fashion industry work for manufacturers who mass-produce garments. It is not uncommon for designers to specialize in a particular classification of clothing, such as junior-size sportswear. Others might work only on accessory items, such as jewelry, shoes, or handbags. Some designers create new designs for home furnishings.

Elements of Design

The designer's main task is to create original designs for fashion products by applying the elements of design. The elements must be chosen according to principles, and then combined effectively to achieve harmony. As introduced in Chapter 1, the main elements of design are color, silhouette, line, and fabric and texture.

The Role of Color

Color is a visual characteristic, representing hue and tone, that is one of the most important elements of fashion design. Research has shown that customers respond to color before any other design element.

SETTING THE TONE Designers choose the color palette or set of colors for a line early in the design process because it sets the tone, or mood, of the collection. For example, bright yellows suggest happiness; whereas grays suggest seriousness. Business suits are made in solid colors or gray pinstripes.

OCCASIONAL COLORS The occasion for which the garment is worn dictates the color of the garmernt. For example, an American wedding gown designer would probably use white or ivory for bridal gowns.

CULTURAL COLORS Different cultures can influence color selection. A designer producing wedding attire for Chinese customers would not choose white because that color is associated with mourning. Red would be an appropriate color for a Chinese wedding because that color symbolizes permanence and joy in the Chinese culture.

color a visual characteristic, representing hue and tone, that is one of the most important elements of fashion design

World Market

New China Fashion

For centuries China's Silk Road was the primary route for imported luxury fabrics from China. Silk and cashmere traveled the Silk Road from China through Asia to Europe until 1949 when foreign trade was halted under communist rule in China.

However, today China's past seems to be giving way to its present. Some luxuries are beginning to appear in China, a country that is receiving fashion icons such as Armani, Gucci, Dior, and Louis Vuitton.

In 2003, the new Asian Fashion Federation was formed, linking China, Japan, and South Korea, to match the traditional fashion circuit of Paris, Milan, and New York. Beautiful Chinese models walk the fashion runways of Beijing and Shanghai wearing designer apparel. Always a cultural compass, fashion is pointing toward a new China.

Should American and European designers be aware of color in China and other countries? Why?

CONNECT
What is the first element of design that you notice when buying clothes for yourself?

silhouette the overall form, or outline, of a garment

line a distinct elongated mark that directs the eye movement when viewing the garment

texture a characteristic of the surface of a material in terms of how it feels and looks

principles of design the standards for creating good design that include proportion, balance, rhythm, emphasis, and harmony

SEASONAL COLORS If styles within a line are similar from one season to the next, color can set the two seasons apart. A different color may give the customer a sense of newness. People also associate certain colors with holidays. For example, many American stores stock red and/or green garments during the December holiday season.

The Role of Silhouette and Line

Once the designer determines the colors for a design, the next consideration is the silhouette, or shape, and the line of the garment. **Silhouette** is the overall form, or outline, of a garment. Because garments are three-dimensional, the silhouette changes as the viewer moves around the item. Designers must develop the overall shape. The silhouette affects the first impact of a design because it can be seen from a distance. As discussed in Chapter 1, most shapes can be classified as natural, bell, tubular, or full.

Not to be confused with the term for a collection of styles, **line** is a distinct elongated mark that directs the eye movement when viewing the garment. It is the element of design that outlines the inner and outer spaces and connecting parts that form details of a garment. Designers attempt to achieve flow with lines from one part of a garment to another through the use of construction details such as seams, darts, topstitching, and trims.

The Role of Fabric and Texture

Styles sketched on paper can take on an entirely different look when the garment is actually made. The fabric used and the texture of that fabric can determine the success or effectiveness of a design. **Texture** is a characteristic of the surface of a material in terms of how it feels and looks. Texture is determined by fibers, yarns, and the method of construction. The surface of fabric can have an appearance such as smooth, shiny, shaggy, or rough.

TEXTURE AND DESIGN Texture influences the shape of a design by causing it to appear bulky, if the fabric is rough—or slender, if the fabric is smooth. The drape of a garment is also affected by the texture. Imagine a prom dress made of heavy wool fabric. Instead of being soft and flowing, it would appear to be stiff and unattractive. Fabric can also serve as the inspiration for a design. The softness or drapeability of a fabric may spark an idea for a long, flowing dress.

TRENDS IN TEXTILES Designers examine the fabric market to identify new trends before they begin to design. They may even work directly with textile mills in developing new fabrics.

Principles of Design

Besides using the basic elements of design, a skilled designer also applies the **principles of design**, or the standards for creating good design, which are proportion, balance, rhythm, emphasis, and harmony. The effective use of these principles allows designers to create fashion products that consumers will accept and buy.

FASHION BABIES

Angelyn de la Garza
Co-owner of Kumquat

Angelyn de la Garza and her cousin Cherylin Sadsad decided to make clothes for preemies after Sadsad's sister-in-law gave birth to a premature baby. No one made clothes that small. Since then, they have expanded their stylish and comfy lines to fit babies and toddlers from 0 to 24 months old. The catalog of little hats, bibs, blankets, and other gear has taken off with help from articles in magazines, appearances on TV shows, and good sales representatives.

What is your job?
"I am the co-owner of Kumquat baby clothes."

What do you do in your job?
"What don't I do? I handle design and development, production, quality control, patternmaking, grading, customer service, shipping, accounting, and marketing. I also clean up!"

What kind of training did you have?
"I took fashion design courses in college. Then I worked for two children's wear companies before starting my own business with my cousin."

What advice would you give students?
"Definitely intern or work for a small company of five employees or less if you want to start your own business. You will learn all aspects of the business this way—including things you could never learn from school or books."

What is your key to success?
"Besides having low overhead and steady growth (since growing too fast can kill you), we hired excellent sales reps, which made all the difference."

What principles of design might be especially important to apply when making clothes for babies and children?

Career Data: Boutique Owner

Education and Training Associate degree or bachelor's degree; certificate in fashion

Skills and Abilities Design, planning, marketing, and accounting skills

Job Outlook Average growth through 2012

Career Path Intern, design/production assistant to designer/production manager to owner of small company

Proportion

Proportion, or scale, is the relationship of all the spaces of the garment. Designers must make sure that all the parts of the design are visually in proportion to each other. Proportion is determined by how the total space of a design is divided—and how the lines of the design are arranged. For example, the size of pockets on a jacket must be scaled to fit the width and length as well as the overall silhouette of the jacket. Sometimes unequal proportions can be more interesting than equal proportions. Designers strive to have a sense of balance in fashion designs.

QUESTION

What are two examples of rhythm in a garment design?

Balance

Balance is the relationship of one side of the garment to the other. Designs can either be *symmetrically* (formally) balanced or *asymmetrically* (informally) balanced. An example of symmetrical balance would be a shirt with buttons down the center and equally sized pockets on each side. Asymmetrical balance occurs when the parts are not equally placed, but the garment appears to be visually balanced, due to the placement or size of details. For example, a one-shoulder evening dress would have asymmetrical balance.

Rhythm

You can hear rhythm in your favorite music, but you can see rhythm in a design. Rhythm gives a sense of movement through the repetition of lines, shapes, and colors. For example, the pleats in a skirt cause the eye to move around the skirt. A row of buttons results in vertical movement from top to bottom. Details and trims such as these create visual rhythm.

Emphasis

Emphasis is the center of interest, or the focal point, of the garment. Emphasis draws the eye to a certain area of a garment. For example, the placement of a large button at the neck of a blouse creates emphasis. However, designers do not place emphasis at unattractive parts of the garment. Usually, garments will not have more than one focal point because too much emphasis is distracting.

Harmony

When the designer has applied the elements and principles of design to a fashion design, harmony is achieved. The design elements work together in a pleasing way. Harmony is apparent in couture designs or formal wear, which tend to be more dramatic. The use of all these elements and principles of design is not always as obvious in mass-produced, ready-to-wear apparel.

Design Process and Schedules

Designers develop their new designs each season before the marketing period begins. A marketing period is generally six months before consumers will purchase the merchandise. Therefore, designers schedule merchandise to be ready two to three months before that. For example, if retailers want to have junior tops in their stores by March, then their buyers will order the merchandise from the manufacturer in August or September of the previous year. Designers have worked on designing these tops months before August.

Steps of the Design Process

Designers are continually at work evaluating the success of designs produced, adding new items to fashion lines, adapting existing designs, and beginning on the next season's designs. Fashion merchandise starts with the idea and moves to the store in six key steps of the design process, as illustrated in **Figure 7.1**.

Figure 7.1

Steps of the Design Process

6. Production

5. Purchase Orders

4. Design Presentation

3. Sales Research Analysis

2. Design Concept and Samples

1. Basic Decisions

PLANNING THE DESIGN
Creating fashion apparel is not a simple process. In order to deliver the right merchandise on time, designers must think ahead. *What step may require the assistance of the most people?*

Step 1—Basic Decisions

Many decisions are made before the designing process ever begins. Considerations can include fabric choice, design ideas for the garment, number of items to be made and sold, and type of promotion to retail stores. When choosing fabric, the season in which the merchandise is sold may determine the weight and color of the fabric. A shirt designed for the summer months would not be made of dark-green corduroy.

Step 2—Design Concept and Samples

Next, the designer develops the concept and appearance of the fashion item, using the design elements and principles of design. Sketches or diagrams are prepared to illustrate the design, incorporating color and fabric choices. Then patterns and samples are produced. Not all proposed designs for a line are actually made. Designers edit and change concepts during this phase so the garments will be suitable for sale. They design by hand or by computer, which is especially helpful when making revisions.

COMPUTER DESIGN In the past fashion designers always manually sketched designs that were converted to patterns and made into garments. Today many designers use **computer-aided design (CAD)** systems, which are computer programs that perform many design functions to create fashion designs. Designers use CAD systems as a tool, like a paintbrush or a piece of charcoal, to produce creations. Designers can incorporate style, color, fabric, and other details about a collection and communicate this information to design staff and retail buyers. CAD software has many features:

- **Sketch pads with electronic pens** allow designers to draw images into the computers. Sometimes the designer creates these sketches and passes them on to the patternmaker. The patternmaker might finalize the sketch and change some stitches or a construction line to make a better garment.

Style Point

TECH-SAVVY CLOTHING
The future has arrived for some manufacturers who offer jackets with features such as cell phones and MP3 players. Some futurists have proposed new clothing designed as wearable tech equipment with built-in wireless computers. The fabric of a jacket would become the computer screen. That would mean you could read your e-mail on your sleeve!

computer-aided design (CAD) computer programs that perform many design functions to create fashion designs

NEW METHODS FOR AN OLD BUSINESS Computer-aided design systems in fashion have revolutionized and enabled the creative design process. *Would fashion designers benefit from having manual drawing skills? Why or why not?*

SOURCE: Courtesy of Gerber Technology

- **Zoom features** allow the designer to focus on specific parts of the garment and give more details to the production staff.

- **Scanning features** allow existing images, such as previous drawings or fabric patterns, to be scanned into the system with equipment that reads an image on paper and enters it into the computer.

- **Electronic graphics features** can interchange garment parts, colors, and prints, allowing designers to experiment with different shapes, colors, textures, and fabrics.

- **3-D imaging** enables a designer to create a three-dimensional design that shows depth and form.

CAD is used by the industry because it allows for quick production. When consumers see a style, they may want it immediately. CAD systems allow designers to react quickly to these demands. They also enhance the creative process, shorten product-development time, and help to reduce costly mistakes.

Step 3—Sales Research Analysis

The designer/manufacturer's sales department plays a key role at this point. The department keeps records that show the history of styles previously offered and the quantities and prices of styles that sold. This information helps a manufacturer determine not only how much should be produced, but also what merchandise should be offered. Records may show that retail stores sold out of certain styles and sizes very quickly. When the line has been previewed and evaluated by retail buyers, the manufacturer may decide to produce a greater selection of styles and increase the quantity of certain sizes.

Step 4—Design Presentation

Now the new collection or line is ready to be shown. Some designers participate in elaborate fashion weeks that are hosted by the major design centers. Others have their merchandise available for preview to buyers in their showrooms in fashion centers. The time that new collections are introduced varies according to each market. Women's lines are shown at different times than men's wear and children's wear.

Step 5—Purchase Orders

Retail buyers will begin purchasing merchandise for their stores when new items have been presented. Certain styles may be eliminated from a line, due to the number of orders placed by the retail buyers.

Step 6—Production

After the orders have been placed by the retail buyers, production begins. The final samples and fittings take place. Then final patterns are made, and sewing is done. Manufacturers use an assembly-line method for production. Computerized equipment aids in constructing each part of a garment. For example, one set of machines may sew all the sleeves, while another may attach the buttons.

Apparel Company Divisions

Apparel manufacturers can be organized into three main divisions: *design, production,* and *sales.* Each division works with other divisions to produce fashion merchandise.

Design Division

The design division must be aware of the company's target market when creating new collections or lines. These lines may be divided into groups of garments that each have a particular theme based on a new fabric, color, or trend. For example, a junior sportswear manufacturer might produce a group of related tops and pants in a summer-weight fabric of various shades of pink.

Production Division

The production division is responsible for producing items in sizes that the retail stores have ordered. Some stores might sell more merchandise in smaller size ranges; therefore, they will order larger quantities in those sizes.

Case Study PART 2

FASHIONS BY KATE SPADE
Continued from Part 1 on page 137

After years of success designing handbags, Kate Spade's company was risking decline after steady growth. So in 2004, Spade introduced a collection of housewares, including five different stainless flatware patterns, nine crystal patterns, and 15 china patterns. These product lines completed a gradual move from accessories into new markets. The expansion originally began with Kate Spade paper and social stationery in 1998, shoes and glasses by 2001, and cosmetics in 2002. With the Kate Spade home collection of housewares and bedding, the brand crossed over from traditional fashion accessories to home accessories.

The key to success in the future involved the name *Kate Spade* and her bold design ideas. Spade explains, "My love of textiles, pattern, and strong geometric shapes inspired the company's signature, iconic design element." The Kate Spade home collection got attention. When 400 brides registered for the line at Bloomingdale's nationwide, her key unlocked another door.

ANALYZE AND WRITE

1. How did Kate Spade expand her business? Write a short paragraph explaining your answer.
2. Why might using the steps of the design process be important to this company? Explain in two sentences.

Selling the Farm

What do a $263-million corporation, hip-hop style, and street smarts have in common? The answer is Russell Simmons' Phat Farm clothing lines—urban clothing with hip-hop roots. Simmons' empire began on the streets of Hollis in Queens, New York, during the 1980s. As Simmons' record label became profitable and hip-hop's influence grew, Simmons launched the Phat Farm clothing company in 1992. Since then Phat Farm's designs, such as baggy clothing, baseball caps, sneakers, and other streetwise fashion, have captured mainstream America.

Corporate America is also aware that the urban-wear trend has been the fastest-growing segment in the fashion industry. Sears and J.C. Penney's carry Simmons' designs, which could be worth more than $100 million to Sears by 2010.

KEEPING IT FRESH

However, fashion trend watchers note that the urban apparel sector is overloaded with labels. Pop culture changes daily, and trendy clothing lines may not draw customers when a style becomes cliché. Simmons knows that hip-hop style may eventually fade. To keep growing business, he sold Phat Farm to Kellwood Manufacturing. He remains CEO as he designs and markets other products such as energy drinks, furniture, and jewelry.

To Simmons, expansion also means giving back to the community while remembering his roots: "We want to be accepted by all without forgetting we're born out of hip-hop."

1. How did Phat Farm designs originate?
2. What impact has urban wear had on the fashion industry?

Sales Division

The sales division markets the lines and acts as the coordinator between the manufacturer and the retail store. Individuals in the sales division work directly with store merchandise buyers or owners.

Interactive Design Production

The elements and principles of design are guidelines used by designers to create designs that sell. The designer's vision must be aligned with the customer's demands so that manufacturers can use all their resources and staff to successfully market fashion.

Quick Check

RESPOND to what you've read by answering these questions.

1. What is the role of the fashion designer?_____

_____

2. What are the five basic principles of design?_____

_____

3. What are the basic steps in the fashion design process?_____

_____

Making Fashion

The Garment Production Process

Clothing manufacturers buy fabrics, design apparel, produce the garments, and sell the finished products to stores. Most clothing today is mass-produced. Because many garments can be made by machine at the same time, the production process is faster and cheaper.

The garment production phase is an important part of fashion marketing. When the designer has created a line, the production staff must take the designer's idea and make the actual garments. In order to get the process started, a pattern, or blueprint, is made so that the manufacturer can construct samples of the garment.

Patternmaking

Patternmaking is the process of transforming the design into the appropriate pieces needed to produce an apparel item. The patternmaker transforms the design into a paper pattern so that the various pieces of the garment can be cut and sewn together to make the garment sample. In the past patterns were made by hand. Today only first patterns may be handmade. The fashion industry uses computer-aided design (CAD) systems to complete patternmaking accurately and efficiently. The production staff can enter information into the computer and make needed adjustments, such as moving seams. Computer systems also facilitate making different sizes. **Grading** is the technical process of increasing or decreasing the sizes of a pattern to correspond to a garment size.

Making Samples

Next, a hard copy of the pattern is made, and samples are created according to the company's sizing structure. Samples are made to a "model" fit size of 6, 8, or 10. Live models or mannequins wear the samples, and the staff can make any final alterations and corrections before the garments are shown to retail buyers.

Costing

After the manufacturer completes the new garment, but before retail buyers see it, the production costs of the garment must be calculated in order to set a wholesale price. This process is called *costing*. **Wholesale** is the price that retail buyers pay for goods they purchase from manufacturers. The wholesale price includes several costs:

- Cost of labor
- Materials
- Markup

patternmaking the process of transforming the design into the appropriate pieces needed to produce an apparel item

grading the technical process of increasing or decreasing the sizes of a pattern to correspond to a garment size

wholesale the price that retail buyers pay for goods they purchase from manufacturers

Patternmaking Software
In the early 1990s, patternmakers had to switch back and forth between two or more computer programs to complete the process. At the time, no single software application could handle every task. Today many companies offer "integrated suites" of software tools that work together. Some of the tasks accomplished by patternmaking software include digitizing, grading, marking, and plotting.

➡Compare the benefits and features of several software products after reviewing the list of patternmaking software suppliers through **marketingseries.glencoe.com**.

computer-aided manufacturing (CAM) a system that automatically moves the garment parts through each phase of the cutting-and-sewing process

CONNECT
Do you think CAM increases the quality of garments produced?

prêt-à-porter French term for designer ready-to-wear clothing

The markup amount includes various costs:

- Commission paid to the sales staff

- Terms, such as discounts to retail stores that pay bills on time

- Overhead, which includes rent, utilities, salaries, insurance, and advertising

- Profit

Order Taking
When retail buyers place their orders, the manufacturer can begin to mass-produce the new garments. Apparel is usually produced in dozens.

Garment Cutting and Sewing
Garments are mass-produced and cut and sewn in an assembly-line manner. Computerized machinery cuts each pattern. Layers of fabric are cut per pattern piece to create multiple pieces. The number of garments cut at a time depends on the number of layers of fabric.

After the pattern pieces are cut, the garments are sewn together. A different machine sews each section. This allows for more efficient and accurate construction because workers are concentrating on only one part of the garment.

Many manufacturers use **computer-aided manufacturing (CAM)**, which is a system that automatically moves the garment parts through each phase of the cutting-and-sewing process. As an operator completes his or her task, the computerized system directs a carrier to automatically move the pieces to the next station.

Quality Control and Labeling
After a garment is constructed, an inspector checks it for flaws or mistakes. If mistakes are found, the inspector returns the garment for correction. Then the garment is pressed, and labels and/or hangtags are placed on the garment. *Hangtags* provide information such as fabric content and care instructions. *Labels* identify the name of the manufacturer or the line of clothing. If a retailer places a large order, the manufacturer might also place price tags with bar codes on the goods. The merchandise is ready for shipping when it is labeled and/or tagged and hung on racks or packed in containers.

Haute Couture vs. Prêt-à-Porter
Haute couture is the French term for high-fashion designer clothing. High-fashion garments are typically original designs made of the finest fabrics. These fabrics are created specifically for the designer. The garments are custom-made by hand to fit the client. Custom-designed items require special fittings, cuttings, and sewing. Construction of high-fashion garments is more complicated and precise. Production of these fashion items differs from production of garments considered **prêt-à-porter**, which is the French term for designer ready-to-wear clothing. Prêt-à-porter is more practical and less expensive and requires very little hand sewing. Prêt-à-porter, however, is important because it generates more income for couture fashion houses.

Size Classifications

A sizing system is a set of sizes based on common assumptions and methods of development. The different groupings within a sizing system in retail stores are known as *size classifications*. The current United States sizing system is based on research available for a large portion of the American population. Men's sizes were originally based on soldiers' sizes during the 1860 Civil War. Women's sizes were based on a 1941 study for the apparel industry. Standard measurements today vary from one manufacturer to another and are influenced by fashion, style, and fit preferences of a particular target market. Different grading processes can also affect the sizes produced by a manufacturer.

Women's Sizing

Size categories in women's apparel are based on the shape of the figure and are identified by numbered sizes. Standard apparel classifications include misses, women's, juniors, and petites. There are some size variations among manufacturers. **Figure 7.2** provides a good overview of women's sizes.

Math Check

ESTABLISHING WHOLESALE PRICE

Henri Bergunsom needs to calculate a wholesale price for his clothing. What factor is missing from his formula that includes cost of labor and materials?

➡ For tips on finding the solution, go to **marketingseries.glencoe.com**.

sizing system a set of sizes based on common assumptions and methods of development

---

Figure 7.2

Women's Size System

SIZE DIVERSITY Sizes are determined by a variety of factors, such as shape and figure, but they vary from manufacturer to manufacturer. This explains why one brand's size 8 might fit you better than a size 8 from another brand. *What size classification is suited for teenagers?*

	MISSES	WOMEN'S/ LARGE	JUNIORS	PETITES
Styling	More conservative adaptations of previous season's designer styles	Same as misses with some junior styles	Young, trendy, figure-conscious styles	Same as misses' styles
Age	25 and up	18 and up	15 to 25	25 and up
Size Range	Even sizes 0–20; stock very few of smallest and largest sizes	Even sizes 16–26W, 16–26WP, or higher	Odd sizes 3–15	Petite 0–14; labeled with P after size number
Figure	Fully developed; 5'5" to 5'9" average weight, height, and proportion	Larger proportioned	Not fully developed	Fully developed; under 5'4"

UNIFORM SIZING Unlike women's apparel, men's slacks, shirts, and tailored garments are sized using measurement numbers. *Do you think this type of sizing would be effective for women's garments? Why or why not?*

Men's Sizing

Men's sizing is more uniform than women's sizing, ensuring a more standard fit. Men's apparel such as slacks, dress shirts, and tailored apparel are sized with a *dual sizing* system, or a combination of two measurements. Slacks are sized according to the waist measurement and the inseam (inside leg), and dress shirts are sized by neck measurements and sleeve lengths. Tailored apparel combines chest measurements with different body types, such as short, regular, long, and extra tall. Most men's sports shirts and sweaters are offered in small, medium, large, and extra large sizes.

Variations in Sizing

Because each company has a different idea about the proportions of its target customer, there is no standard sizing system in the apparel industry. The way the items fit customers may be very different. There are several factors that might influence a manufacturer's sizing structure.

COST SAVING A fashion company may reduce production costs by making its sizes smaller. A size 10 garment might be cut smaller to save on fabric. Reducing a size by one inch could save hundreds of yards of fabric costing thousands of dollars. However, the customer might have to purchase a larger size to fit into the garment.

VANITY SIZING Some manufacturers of expensive fashions downsize their lines. For example, a size 12 or 14 jacket from a budget manufacturer might be a size 10 from a more upscale company. This sizing is called *vanity sizing,* because it gives the customer the illusion of being able to fit into a smaller size.

QUESTION
What was the origin of the first U.S. sizing system?

The Value of Production

The entire garment production process transforms a creative idea into a finished apparel item. Clothing manufacturers perform many functions. They buy fabrics, design a line, produce the garments, and sell the completed apparel to stores.

Quick Check ✓

RESPOND to what you've read by answering these questions.

1. What are the six key steps in the apparel production process?_____

_____

2. What are the production differences between haute couture and prêt-à-porter?_____

_____

3. What is the difference between women's and men's sizing?_____

_____

Name _____ Date _____

Worksheet 7.1

Divisions of Apparel Manufacturers

Use the graphic organizer below, or create one of your own, to illustrate the connection between the three main divisions of apparel manufacturing. Write the function of each division in the space provided.

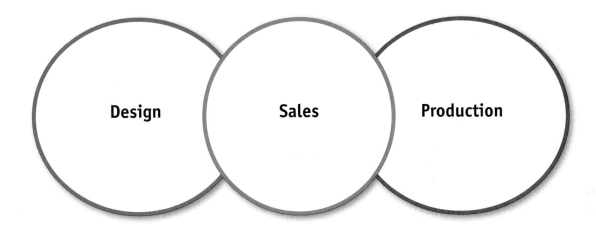

Design

_____

_____

_____

_____

Production

_____

_____

_____

_____

Sales

_____

_____

_____

_____

Worksheet 7.2

Your Favorite Designer

Look in your closet and pick your favorite clothes. Identify the clothing designers or design companies. Then answer these questions:

1. Who are your top-three favorite designers?

_____

_____

_____

2. What do you like most about these designs?

_____

_____

_____

_____

_____

3. Is there a difference in the sizing of the designers? If so, what is that difference?

_____

_____

_____

_____

_____

4. What advantages do your favorite designers have over the competition?

_____

_____

_____

_____

_____

5. Use the Internet to research your designers. Write two facts about each designer.

_____

_____

_____

_____

_____

PRINCIPLES OF DESIGN

Use different colors of markers and different lines to create a symbol for each of the five principles of design: proportion, balance, rhythm, emphasis, and harmony. Label each of your symbols.

Example: Use red and yellow to draw a box within a box to represent *proportion*.

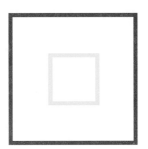

Add this page to your career portfolio.

CHAPTER SUMMARY

Section 7.1 **The Design Process**

collection (p. 138)
color (p. 139)
silhouette (p. 140)
line (p. 140)
texture (p. 140)
principles of design
   (p. 140)
computer-aided design
   (CAD) (p. 143)

- The different types of fashion designers can include self-employed designers, design-house designers, and designers for manufacturers.

- The basic design elements include color, silhouette, line, and texture. The principles of design are standard for creating good design, which include proportion, balance, rhythm, emphasis, and harmony.

- The fashion design process begins each season before the marketing period and involves six steps: basic designs, design concept and samples, sales research analysis, design presentation, purchase orders, and production.

Section 7.2 **Making Fashion**

patternmaking (p. 147)
grading (p. 147)
wholesale (p. 147)
computer-aided manufac-
   turing (CAM) (p. 148)
prêt-à-porter (p. 148)
sizing system (p. 149)

- The steps in the garment production process include patternmaking, making samples, establishing costs (costing), garment cutting and sewing, inspection, labeling, and shipping.

- Haute couture and prêt-à-porter differ because haute couture uses fine fabrics, customizes garments, has more complex construction, and is more expensive.

- Men's apparel is sized more uniformly than women's apparel. There is less size variation in men's apparel because men's sizing uses a dual-sizing system.

CHECKING CONCEPTS

1. **Name** at least two tasks of a designer.
2. **Identify** four aspects of the role of color.
3. **Explain** the role of harmony as a principle of design.
4. **List** the divisions of an apparel company.
5. **Define** the term *grading*.
6. **Define** the term *prêt-à-porter*.
7. **Name** two computer systems used in fashion manufacturing.

Critical Thinking

8. **Explain** why women's sizes may be less standard than men's sizes.

CROSS-CURRICULUM SKILLS

Work-Based Learning

Thinking Skills—Creative Thinking

9. You have been hired by a fashion designer to market his new line of beach wear. Write ten creative marketing ideas.

Basic Skills—Speaking

10. Choose your favorite fashion or home-furnishings designer and present a five-minute speech about him or her.

School-Based Learning

Math

11. What is the markup amount on the retail price for a designer T-shirt that costs $24 to manufacture wholesale? The retail price of the T-shirt is $60.

Social Science

12. Choose a country, and then use the Internet or library to research a fashion designer from that country. How does the culture of that country affect the designer's work?

Role Play: Assistant Manager, Clothing Store

SITUATION You are to assume the role of assistant manager of a family clothing store. Your store is located in the main shopping area of a small town. Most of your customers are residents of the town and the nearby areas. Several customers ask why there are different types of sizes for the clothing in the store. You have decided to discuss the store's sizing classifications during the next staff meeting.

ACTIVITY You must explain to your sales staff (judge) the reasons for the various sizing classifications and how to distinguish each one.

EVALUATION You will be evaluated on how well you meet the following performance indicators:

- Acquire product information for use in selling.
- Use garment-construction methods to identify benefits.
- Explain the nature of sales training.
- Handle customer inquiries.
- Demonstrate a customer-service mindset.

INTERNET ACTIVITY

Use the Internet to access the U.S. Department of Labor Web site. Then answer the following questions:

- How many designers are self-employed?
- What degrees are desirable in the industry?
- Is there much competition in the industry?

➡️For a link to a Web site to help you do this activity, go to **marketingseries.glencoe.com**.

Chapter 8

Creators of Fashion

Chapter Objectives

- Discuss haute-couture design houses.
- Explain the process of buying haute couture.
- Discuss the background of haute couture.
- Describe prêt-à-porter and ready-to-wear garments.
- Identify some current ready-to-wear designers.

CATALOG DESIGNS

The first Chico's women's apparel store opened in 1983 as a small shop in Sanibel Island, Florida. The owners, Marvin and Helene Gralnick, sold Mexican folk art and cotton sweaters. Today Chico's is a retail chain that includes 418 stores and a dozen franchisee stores nationwide. The chain specializes in "exclusively designed, private-label women's casual clothing and related accessories."

In November 2002, sales results for a four-week period were reported at nearly $33 million, up 37 percent from the year before. Pam Danziger, President of Unity Marketing, credits this kind of growth to word-of-mouth marketing. Sixty percent of the consumers she surveyed said that the recommendations of friends and associates influence the purchase of a luxury item. How has Chico's managed to be successful by selling exclusive designs? What's the secret behind the success of the women's apparel chain?

ANALYZE AND WRITE

1. What type of apparel does Chico's offer?
2. What might be the difference between exclusively designed, private-label clothing and high-fashion designer clothing? Write your response in one paragraph.

Case Study Part 2 on page 163

POWER READ

Be an active reader and use these reading strategies:

PREDICT what the section will be about.

CONNECT what you read with your life.

QUESTION as you read to make sure you understand the content.

RESPOND to what you've read.

Haute Couture

YOU WILL LEARN

- To discuss haute-couture design houses.
- To explain the process of buying haute couture.
- To discuss the background of haute couture.

WHY IT'S IMPORTANT

The haute-couture industry has a long tradition of setting the standards for fashion. Design houses create high fashion and custom-made designs that influence ready-to-wear, mass-produced fashion.

KEY TERMS

- Fédération Française de la Couture
- custom-made
- vendeuse

PREDICT

In what ways might haute-couture garments differ from mass-produced garments?

Fédération Française de la Couture the French Fashion Federation, the organization that regulates the haute-couture industry

What Is Haute Couture?

Haute Couture, or high fashion, is the branch of the apparel industry that creates the most fashionable, expensive, and exclusive designer clothing. The French term translates as "high dressmaking." Haute couture involves the highest level of workmanship, using the highest-quality fabrics. The industry focuses on the design, production, and sale of these fashion garments. The city of Paris plays an important role as the original fashion capital of the world and the birthplace of haute couture, or fine dressmaking.

Haute-Couture Designer Houses

Most clothing manufacturers are found in design centers that are situated in commercial districts. However, in the couture segment of the industry, designers have fashion houses where haute couture is created, with many of them in Paris, the center of fashion activity. Only a few of the designers operate showrooms or boutiques in New York on Manhattan's Seventh Avenue. A fashion house is named after its designer or originator. Some legendary designers are no longer alive; however, their houses retain their names as other designers produce apparel under the particular name or label. One example of such a legendary designer is Coco Chanel and her House of Chanel.

The Fédération Française de la Couture

Not every designer creates haute couture. In France, this title is reserved for only a select few. There are specific requirements for a designer and design house to be included in this category. The **Fédération Française de la Couture**, or the French Fashion Federation, is the organization that regulates the haute-couture industry. Formed in the 1800s, it establishes the qualifications for membership and regulates the fashion showings. Membership is based on the talent and success of the couturier, or designer, and decided by a special commission of the French Department of Industry. Membership rules also include codes that control copying, number of showings allowed, minimum number of original styles in collections, and regulations concerning staffing and shipping dates. For example, members must employ 15 or more people in a fashion house and present their collections twice a year. Each presentation must include at least 35 separate designs for day and evening wear. The federation has had members such as fashion giants Coco Chanel, Christian Dior, and Pierre Cardin. The houses produce more than a billion dollars in yearly sales and employ thousands of people.

FEDERATION BRANCHES The three branches of the French Fashion Federation are:

- **Chambre Syndicale de la Couture Parisienne**—promotes and protects the couture houses

- **Chambre Syndicale de Prêt-à-Porter**—represents ready-to-wear branches of couture and the best of French prêt-à-porter

- **Chambre Syndicale de la Mode Masculine**—represents men's wear industries of couture

FEDERATION EDUCATION In addition to regulatory functions, the federation conducts other activities. It sponsors a school to educate individuals seeking apprenticeships in the couture industry. The French Fashion Federation also handles any disputes or concerns with the government regarding issues such as working conditions, hours, and wages.

FEDERATION FASHION SHOWS One of the major functions of the federation is the coordination and scheduling of fashion shows. This includes the registration of attendees. The press and individual customers are allowed to attend at no charge. However, a *caution fee* is charged to trade buyers from apparel manufacturers, retailers, and pattern companies. The fee, which is usually a large payment, serves two functions. First, it discourages copying of designs. It can also serve as an agreement to purchase specific amounts and can be applied to these purchases. Larger fees are charged to trade buyers than to individual customers, because trade buyers are purchasing copying rights. For example, if a new style of jacket is presented at a show, the trade buyer can take this idea back to his or her company to legally copy and sell.

Purchasing Haute Couture

An individual purchasing a haute-couture design buys a garment that is **custom-made**, or made specifically to the customer's measurements. A couture house such as Chanel has about 150 regular clients who buy couture each year. A house such as Dior will make about 20 couture bridal gowns annually.

The Purchasing Process

The first step in having a haute-couture garment made is to schedule an appointment with a design house prior to a visit to Paris. Then the customer previews samples of garments in the design salon. The couture house must make sure the model or sample garments from collections are available at the house because garments may be out of the country being shown to other customers or trade buyers. Another method of previewing is by video tape. This option is available to serious buyers. When the customer has chosen the garments, the tailoring process begins, which typically requires three fittings.

Math Check

CONNECT
Do you prefer or not prefer special service when you shop for clothing? Why?

custom-made made specifically to the customer's measurements

vendeuse the haute-couture sales associate who works with a customer and is paid by commission on the clothes that customers purchase

➤ **CATERING TO THE CUSTOMER** For those who are willing to pay for high-fashion service, haute-couture design houses are unparalleled with private viewings, custom fittings, and continuing attention after the sale. *Do you think that patrons of haute-couture houses remain customers because of the designs or because of the service? Explain.*

Sales and Service

The customer is assigned a **vendeuse**, the haute-couture sales associate who works with a customer and is paid by commission on the clothes that customers purchase. In addition to supervising all the fittings and order taking, the vendeuse helps smooth out any problems that might occur. For example, the vendeuse makes sure that customers living in the same city do not buy the same or similar designs. It would be bad business if two customers were to attend the same event wearing the same haute-couture design, for which they have both paid thousands of dollars.

The High Cost of High Fashion

It can take 100 to 1,000 hours and thousands of dollars to make a haute-couture garment, depending on the design house and the actual garment. One dress may cost from $26,000 to over $100,000. A tailored suit may start at $16,000. Some Chanel couture suits cost as much as $30,000. An evening gown may cost over $60,000. The high price of haute couture explains why few men and women throughout the world can afford these garments. There are fewer men and women who buy them on a regular basis.

GARMENT EXPENSES The reason these garments are so expensive is due to the service, workmanship, and originality of the designs. A specific design or color might be used only by that design house. The garment may be made of luxurious fabrics, such as expensive silks, fine wools, leather, or furs. The trim work on a garment adds to the expense of the garment. For example, embroidery and beading on an evening gown increases the overall price of the gown. **Figure 8.1** lists the elements that the design houses of Paris consider when pricing haute couture.

 marketingseries.glencoe.com

Figure 8.1

Haute-Couture Costs

Christian Dior

Christian Lacroix

$ Service

$ Workmanship and labor

TORRENTE

$ Custom-made designs

CHANEL

$ Exclusive designs

$ Special colors

Dominique Sirop

$ Luxurious fabrics

$ Expensive trim work

Jean-Louis Scherrer

Jean-Paul Gaultier

ELITE EXPENSES Many exclusive design houses of Paris have discontinued the expensive tradition of haute couture in favor of making ready-to-wear designs. As of 1996, 18 houses were members of the haute-couture elite. However, only seven houses now offer the most expensive and finely made apparel. *Do you believe the quality of haute couture can be offered in ready-to-wear designs? Why or why not?*

The Era of Modern Haute Couture

Every year during the Academy Award ceremonies, the celebrities are asked about the designer attire they are wearing to the event. Notable designers such as Vera Wang are popular; however, designs by newcomers such as Narciso Rodriguez are visible as well. Prior to the event, there is much public discussion about the designer fashions the celebrities will be wearing. This kind of public interest in fashion is not a new phenomenon. Women have placed value on designer fashions dating back to the 1800s and Charles Frederick Worth.

The Father of Haute Couture

Charles Frederick Worth is considered the father of haute couture. He did not invent fashion but was a principal player in the Parisian fashion world of the 1800s. There were many well-known dressmakers during his time, but he holds this title because he was the first professional clothing designer for women. He was also the first designer to become internationally famous.

A BRIT IN PARIS Born in England, Worth came to Paris when he was 20 years old. After he established himself as a quality designer at a clothing shop, he opened his own design house. He was one of the first designers to show samples on live models and the first to have customers come to a fashion establishment, or design house.

ROYAL DESIGNER Worth's career advanced when he began designing for the royalty of his time. After noticing one of his designs, Empress Eugénie, wife of Napoleon III, became one of his faithful customers and established his reputation among royalty. This work gave him the opportunity to become a trendsetter of fashion and style in the 1800s.

ETHICS & ISSUES

Free Samples

One way that fashion designers and cosmetic makers get consumers' attention is by sending samples to celebrities and members of the fashion press. The idea is that celebrities or fashion editors will try their products and give favorable endorsements. For example, in 2003, all nominees for the Academy Awards received gift baskets, which were valued at $45,000. Included in the baskets were certificates for penthouse accommodations at exclusive resorts as well as top-quality cosmetics. *Do you think it is ethical for celebrities and the press to receive free products while the consumer pays full price? Why or why not?*

WORTH'S TRADEMARKS Charles Frederick Worth was known for using detail, special fabrics, colors, and trims. He also used certain design techniques that enabled him to produce the special and unique shapes of that time period. Worth is credited for introducing the hoop skirt and the walking skirt. His designs were very expensive. Worth's customers paid for fine fabrics and detailing used for his garments and for the privilege of wearing his apparel. In the 19th century, a Worth design could cost up to $2,500.

Haute Couture in Today's World

Today haute-couture fashion houses produce extravagant outfits, which are seen on the runways but rarely worn in real life. Likewise, each year automakers produce concept cars to feature at special auto shows. The cars are not meant for mass production because they are extremely expensive. However, they do create excitement.

Hot Property

Museum-Quality Designs

The Bata Shoe Museum in Toronto is home to the world's largest, most comprehensive collection of shoes and footwear-related objects. The collection is comprised of over 12,000 artifacts that span 4,500 years of history from many of the world's contemporary and historic cultures. Mrs. Bata and architect Raymond Moriyama designed the award-winning five-story building to resemble a shoe box ready to explode and reveal history's finest footwear.

Shoes are the focus of this unusual Canadian museum because they are a human necessity, worn by every culture around the world. Shoes protect feet and allow for long-distance travel. Protection from a harsh climate is not the only reason why humans wear shoes. They can also indicate personal style, religion, occupation, gender, and social status. Historians can trace the development of humanity, economics, technology, politics, and even fashion through a chronological study of shoes.

ECLECTIC COLLECTION

The museum conducts school tours and group tours of the exhibits. Students, tourists, academic researchers, and designers visit the Bata Shoe Museum to understand humanity, through footwear. Where else could you find French chestnut-crushing boots, Chinese silk shoes for women with bound feet, pre-Columbian sacrificial boots, soft-soled deerskin moccasins for a Cree woman, ivory toe-knobs from India, Marilyn Monroe's red-leather stiletto shoes, and sealskin boots from Siberia all together in one giant shoebox? Fashion designers as well as curiosity-seekers who visit the Bata Shoe Museum are sure to find inspiration from the past.

1. Name some cultures whose shoe designs are represented at the museum.
2. Can designers of high-fashion and ready-to-wear shoes get ideas for new designs from historical designs? Why or why not?

Markets for Haute Couture and RTW

Only about 2,000 people in the world buy couture clothes, 60 percent of whom are American. Further, it is estimated that only 200 people are regular customers. Designers lend or give clothes to movie stars or other public figures for the publicity. However, many designers are leaving the couture world because the client base has decreased. It has become expensive for the couture houses to produce fashion shows, present the model samples, order fabrics, wait for delivery, and then have clients sit for three fittings. Instead, many haute-couture designers have decided to shift their efforts and resources to less expensive ready-to-wear lines. For example, couturiers Emanuel Ungaro and Gianni Versace discontinued designing haute couture. Other designers who have stopped making haute couture include Yves Saint Laurent, Louis Féraud, and Nina Ricci.

Haute-Couture Advantages

Haute-couture design houses serve as places of creativity and inspiration. Aspiring young designers train and showcase their talent in these design houses. Despite the small market, designers maintain haute-couture operations because the prestige helps sell other products, such as perfume, cosmetics, and their ready-to-wear lines available in stores. Extravagant fashion shows are costly and do not produce a profit, but the couture status of the designer and shows helps to generate sales of other fashion products.

Case Study PART 2

CATALOG DESIGNS

Continued from Part 1 on page 157

Continued from Part 1 on page 157

According to marketer Pam Danziger, Chico's unique sizing system and dedication to mix-and-match comfort has promoted Chico's. For example, the store's ready-to-wear clothing comes in sizes extra-small to large, which give women more size options. The company's focus on comfort inspired the sizing policy. The clothing lines are designed to be mix-and-match and include wrinkle-free travel garments and colorful accessories. These innovative concepts have brought customers in the door via word-of-mouth. In addition, customer-discount programs combined with direct-mail announcements of special offers and birthday discounts keep customers coming back.

ANALYZE AND WRITE

1. Do you think customers can identify Chico's styling as unique Chico designs? List reasons for your answer.
2. Would you classify Chico's clothing as haute couture or ready-to-wear? Write a sentence explaining your response.

Quick Check ✓

RESPOND to what you've read by answering these questions.

1. Why are haute-couture garments so expensive? _____

   _____

2. Why was Charles Frederick Worth important to the haute-couture industry? _____

   _____

3. Why have some designers discontinued creating haute couture? _____

   _____

Everyday Designers

AS YOU READ...

YOU WILL LEARN

- To describe prêt-à-porter and ready-to-wear garments.
- To identify some current ready-to-wear designers.

WHY IT'S IMPORTANT

The ready-to-wear industry is responsible for producing fashion for the largest number of people. It includes mass-produced garments in standard sizes as well as custom-made creations.

KEY TERMS

- demi-couture
- ready-to-wear (RTW)
- bridge line

PREDICT

Give your own definition of ready-to-wear clothing.

demi-couture ready-to-wear designs produced by fashion houses but not mass-produced

ready-to-wear (RTW) standard-sized garments made in advance and offered for sale to any purchaser

bridge line a secondary line that is the most expensive category of ready-to-wear

Demi-Couture

Many design houses are employing young designers, which has resulted in a new trend in the couture world, called **demi-couture**, which is ready-to-wear designs produced by fashion houses but not mass-produced. Not a single stitch or tuck has been specially fitted and adjusted for the customer. There is also no guarantee that five other women will not come to the same party wearing the same garment. However, the haute-couture salons prevent this situation by keeping precise client records, noting who has ordered the same apparel. Customers might pay $6,000 for a demi-couture dress instead of $60,000 for an haute-couture dress. Hot new styles can be in the stores just a few weeks after the fashion show presentations—and sometimes before they are in the shops of the designers who created them. Stella McCartney, the designer at Chloe, is an example of a demi-couture designer.

Prêt-à-Porter Apparel

Haute couture is the prestigious front for French creative fashion by designers who influence all fashion. The haute-couture designs ultimately translate into the lesser-priced but still costly French designer ready-to-wear known as prêt-à-porter. The designer ready-to-wear industry is extremely important to fashion houses as it helps generate more income. It bridges the gap between ready-to-wear and haute couture by bringing couture to those who want to wear designer fashions but will not pay the highest prices. The styles are not as extravagant or eccentric, and the fabrics are not as unique. The advantage is that the customer gets a high-quality, high-fashion garment with a prestigious designer label.

Ready-to-Wear

Ready-to-wear (RTW) are standard-sized garments made in advance and offered for sale to any purchaser. In the American designer market, a well-known designer may offer a **bridge line**, which is a secondary line that is the most expensive category of ready-to-wear. Some of the design houses making new strides with their collections are:

- Tommy Hilfiger
- Perry Ellis
- Calvin Klein

STYLE ON A BUDGET
Making fashion accessible to everyone is one benefit of the trend toward ready-to-wear fashion. *Identify the ready-to-wear category for designer clothing sold at stores such as Target.*

Categories of Ready-to-Wear

Other categories of ready-to-wear include *better, moderate,* and *budget.* While offering collections at better stores, even a high-fashion designer such as Isaac Mizrahi has ventured into discount markets with his garments sold at Target stores.

History of Ready-to-Wear

The majority of women in the 19th century made clothes at home. By 1860 in the United States, however, there were 96 factories producing ready-to-wear garments. Though the first garments lacked quality, manufacturing procedures improved rapidly. Technological developments enabled the new industry to grow. The invention of the sewing machine by Elias Howe in 1845, with improvements by Isaac Singer, allowed for volume production of clothing in factories.

20th CENTURY RTW The labor force grew during the latter 19th and early 20th centuries with the arrival of immigrants from Central and eastern Europe. Textile technology advanced during this time, and retailers learned new methods of distribution and advertising. Women were entering the workforce and had little time for home sewing. All these factors combined to stimulate the ready-to-wear clothing industry—and created the need for designers in America and abroad.

Design Awards

Each year various fashion associations and businesses present awards to designers for their achievements and contributions to the fashion industry within their fields of design. These designers influence style for consumers around the world. (See **Figure 8.2** on page 167.)

CONNECT
How much time would you need to make a shirt?

THE Electronic CHANNEL

McCall's Online

In the past, people who sewed and designers who wanted clothing patterns would flip through large pattern books at fabric stores in order to find patterns. Today pattern catalogs have gone online. McCall's is a well-established pattern company. Its Web site allows customers to search catalogs online, view complete patterns, analyze sewing and measurement details—and purchase the patterns in a secure online environment.

➡️Make a list of the pros and cons of browsing McCall's online catalog after viewing two patterns you like through **marketingseries.glencoe.com**.

AN EYE FOR FASHION

Roger Neve
Fashion Photographer

What is your job?
"I'm a freelance fashion photographer."

What do you do in your job?
"I take photographs of fashion products and models. For magazine articles, I deal directly with the editors to come up with image ideas and give the photographic session, or shoot, a personal touch. I work with my agent to present my portfolio to clients in New York, London, and Amsterdam. My agent handles the booking and finances so I can stay behind the camera."

What kind of training did you have?
"I studied photography at the School of Photography in The Hague in the Netherlands, the country where I was born. I got into fashion photography because I love capturing images of people. I started taking pictures of my girlfriend and was noticed by some agencies. I got some magazine work in Holland, and my career grew from there."

What advice would you give students?
"You need a good eye, but you also need good communication skills. You need to be able to make people feel good. From the model, to the stylist, to the art director, you want to get everyone on the same page so you can get the best picture."

What's your key to success?
"Fashion photography is great because it changes so quickly, and you are constantly reinventing. I keep my eyes open and pay attention to everyone, from the crew to other creative people. I stay open to ideas to create a better product."

What can a photographer do to enhance the fashion designer's clothing designs?

Career Data: Photographer

Education and Training
Associate degree or bachelor's degree and apprenticeship

Skills and Abilities
Photographic, lighting, composition, photo-developing, retouching, communication, and business-management skills

Career Outlook As fast as average growth through 2012

Career Path Photographer's assistant, photographer to commissioned photographer

---

QUESTION
What trade association gives awards to top U.S. designers?

- **Council of Fashion Designers of America (CFDA)** is the trade association for top U.S. designers. It gives awards each year to designers in several categories, such as women's wear, men's wear, and accessories. The award includes the Lifetime Achievement Award, the Best New Fashion Talent award, and the Perry Ellis Awards for Ready-to-Wear and Accessory Design. It also recognizes fashion achievements in various fields, such as publishing, retailing, photography, and entertainment.

- **The Coty Award** was one of the most prestigious U.S. fashion awards from the 1940s to the 1970s. It was given to the most creative and outstanding women's wear, accessories, and men's wear designers. Anyone receiving the award in three different years was named to the Coty Hall of Fame. Designer Donna Karan is a Hall of Fame inductee. These same awards were renamed the Cutty Sark Awards through the early 1980s, but were later discontinued.

- **The Neiman Marcus Award** was created by the well-known retail store. It is an award for a designer who has designed, publicized, or worn fashion that has influenced the public. Recipients of this award have included Coco Chanel, Christian Dior, and Princess Grace of Monaco.

Style Point !

→ **GETTING READY-TO-WEAR**
The first ready-to-wear clothing in the United States was made for men—not women. During the 1800s, most women made their own clothing using instructions printed in women's magazines.

Figure 8.2

Influential Designers

Designer	Style
Pierre Cardin	French designer of "unisex" apparel for men and women; first to set trend for licensing
Gabrielle "Coco" Chanel	Most famous French couturier of sophisticated styles who designed "the little black dress" and boxy, collarless jackets for women's suits; first to design pants for women
André Courrèges	Designer of "go-go" boots for women
Christian Dior	French designer who created The New Look featuring long, full skirts
Mariano Fortuny	Designer of the Art Nouveau movement who created special pleating that has not been duplicated
Jean-Paul Gaultier	High-fashion designer who applied "punk" influence
Hubert de Givenchy	French designer known for simple, elegant, beautifully made gowns worn by stars such as Audrey Hepburn
Claire McCardell	Designer who defined American sportswear
Mary Quant	Designer who popularized the mini-skirt
Elsa Schiaparelli	French designer who was first to design fitted sweaters with collars, bows, and other details; introduced the color "shocking pink"

TRENDSETTING COUTURIERS
The creativity of these designers during the 20th century has influenced fashion by defining style for many generations. *Do you think high-fashion styles have a greater impact on trends than do popular street styles? Why or why not?*

From Mod to Funk

Carnaby Street in London was the "mod" fashion place to be in the 1960s, made famous by designer Mary Quant, British rock stars, and international celebrities. However, it lost favor during the 1980s and 1990s. Carnaby Street is located at the center of a collection of side streets, including Foubert's Place, Ganton, Kingly, Marshall, Broadwick, Newburgh, and Beak Streets. Today, however, this fashion district is the new "in" place. International retail businesses are standing in line for a space in the stylish shopping area.

Shoppers have a wide range of choices, from trendy to upscale fashion shops. One must-stop boutique for young women is Chili Pepper, which carries its bright, funky, fashion brand aimed at women from 16 to 30. The store also carries a line of men's denim jeans, T-shirts, and shorts. For the more upscale urban male, there is Dispensary Boys.

If you are searching for the latest fashion trends in any part of the world, Carnaby Street is still the place to go.

Would you expect to find haute-couture, demi-couture, prêt-à-porter, or ready-to-wear clothing in the Carnaby Street shops?

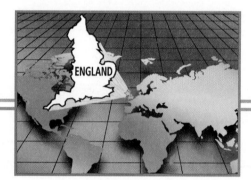

The Importance of Affordable Fashion

Fashion designers are creative and technical professionals whose designs leave a lasting impression on fashion. (See **Appendix 1** for an expanded list of designers.) With more haute-couture designers moving to ready-to-wear designs for the masses, the trend toward affordable style will continue, making it possible for more people to enjoy fashionable clothing.

Quick Check ✓

RESPOND to what you've read by answering these questions.

1. What is demi-couture?_____

_____

2. Why is designer ready-to-wear important to fashion houses?_____

_____

_____

3. What are three important fashion awards given by the CFDA to designers?_____

_____

Worksheet 8.1

Haute Couture

Use the Internet to research one haute-couture fashion designer. Then answer these questions:

1. What is the name of the designer?

_____

2. What makes this designer unique among his or her peers?

_____

_____

_____

3. In what fashion shows does this designer participate?

_____

_____

_____

4. How much does one of his or her designs cost?

_____

_____

_____

5. What awards has this designer won?

_____

_____

_____

6. Does the designer also have a ready-to-wear line? If so, what types of clothes?

_____

_____

_____

7. What other products, such as perfume, does the designer offer?

_____

_____

_____

8. Describe why this designer's style might appeal to you.

_____

_____

_____

Worksheet 8.2

Hot Designers

Use the Internet to research a hot fashion designer of ready-to-wear fashion. Then answer these questions:

1. What is the name of the designer?

_____

2. What makes this designer unique among his or her peers?

_____

_____

_____

3. Have you seen any of this designer's clothes? If so, where did you see them?

_____

_____

_____

4. How much does one of his or her designs cost?

_____

_____

_____

5. How is this designer influencing today's fashion?

_____

_____

_____

_____

_____

6. Does the designer offer any other products? If so, what are they?

_____

_____

_____

7. Describe why this designer's style might appeal to you.

_____

_____

_____

HAUTE-COUTURE BROCHURE

You have been hired to create a brochure for a design house. Your brochure should include information on this (imaginary) haute-couture house, such as its designs, designers, awards received, and an upcoming show. Use the Internet or the library to research different houses before you write the brochure. Then write a summary of information that will go into the brochure.

Name of Design House:

_____

_____

Design House Information:

_____

_____

_____

_____

_____

_____

_____

Information for the Brochure:

_____

_____

_____

_____

_____

_____

_____

_____

_____

Add this page to your career portfolio.

CHAPTER SUMMARY

Section 8.1 Haute Couture

Fédération Française de la Couture (p. 158)
custom-made (p. 159)
vendeuse (p. 160)

- Most haute-couture design houses are located in Paris, France, but some have showrooms in New York. Haute-couture designers create the most fashionable, expensive, and exclusive clothing. A fashion house is named after its designer or originator. Only haute-couture designers with houses are members of the elite Fédération Française de la Couture.

- To purchase haute-couture apparel, a customer schedules an appointment with a design house. Then the customer previews samples of garments in the design salon or by video tape. The customer is assigned a vendeuse, who is the sales associate responsible for working with the customer. When garments are chosen, the customer is given at least three fittings.

- The father of modern haute couture is Charles Frederick Worth, an Englishman who worked in Paris during the 1800s. He was the first professional clothing designer for women and was the first to show samples on live models.

Section 8.2 Everyday Designers

demi-couture (p. 164)
ready-to-wear (RTW) (p. 164)
bridge line (p. 164)

- Haute couture designs translate to lesser-priced but costly French designer ready-to-wear known as prêt-à-porter. The designer ready-to-wear industry is extremely important to fashion houses because it generates income. Prêt-à-porter bridges the gap between ready-to-wear and haute couture. Ready-to-wear (RTW) garments are standard-sized garments made in advance.

- Some current ready-to-wear designers include Tommy Hilfiger, Perry Ellis, Calvin Klein, Donna Karan, and Isaac Mizrahi.

CHECKING CONCEPTS

1. **Identify** the industry regulated by the Fédération Française de la Couture.
2. **List** the basic steps of buying haute couture.
3. **Define** the term *vendeuse*.
4. **Discuss** some task performed by the vendeuse.
5. **Identify** the expenses involved in making haute couture.
6. **Name** the father of haute couture.
7. **Describe** ready-to-wear garments.

Critical Thinking
8. **Describe** the difference between demi-couture and prêt-à-porter.

CROSS-CURRICULUM SKILLS

Work-Based Learning

Basic Skills—Listening/Writing

9. Write or call the buyer of a clothing store or a department store. Interview the buyer to learn about the different designers from whom they buy. Write an article based on your interview.

Interpersonal Skills—Participating as a Team Member

10. Form a fashion award panel of eight to ten students. Name your group's award. Each member will submit the name and qualifications of a designer. The panel will then vote for the best designer submitted. Present your award in class.

School-Based Learning

Language Arts

11. Research your favorite fashion designer. Write a two-page biography about the designer.

Arts

12. With four or five students, prepare and present a multimedia presentation about a fashion design house.

Role Play: Assistant Manager, Designer Store

SITUATION You are to assume the role of assistant manager of an upscale store located in a mall. Your store carries clothing created by a well-known young designer of both haute couture and prêt-à-porter. Several customers have asked about the price difference in the two lines and about the differences in the merchandise. You have decided to discuss these questions with the sales staff (judge).

(ACTIVITY) You are to explain the difference between haute couture and prêt-à-porter to your sales staff (judge).

EVALUATION You will be evaluated on how well you meet the following performance indicators:

- Explain the role of fashion designers.
- Explain fashion brand images.
- Explain the use of brand names in selling.
- Handle customer inquiries.
- Conduct staff meetings.

INTERNET ACTIVITY

Use the Internet to access the Style Web site from the editors of *Vogue* and *W* magazines.

- Click News and Trends.
- Click Trend Reports.
- Click any trend.
- What are the fashion trends in this category?

➥For a link to the Web site to help you do this activity, go to **marketingseries.glencoe.com**.

BusinessWeek News

TEENTAILERS: TOO HOT NOT TO COOL DOWN

Investing in "teentailers," such as teen-focused retailers Abercrombie & Fitch or American Eagle Outfitters, is bewildering. The five with market values of at least $1 billion this year returned an average of 57 percent through June 29, 2004. Yet, further gains will be more grudging, given the crowded market for teen apparel.

At the Florida Mall in Orlando, [you will find] Abercrombie and American Eagle, Pacific Sunwear, Rave, Urban Planet, Billabong, Aeropostale, Gadzooks, No Fear, dELiA's, Wet Seal, Surf Zone, Hot Topic, and more. There are differences, naturally. Music blares loudest at Abercrombie; PacSun displays the most frantic clearance signs ("Girls' tank tops 2 for $20"). Yet store to store, most striking is how many of the garments look interchangeable. Cristina Ortiz, 15, and Ciara Rosario, 16—their favorite store? Cristina shrugs and points to her T-top with Aeropostale's logo. "They always have a lot of sales," she says. Glancing back at American Eagle, she adds: "There's not really much difference. They have the same clothes."

The newer, tonier Mall at Millenia has many of the same teen stores. There, 19-year-olds Jamie Contractor and Rachel Streitfeld roll their eyes at today's dominant style. "It's not that we don't like Abercrombie," Rachel says. "It's just that look— like, 'Summer Girl'—is really annoying. It's really cookie-cutter." They prefer the "wacky" thrift-store mix of Urban Outfitters, with housewares and toys. Yet the clothes, from Converse sneakers to $24 scoop-necked jerseys, on sale at $15, might also be found at many competing stores.

Healthy but Slower

Teentailers aren't about to go bust. Abercrombie has a debt-free balance sheet and began this year to pay a dividend. American Eagle's board is weighing its dividend more seriously, too. But slower earnings growth is in store for the coming year. American Eagle's chief financial officer, Laura Weil expects profit margins to keep widening this year and next. "We know we can improve," she says. But quarterly comparisons will inevitably get tougher. Teentailers are volatile, [and] investors are better off loving them only when they are down.

CREATIVE JOURNAL

In your journal, write your responses:

CRITICAL THINKING

1. List the clothing manufacturers mentioned in the article and compare each company's apparel style.

APPLICATION

2. Create a graphic organizer of the fashion cycle, using examples of clothing styles mentioned in the article to illustrate the fashion cycle.

See the Teacher Manual for answers.

 Go to businessweek.com for current *BusinessWeek* Online articles.

UNIT LAB

House of Style

You've just entered the real world of fashion. The House of Style assists fashion businesses and individuals to conceive, plan, produce, and sell the latest and most popular fashion products. Acting as the owner, manager, or employee of the House of Style, you will have the opportunity to work on different projects to promote the success of this fashion business.

Fashionable Accessories—Budget the Business

SITUATION You are assisting a designer and his silent partner who want to design and make fashionable fabric handbags and fabric belts. They have enjoyed excellent success selling limited numbers of the accessory items they have created to friends. However, you inform them that to sell to local retailers, they will have to produce greater quantities of each of the items. You also realize that they will need money to finance the purchase of supplies and extra space to produce the items.

ASSIGNMENT Complete these tasks:
- Determine the retail market for the handbags and belts.
- Estimate the approximate amount of money needed for start-up and operating costs of the new business.
- Make a report to the partners.

TOOLS AND RESOURCES To complete the assignment, you will need to:
- Conduct research at the library, on the Internet, or by talking to local retailers.
- Ask a banker about the loan process and information required for a loan application.
- Have word-processing, spreadsheet, and presentation software.

RESEARCH Do your research:
- Research the demographics and psychographics of the target-market population.
- Determine the quantities of each style the retailers would purchase.

- Determine the approximate start-up costs for the business.

REPORT Prepare a written report using the following tools:
- *Word-processing program:* Prepare a written report listing the demographic and psychographic characteristics for the target-market customer of each retailer.
- *Spreadsheet program:* Prepare a chart comparing the target-market data for each retailer in the target market. Prepare a chart to illustrate the number of items to be purchased by each retailer.
- *Presentation program:* Prepare a ten-slide visual presentation with key points, photos of each handbag and belt design, and key descriptive text.

PRESENTATION AND EVALUATION You will present your report to the designer and silent partner and the bank that may finance the plan. You will be evaluated on the basis of:
- Your knowledge of your target retail market and start-up costs
- Continuity of presentation
- Voice quality
- Eye contact

PORTFOLIO

Add this report to your career portfolio.

UNIT 3

FASHION MARKETING AND MERCHANDISING

> ❝It is change, continuing change, inevitable change that is the dominant factor in society today.❞
>
> —Isaac Asimov
> Author

UNIT OVERVIEW

There are many aspects to marketing and merchandising fashion products. Unit 3 will explore product planning and research, buying and selling, pricing, merchandising, and advertising and promotion.

Chapter 9 focuses on how fashion products are selected and how research is used to determine the best mix. The process of buying and selling fashion is the focus of Chapter 10. In Chapter 11, you will learn about pricing in the fashion industry and the many applications of technology. Chapter 12 focuses on promoting fashion merchandise through visual merchandising in retail stores and different methods of advertising and promotion.

UNIT LAB Preview

House of Style

Think about the fashion shops in a mall. Why are the look and atmosphere of every store different if the stores all sell fashion?

Functions of Marketing

- Marketing-Information Management
- Financing
- Selling
- Pricing
- Distribution
- Promotion
- Product/Service Management

Foundations
- Professional Development
- Economics
- Business, Management, Entrepreneurship
- Communication, Interpersonal Skills

Academic Concepts • Technology

These functions are highlighted in this unit:

- Marketing-Information Management
- Products/Service Management
- Distribution
- Financing
- Pricing
- Promotion
- Selling

177

Chapter 9

Fashion Products and Research

Chapter Objectives

- Describe fashion products.
- Explain trade associations.
- Explain trade publications and fashion magazines.
- Discuss aspects of product planning.
- Describe the methods used to do market research.
- Explain market segmentation and target market research.
- Define merchandise information systems.

ON TARGET

Discount stores have existed since the 1960s. They have struggled with their image: stores that sell low-quality goods at low prices. Target stores were launched in 1961 in the same year as Kmart and Wal-Mart. All of these stores built their reputations on offering products at low prices. But Target remained a regional Minnesota-based retailer, while Kmart and Wal-Mart stormed the nation. Then in the 1990s, Target began to expand beyond the Midwest, giving the chain an opportunity to revise its identity.

Ron Johnson is Vice President/Merchandise Manager for home décor at Target. He says, "In the last 15 to 20 years of retailing, there has been an overly high focus on the price of products and a minimization of the importance of product design. But historically, design has been the most important aspect in retailing." Therefore, in 2000, Target began offering something more—original design. With a marketing strategy based on well-designed but affordable products, Target began offering high-quality fashion at low prices. How well did the strategy work?

ANALYZE AND WRITE

1. Make a list of some typical fashion products you might find at a Target store.
2. Write a paragraph about how Target's customers have changed over the years.

Case Study Part 2 on page 191

POWER READ

Be an active reader and use these reading strategies:

PREDICT what the section will be about.

CONNECT what you read with your life.

QUESTION as you read to make sure you understand the content.

RESPOND to what you've read.

Fashion Products and Planning

AS YOU READ ...

YOU WILL LEARN

- To describe fashion products.
- To explain trade associations.
- To explain trade publications and fashion magazines.
- To discuss aspects of product planning.

WHY IT'S IMPORTANT

To understand and market fashion, it is important to know what and how fashion products are planned.

KEY TERMS

- rag trade
- trade association
- trade publication
- fashion magazine
- product mix
- product assortment

PREDICT

What might be the difference between trade publications and fashion magazines?

rag trade the slang term meaning the garment industry

Fashion Products: Goods and Services

The fashion industry includes a variety of businesses involved in the design, production, distribution, promotion, and sale of textile, apparel, and other fashion products. Fashion products include goods that are produced and services that are performed. The fashion industry is comprised of many businesses that create fashion products.

Fashion Goods

Goods are tangible items that are made, manufactured, or grown. They include apparel, textiles, accessories, and other fashion products, from cosmetics and perfumes to furniture and cell phones. For example, the goods made by manufacturers include the textiles created from raw materials, the fabrics to make garments, and the finished garments sold in retail stores.

Fashion Services

Services are intangible things that people do, such as tasks performed for customers. Fashion services are provided by producers, retailers, cosmeticians, stylists, and other individuals who bring fashion to consumers.

VARIETY OF SERVICES People in all segments of the fashion market—primary, secondary, or tertiary markets—offer services. For example, marketing specialists in each segment can provide current information concerning market trends and new products. People involved in sales and service target fashion products on the right buyers. Sales associates in the design segment provide information to production people. The production sales staff works with retail buyers who stock the right goods in their stores. Other services in the production segment might include fashion show production, such as fashion week presentations and advertising assistance. In addition, retail services might include providing credit, personal shopping, and gift-wrapping services. All segments of the fashion industry offer some form of service to attract and keep customers.

The Fashion Trade

As a dominant segment of the fashion industry, the garment industry is sometimes called the **rag trade**, which is a slang term meaning the "garment industry." The rag trade has its own trade associations.

Trade Associations

A **trade association** is a nonprofit organization that provides services to specific groups who develop, make, and sell products within an industry. In addition to promoting a specific group, a trade association sets standards and provides a means of communication among its members. These associations are also active in the legislative process. For example, the American Apparel and Footwear Association (AAFA) stays informed about current legislation relating to imports and exports, focusing on taxes, labor, and environmental issues.

TYPES OF TRADE ASSOCIATIONS Many associations in the garment industry serve businesses that deal with soft-goods products:

- American Fiber Manufacturers Association—fiber production
- American Yarn Spinners Association—yarn production
- American Textile Manufacturers Institute—fabric manufacturing
- American Association of Textile Chemists and Colorists—fabric finishing
- Council of Fashion Designers of America—apparel designing
- American Apparel and Footwear Association—apparel manufacturing and sales
- National Retail Federation—retail activities

THE FASHION GROUP The Fashion Group International, Inc., is a trade association representing all segments of the fashion industry. Its membership consists of women and men who are successful in the fashion business. The members work as fashion designers, magazine editors, retail executives, and other fashion professionals. The group provides a forum for its members to share information and resources about career opportunities and ideas concerning the fashion industry.

The headquarters of the Fashion Group is located in New York City. American cities such as Los Angeles and Chicago that serve as fashion centers have regional chapters. These chapters host local meetings and send representatives to national conferences. In addition, Fashion Group chapters are located in key fashion cities around the world.

SPECIALIZED ASSOCIATIONS Some trade associations deal with specific facets of the industry. The National Shoe Retailers Association is an example of a major accessory organization. In the home furnishings industry, the American Society of Interior Designers (ASID) serves interior designers. The home-sewing industry is represented by the Home Sewing Association (HSA).

Different countries have fashion-related organizations. For example, the Hong Kong Trade Development Council, which sponsors the bi-annual Hong Kong Fashion Week, provides details on all aspects of doing business with Hong Kong. Each association has different types of memberships, but all associations have a common goal—to help members succeed by improving their segment of the fashion industry.

trade association a nonprofit organization that provides services to specific groups who develop, make, and sell products within an industry

Trade Publications

trade publication a magazine, newspaper, book, or journal offering a variety of information to a certain industry or a segment of an industry

Many organizations within the fashion industry publish their own trade publications. A **trade publication** is a magazine, newspaper, book, or journal offering a variety of information to a certain industry or a segment of an industry. These publications are also types of fashion products, though they are not always sold commercially. They provide fashion companies with information they can use to develop new products. Trade publications focus on current trends and report on new developments in the textile, apparel-production, and retail industries.

WOMEN'S WEAR DAILY The major American fashion trade publication is *Women's Wear Daily*. It is published five days a week, with each day dedicated to different features concerning fashion trends, designs, and manufacturing information. The paper also lists schedules for fashion events, such as designer and fashion week shows. Other special supplements include information about accessories, sportswear, or swimwear. In addition to style news, *Women's Wear Daily* also reports important business and financial news regarding the women's apparel trade.

CONNECT

What kind of information is provided in *Women's Wear Daily*?

Hot Property

Lucire, Global Fashion Magazine

Do you want to know what the international A-list celebs are wearing in Cannes this year? What is in style at the International Design Competition and what is hot on this season's catwalk? To find out what is happening in the world of fashion, log on to *Lucire,* the online global fashion magazine.

England, New Zealand, Sweden: Wherever you may be, this fashion magazine gives a glimpse of hot fashion items all over the world. Lucire's Web site provides fashion features, style talk, a shopping guide, travel destinations, gift guides, and designer profiles.

Truly international, this Web-based magazine was launched on October 20, 1997, from Alexandria, Virginia, with art direction taking place in Wellington, New Zealand. Editing was done in London, and design was completed in New York and other locations.

RAVE REVIEWS

From the start, *Lucire* has been an award-winning magazine. In 2003, *Lucire* received a nomination for a Webby Award, given for excellence in Web design, creativity, and functionality. Respected in the fashion world and in the media, *Lucire* has been praised in both print and online magazines, in newspapers, and on television. *The San Diego Union-Tribune* notes that "From the reviews of the fall collections to a global directory for shopping, *Lucire* is one of the world's leading fashion magazines for fashion with a global perspective." In 2003, *Lucire* became the United Nations Environment Programme's first Fashion Industry Partner.

1. Is *Lucire* a fashion magazine or a trade publication? Explain your response.
2. Which magazine would be more helpful to someone in fashion merchandising—*Lucire* or *Women's Wear Daily*? Explain your answer.

FASHION MAGAZINES
Fashion magazines help fashion businesses and retailers promote their products. *Would you consider this type of communication to be a service?*

OTHER TRADE PUBLICATIONS Some publications are created for specific segments of the fashion industry. The five-day publication for the textile and men's wear industries is the *Daily News Record.* The children's fashion industry has trade publications such as *Earnshaw's* and *Children's Business.* The sportswear market publishes *Sportswear International,* and accessories professionals read *Footwear News* magazine and *Accessories* magazine. In the retail segment, *STORES, Retail Week, Chain Store Age, Visual Merchandising and Space Design (VMSD),* and *Retail Ad Week* are examples of the publications that are read by store managers. Market centers also participate in publicizing fashion news through publications such as the *Chicago Apparel News, Dallas Apparel News,* and *California Apparel News.*

Fashion Magazines

Individuals in the fashion industry read trade publications for current information on fashion products, but the public gets most fashion news from magazines, which are also fashion products. A **fashion magazine** is a consumer magazine sold commercially, featuring articles, illustrations, and advertisements with an international emphasis.

POPULAR MAGAZINES Some popular titles include *Vogue, Marie Claire, Glamour, Cosmopolitan,* and *InStyle.* Publishers also target specific groups with magazines such as *GQ (Gentlemen's Quarterly)* for men and *Teen Vogue, Teen Glamour,* and *Seventeen* for teenagers. These magazines also allow retailers to identify what consumers want to purchase in their stores. Fashion publications offer fashion direction and target specific consumers.

MARKETING SERIES *Online*
Remember to check out this book's Web site for information on fashion products and more great resources at **marketingseries.glencoe.com.**

fashion magazine a consumer magazine sold commercially, featuring articles, illustrations, and advertisements with an international emphasis

MARKETING PHENOMENON

Estée Lauder
Cosmetics Engineer
Businesswoman

E stée Lauder Companies, Inc., sells products in over 120 countries. In addition to Estée Lauder brand cosmetics, the company also produces Aramis, Clinique, Prescriptives, Origins, M.A.C., and Bobbi Brown cosmetics. In 2004, the founder of the company, Estée Lauder, died at age 97. She started the business in 1946, making cosmetics on her stovetop.

What kind of training did she have?

Taught by an uncle who was a chemist, Estée Lauder started making cosmetics out of her New York home. Beyond making cosmetics, Lauder was also a phenomenal sales woman and marketer.

What did she like most about her job?

She recalled that she got her start in the 1930s: "During every possible spare moment, I cooked up little pots of cream for faces. I always felt most alive when I was dabbling in the practice cream."

What's her key to success?

Lauder once said, "If I believe in something, I sell it, and I sell it hard." After her business took off, she would still get behind the counter and sell cosmetics herself. She also pioneered the idea of a free gift with purchase, which helped her boost sales and set a precedent for selling new products. In 2003, the company reported sales of $4.7 billion.

Why would Estée Lauder's products be classified as fashion products?

Career Data: Cosmetologist

Education and Training High school diploma, cosmetology school degree, apprenticeship

Skills and Abilities Cosmetic, hair, nail, and facial treatment knowledge and skills

Career Outlook As fast as average growth through 2012

Career Path Apprentice to license practitioner to product sales representative to entrepreneur or business owner

FASHION MAGAZINES OF THE PAST Since 1892, when *Vogue* was first published, women have acquired fashion news by reading fashion magazines. *Harper's Bazaar,* first published in the 1920s, also showcased the latest styles. In 1935, *Mademoiselle* debuted as a fashion magazine for women between the ages of 17 and 35. For decades, people have enjoyed viewing photographs of models wearing stylish apparel in photo studios or at fashion shows. Fashion magazines continue to influence the consumer's knowledge of fashion news and to promote sales of other fashion products.

Fashion Product Planning

Fashion businesses in every segment of the industry make products. Companies in all industries must do planning to market products that customers will want and buy. Product planning includes doing market research (see Section 9.2) as well as making decisions about which products to include in a product mix and product assortments. Complete product development includes a number of factors, steps, and decisions before a fashion product is sold in stores. (See **Figure 9.1**.)

Fashion Product Mix

The planning process includes developing a product mix and product assortment that will satisfy the needs and wants of the market. The **product mix** is the total selection of goods and services that a company makes or sells. Manufacturers offer different lines of products, garments, accessories, household goods, cosmetics, and other fashion items. Retailers offer products such as garments, but their products differ in the variety of assortments they sell. For example, retailers may offer men's shirts, women's dresses, and children's wear—all made by different manufacturers. They may also offer services, such as personal help from sales associates and gift wrapping.

Math Check

SELLING GLOBAL PRODUCTS

Mei sells hand-knit sweaters from Peru. Mei pays $60 for each sweater. Import tax is 25 percent. What is the total cost of each sweater?

➥For tips on finding the solution, go to **marketingseries.glencoe.com**.

product mix the total selection of goods and services that a company makes or sells

---

Figure 9.1

Product Development

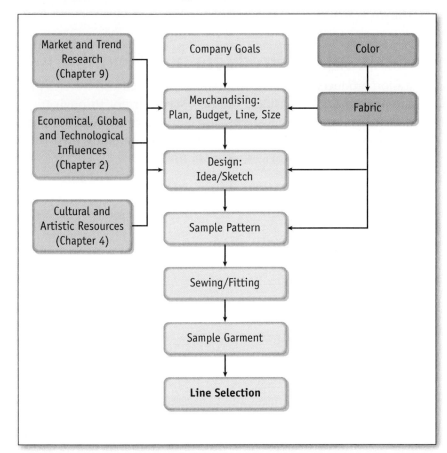

CREATING A PRODUCT For apparel production, many steps lead to the final product. *When would a business decide on its product assortment and perform market research?*

QUESTION

Are services included in a company's product mix?

ETHICS & ISSUES

Product Promises

For branding to be effective, consumers must trust that a company can deliver what it promises. One of the downfalls of failed businesses during the 1990s dot-com era was they could not keep promises. For example, eToys' promise of same-day shipping was broken when the company could not deliver.

Sometimes a company's promises can be more subtle. For example, by using celebrities to endorse and advertise products, a cosmetic company may imply that a consumer will look like the star in an ad.
Do you think that certain fashion products make indirect promises? If so, is this an ethical practice? Why or why not?

product assortment the range of items or merchandise within categories that a company sells

Product Assortments

The **product assortment** is the range of items or merchandise within categories that a company sells. For example, a textile company's assortment of natural fiber fabrics may include only wool and cotton. A garment manufacturer may offer an assortment of coats. A retailer, whose target market is young women, will stock a product assortment appropriate for that group. However, sometimes the terms *product mix* and *product assortment* are used interchangeably.

ASSORTMENT BREADTH The number of different items offered within a classification of products is called assortment *breadth*. If a company offers a large variety of goods, its assortment is wide or broad. For example, a wool textile producer might offer a wide assortment of fabrics made from different animal sources, such as lamb, goat, rabbit, or llama. Coat manufacturers may produce a wide assortment of coats, ranging from long coats to windbreakers to blazers. A retailer with a wide assortment might sell coats made by many different manufacturers.

ASSORTMENT DEPTH A product assortment has *depth* if it consists of a large quantity of the goods offered. For example, the textile producer's assortment has depth if its lamb's wool fabric comes in many colors. The coat manufacturer may offer depth of assortment if many styles of coats, such as single-breasted, double-breasted, and coats with or without belts. The retailer's coat assortment has depth if it stocks a large selection of sizes and colors of a single-breasted style. However, if only a few choices of product are available, the product assortment is shallow or narrow.

Understanding Products and Planning

Fashion products include goods that are produced and services that are performed. The fashion industry stays current through trade associations and trade publications, and consumers use fashion magazines to stay informed. Fashion businesses must carefully plan their selections of goods and services to suit consumers.

Quick Check ✓

RESPOND to what you've read by answering these questions.

1. What are the two types of fashion products?_____

_____

2. What trade association represents all segments of the fashion industry?_____

_____

3. What are the two characteristics of assortment?_____

_____

Fashion Market Research

Market Research and Fashion

Market research is an essential part of the product planning process in the fashion industry. Producers and retailers must know what products consumers want. Designers create new styles for consumers to purchase. However, if the products are not what consumers want, they will not sell. Therefore, companies must perform studies to determine consumer tastes and trends. This process, called **market research**, is the systematic gathering, recording, analyzing, and presentation of information related to marketing goods and services.

Market Analysts

Market analysts are specialists who gather marketing information, analyze data, compile reports, and assist all segments of the fashion industry by providing information. With information about new interest in fabrics, textile scientists will produce new fabrics, and manufacturers will keep supplies at levels to meet production needs. Designers can respond to new trends in apparel by reading current research reports. This market research also allows retailers to react accordingly. For example, when research shows a trend moving toward shorter skirts, stores will stock a wide assortment of that style.

Gathering Marketing Information

There are several formal methods used by market analysts to gather information to apply to product planning—survey, observation, experimental, and focus-group methods. In addition to such formal research, many fashion marketers read trade publications and fashion magazines to observe trends and consumer tastes.

Survey Method

The **survey method** is a research method that involves gathering specific information from people through surveys or questionnaires. Retail stores use surveys to determine how often customers shop, the quality of customer service, and which items are purchased.

Observation Method

The **observation method** is a research method that involves watching people and recording consumer behavior through cameras or individuals. This method can provide information to designers about what styles are being purchased and worn in different locations. One effective technique is observing people on the streets.

AS YOU READ ...

YOU WILL LEARN
- To describe the methods used to do market research.
- To explain market segmentation and target market research.
- To define merchandise information systems.

WHY IT'S IMPORTANT

Fashion businesses use market research to identify target markets, product opportunities, and to make product development decisions.

KEY TERMS
- market research
- survey method
- observation method
- experimental method
- focus group
- merchandise information system

PREDICT

What are some ways that fashion companies find out what customers want?

market research the systematic gathering, recording, analyzing, and presentation of information related to marketing goods and services

survey method a research method that involves gathering information from people through surveys or questionnaires

observation method a research method that involves watching people and recording consumer behavior by cameras or individuals

experimental method a research method whereby a researcher observes the results of changing one or more marketing variables while keeping other variables constant

focus group a panel of six to ten consumers who discuss opinions about a topic under the guidance of a moderator

Experimental Method

The **experimental method** is a research method in which a researcher observes the results of changing one or more marketing variables while keeping other variables constant. A *variable* is an aspect that may change or be unpredictable. A variable may influence the result of an experiment. Textile companies also perform experiments to record characteristics and performance levels of fibers and fabrics as they develop new textiles.

Focus-Group Method

A **focus group** is a panel of six to ten consumers who discuss opinions about a topic under the guidance of a moderator. Companies conduct this type of research to get feedback on their products and services. This method can be very effective because participants focus their opinions on specific products or ideas. For example, a retailer might conduct a focus group to determine what fashion merchandise customers want in the store by asking about specific brands, sizes, and other preferences.

World Market

Fashion at Midnight

Fashion in Iceland has come a long way since the wooly sweaters that were popular in the 1960s. In 2003, 40 years later, new and emerging fashion designers from around the world gathered in Iceland to present their creations at perhaps the world's largest and most unique open-air fashion event, Iceland Fashion Week—under the midnight sun. Because of its location near the North Pole, the sun never completely sets in Iceland during the summer months, creating a permanent daylight in summer (and permanent night in winter).

Famous for natural geothermal pools, Iceland has hosted fashion shows staged in unique environments. The first year, a show took place at below-freezing temperatures on top of Iceland's biggest glacier *Vatnsjokull*. During the second year, a show took place on the Icelandic volcano *Vestmannaeyjar*. In 2002, Iceland's

black sand desert *Landmannalaugar* served as the backdrop for global fashion.

The fashion shows were organized by Kolbrun Adalsteinsdottir, owner of Icelandic Models model agency, who has contacts in the fashion industry around the world. Over 30 design collections come to Iceland from countries such as France, the United Kingdom, Spain, Sweden, Norway, Denmark, Iceland, Greenland, the Faroe Islands, and Israel to shine under the midnight sun.

What type of customers might be interested in buying fashion showcased in natural environments such as Iceland?

SKATER KIDZ **Market researchers who want to get information about active teenage consumers and their preferences have a perfect laboratory at a skate park.** *What other fashion products, besides skate-surf apparel, might be purchased by these teens?*

Market Segmentation

I t is not possible to serve all consumers in a market. A company must decide which customers to serve to achieve the greatest success. Market segmentation is a way of dividing the total market into smaller groups and analyzing each group by specific characteristics.

Target-Market Research

Market research is an ongoing process. No matter what method is used, researchers gather and analyze information that relates to specific groups of customers or target market. A business selects those customers who might buy the most products. The strategy of market segmentation allows companies to target their primary customers. Using market segmentation to identify and define a company's target market is extremely important to maximize sales. The research must be focused in order to be useful. The fashion marketer bases many decisions on the research about the target consumer.

Case Study: Targeting Research

It would not be useful for the retailer Pacific Sunwear (PacSun) to conduct a focus group with people who live in a retirement community near a golf course. PacSun's customer base includes teens who skateboard or surf. A skate park might be the best location for conducting research to determine current styles and trends worn by PacSun's target market.

SERVICES RESEARCH Fashion marketers can also use market research to improve and enhance their communications and services to their customers. For example, PacSun might conduct a survey and learn that customers prefer to listen to certain music. The retailer might play this music in the PacSun stores to draw customers.

OTHER APPLICATIONS The research might also identify certain role models of the particular target audience. These role models could be integrated into an advertising campaign. For example, PacSun's sales may increase if the retailer sponsors a contest or special event featuring a customer favorite such as professional skateboarder Tony Hawk.

CONNECT

W hat fashion products might be targeted at you and your friends?

Style Point !

THE NAME GAME
A company called Looking Glass has developed a market segmentation tool called *Cohorts* that can be used by businesses, including fashion companies. It classifies groups of customers who have similar demographic characteristics and names each group with personal names such as Rachel, Ryan, or Megan.

Figure 9.2

Future Demographics: U.S. Apparel Consumers

PREDICTING TRENDS Fashion businesses pay close attention to statistics gathered by the government and base their decisions about making products on factors such as population trends. *What demographic group could be the largest by 2025? The smallest?*

Ages	Markets	2005	2010	2015	2020	2025	% Change over 20 yrs.
Under 5	Children	19,127	20,011	21,174	21,978	22,498	+15.0%
5–14	Girls	19,593	19,380	19,894	20,904	21,881	+10.5%
	Boys	20,554	20,340	20,901	21,978	23,006	+10.7%
15–24	Women	20,076	21,032	21,110	20,907	21,448	+6.4%
	Men	20,882	21,884	21,959	21,755	22,322	+6.5%
25–34	Women	18,291	19,301	20,691	21,615	21,715	+15.8%
	Men	18,014	18,991	20,393	21,319	21,405	+15.8%
35–44	Women	21,273	19,527	18,120	20,146	21,543	+1.3%
	Men	20,892	18,993	18,479	19,466	20,847	-0.2%
45–54	Women	21,203	22,239	21,078	19,393	19,011	-11.5%
	Men	20,304	21,325	20,118	18,347	17,878	-13.6%
55–64	Women	15,440	18,362	20,573	21,595	20,494	+24.7%
	Men	14,166	16,921	19,077	20,120	19,047	+25.6%
65–74	Women	9,961	11,305	13,970	16,595	18,598	+46.4%
	Men	8,409	9,753	12,273	14,791	16,826	+50.0%
75+	Women	11,019	11,216	11,619	12,847	15,267	+27.8%
	Men	6,779	7,135	7,705	8,986	11,260	+39.8%
Totals		285,983	297,705	309,134	322,742	335,046	+14.6%

SOURCE: Bureau of Census, U.S. Department of Commerce

(Numbers in thousands)

Demographics

As discussed in Chapter 2, demographics are statistics that describe a population in terms of personal characteristics, such as age, gender, income, and other aspects. Demographic data serves as useful sources of information for market researchers. They can identify special target markets for their products by using this information. The U.S. Bureau of the Census can provide much demographic information.

SAMPLE DATA For example, **Figure 9.2** lists the population by markets that are segmented by age brackets, such as 15–24, 25–34, and 35–44. Data collected by this government bureau also provides demographic information concerning where people live, what they do, and how much money they are willing to spend.

APPLYING DEMOGRAPHICS A retailer might follow this example: A women's boutique specializing in high-end apparel is considering opening an additional store near a new housing development. Market research could influence the decision to open the new store. Demographic information can determine if the income level of the neighborhood or town could support the expensive apparel store. Also, the information gathered from research can help the store owner to select the vendors and prices that would be appropriate for the customers who live in the area.

Merchandise Information Systems

When research is conducted, the information must be collected, stored, and analyzed. The set of procedures and methods for handling this data is called a **merchandise information system**, a system that produces, stores, and analyzes information that enables fashion marketers to make decisions about merchandise for sale. Businesses depend on accurate information so they can produce for and sell to their target market. Because information may change, market researchers must collect data on a continual basis.

This information can be obtained from the following sources:

- Sales records and supplier data

- Competitors' records relating to prices, location, and market share

- Customer profile data, such as research relating to buying behavior, shopping patterns, and lifestyles

- Government data, such as price trends and projections

Textile producers, garment manufacturers, and retailers alike maintain detailed records of sales and purchases relating to quantities, sizes, colors, fabrics, styles, and prices. This information helps each segment of the fashion industry determine what and how much merchandise to have available for sale.

Case Study | PART 2

ON TARGET

Continued from Part 1 on page 179

When Target stores expanded in the 1990s, the company launched an image campaign. According to Fashion Creative Director Minda Gralnek, "Our image campaign was launched because we were going into many markets where people weren't familiar with us or what they can get at Target." Customers can now purchase household and fashion items designed by top designers at discount prices.

In 1999, Target recruited a renowned product designer, Michael Graves, to create a line of everyday items for the store. Graves agreed with Target that good design doesn't have to be expensive. The Graves collection included over 200 products. Target also hired high-fashion designers Mizrahi and Mossimo, who created clothing collections for the store. These designer products pleased Target's *target* customers in 1,107 stores in 47 different states nationwide and earned the discount chain $40 billion in annual sales.

ANALYZE AND WRITE

1. Write a paragraph explaining why moving into new markets was successful.
2. How might a store such as Target determine what its customers want? Write your response in a few sentences.

QUESTION

What information that relates to competitors is collected by companies?

merchandise information system a system that produces, stores, and analyzes information that enables fashion marketers to make decisions about merchandise for sale

Market Research and New Products

Businesses must respond to market research on a timely basis so that the research will be productive. The information can help solve problems and acquire new business. It can also bring about the development of new fashion products and services to the industry. When new products are developed, the process starts with the idea and ends with the actual product that the customer buys.

Applied Research

In the past, market research indicated an increase of working women and a decrease in time spent on household tasks. The need developed for easy-to-care-for garments that were stain resistant. Therefore, textile manufacturers created fibers that could be made into fabrics with those characteristics. Then clothing producers made garments from those fabrics for retail stores to sell to customers. In addition, market research provided information about consumer issues regarding animal fur. When research showed that people objected to using real animal fur to make garments, the textile industry developed *faux fur,* a synthetic fabric that has the appearance of fur.

Changing Products

The fashion industry is constantly looking for new fashion products, whether it is fiber, fabric, or style, to stay current and satisfy the ever-changing desires of consumers.

Quick Check ✓

RESPOND to what you've read by answering these questions.

1. What is market research?_____

_____

_____

_____

2. What are four methods used to collect data in a merchandise information system?_____

_____

_____

_____

3. How does market research influence new products?_____

_____

_____

_____

 marketingseries.glencoe.com

Worksheet 9.1

Trade and Fashion Publications

Find a trade publication at a local bookstore, magazine stand, or library. Examples are *Women's Wear Daily* or *Sportswear International*. Then find a copy of a fashion magazine such as *GQ* or *Marie Claire*.

Make a list of the titles of the articles and features in each publication.

**Name of
Trade Magazine:**

_____

**Name of
Fashion Magazine:**

_____

Article Titles:

_____

_____

_____

_____

_____

_____

_____

_____

_____

_____

Article Titles:

_____

_____

_____

_____

_____

_____

_____

_____

_____

_____

Compare and contrast the two magazines:

_____

_____

_____

_____

_____

_____

_____

_____

_____

_____

Worksheet 9.2

Mall Survey

Visit a local mall or shopping center. Take a survey of the people shopping: Ask them where they shop, what they buy in these stores, and why they shop in these stores. Survey people of different ages, genders, and types of dress. Create a chart to organize the information. Then answer the questions below.

1. What are the top three stores?

   _____

   _____

   _____

2. Why are these stores popular?

   _____

   _____

   _____

TRADE ASSOCIATIONS

Use the Internet or library to research each of the following trade associations.

American Fiber Manufacturers Association

Purpose: _____

Contact information: _____

_____

American Textile Manufacturers Institute

Purpose: _____

Contact information: _____

_____

American Association of Textile Chemists and Colorists

Purpose: _____

Contact information: _____

_____

Council of Fashion Designers of America

Purpose: _____

Contact information: _____

_____

Fashion Group International, Inc.

Purpose: _____

Contact information: _____

_____

American Apparel and Footwear Association

Purpose: _____

Contact information: _____

_____

National Retail Federation

Purpose: _____

Contact information: _____

_____

Add this page to your career portfolio.

CHAPTER SUMMARY

Section 9.1 Fashion Products and Planning

rag trade (p. 180)
trade association (p. 181)
trade publication (p. 182)
fashion magazine (p. 183)
product mix (p. 185)
product assortment
    (p. 186)

- Fashion products include goods and services. Goods are the tangible items made, manufactured, or grown, such as apparel or textiles. Services are intangible things people do, such as tasks performed by cosmeticians and market researchers.

- Trade associations are voluntary, nonprofit organizations that provide services to special groups who develop, make, and sell fashion products.

- Trade publications are magazines, newspapers, books, or journals, offering a variety of information to a certain industry or segment of industry. Fashion magazines are consumer magazines sold commercially, featuring articles, illustrations, and advertisements.

- Fashion companies must do product planning, which includes doing market research and making decisions about which products to include in their product mix and product assortments.

Section 9.2 Fashion Market Research

market research (p. 187)
survey method (p. 187)
observation method
    (p. 187)
experimental method
    (p. 188)
focus group (p. 188)
merchandise informa-
    tion system (p. 191)

- Market research methods include the use of survey, observation, experimental, and focus group methods.

- Market segmentation is a way of dividing the total market into smaller groups and analyzing each group by specific characteristics, which helps determine target markets.

- A merchandise information system produces, stores, and analyzes information that enables fashion marketers to make decisions concerning merchandise they have available for sale.

CHECKING CONCEPTS

1. **Name** two fashion products, including goods and services.
2. **Describe** the services provided by trade associations.
3. **Identify** the difference between trade and fashion publications.
4. **Explain** two tasks involved in product planning.
5. **Identify** the market research method that involves a group of possible customers.
6. **Name** one source of demographic information.
7. **List** the kind of data obtained by merchandise information systems.

Critical Thinking

8. **Explain** the importance of doing fashion market research.

CROSS-CURRICULUM SKILLS

Work-Based Learning

Basic Skills—Speaking

9. Choose one of the fashion trade associations. Prepare and present a five-minute speech about the association.

Interpersonal Skills—Exercising Leadership

10. Imagine a fashion apparel product such as denim jeans. Write ten questions to survey potential customers about their interest in this product. Form a focus group and ask your questions.

School-Based Learning

Social Science

11. Choose a country. Use the Internet to research fashion trade associations in that country. Write about your findings.

Language Arts

12. Spend two hours observing and recording people's buying habits in two stores at a local mall. Write a report.

 CONNECTION

Role Play: Sales Associate for Juniors

SITUATION You are to assume the role of a sales associate for the juniors clothing department of a large department store. You are being considered for the position of assistant buyer. The buyer (judge) has decided to ask you about fall merchandise purchases as a way of assessing your suitability for the position. The buyer (judge) has asked for your opinion about beaded-and-sequined tops. The buyer (judge) wonders if that look has reached its peak of popularity.

ACTIVITY You are to make your recommendations and give reasons for them to the buyer (judge) in a meeting.

EVALUATION You will be evaluated on how well you meet the following performance indicators:

- Explain the nature of the fashion cycle.
- Identify the impact of product life cycles on marketing decisions.
- Identify fashion trends.
- Describe the need for marketing information.
- Describe information helpful to retailers in planning.

 INTERNET ACTIVITY

Use the Internet to access the Fashion Group International, Inc. (FGI) Web site to gather information about membership in that trade association.

- Click Skip Intro.
- Click Benefits.
- List six membership benefits.

➡ For a link to a Web site to help you do this activity, go to **marketingseries.glencoe.com**.

Chapter 10

Fashion Distribution

Section 10.1

Buying Fashion

Section 10.2

Selling Fashion

Chapter Objectives

- Explain the role of the fashion buyer.
- Discuss the steps in the buying process or merchandising cycle.
- Identify the types of fashion retailers.
- Discuss buying motives.
- Explain the steps in the personal-selling process.
- Discuss the importance of math skills in the fashion industry.

THE GUCCI IMAGE

Gucci is known internationally as an exclusive luxury brand. Gucci products are made with fine fabrics and Italian leather using high-quality production, and Gucci selectively distributes its products. In 1921, Guccio Gucci founded the company in Florence, Italy. He started with a luxury leather-and-luggage shop, where his logo-stamped products quickly became status symbols among Europe's elite. But in the 1990s, the Gucci company was in turmoil. Family feuding and poor management forced the family-run business to sell an interest to a London-based investment firm.

During this period, Gucci broadened distribution to thousands of retailers who had never before sold Gucci products. However, this strategy weakened the brand and hurt Gucci's 70-year-old reputation for exclusivity and luxury. Selling products to anyone anywhere damaged Gucci's image. How could Gucci recover its exclusive identity and return to profitability and growth?

ANALYZE AND WRITE

1. What type of store would sell Gucci products? Make a list of at least three types of stores.
2. How did choices about distribution affect Gucci's image? Write a paragraph explaining your answer.

Case Study Part 2 on page 205

POWER READ

Be an active reader and use these reading strategies:

PREDICT what the section will be about.

CONNECT what you read with your life.

QUESTION as you read to make sure you understand the content.

RESPOND to what you've read.

Buying Fashion

AS YOU READ ...

YOU WILL LEARN

- To explain the role of the fashion buyer.
- To discuss the steps in the buying process or merchandising cycle.
- To identify the types of fashion retailers.

WHY IT'S IMPORTANT

The buying process, or merchandising cycle, includes the planning, buying, and selling of merchandise. Consumers have a variety of choices when purchasing fashion merchandise.

KEY TERMS

- merchandise buying
- department stores
- specialty stores
- boutiques
- designer stores
- outlets
- discount stores

PREDICT

What might be the difference between designer stores and specialty stores?

Making Fashion Available

As discussed in Chapter 2, *place* is one of the four Ps of the marketing mix. Place refers to product distribution. The channel of distribution, or path that a product takes from producer to the consumer, involves manufacturers, wholesalers, and retailers. Fashion merchandising and distribution includes all the activities involved in offering the right merchandise blend to customers—planning, buying, and selling.

The Fashion Buyer's Job

The fashion buyer is responsible for making sure the merchandise that consumers want is available in stores. Buyers purchase goods from manufacturers or vendors. They must be able to predict what consumers want six months to a year before the goods reach stores. Buyers constantly monitor items that are selling as well as the latest styles and trends featured in fashion publications such as *Vogue* and *Bazaar*. Fashion buyers also read trade publications such as *Women's Wear Daily*. It is important to be aware of current fashion news because trends can affect profits for fashion businesses. Therefore, a buyer must have good fashion sense as well as keen business skills.

Types of Buyers

An individual who owns his or her own store usually serves as the buyer. The buyer is responsible for purchasing all merchandise, which might include apparel, accessories, or other fashion items. Buyers for larger retail operations are known as classification, or central, buyers. Stores that have catalog operations, such as J.C. Penney, may also have a separate buying staff for the catalog division.

A buyer may specialize in a category of goods, such as:

- Women's sportswear
- Women's handbags
- Men's suits
- Boys' clothing
- Teen boys' clothing
- Girls' clothing
- Teen girls' clothing

The Buying Process

There are three steps to the buying process, also known as the merchandising cycle:

1. Merchandise planning
2. Merchandise buying
3. Merchandise selling

Merchandise Planning

The first step of merchandise planning involves estimating, as accurately as possible, the various styles, colors, sizes, and prices of goods consumers will purchase. Buyers use many resources for planning:

- **Sales Records**—The main resource is the past records of goods that are sold. These records tell buyers not only the quantities of specific styles sold, but also the sizes and colors. For large retailers, records will indicate which stores sold particular items. Buyers will not always purchase the same styles and quantities for each store. For example, a Wal-Mart coat buyer will place more coats in stores located in the northern regions than those in the south.

- **Vendor Information**—Buyers also depend on information supplied to them by vendors. Vendor sales representatives keep on top of current trends and can advise the retail buyer about making purchases.

- **Market Week Previews**—Buyers attend market weeks to preview the upcoming season's merchandise and to buy merchandise.

Style Point !

SHOPPING LIST

A buyer goes to market prepared with a shopping list—but it's called a *buying plan*. Buying plans list the types, sizes, quantities, and prices of merchandise that the buyer will purchase from a vendor during a specific period. The target sales for each category of merchandise and spending limits are also included on the buying plan. But most buyers plan for some "impulse" purchases if items are not available.

SHOPPING TRIP **Buyers must have good timing, good fashion sense, and good business sense to purchase fashion items that will be popular and sell.** *What recent fashion item do you think would be the wrong choice to buy because it is about to go out of style?*

Virtual Dressing Room

Getting the right fit can be a challenge for people who shop online for clothing. Some fashion retailers, such as Lands' End, use My Virtual Model™ software on their Web sites, which allows customers to "try on" clothing in a virtual dressing room. By entering measurements and details about your build and features, you can create a 3D figure of yourself. The figure can be rotated and viewed from different angles or even sent by e-mail to a friend for a second opinion. For customers unsure of buying without trying, getting the right virtual fit can make the sale.

➡️Create your own virtual model and describe the results after visiting an online retailer through **marketingseries.glencoe.com**.

merchandise buying the process of purchasing merchandise for resale from manufacturers or vendors during buying trips

CONNECT

Do you think most sales associates are trained to help customers? Why or why not?

department store a retail operation that carries different kinds of merchandise and houses them in separate sections, or departments

Merchandise Buying

Buyers conduct **merchandise buying**, which is the process of purchasing merchandise for resale from manufacturers or vendors during buying trips. These buying trips are integrated into the planning process so that orders can be placed effectively.

SHIPPING DATES The shipping date of merchandise is an important consideration when placing orders. This date is vital because buyers want the merchandise in their stores during peak selling periods to earn maximum profits. Bad timing can cause financial loss. For example, swimsuits received in late August would miss the swimsuit selling season, and a store would have to mark down swimsuit prices, causing profit loss.

Merchandise Selling

This step in the buying process is the exchange of goods for money, from the retailer to the customer. Buyers were once very involved in the selling process. Their offices were located in the main store of a department store chain. They could watch the movement of the merchandise they bought on a daily basis and could be actively involved with the selling staff. Today buying staffs are located in central buying offices or company headquarters, which may be separate facilities.

SALES TRAINING Store personnel are responsible for training the sales staff. The buyers provide information to the staff, helping them to effectively sell the merchandise. Depending on the specialty of the merchandise, buyers schedule seminars for the sales staff. A vendor representative may conduct these seminars. For example, a lingerie or foundations buyer might arrange training classes for lingerie sales staff to instruct them on proper fitting techniques.

Types of Fashion Retailers

The final link between the designer, manufacturer, and consumer is the retail operation where merchandise selling takes place. **Figure 10.1** lists some top retailers that sell merchandise including apparel in the United States. Today consumers have a variety of locations where they can buy fashion merchandise. From traditional department stores and boutiques to kiosks in airports and online e-tail stores, retail distribution options are limitless.

Department Stores

A **department store** is a retail operation that carries different kinds of merchandise and houses them in separate sections, or departments. Some large department stores around the world include Macy's in the United States, Seibu in Japan, and Harrods of London. The U.S. government defines a department store as a store that employs at least 25 people and sells at least three groups of general merchandise: apparel and accessories, home furnishings, and household linens.

Figure 10.1

Top Retailers

Country of Origin	Name of Company	2002 Retail Sales (US$ millions)
United States	Wal-Mart	229,617
United States	Target	42,722
United States	JC Penney	32,347
United States	Gap	14,455
United States	May Department Stores	13,491
United States	TJX Companies (TJ Maxx)	11,981

SOURCE: Top 200 Global Retailers, www.stores.org, © 2004

VARIETY OF STORES Of the Top 50 global retailers, these American stores also distribute fashion. *What type of retailer is each store, and which stores also have online stores?*

GROUPS, CATEGORIES, AND CLASSIFICATIONS Within the apparel group, store merchandise can be subdivided into other categories, such as women's wear, juniors, children's, and men's wear, each with a wide range of colors, sizes, and styles. Within these categories, merchandise is divided into classifications, such as women's sportswear and dresses.

PRICE RANGES Retailers may also classify merchandise according to price ranges, such as "better" women's dresses or "budget" sportswear. Although department stores offer many different prices to attract a variety of customers on various income levels, most prices are set for households in the middle- to upper-middle income brackets.

DEPARTMENT STORE SERVICES Department stores offer services such as credit, gift wrapping, home delivery on large purchases, and bridal registry services.

Specialty Stores

A **specialty store** is a retail operation that offers only one category or related categories of fashion merchandise. This type of operation has been successful because a store is able to focus on a particular segment of the market. Specialty stores generally emphasize certain styles, such as classic or trendy. They target their merchandising to specific age groups and price ranges. Examples of specialty stores include the Gap, Pacific Sun, Claire's, and The Limited.

SPECIALTY STORE SERVICES Specialty stores may offer services such as credit accounts and gift wrapping. However, they usually give more personalized attention. For example, sales associates may advise customers on selections and make fashion recommendations.

QUESTION

What are the main categories used to group merchandise?

specialty store a retail operation that offers only one category or related categories of fashion merchandise

Boutiques

boutique a type of small specialty store that offers a more limited selection of merchandise and may focus on few-of-a-kind items

Another retail operation is the **boutique**, which is a type of small specialty store that offers a more limited selection of merchandise and may focus on few-of-a-kind items. Apparel and accessories carried by boutiques tend to be more trendy.

BUYING FOR BOUTIQUES The target market group who shops at boutiques is smaller, so boutique buyers must plan purchases carefully. These buyers might even go to market with specific customer preferences in mind, and then sell merchandise to a few customers.

Designer Stores

designer store a designer-manufacturer retail operation that owns and operates the retail store and carries only its own lines

A **designer store** is a designer-manufacturer retail operation that owns and operates the retail store and carries only its own lines. This concept is called vertical retailing. The designer or manufacturer controls the product from original concept to the final sale. By selling directly to the customer, designer stores earn bigger profits. Some examples of these stores include Gucci, Chanel, Guess?, and Ralph Lauren.

outlet a discount store that is owned by a manufacturer that sells its own merchandise in the store

Outlets

Another type of retail operation is the **outlet**, or off-price retailer, which is a discount store that is owned by a manufacturer or department or specialty-store chain that sells its own merchandise in the store. The goods offered may be overruns, damaged items, or leftovers from a prior season.

Hot Property

Fun in the Sun

Walk along any California beach and check out the surfers' clothing. Chances are they bought their Quiksilver, O'Neill, and Billabong shirts and boardshorts at Pacific Sunwear of California—or PacSun. The same is true of skate-boarders and snowboarders across the nation. In fact, you can find a PacSun retail store just about anywhere in the United States.

PacSun started out on the edge of the active wear trend in 1980 as a surfboard shop in Newport Beach, California. By 1981, this board-and-wax store was the first to move inside during the off-season as cool weather sent beachgoers to the mall. PacSun's first mall store opened at Santa Monica Place. Flash forward to 2004, and over 900 PacSun stores and outlets were open for business in 50 states and Puerto Rico. Customers can also find their favorite fashions at the 24/7 online store.

The specialty retail chain owes its success to listening to young people and providing the clothes teens and young adults want. PacSun caters to young people aged 12 to 22. By offering a selection of popular and emerging brands, along with its own brands, PacSun doesn't just ride the waves of fashion trends—it creates them.

1. Are the clothes carried by PacSun classified as haute couture? Why or why not?
2. What do you think has made PacSun a successful distributor of fashion?

OUTLET LOCATIONS The original concept of an outlet developed from a manufacturer's factory store that sold surplus goods produced by the factory. Today groups of outlet stores are located in centers called *outlet centers*. These centers can be located in outlying areas, far from populated shopping areas, because they do not want to compete with standard retailers selling goods at regular prices.

Discount Stores

A **discount store** is a retail operation that offers volume merchandise and limited service and sells goods below usual retail prices. Discount stores also offer private-label and national brands. The target market customer has a moderate budget and purchases clothing at lower prices. Originally, discount stores could afford to sell merchandise at lower prices because they had fewer operating expenses, such as rent, employee salaries, and services. However, today discount stores function like department stores, but they can offer discount prices because they purchase manufacturer's overruns and end-of-season goods. Discount stores usually receive special deals from manufacturers because of the large quantities they purchase. Because of this lower cost to the store, the customer pays less. Wal-Mart and Target stores are examples of discount stores.

DISCOUNT-STORE SERVICES Customers do not expect the same level of customer service in a discount store that they would receive in a traditional department store. Customers make purchases at a central check-out area, instead of at individual department check-out areas. However, many discount operations do offer their own credit cards as a service.

DISCOUNT-STORE TRENDS A trend in discount retail operations is the focus on image upgrading while maintaining discount prices. Target has experienced success with this strategy by offering merchandise created by designer Isaac Mizrahi. A three-time winner of the Fashion Designers of America's (CFDA) Designer of the Year Award, Mizrahi pioneered designer fashions at discount prices. Consumers who previously could not afford his fashions are now able to buy style.

Case Study **PART 2**

THE GUCCI IMAGE
Continued from Part 1 on page 199

Decades of family feuding and poor management choices had nearly crippled Gucci. The company was not directing how its products were marketed and sold, and sales slumped. However, under the new creative direction of Tom Ford and management of CEO Domenico De Sole, Gucci began to experience a revival.

Their strategies involved revitalizing product design. In addition, they focused attention on the high quality of Gucci's core products and the exclusivity of the Gucci brand name. Then they reestablished selective distribution of the products. Selective distribution is a method of carefully choosing the stores where a product is distributed to consumers. Marketers can control the reputation of the vendors selling the product and the type of customer who has access to the product. Gucci cut its distribution channels in half and began selling at Gucci owned-and-operated stores. By 2002, Gucci's sales topped $1.5 billion at 174 Gucci stores and 31 franchised stores.

ANALYZE AND WRITE

1. How does selection of distribution channels affect a product's reputation? Write a brief paragraph explaining your answer.
2. What are the benefits of businesses using their own distribution channels? Write a paragraph explaining your answer.

discount store a retail operation that offers volume merchandise and limited service and sells goods below usual retail prices

Distributing Online Fashion

How does e-commerce affect fashion distribution and sales? Online shopping eliminates the need for the storeowner, stock clerk, and sales associate. Shoppers can find what they want online and purchase it. The product is shipped straight to the customer without stopping in a store to be unpacked, steamed, displayed, tried on, bought, packed up and sent home. In a 2003 *Retail Consumer Survey Report,* 89 percent of the people surveyed said they would shop with online retailers who offered free shipping. Low shipping fees can help online retailers be more competitive.

➡Look into making an online purchase and calculate the shipping fees through **marketingseries.glencoe.com.**

Mail-Order Retailers

Mail-order, or direct-mail marketing, is a type of retail operation in which a business sells merchandise in a catalog and sends it by mail to customers who purchase it. People use catalogs for shopping because of convenience. Merchandise offerings can range from discount to moderately priced merchandise.

VARIETY OF MAIL ORDER Mail-order companies can be strictly catalog retailers, such as Lands' End, or have actual "brick-and-mortar" stores, such as well-established department stores Sears and J.C. Penney. Higher-priced and luxurious items can also be found through mail-order catalogs. Neiman Marcus department store is renowned for its special Christmas catalog offering expensive and unusual gifts.

Online Retailers

One of the fastest-growing trends is online shopping, or Internet shopping. Almost every type of retailer—whether department store, boutique, discounter, or designer—offers online services. Customers are able to shop at any time of the day or night, seven days a week, on e-tail Web sites and have merchandise shipped directly to their homes. In addition, some retailers give special discounts for Internet purchases.

Buying to Sell

As part of the distribution process, planning and buying fashion merchandise is the job of buyers on behalf of retailers who ultimately distribute and sell goods and services to customers. With the wide variety of distribution channels and types of stores available, fashion retailers and marketers can be sure to offer consumers the products they want when they want them.

Quick Check ✓

RESPOND to what you've read by answering these questions.

1. What is the job of the fashion buyer?_____

_____

_____

2. What are the three steps of the buying process or merchandising cycle?_____

_____

3. What are some advantages of online shopping?_____

_____

_____

Selling Fashion

Why People Buy Fashion

Fashion fulfills more than just the basic need for clothing. People also wear clothes to enhance appearance and to fit in socially. These cultural, social, and psychological factors affect **buying behavior**, or the way consumers react to satisfying a need or want when making a purchase. Retailers, buyers, and sales associates must be aware of these factors whether planning, buying, or selling fashion.

Rational and Emotional Buying

Buying behavior can either be *rational* or *emotional*. Rational behavior involves logical thinking and decision making. For example, a customer on a limited budget may need a pair of shoes to wear to a job that requires standing. Therefore, that person would consider price and comfort in making a selection. Emotional behavior, on the other hand, is based on feelings. For example, a teen might observe a popular group at school wearing a new jean style. The teen may purchase that same style to be affiliated with the group. Fashion marketers attempt to influence consumers' emotional behavior through magazines and television because people tend to react to what they see other people wear.

Influences on Fashion

Different forms of media have had a tremendous influence on fashion. Consumers are aware of people in the news, which affects fashion on an ongoing basis. Fashion also affects popular media, such as television, magazines, music, and the Internet. The role of fashion in popular culture has a significant impact on people's lives and the purchases they make.

Television and Films

Television and film stars can start new trends just by appearing at an award ceremony wearing a new and aspiring designer's clothes. The Initial Necklace, worn by Sarah Jessica Parker, was seen by millions on television, and it immediately became a must-have item. Chandelier earrings became popular after various stars were seen wearing them at the Academy Awards. Music styles and stars have also played an important role in current fashion. For example, urban-wear fashion is inspired by hip-hop music.

AS YOU READ ...

YOU WILL LEARN
- To discuss buying motives.
- To explain the steps in the personal-selling process.
- To discuss the importance of math skills in the fashion industry.

WHY IT'S IMPORTANT
All segments of the fashion industry rely on personal selling to sell products. The basic selling process is comprised of seven key steps.

KEY TERMS
- buying behavior
- nonpersonal selling
- personal selling
- steps of selling

PREDICT
How would you define personal selling related to fashion merchandise?

buying behavior the way consumers react to satisfying a need or want when making a purchase

---

nonpersonal selling the type of selling that does not involve interaction between people

personal selling the type of selling that involves direct interaction between sales associates and potential buyers by telephone or in person

steps of selling the basic selling process that includes seven steps: Approach the customer, determine needs, present the product, overcome objections, close the sale, perform suggestion selling, and follow up

Magazines

Fashion magazines, including *Vogue, Glamour, Seventeen, Ebony,* and *GQ (Gentlemen's Quarterly),* print articles and ads for readers. In addition, some magazines research fashion trends as a service to advertisers. Research reports predict styles, colors, and fabrics that people will wear next season. Magazines carry articles about fashion trends and clothing care, interviews with designers, and photos of fashion collections. *Vogue, Bazaar,* and *Glamour* have been the main fashion magazines for consumers, but today's market also includes *People, Lucky,* and *Us.*

Personal Selling

Nonpersonal selling is the type of selling that does not involve interaction between people. Advertising, sales promotion, and publicity are types of nonpersonal selling. However, the selling process occurs when sales associates communicate through **personal selling**, which is the type of selling that involves direct interaction between sales associates and potential buyers by telephone or in person. Once a customer is attracted to a product by advertising, sales promotion, or publicity, personal selling helps to complete the sale. Fashion sales representatives can use information provided by direct contact with the buyer or customer. Personal selling is therefore the most flexible and individualized of the promotion techniques. It is often more persuasive than advertising and other forms of promotion because the message can be customized to fit the customer.

Selling in All Segments

All segments of the fashion industry rely on personal selling to sell products. Textile producers have representatives who sell "piece goods" to the apparel industry. Apparel producers sell directly to retailers after the garments are manufactured. Garment samples in a line are typically presented to retailers six months ahead of the wearing season. A sales presentation is a formal, well-prepared showing of a company's goods to potential customers. The sales professional answers questions concerning the line and takes orders. Representatives can also make sales calls to the retail buyer in their store location.

The Selling Floor

The center of action for the retail segment is the selling floor. This is where the buyer and seller interact. There are proven methods and techniques for successful selling. The most important ingredient, however, is the sales associate's willingness to provide a quality product, good value, and exceptional customer service.

The Steps of Selling

Successful sales associates use the **steps of selling**, or the basic selling process that includes seven steps: Approach the customer, determine needs, present the product, overcome objections, close the sale, perform suggestion selling, and follow up. (See **Figure 10.2**.)

Figure 10.2

The Steps of Selling

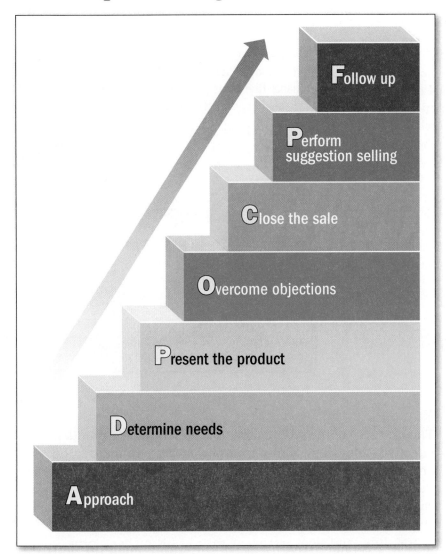

Follow up

Perform suggestion selling

Close the sale

Overcome objections

Present the product

Determine needs

Approach

THE METHOD OF SELLING
Customers respond to sales associates who listen and communicate, using this step-by-step method to make a sale. *How can a sales associate best determine a customer's needs?*

Approaching the Customer
Sales associates meet and greet customers when they enter the store, usually by saying "hello" and acknowledging their presence. The process of approaching the customer is critical to establishing a relationship that enables the selling process to continue.

Determining Needs
Good sales associates determine needs by learning as much as possible about a customer's preferences in order to decide which products to show the customer. They use open-ended questions to classify customers according to their needs. They encourage the customer to do most of the talking and avoid questions with possible "yes" or "no" responses. A talented sales associate listens and determines what garments or accessories to present to the customer. By concentrating on what the customer is saying, they let the customer know that they really are listening.

CONNECT
What selling step do you think is the most important? Why?

To Russia With Shopping List

In St. Petersburg, all roads lead to *Nevsky Prospekt,* which is a street in the heart of the city where everything can be found—the best hotels, plenty of restaurants and cafés, movie theaters, banks, churches, concert halls—and the best shopping anywhere. Stroll down this long street, and you will be greeted by souvenir peddlers, musicians, money changers, and street vendors outside of upscale and ready-to-wear shops.

Located on Nevsky Prospekt is St. Petersburg's largest and most famous department store, *Gostiny Dvor.* It used to be one huge store with 164,690 square feet of selling space. Now the department store rents out space to smaller shops, and Gostiny Dvor is the anchor store.

Whether shopping for fresh vegetables, hand-crafted goods, clothes, or outdoor gear, you will probably find what you need on Nevsky Prospekt, St. Petersburg's most festive street.

Do you think the selling steps used by sales people in a shop on Nevsky Prospekt are different from those used in the United States? Why or why not?

RUSSIA

MARKETING SERIES *Online*

Remember to check out this book's Web site for fashion distribution information and more great resources at **marketingseries.glencoe.com**.

Presenting the Product

The next step of the selling process is presenting the product. To be effective, salespeople must translate *product features,* or physical characteristics of items, into *benefits* for the customer. Customers do not buy product features; they buy the benefits and solutions that the product provides. Benefits may include comfort, saving time or money, safety, or ease of care. For example, someone who is traveling, and does not want to iron his or her clothes, needs wrinkle-free garments. However, a person who has limited funds may choose wash-and-wear garments that do not require expensive dry cleaning.

Overcoming Objections

After presenting the product, the next step in the sales process is overcoming objections. Sometimes customers have spoken or unspoken objections to certain aspects of the product. Objections are concerns, hesitations, doubts, or other honest reasons a customer has for not making a purchase. These objections might involve the product, price, timing, or even the sales associate. In order to overcome objections, an effective sales associate will use a positive approach. They will try to determine the objections and take the opportunity to provide additional information to the customer. The ultimate goal is to help the customer make a satisfying buying decision.

Closing the Sale

Closing the sale means the customer agrees to buy the merchandise. Until this step of the sale, all of the sales associate's efforts have been directed to helping the customer make buying decisions. In closing the sale, a sales associate observes the customer for signs that he or she is ready to make a positive purchasing decision. Sales associates summarize benefits and formulate an action plan.

QUESTION

What does closing the sale mean?

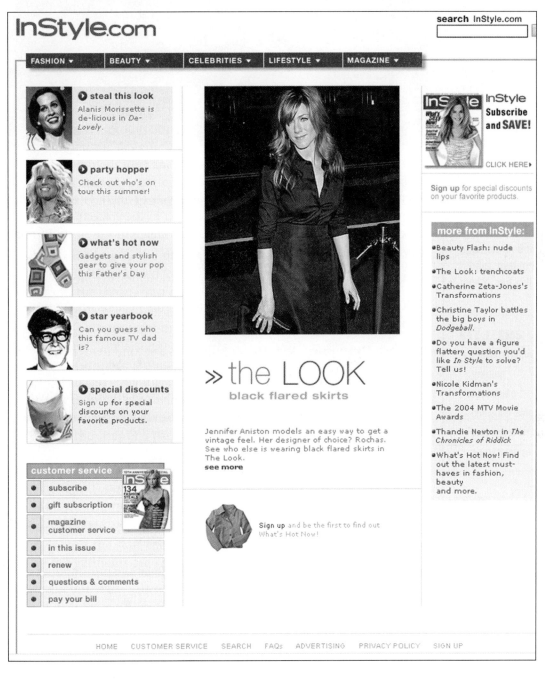

 FASHION NEWS AND SALES Another outlet for nonpersonal selling is found on fashion-related Web sites, such as online magazine sites that offer the latest hot items and special discounts. *Do you think magazine readers are interested in making purchases when getting fashion news? Why or why not?*

THE PERFECT MATCH
A good sales associate can help the particular customer find the right accessories. *What step of the selling process is portrayed in this picture?*

Suggestion Selling

Suggestion selling is selling additional goods or services to the consumer. It is a way to increase sales by adding to the customer's original purchase by directing customers to other merchandise or additional services. Suggestion selling includes:

- **Add-on**—A customer purchases an additional related item.

- **Trading up**—A customer substitutes an item that is higher priced or of better quality.

- **More than one**—A customer purchases a second item, possibly in a different color.

- **Special offer**—A customer takes advantage of an opportunity to receive an additional item that can be obtained as a result of purchasing a specific item.

Follow-Up

Closing the sale is not the end of the selling process, but rather the beginning of the *relationship building* process. Relationship building involves following up with a customer, building a strong rapport, and maintaining that relationship with the customer.

WAYS TO BUILD RELATIONSHIPS Relationship building can be accomplished in several ways. A relationship with the customer starts when a sales associate gives honest and positive statements during the buying process. In the retail segment, this is particularly critical. Telling a customer that a style is flattering when it is not can result in merchandise returns and the loss of a customer. This relationship can continue by *bonding* with the customer, which is the process of taking actions to maintain the relationship. It can be achieved by keeping records of purchases. The records might note favorite brands or styles and important dates, such as birthdays and anniversaries. The sales associate is then able to suggest purchases.

212 Unit 3 **Fashion Marketing and Merchandising**

DOOR-TO-DOOR DISTRIBUTION

Madam C.J. Walker
Cosmetics Engineer
Businesswoman

Madam C.J. Walker was born Sarah Breedlove in Louisiana in 1867. She invented a line of hair-care products and cosmetics that became popular with African-American women. More importantly, she innovated a system of selling door-to-door and recruiting agents to sell her hair treatment. The success of her system made her one of the first African Americans and one of the first women to become a self-made millionaire. Distributing her products was a way to promote "cleanliness and loveliness" as assets. Her goal was to help improve the self-respect and appearance of millions of people.

What was the key to her success?

As one of the pioneers of the personal-care products industry, Madam C.J. Walker employed a well-developed marketing strategy and carefully built a recognizable brand. She employed "Walker agents" to sell her products door-to-door, demonstrating the hair treatment to ladies in their homes. Walker products were branded with a portrait of Madam Walker on the package. She also advertised heavily in African-American newspapers and magazines. Her products were used internationally as well, by stars such as Josephine Baker. In addition, Madam Walker's public philanthropy and political activism contributed to the successful promotion and expansion of her brand.

Do you think the steps of selling would be more or less useful when selling products door-to-door? Why or why not?

Career Data: Cosmetician

Education and Training High school diploma, apprenticeship or cosmetology school degree and licensing, associate degree or bachelor's degree in business or marketing

Skills and Abilities Cosmetic, business, and interpersonal skills

Career Outlook As fast as average growth through 2012

Career Path Apprentice to licensed practitioner to product sales representative to entrepreneur or business owner

Math and Selling Fashion

Mathematical calculations are used in all segments of the fashion industry. Acquiring basic math skills, such as performing basic computations of addition, subtraction, division, and multiplication, is essential. People in the fashion industry use these basic math skills to determine the cost, the markup or markdown, and the final selling price of fashion products.

Math Check

MARKDOWNS

Court's Department Store is having a 10 percent sale on all home furnishings. Jarel purchased a recliner for $250. What was the original price of the recliner?

➡️For tips on finding the solution, go to **marketingseries.glencoe.com**.

Calculating Markups and Markdowns

Math is also useful when computing the final sales price after a series of markups and markdowns. In the textile segment, math is used to determine the cost of producing a fabric. A markup amount is calculated and added before the fabric is sold to a garment manufacturer. The same principle applies when the manufacturer sells garments to a retailer, and a retailer sells to the customer. Sales associates use math in handling sales transactions and accounting for merchandise in their departments. They must be familiar with mathematical calculations relating to returns, exchanges, sales tax, and shipping charges, as well as those necessary to conduct inventory counts. Math skills are critical to the success of professionals in the fashion industry.

Selling Fashion

All segments of the fashion industry rely on personal selling to sell products to customers. Personal selling is the most flexible and individualized of the promotion techniques. Sales associates for wholesale and retail fashion products can apply the steps of selling to specific customers. Fashion merchandising and distribution include all the activities involved in offering the right merchandise blend to customers—planning, buying, and selling. Distribution, or place, is just one component of the overall fashion marketing mix used to provide consumers with a variety of fashion products.

Quick Check

RESPOND to what you've read by answering these questions.

1. What are the two types of buying behavior?_____

_____

_____

_____

2. What are the seven steps in the selling process?_____

_____

_____

_____

3. What are four types of suggestion selling?_____

_____

_____

_____

_____

Name _____ Date _____

Worksheet 10.1

Predicting Fashion Trends

You are a fashion buyer for the teen department of a national department store. Choose the teen boys' or teen girls' department as your specialty. Go to the library and look through several fashion magazines. Then predict some new fashion trends for next season. For example, some trends might focus on the length of hemlines; the look of jeans: bell bottoms, straight leg, baggy, or tight; T-shirt looks; or a California beach look. Include colors that you predict will be popular.

I predict some fashion trends for teen girls/boys will be:

_____

_____

_____

_____

_____

_____

_____

_____

_____

_____

_____

_____

_____

_____

_____

_____

_____

_____

_____

_____

_____

_____

_____

_____

Name _____   Date _____

Worksheet 10.2

The Selling Process

Choose a product you want to purchase. Visit two different stores that sell the product. Evaluate how well the sales associate handles selling the product. You may or may not choose to go through with closing the sale. Answer the following questions.

Store #1:

1. Were you comfortable with the sales associate's approach? Why or why not?

_____

2. Rate how well the sales associate determined your needs. Circle one.

Very well   Okay   Not very well

3. Rate how well the sales associate presented the product. Circle one.

Very well   Okay   Not very well

4. Rate how well the sales associate overcame objections. Circle one.

Very well   Okay   Not very well

5. Rate how well the sales associate closed the sale. Circle one.

Very well   Okay   Not very well

Store #2:

1. Were you comfortable with the sales associate's approach? Why or why not?

_____

2. Rate how well the sales associate determined your needs. Circle one.

Very well   Okay   Not very well

3. Rate how well the sales associate presented the product. Circle one.

Very well   Okay   Not very well

4. Rate how well the sales associate overcame objections. Circle one.

Very well   Okay   Not very well

5. Rate how well the sales associate closed the sale. Circle one.

Very well   Okay   Not very well

Which sales associate did you prefer? Explain your answer.

_____

_____

_____

TYPES OF FASHION RETAILERS

Under each type of fashion retailer, add a few facts that will help you remember the purpose of each retailer.

Department Store

_____

_____

Boutique

_____

_____

Outlet

_____

_____

Mail-Order Catalog

_____

_____

Specialty Store

_____

_____

Designer Store

_____

_____

Discount Store

_____

_____

Online Store

_____

_____

Add this page to your career portfolio.

CHAPTER SUMMARY

Section 10.1 Buying Fashion

merchandise buying
(p. 202)
department store (p. 202)
specialty store (p. 203)
boutique (p. 204)
designer store (p. 204)
outlet (p. 204)
discount store (p. 205)

- The fashion buyer is responsible for making sure the merchandise that consumers want is available in stores. Buyers purchase goods from manufacturers or vendors. They must predict what consumers want six months to a year before goods reach the stores. Buyers monitor the latest styles and trends.

- There are three steps to the buying process, also known as the merchandising cycle: merchandise planning, merchandise buying, and merchandise selling.

- The different types of fashion retailers are distributors such as department stores, specialty stores, boutiques, designer stores, outlets, discount stores, and non-store retailers, such as catalogs and online stores.

Section 10.2 Selling Fashion

buying behavior (p. 207)
nonpersonal selling
(p. 208)
personal selling (p. 208)
steps of selling (p. 208)

- Buying behavior can be either rational or emotional. Rational behavior involves logical thinking and decision making. Emotional behavior is based on feelings.

- Successful sales associates use the steps of selling, or the basic selling process that includes seven steps: Approach the customer, determine needs, present the product, overcome objections, close the sale, perform suggestion selling, and follow up.

- Mathematical calculations are used in all segments of the fashion industry to determine the cost, the markup or markdown, and the final selling price of fashion products.

CHECKING CONCEPTS

1. **Identify** three tasks performed by fashion buyers.
2. **Describe** the merchandise-planning step of the buying process.
3. **Define** *merchandise buying*.
4. **Name** the types of retailers that distribute fashion merchandise.
5. **Identify** types of consumer buying behavior.
6. **Explain** the first two steps of the selling process.
7. **List** two reasons math skills are essential in the fashion industry.

Critical Thinking

8. **Discuss** ways that sales associates build relationships with customers.

CROSS-CURRICULUM SKILLS

Work-Based Learning

Interpersonal Skills—Participating as a Team Member

9. Work with three or four other classmates. Prepare and creatively present a lesson on the different types of fashion retailers. Give your lesson to the class.

Basic Skills—Math

10. At your store, you sell sweaters for $15 each. Last week the sweaters went on sale at 20 percent off. You sold 26 sweaters at the full price and 36 at the sale price. What is the total amount of your sales?

School-Based Learning

Language Arts

11. You are a fashion buyer for Gap clothing store. Write a journal entry about a typical day on the job.

Computer Arts

12. Use computer graphics to create a chart that illustrates the steps of selling. Display your chart in the classroom.

Role Play: Assistant Manager of Shoe Store

SITUATION You are to assume the role of assistant manager of a large, family shoe store. In addition to shoes, the store carries a full line of accessories and supplies: women's handbags, cleaning products, storage items, and other related products. Your manager has recently hired several new sales associates. One of the new sales associates (judge) is not meeting his or her sales goals and needs some additional sales training, especially in the area of suggestion selling.

(ACTIVITY) Your manager has asked you to explain the selling process to the new employee (judge).

EVALUATION You will be evaluated on how well you meet the following performance indicators:

- Explain the selling process.
- Identify customer's buying motives for use in selling.
- Demonstrate suggestion selling.
- Assess customer/client needs.
- Acquire product information to use in selling.

As a class, make a list of online purchases you have made. Include the name and URL of the Web sites used.

- Choose one of the Web sites to visit.
- Write a short description of the products available through this Web site.

➡️ For a link to a Web site to help you do this activity, go to **marketingseries.glencoe.com**.

Chapter 11

Fashion Pricing and Technology

Section 11.1

Pricing and Credit

Section 11.2

Using Technology

Chapter Objectives

- Describe the five price levels of fashion apparel.
- Identify the considerations used by fashion makers to determine prices.
- Explain how manufacturers use credit.
- List types of credit offered by retail stores.
- Explain computer-integrated manufacturing.
- Describe inventory control and systems used in retail stores.

OFF-PRICE POWER

T.J. Maxx is the largest off-price retailer in the United States. Off-price stores resell manufacturer's overruns, returns, irregulars, and off-season merchandise. Operated by TJX Companies, T.J. Maxx was founded in 1977 in Framingham, Massachusetts. The store offers brand-name and designer-label apparel and home products at deeply discounted prices. Products are priced as low as 60 percent off department store prices. In addition to selling seconds or returns, the company saves the customer money by operating low-overhead stores. Clothes are placed together by section, and the staff does not actively sell to customers. Instead, they maintain stock and run the store. Customers sort through clothing racks looking for bargains. T.J. Maxx has few in-store luxuries to attract customers, and they do very little advertising. Also, online discount marketers such as Sierra Trading Post are offering consumers similar bargains from the comfort of home. Can T.J. Maxx keep customers coming through the door as online competition heats up?

ANALYZE AND WRITE

1. List the advantages and disadvantages of off-price merchandise?
2. Is shopping at discount stores fashionable to the consumer? Write a paragraph explaining your answer.

Case Study Part 2 on page 227

POWER READ

Be an active reader and use these reading strategies:

PREDICT what the section will be about.

CONNECT what you read with your life.

QUESTION as you read to make sure you understand the content.

RESPOND to what you've read.

Section 11.1

Pricing and Credit

AS YOU READ ...

YOU WILL LEARN

- To describe the five price levels of fashion apparel.
- To identify the considerations used by fashion makers to determine prices.
- To explain how manufacturers use credit.
- To list types of credit offered by retail stores.

WHY IT'S IMPORTANT

Fashion marketers must be familiar with classifications and factors that determine the price of fashion products. Credit plays an important role in all segments of the industry.

KEY TERMS

- selling price
- better garments
- moderate lines
- budget lines
- cost of product
- operating expenses
- markup

PREDICT

List some operating expenses for a retail store.

selling price retail price, or the amount the consumer pays

better garments more reasonably priced garments that maintain high quality

The Price of Fashion

Consumers want to feel confident about the price and value of a fashion product. Makers of fashion products give careful consideration to specific price ranges, design styles, and the target customer. Pricing for apparel starts with the textile phase, according to the quality and construction of the fabric. In the production phase, the reputation of the designer, the type and amount of labor used, the complexity of the style, and the construction of the garment affect the price. Then the retailer establishes a **selling price**, or retail price, which is the amount the consumer pays for merchandise.

Fashion Price Levels

The fashion industry has different classifications for pricing merchandise. There are five price levels that are associated with the quality of the fashion product:

1. **Couture**—custom-made designer garments in the highest-priced category. Garments by Dior and Chanel are examples of couture.

2. **Bridge lines**—secondary lines of well-known designers, priced between the couture and better categories. This category represents the most expensive ready-to-wear apparel. Some designers sell these lines in individual boutiques, located on 5th Avenue in New York City or on Rodeo Drive in Beverly Hills. An example of a bridge designer is Linda Allard for Ellen Tracy.

3. **Better garments**—more reasonably priced garments that maintain high quality. These items are found in specialty stores and department stores. Liz Claiborne, CK by Calvin Klein, and Chaps by Ralph Lauren are examples of better garments.

4. **Moderate lines**—medium-priced garments with well-known brand names, such as Levi's, and private brands seen in department stores. Charter Club and I.N.C. are private labels for Macy's department stores.

5. **Budget lines**—the least expensive category of garments that are knockoffs or downscaled duplications of designer styles, which are mass-marketed. Less expensive fabrics with cheaper trims are used in budget lines, and the details are simpler. Fashion merchandise found at Wal-Mart and Target is categorized as budget lines.

222 Unit 3 **Fashion Marketing and Merchandising**

Determining Prices of Fashion Goods

The selling price is the amount the consumer is willing to pay to the retailer for merchandise. Because consumers are concerned about value and quality when making purchases, fashion marketers use four main considerations when establishing prices:

- Achieving the most profit

- Obtaining the most sales volume

- Being competitive

- Presenting an image

Calculating Price

The selling price is calculated by adding together the cost of the product, operating expenses, and profit. The largest component is the **cost of product**, which is the cost of the merchandise from the manufacturer. **Operating expenses** are all costs associated with the actual business operations: cost of buildings or rents, salaries, and taxes. The profit amount is then added, according to what the company wants to receive.

moderate lines medium-priced garments with well-known brand names, such as Levi Strauss, and private brands seen in department stores

budget lines the least expensive category of garments that are knockoffs or downscaled duplications of designer styles, which are mass-marketed

cost of product the cost of the merchandise from the manufacturer

operating expenses all costs associated with the actual business operations: cost of buildings or rents, salaries, and taxes

Hot Property

Pop Beauty

What girl does not want "Boo-Boo Zap," a potent blend of salicylic acid and camphor that sabotages blemishes with lightning speed? Then there is that famous eye shadow called "Busy Signal." Most fashion makeup connoisseurs know these famous cosmetics. They are the brain children of twin sisters Jean and Jane Ford of the world-renowned Benefit cosmetics line.

Opening as The Face Place in San Francisco in 1976, the Benefit makeup boutique has grown to nearly 600 cosmetic counters worldwide. Found in such sophisticated stores as Henri Bendel in New York City and Harrods and Selfridges in London, Benefit has become synonymous with fresh solutions for women's skin. For example, if laugh lines appear while smiling at the products' whimsical names, Benefit has a product to conceal those laugh lines.

Benefit products are practical as well as fun. One product advertises to "de-shine the invisible way. Whether worn on bare skin or over makeup, this light balm with Vitamin C fills in fine lines and pores and evens out your complexion." Or there is Ooh La Lift—"a miracle in a wand for de-puffing and firming the delicate eye area, thanks to reflective pigments and cooling and firming botanicals."

From ages 16 to 65, women are willing to pay for Benefit, the hot cosmetics with the cool sense of humor.

1. How might image determine Benefit's prices?
2. What type of operating expenses might Benefit incur?

markup the difference between the cost of the product and the retail price

MARKUP **Markup** is the difference between the cost of the product and the retail price. The markup amount must be enough to cover the cost of the product, expenses associated with doing business, and a profit.

MARKUP CALCULATION To simplify the process of calculating markup, fashion marketers may use a markup amount that is a percentage of the total retail value. This method is used because expenses and profits are expressed as a percentage of the net sales, which is based on retail value. To determine the retail price, retailers often use a *keystone markup*, which is a price that is twice the wholesale cost.

Pricing at Each Stage

At each stage in the process of bringing fashion to the consumer, markups are added before a product is sold to the next segment. For example, the textile manufacturer will add an additional amount, or markup, to the cost of producing the fabric so that a profit can be made.

The garment producer then establishes the *wholesale price*, which is the price charged to the retailer. The wholesale price of the garment is determined by calculating the cost of the labor, materials, and markup. (See **Figure 11.1**.)

Figure 11.1

Wholesale Jacket Price

BEFORE YOU PAY FOR IT
Many of these wholesale costs vary, but you can be sure that the retailer will mark up the wholesale price of this jacket. *What profit did the wholesale company make?*

Materials	$14.05
Wool-blend fabric	12.40
Lining	1.10
Thread	.20
Zipper	.15
Button	.20
Labor	$7.65
Cut/sew/finish	2.15
Factory	4.30
Warehousing/distribution	1.20
Packing costs	$ .95
(tags, labels, hangers, pins, bags)	
Overhead	$7.59
Sewing expense	1.54
Administrative expense	4.32
Financing	.40
Returns and allowances	1.32
Trade discount	$2.80
Taxes	$1.18
Net profit	$1.78
Wholesale price	$36.00

BUILDING GOOD CREDIT
Building relationships is dependent upon trust, especially when it relates to credit purchases. *What items might a designer want to purchase on credit?*

The garment producer's markup may include:

- Sales commission
- Terms (amount of discount to retail stores if they pay on time)
- Overhead (rent, insurance, and utilities)
- Profit

After the retailer has purchased merchandise from the garment producer, the retailer establishes a retail price, or the amount the consumer pays. Retailers mark up the wholesale cost to the retail price by adding these expenses together:

- Salaries
- Advertising
- Overhead
- Allowances for marking down prices of merchandise
- Profit

Example:

- Cost of producing a garment by designer/manufacturer = $50
- Markup at 120 percent to establish wholesale price = $110
- Wholesale price increased by keystone markup to retail price = $220

Other Pricing Strategies

A retailer must consider the prices set by competitors. If a competing store sells the same merchandise for less, a retailer may have to cut expenses and/or reduce profit. Many discount stores sell off-price, or deeply discounted, merchandise.

Math Check

HOMEWORK FURNITURE
Roby's is a manufacturer of home-office furniture. The company borrowed $10,000 at 7 percent interest for one year. Calculate the amount of interest that Roby's will pay.

➥For tips on finding the solution, go to **marketingseries.glencoe.com**.

SELLING TO SALESPEOPLE

Leslie Haddon
Apparel Showroom Owner
Cole Haddon, Ltd.

What is your job?

"I function as the go-between for apparel manufacturers and boutique owners. This means that I show and sell products which come directly from apparel manufacturers to a network of retailers who purchase the items to sell in their boutiques."

What do you do in your job?

"My job involves a lot of travel and a lot of phone work. We are the Midwest representatives for our manufacturers, so I take all our collections on the road and show them to boutiques in a ten-state sales area."

What kind of training did you have?

"I graduated with a degree in fashion merchandise from the International Academy of Merchandise and Design in Chicago. I started out in retail. A good friend of mine, who was a buyer, helped get me a job in a showroom. I worked my way up from there."

What advice would you give students?

"Get an internship in either a manufacturer's showroom or an independent showroom like mine. This will give you a good idea of what the job involves. It's a fun job, but it's also a lot of work requiring long hours. You really need to love to sell and love clothes. You need to work hard and be determined. You also need a good attitude."

What's your key to success?

"This business is about keeping your manufacturers happy and your clients happy. In a competitive industry such as fashion, good relationships can make or break a business."

Why might an apparel company representative need to be aware of price levels?

Career Data: Retail Buyer/ Wholesale Representative

Education and Training
Associate degree or bachelor's degree

Skills and Abilities
Organizational, scheduling, sales, communication, and negotiation skills

Career Outlook Faster than average growth through 2012

Career Path Trainee, buyer, sales representative to account manager

ODD/EVEN PRICING Some retailers use additional pricing strategies, such as *odd pricing,* to set the retail price. For example, a fashion marketer selling a coat might calculate the retail price at $300. However, the retailer might ticket the coat at $299.99 because the price appears to be less expensive. This pricing method is a psychological strategy. To give the coat a prestigious image and attract a high-end market, a retailer may use *even pricing* and set the price higher at an even $300.

CONNECT

Do you respond to even or odd pricing when you want to buy a specific item?

Credit in the Fashion Industry

Offering good prices on fashion merchandise is an incentive for customers to buy merchandise. Facilitating the buying process by offering credit to customers can also increase business. Consumer credit enables consumers to receive merchandise immediately and pay for it later. Immediate response is very important in the world of fashion, because consumers want to wear the latest fashions when they become available in the retail stores. Fashion businesses may also offer credit to industry customers, such as designers, buyers, and retailers, in an attempt to increase sales. Fashion marketers use credit to develop their businesses.

Designers and Credit

Designers might establish credit as a source of funds to purchase new fabrics or to pay for market information from trend forecasting services. Designers may also need to hire workers to complete a line. New expensive tools, such as computer-aided design equipment, might also be purchased on credit, allowing the designer to use modern technology now and pay for it later when profits are realized.

Manufacturers and Credit

Business credit, or trade credit, is very similar to consumer credit. A manufacturer purchases materials, such as fabric, from a supplier. The supplier invoices, or bills, the manufacturer for the fabric with specific terms of payment, such as 30 days or 60 days to pay from the date of purchase.

MANUFACTURER AND RETAIL BUYERS

Manufacturers also offer credit to retail buyers who purchase garments for their stores. Manufacturers typically accept a purchase order from a retail store when credit has been established. Amounts owned by the retailer are usually due in 30 to 60 days, depending on the terms of the purchase. Retailers that do not meet the terms of these agreements and do not pay manufacturers on time have difficulty obtaining credit in the future.

Retailers and Credit

Many retailers rely on credit to make other purchases for their businesses. Credit can be used to purchase merchandise, fixtures, and supplies. Purchasing these items with credit means the retailer can use available cash to pay other bills.

Case Study — PART 2

OFF-PRICE POWER
Continued from Part 1 on page 221

According to *Forbes* magazine, a failing economy at the end of the 1990s caused an increase of off-price shopping because consumers became less willing to pay full price at department stores. According to retail analyst Ed Nakfoor, "The stigma of (off-price) shopping is gone. People have programmed themselves to save wherever they can." T.J. Maxx has taken advantage of this trend by continuing to offer deep discounts and promote its stores.

In the face of competition from online off-price retailers, T.J. Maxx has limited its online activity to keyword advertising on search engines. Online customers steered to T.J. Maxx's Web site are encouraged not to shop online. Instead, the company wants customers to use the online store locators and sign up for e-mail notices. This marketing strategy is designed to keep people coming to the off-price retail store that delivers on its promise: "Brand names at discount prices." With 2004 sales at $13.3 billion, up 39 percent from 2000, it seems people are willing to shop at the store.

ANALYZE AND WRITE

1. Describe the type of prices at T.J. Maxx.
2. Do you think T.J. Maxx offers credit to customers? Research the answer on the Internet and write your answer.

QUESTION

List the items that retailers might purchase with credit?

Consumers and Credit

Stores also accept consumer credit cards from customers to increase the average purchase amount and increase overall sales. Consumers usually spend more money on fashion products when they can buy with credit instead of having to pay with cash. There are three types of consumer credit cards accepted by retail stores: third-party, proprietary, and private-label credit cards.

THIRD-PARTY CREDIT CARDS This type of credit card is the most widely used by consumers. Examples include MasterCard, Discover, American Express, and VISA.

PROPRIETARY CREDIT CARDS Many retailers offer their own credit cards imprinted with the store's name and logo. These cards are store-issued credit cards that are owned and managed by the retail company. This type of credit is beneficial to retailers because they can also send special mailings and include inserts in bills. For example, Old Navy can send coupons or information about a sale in the same envelope with a monthly bill. Stores can also gather customer information from the credit application for marketing purposes.

PRIVATE-LABEL CREDIT CARDS These consumer credit cards are imprinted with the store's name and logo, but they are issued and managed by a bank. Retailers benefit because they can also offer special mailings and bill inserts with monthly statements. In addition, the store's credit management problems are reduced because billing and administration are handled by a financial institution.

Quick Check

RESPOND to what you've read by answering these questions.

1. What are the five price levels of women's garments? _____
   _____
   _____
   _____

2. What are the four main considerations when establishing the price of a fashion product?
   _____
   _____
   _____

3. What are three types of consumer credit cards accepted by retailers? _____
   _____
   _____
   _____

Using Technology

Technology in the Fashion Industry

Advances in technology have had a major impact on the apparel industry. Technology affects textile production and apparel manufacturing, distribution, and retailing. **Computer-integrated manufacturing (CIM)** is the technological production process that combines two systems: CAD and CAM. Computer-aided design (CAD) is a computer system used for designing textiles, apparel, and other products. Computer-aided manufacturing (CAM) is electronically controlled production. Both forms of technology have dramatically advanced the fashion industry.

Communication and Technology

Each segment in the fashion industry has computer-related equipment developed specifically for the particular area of the industry. The most important technology involves communication systems that link the segments of the apparel industry together. Manufacturers must be able to respond to consumer and retailer demand quickly. Because so much garment production is done overseas, the industry must have technology that can manage information to global partners. For example, software programs must be able to convert U.S. measurements to metric-system measurements for a manufacturer in a foreign country. Various forms of technology have allowed the fashion industry to adapt quickly to change.

Textiles and Technology

The textile industry is one of America's largest manufacturing industries. Its success is critical to the economic well-being of the country. The fiber/textile/apparel (FTA) industry is considered one of the most productive in the world due to its application of sophisticated technology. Computer innovations have improved textile design and made manufacturing faster and more efficient. CAD and CAM technology has improved the quality of goods produced and has lowered production costs.

Textile Research and Development

CAD technology helps create innovations in designs, but original research and development plays an important role in creating innovations in textile technology. For example, new fabrics are designed to be more absorbent and quicker to dry.

AS YOU READ ...

YOU WILL LEARN
- To explain computer-integrated manufacturing.
- To describe inventory control and systems used in retail stores.

WHY IT'S IMPORTANT
Technology plays a critical role in all segments of the fashion industry. New technological advances improve the efficiency in the industry and help meet consumer demand.

KEY TERMS
- computer-integrated manufacturing (CIM)
- bar codes
- inventory control

computer-integrated manufacturing (CIM) the production process that implements various technological systems: computer-aided design (CAD) and computer-aided manufacturing (CAM)

PREDICT
Why should a store keep track of its inventory?

CONNECT

What fabric do you prefer for a bathing suit or swimming trunks? Why?

HIGH-PERFORMANCE FABRICS One of the most recent innovations in textiles is high-performance fabrics. These fabrics are made into garments used for action sports, such as skateboarding, surfing, and skiing. The garment producers for these sports products want fabrics that are durable and protective but allow the body to breathe.

FABRIC RESEARCH Sole Technology, Inc. (STI), is one company that targets these customers by selling through national, mall-based specialty retailers such as Pacific Sunwear of California (PacSun). The STI facility houses a biomechanics laboratory for studying the movement of the body during skateboarding and the impact of skateboard jumps on the body. To participate in STI studies, skateboarders suit up in outfits covered with infrared sensors. The participants then ride and jump across laboratory props in an urban skateboarding environment. The athletes' movements are captured by a computerized camera system that records pressure levels on different parts of their bodies as they move. The results of this type of research help STI produce fabric that is appropriate for garments worn for action sports.

Design and Technology

In the past, fashion designers hand-sketched designs that were converted to patterns and made into garments. Today designers use CAD equipment as a tool, like a paintbrush or a piece of charcoal, to draw their creations. Designers can use CAD to incorporate style, sizing, and component details about a collection and communicate this information to the production staff and retail buyers.

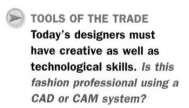

TOOLS OF THE TRADE
Today's designers must have creative as well as technological skills. *Is this fashion professional using a CAD or CAM system?*

International Cotton

Brazilian farmer Ronaldo Spirlandelli de Oliveria is part of a new wave of cotton growers in Brazil who benefited by the World Trade Organization (WTO) ruling in June 2004. The ruling stated that the U.S. government cotton-subsidies program violates international trade rules. The Brazilian complaint contended that the $3 billion in annual subsidies paid to American cotton growers leads to an increase in output and depresses global prices. This robs Brazil of potential export markets and undercuts the livelihood of Brazilian farmers.

Woody Anderson, chairman of the National Cotton Council in the United States, stated that U.S. cotton growers plan to appeal the ruling. He said that the U.S. cotton program is an important component of the agriculture policy of the United States and was designed to comply with WTO obligations.

Regardless of whether the ruling stands, cotton production is on the increase in Brazil. In 2004, Brazil harvested 1.38 million tons of cotton, more than twice as much as it had produced five years before.

How might the global price of cotton affect how prices of fashion goods are determined?

CAD Features

As mentioned in Chapter 8, CAD terminals can include sketch pads with electronic pens for drawing images into the computers. *Electronic graphics interchange* allows garment parts, colors, and prints to be changed by the computer so that designers can experiment with shapes, colors, textures, and fabrics. *3-D imaging* enables a designer to create a three-dimensional design that shows depth and form.

CAD is used by the fashion industry because of the need to create and produce fashions quickly. When a consumer sees a new style on TV or in a music video, he or she wants it immediately. These systems allow designers to react quickly to these demands. CAD enhances the creative process, shortens product-development time, and reduces costly mistakes.

Design to Pattern

Sometimes the designer creates the sketches and passes them on to the patternmakers. The patternmaker might finalize the sketch and even change some stitches or a construction line to make a better garment. Software allows the patternmaker to zoom in on specific parts of the garment and provide more details for the production staff. Existing images, such as previous drawings or fabric patterns, are scanned into the system using a scanner that can read an image on paper and enter it into the computer. Thus, precise patterns are ready to be used in the manufacturing phase of fashion creation.

Manufacturing and Technology

High-tech computer technology and equipment have significantly changed the apparel-production industry. In addition to CAD systems, garment producers use CAM systems. These systems include a variety of equipment:

- Patternmaking equipment

- Computerized, programmable sewing machines

- Automatic workstation units to perform multiple sewing tasks

- Robotics, or machinery programmed to do mechanical tasks

New Technology

Garment producers, such as Haggar Clothing Company, now use 3-D imaging software that is similar to software used by designers. Information about fabric characteristics, such as its thickness and weight, is fed into a CAD system. This software allows the manufacturer to apply the fabric qualities to 3-D mannequins, or avatars. Garment producers can see the end result before patterns are cut and garments sewn together. They can make changes and corrections without the cost of making samples. Producers can then show the *virtual* samples to retail buyers. The goal of all segments of the industry is to make a profit. With less cost involved, the garment producer can make more money.

QUESTION

What is a virtual sample?

Trade Shows and Technology

The fashion industry is continually introducing new equipment which is usually exhibited at trade shows, such as the American Apparel and Footwear Association Conference. At these exhibitions innovative machinery and equipment, new fabric findings, and information technology are presented. As a result of new technology and automation, manufacturers have lower production costs, higher-quality goods, and faster turnaround time. In fact, technology has improved other processes in the fashion industry, including retail sales transactions.

Retailers and Technology

Going to New York City on a buying trip is considered one of the perks of being a retail apparel buyer. Depending on the market, apparel buyers visit New York City from three to five times per year, making the rounds at garment district showrooms. Because New York City is an expensive travel destination, the buyer's overhead increases due to buying trips. However, in order to reduce costs, buyers are exploring Internet technology that can help them browse design collections, place orders, and streamline the business of fashion without travel. Video conferencing is also widely used.

Figure 11.2

Bar Code

ISBN 0-07-830599-3

9 780078 305993

90000>

BUYING CODE This Universal Product Code translates to information about a fashion product, which helps retailers keep the most popular items in stock. *What other products use bar codes on their merchandise tickets?*

Cost-Effective Technology

Though technology might seem expensive, it is actually very cost effective. Expenses can be saved due to less employee time and less company travel. In addition, more people can participate in the decision-making process, and response time is improved.

Retail Operations and Technology

Retail operations have benefited from technology and software development. As a result of management software, retailers can more accurately record sales and maintain merchandise stock levels. These systems can mark merchandise tickets, using a code printer, and record a sales transaction by electronically reading bar codes on tags.

BAR CODES Bar codes are standardized symbols made up of dark vertical bars and white spaces that carry information such as vendor, style, size, and color. Codes are printed onto machine-readable merchandise tickets or labels. Bar codes are used throughout the fashion industry on raw materials, parts going through production, shipping containers, and finished products for sale to consumers. The *Universal Product Code (UPC)* is the most familiar bar code and has been endorsed by retailers as the marking standard of the industry. (See **Figure 11.2**.) Electronic optical scanners read the bar codes and carry the information to a computer. Optical scanning wands and handheld laser readers are also used at retail checkout counters.

EPR Because consumers today want more selection, better quality, and faster service, retailers and manufacturers have developed new methods to handle consumer demand. The *Enterprise Resource Planning (ERP)* system extracts data from sales transactions in the retail store and enables the retailer to reorder merchandise on a timely basis. For example, a cash register scanner records the sale of the last size 15, blue, pin-striped shirt in stock. It can automatically place an order; then the factory can make another shirt in 28 minutes and ship it to the store by the end of the day.

TECH NOTES

Smart Tags

Radio frequency identification (RFID) offers many benefits to the fashion industry. An RFID tag contains a tiny computer chip and antenna. When the tag is attached to a product, the tag enables everyone to track the item as it moves through the supply chain. RFID tags may be used to provide retailers with information about customers, such as how often they visit a store and what they have bought in the past.

➡ Explain privacy issues related to RFID technology after reading the reference material at **marketingseries.glencoe.com**.

bar codes standardized symbols made up of dark vertical bars and white spaces that carry information such as vendor, style, size, and color

inventory control the process used to track the buying and storing of products for sale as well as costs for ordering, shipping, handling, and storage

INVENTORY-CONTROL SYSTEMS *Inventory,* or the supply of goods to be sold, represents a large investment to all segments of the fashion industry. It must be well managed to maximize profits for the business. **Inventory control** is the process used to track the buying and storing of products for sale as well as costs for ordering, shipping, handling, and storage. Software used by the industry includes programs that track merchandise, from the design and production stages to distribution to the retail store. Inventory control systems track when merchandise is received at the store. Specific details about each item at the store are also maintained in the system, such as items sold, returned, transferred to another store, damaged, or stolen.

RFID SYSTEMS Retailers, such as Wal-Mart and Target, require manufacturers to use *Radio Frequency Identification (RFID) Systems.* This system tags pallets and cases for automatic processing of merchandise shipments. It helps the retailer identify, track, and manage large quantities of goods as they move through the supply chain. Merchandise tagged with RFID can be tracked to its exact location. This enables companies to reduce warehousing and distribution costs through inventory control.

Internet Technology and Fashion

The use of the Internet has also impacted fashion marketers. As retailers began developing Web sites, they had to develop software that could respond to customer orders. In the past, stores believed that Internet sales would reduce in-store retail business. However, they have discovered that one type of channel supports the other. Customers look to the Internet to find options, and then go to the stores to purchase.

The Importance of Technology

Technology plays a critical role in all segments of the fashion industry. New technological advances continue to improve the efficiency of the industry in order to meet consumer demand.

Quick Check

RESPOND to what you've read by answering these questions.

1. What does 3-D imaging software do? _____

_____

2. What bar code is endorsed by retailers as the marking standard of the industry? _____

_____

3. What are some advantages of RFID systems? _____

_____

_____

Worksheet 11.1

Merchandising Fashion Apparel

Visit two different stores or departments within a department store. One store or department should carry better garments, and the other store or department should carry a budget line. Notice how the apparel is merchandised in each store or department. Compare and contrast the two stores or departments. Notice such things as lighting and the way the merchandise is laid out on tables or hung on racks. How many salespeople are there? Are you given more personal attention in one of the stores or departments?

Write your observations:

_____

_____

_____

_____

_____

_____

_____

_____

_____

_____

_____

_____

_____

_____

_____

_____

_____

_____

_____

_____

_____

_____

_____

Worksheet 11.2

Observing Trends in the Fashion Industry

When consumers see a trend on TV or in a music video, they may want it immediately. Computer-aided design (CAD) allows designers to quickly turn trends into ready-to-buy apparel. Over the next few weeks, notice how quickly a new style becomes available in stores.

Type of fashion apparel

_____

Date seen

_____

Seen on TV, music video,
awards show, other media

_____

Date apparel in store

_____

Type of fashion apparel

_____

Date seen

_____

Seen on TV, music video,
awards show, other media

_____

Date apparel in store

_____

Type of fashion apparel

_____

Date seen

_____

Seen on TV, music video,
awards show, other media

_____

Date apparel in store

_____

Type of fashion apparel

_____

Date seen

_____

Seen on TV, music video,
awards show, other media

_____

Date apparel in store

_____

TECHNOLOGY AND FASHION RETAILERS

Under each type of fashion retailer, list the types of technology each store might use.

Department Stores

_____

_____

_____

_____

_____

Specialty Stores

_____

_____

_____

_____

_____

Boutiques

_____

_____

_____

_____

_____

Designer Stores

_____

_____

_____

_____

_____

Outlets

_____

_____

_____

_____

_____

Discount Stores

_____

_____

_____

_____

_____

Mail Order

_____

_____

_____

_____

_____

Online Shopping

_____

_____

_____

_____

_____

Add this page to your career portfolio.

CHAPTER SUMMARY

Section 11.1 Pricing and Credit

selling price (p. 222)
better garments (p. 222)
moderate lines (p. 222)
budget lines (p. 222)
cost of product (p. 223)
operating expenses
   (p. 223)
markup (p. 224)

- The five price levels of fashion apparel include: couture, bridge lines, better garments, moderate lines, and budget lines.

- Besides costs of manufacturing, fashion makers consider certain factors when determining price: achieving the most profit, obtaining the most sales volume, being competitive, and presenting an image.

- Manufacturers use credit to purchase materials, such as fabric, from a supplier. They also offer credit to retailers who buy from them.

- Retail stores offer three basic types of credit: third-party credit, proprietary credit, and private-label credit.

Section 11.2 Using Technology

computer-integrated
   manufacturing (CIM)
   (p. 229)
bar codes (p. 233)
inventory control
   (p. 234)

- Computer-integrated manufacturing (CIM) is the production process that implements various technological systems: computer-aided design (CAD), a computer system used for designing textiles, apparel, and other products; and computer-aided manufacturing (CAM), which is electronically controlled production.

- Inventory must be well managed to maximize profits for a business. Inventory control is the process used to track the buying and storing of products for sale as well as costs for ordering, shipping, handling, and storage. Computer systems are used to track merchandise, from the design and production stages to distribution to the retail store.

CHECKING CONCEPTS

1. **List** the price levels of fashion apparel.
2. **Name** the price level of apparel sold in discount department stores.
3. **Identify** considerations for pricing.
4. **Explain** how textile makers use credit.
5. **Identify** the type of credit that stores offer that is handled by a bank.
6. **Describe** the technology used in retailing.
7. **List** types of information included in a bar code.

Critical Thinking
8. **Explain** the advantages of RFID technology.

CROSS-CURRICULUM SKILLS

Work-Based Learning

Personal Qualities—Self-Esteem

9. How would self-esteem help someone who sells couture-priced clothing?

Interpersonal Skills—Serving Clients/Customers

10. Design a poster that illustrates to stores and to their customers the benefits of using a Universal Product Code (UPC).

School-Based Learning

Math

11. You buy athletic shoes for $50 wholesale. You then use a keystone markup to set the price. What is the retail price?

Arts

12. As a class, design a mural about credit: how credit is used, ways to use credit, and ways credit can cause trouble.

Role Play: Sales Manager, Retail Chain

SITUATION You are to assume the role of sales manager for a large international retail chain. Your store carries a line of high-quality clothing and accessories for men and women. Computers link all of the stores' inventories. This enables a sales associate (judge) to locate a specific style or color for a customer from any store worldwide. You have just taken a phone call from a customer (judge) who is frantically searching for a dress. The only size in stock at her local store did not fit. The customer (judge) is upset because the sales associate did not offer to help the customer (judge).

ACTIVITY You have decided to conduct a class about customer service and the use of a computer network to find the correct size and color garment for each customer.

EVALUATION You will be evaluated on how well you meet the following performance indicators:

- Demonstrate a customer-service mindset.
- Handle customer inquiries.
- Use a database for information analysis.
- Explain the role of customer service in positioning/image.
- Conduct training class/program.

INTERNET ACTIVITY

Click on the Web site for Fashion CAD to learn more about patternmaking with this type of CAD.

- Read about the benefits of Fashion CAD.
- Write a fact sheet about Fashion CAD and how it is used in patternmaking.

➡️ For a link to a Web site to help you do this activity, go to marketingseries.glencoe.com.

Chapter 12

Promoting Fashion

Chapter Objectives

- Explain the purpose of visual merchandising in the fashion industry.
- Describe the display areas of a store.
- Identify the design elements of displays.
- Explain the four components of the promotional mix.
- Describe a fashion promotion plan.
- Discuss how designers and manufacturers use branding and licensing.

BROADCAST STYLE

Style Network was created by E! Entertainment as a cable channel dedicated to high fashion. The original concept focused on designer clothes, supermodels, and fashion trends. However, the Style Network did not attract much of an audience. Gavin Harvey, Senior Vice President of Marketing for E! Entertainment says, "Marketing to consumers [on cable TV] is relentlessly difficult. We win or lose every day." Style Network was losing. Viewers were not connecting with the exclusive-designer programming.

Then in 2002, the E! Channel transformed its brand and programming to appeal to a wider demographic audience. It worked. The year 2003 was E!'s most-watched year ever, with almost 85 million viewers. Would similar re-branding and re-programming help the Style Network attract more viewers while promoting the world of fashion?

ANALYZE AND WRITE

1. Do programs about fashion appeal to all viewers? Write a paragraph explaining your answer.
2. Why is Style Network an important medium for promoting fashion? Write a paragraph explaining your answer.

Case Study Part 2 on page 253

POWER READ

Be an active reader and use these reading strategies:

PREDICT what the section will be about.

CONNECT what you read with your life.

QUESTION as you read to make sure you understand the content.

RESPOND to what you've read.

Visual Merchandising and Display

AS YOU READ ...

YOU WILL LEARN

- To explain the purpose of visual merchandising in the fashion industry.
- To describe the display areas of a store.
- To identify the design elements of displays.

WHY IT'S IMPORTANT

Visual merchandising uses various techniques and fixtures to showcase merchandise and promote a positive image of a fashion store. The elements of visual merchandising can be applied to a variety of themes to promote interest and increase sales.

KEY TERMS

- visual merchandising
- display
- fixtures

PREDICT

What is the purpose of a display?

visual merchandising the integrated look of an entire store

display a presentation of merchandise to attract customers so they will examine it and buy it

Visual Merchandising for Customers

Visual merchandising has existed since retail vendors began selling merchandise to customers. Vendors arrange goods to be more attractive to promote sales. For example, a farmer puts the biggest and ripest apples on top of the basket for consumers to see and touch, just as fashion merchandisers put complete outfits together and use mannequins as models so customers can visualize wearing the clothing.

Visual Merchandising Today

Today visual merchandising is very sophisticated. **Visual merchandising** is the integrated look of an entire store. All the physical elements in a place of business are coordinated to project the right image to customers. For example, imagine shopping during the holiday season and seeing colorful, festive decorations along with holiday fashions lining the aisles of your favorite store.

The Role of Display

Fashion marketers strive to present or display merchandise to grab customers' attention and increase sales. A **display** is a presentation of merchandise to attract customers so they will examine it and buy it. Most displays present the visual and artistic aspects of a product to target a specific group of customers. Through visual merchandising, stores communicate their fashion message to customers every day.

Creating Visual Merchandising

The goal of effective visual merchandising is to sell goods by promoting the store image and creating a positive shopping experience for the customer. Retail stores use four display areas to achieve this goal:

- Storefront
- Store layout
- Store interior
- Interior displays

The Storefront

The *storefront,* or exterior of a store, gives the first impression of a store. Exterior visual merchandising features include:

- Signs
- Marquees
- Entrances
- Window displays

Window Displays

Stores located in malls generally do not have traditional front window displays. Free-standing stores, such as Saks Fifth Avenue in New York City, present elaborate displays. The holiday window displays at Saks are a major tourist attraction each year. Visitors to the city line up around the block to view the spectacular presentations. For example, one year Calvin Klein produced a window display that featured Santa Claus wearing a leather jacket while sitting on a motorcycle, which was suspended from the ceiling.

The Store Layout

Inside the store, the *store layout* is the arrangement of floor space in order to promote sales of fashion products. The customer should be able to walk through the store and easily view the merchandise. There are several standard layouts: free-flow, spine, loop, and grid layouts. (See **Figure 12.1** on page 244.) Visual merchandisers help determine the best location for each fashion product.

The Store Interior

Several other visual merchandising techniques are used inside of the store, or *store interior:*

- Lighting
- Color schemes
- Store fixtures

Interior Displays

Interior or *in-store* displays are a critical part of the general store interior. Visual excitement is created by using:

- Space design
- Fixtures and hardware
- Mannequins
- Floor and wall coverings
- In-store signage

TECH NOTES

Whispering Windows™
Fashion retailers can add sound effects to storefront window displays with new technology that turns large, flat surfaces into giant speaker systems. Two small transducers, about the size of hockey pucks, attach to the window and convert audio signals into vibrations. The transducers are made of "smart metals" that expand and contract when they receive certain types of electrical stimulation. The vibrations distribute across the surface of the window and broadcast music, advertising messages, and sound effects to customers.

➡ List three ways that Whispering Windows benefits fashion retailers after reading information through *marketingseries.glencoe.com.*

CONNECT

What exterior store feature gets your attention the most: signs, marquees, entrances, or window displays?

Figure 12.1

Types of Layout

INTERIOR DESIGNS The layout for a fashion store should encourage customers to move easily as they see all the merchandise. *What type of layout might be appropriate for a discount fashion store? Why?*

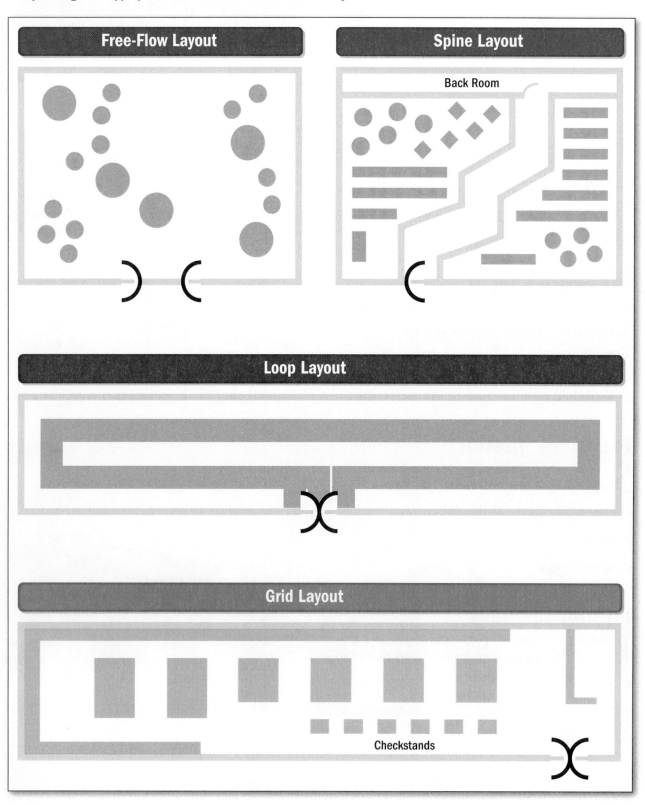

Free-Flow Layout

Spine Layout

Back Room

Loop Layout

Grid Layout

Checkstands

Display Styles

Different stores allow various degrees of flexibility and creativity in visual display styles. Stores such as the Gap adhere to specific guidelines for their display presentations. These guidelines may include diagrams illustrating what merchandise is to be used and how it is to be presented. Visual merchandisers for high-end specialty stores, such as Neiman Marcus, have more flexibility in creating their displays. They might use ornate props or special lighting to feature merchandise.

Display Staff

Retail stores have staffs of people responsible for displaying the merchandise in the store. In larger operations, such as Dillard's department stores or the Gap, a regional merchandise director works with buyers to develop visual presentations that are forwarded to the in-store display personnel. Smaller stores have display teams.

Design Elements of Display

Visual merchandisers focus their efforts on everything from designing the visual floor plan of the store to the well-dressed mannequins that grace the selling floor. No matter what type of retail environment, visual display personnel generally use three design elements to create displays. These elements are *color, lighting,* and *harmony.* Harmony is achieved through the use of balance, proportion, rhythm, and emphasis. All the elements give the store a personality and image.

Fashion Display Themes

Visual merchandisers use the display elements when developing their fashion or merchandising themes. A theme gives a store focus and provides a consistent look within the store and within a group of stores. For example, a department store with several locations wants customers to see the same theme displayed in all the stores.

Theme Planning

Themes are planned well in advance. Calendars are developed to coordinate the implementation of visual presentations. The themes can vary and are centered on ideas and events such as:

- Recent or upcoming events
- Cultural activities
- Historical events
- Store promotions
- Seasonal color palettes
- Current fashion trends

Sample Themes

A store may want to focus on a dominant color theme for the season. Display designers would feature merchandise in that color throughout the store or in the windows. Also, current fashion trends may inspire a theme-based display. For example, hip-hop stars DJ Funkmaster Flex, Birdman, and Jay-Z have a line of athletic footwear. This fashion trend might inspire an urban-themed display.

Style Point !

MANNEQUIN HISTORY
Established in 1885, Gems Wax Models was one of the first suppliers of mannequins for stores. Made of wax, wood, or heavy fabric, these life-size dolls were expensive at $15 each. By the turn of the century, mannequins were the center of a new industry called "display," which would become visual merchandising. The first known book about visual merchandising was written by L. Frank Baum, author of *The Wizard of Oz,* in which he devoted a chapter to the importance of mannequins for attracting customers.

QUESTION
Why are themes used for visual displays?

Diamonds on Display

Few people think of Canada when they think of the elegant diamond. Yet Canada's diamond industry has become a $1.7 billion business. All indicators point to continuing growth. Although diamond exploration in Canada began during the 1960s, it was not until the 1980s that the first kimberlite was discovered. Kimberlite is the stone that contains diamonds. The first deposit was discovered in 1991 in the Lac de Gras area of Canada's Northwest Territories. By 1999, that mine produced one million carats of diamonds.

In January 2003, a second mine began production with a life expectancy of 20 years. Five percent of the world's future diamond supply may come from the second mine, totaling six to eight million carats a year. (A carat is a unit of weight equaling 0.007 ounce.) By 2007, Canada will be the third largest producer of diamonds used by jewelers around the world to create everything from elegant Tiffany tiaras to simple friendship rings.

Describe a visual display and fixtures in a retail store using the theme of Canadian diamonds. Describe the type of store and the location of the display in the store.

Types of Stores and Themes

The overall store image greatly influences its visual merchandising. For example, home furnishing stores use themes and present goods so customers will purchase them. Visual merchandisers will group merchandise such as pictures, floral arrangements, dinnerware, and table linens as they coordinate colors, fabrics, and styles. This is referred to as "life styling." These kinds of displays appear during seasons such as Thanksgiving when the home décor presentations use fall colors. PacSun stores have a distinct overall store image. The visual presentations are directed to a young, active market of customers. The merchandise is orderly but presented in a free-spirited way. Visual merchandising can influence how shoppers feel about being in a retail space. The longer they stay, the more likely they are to buy.

Fixtures

fixtures permanent or movable store furnishings that are used to hold or display merchandise

Fixtures are permanent or movable store furnishings that are used to hold or display merchandise. Display cases, counters, shelving, racks, benches, and tables are examples of fixtures.

Required Fixtures

Some vendors, such as Liz Claiborne and Ralph Lauren, require that stores present their merchandise on special fixtures that display the designer name. An agreement may be made between the retailer and a vendor to purchase the special fixtures. Manufacturers such as Levi Strauss use the Internet to show retail merchants the required display racks and how many garments should be placed on each rack.

FIRST IMPRESSION, BEST IMPRESSION The store window is the first thing customers see. Good displays can draw people inside the store. *Do you prefer simple or elaborate window displays? Why?*

Other Fixtures

Other types of display fixtures include mannequins, platforms, ladders, poles, and special equipment or props for jewelry and accessories. These types of fixtures are not meant to hold quantities of merchandise but to highlight merchandise and themes.

Importance of Visual Merchandising

A visual merchandiser's challenge is to inform the target customer about the store and its image. Clear communication is the key to visual merchandising success. Visual merchandising promotes the image and merchandise of a fashion business, as do promotion and advertising discussed in the next section.

Quick Check ✓

RESPOND to what you've read by answering these questions.

1. What are the four key display areas in a store?_____
   _____
   _____

2. What are the types of fixtures used in retail stores?_____
   _____
   _____

3. What are the common themes used in visual merchandising?_____
   _____
   _____

Fashion Advertising and Promotion

AS YOU READ ...

YOU WILL LEARN

- To explain the four components of the promotional mix.
- To describe a fashion promotion plan.
- To discuss how designers and manufacturers use branding and licensing.

WHY IT'S IMPORTANT

As part of the marketing mix, promotion is used in the fashion industry to inform, persuade, and increase sales.

KEY TERMS

- promotion
- promotional mix
- sales promotion
- fashion shows
- public relations
- publicity
- advertising
- fashion promotion plan
- brand
- licensing

PREDICT

How might advertising differ from public relations?

promotion any form of communication a business uses to inform, persuade, or remind people about its products or to enhance its image

Promotion and the Promotional Mix

Promotion is any form of communication a business uses to inform, persuade, or remind people about its products or to enhance its image. It is a component of the marketing mix.

Promotional Mix and Fashion

The **promotional mix** is any combination of the four components of promotion:

- Sales promotion
- Public relations and publicity
- Advertising
- Personal selling

Each component plays a critical role in promoting fashion businesses and their products. Sales promotion, public relations and publicity, and advertising are all forms of non-personal selling, which is indirect communication with customers. As discussed in Chapter 11, personal selling requires direct contact with the customer. It can take place in any of the fashion industry segments. It is the final stage of a sale after the customer has been prompted by sales promotion, public relations and publicity, or advertising. Fashion marketers decide on the promotional mix that will be most effective.

Sales Promotion

One component of the promotional mix is sales promotion. **Sales promotion** is a short-term incentive used to interest customers in buying products. Companies in every segment of the textile and apparel industries promote their fashion products to each other and to their customers. There are two main types of sales promotion— trade promotion and consumer promotion.

Trade Promotion

Trade promotion occurs within the industry. A business directs this promotion to the next segment in the distribution chain. For example, fiber and fabric companies promote their textiles to apparel designers and manufacturers. Apparel manufacturers promote their styles and lines to retailers. Trade promotion includes activities such as trade shows and conventions. Manufacturers may provide retailers with photographs for displays or videotapes for sales training.

Consumer Promotion

Consumer promotion is used by manufacturers and retailers and is directly targeted to the consumer. Though they do not sell directly to consumers, textile and apparel manufacturers may use consumer promotion to get recognition for their lines. For example, the cotton textile industry, represented by Cotton Incorporated, promotes the benefits of apparel made with cotton to consumers.

Other examples of consumer promotions include:

- Fashion shows

- Special appearances by designers

- Trunk shows (a complete collection shown at a store for a limited time)

- Contests

- Sales

- Premiums

- Free samples

- Free services (such as makeovers)

- Coupons

- E-mail offers

The Role of Fashion Shows

Fashion shows are special theatrical events with live models presenting fashion apparel and accessories. Like the other promotional activities, fashion shows can be targeted to different audiences. New lines of couture-designer collections are shown to selected customers and the press. Apparel manufacturers will present shows featuring their lines to retail buyers. Consumer fashion shows are hosted by retailers at the beginning of a fashion season to showcase new merchandise and the latest fashions to their customers. Fashion shows can range from high-dollar productions to simple shows in retail stores. (See **Appendix 2** for sample forms for planning a fashion show.)

Public Relations and Publicity

Public relations is a promotional technique that uses any form of communication to create a positive image for the business. The exposure and goodwill generated by public relations is valuable because they may promote sales and create a good image. For example, fashion businesses and marketers often get involved with non-profit organizations and community service activities. These activities may range from hosting various events, such as fashion shows, to raising funds for charities. Revlon sponsors the Run/Walk for cancer research and programs each year. Companies spend money on these functions, though there is no guarantee of a customer purchase because such activities are a form of public relations.

ETHICS & ISSUES

Bogus Popularity

The "link popularity" of a particular Web site is determined by the number of other Web sites providing a link to it. Search engines, such as Yahoo, give the more popular links a higher ranking. The popular sites pop up faster when someone searches for a product. Retailers want to be at the top of the link list when a customer uses a search engine. When setting up Web sites, retailers carefully choose the right key words—and pay other popular sites to link to them. However, *link spamming* is a way of artificially increasing the popularity of a link. Link spammers use mass e-mails that include links to their sites to make them appear more popular. *Do you think link spamming is ethical even though it is not illegal. Why or why not?*

promotional mix any combination of the four components of promotion: sales promotion, public relations and publicity, advertising, and personal selling

sales promotion a short-term incentive used to interest customers in buying products

fashion shows special events that are theatrical with live models presenting fashion apparel and accessories

public relations a promotional technique that uses any form of communication to create a positive image for the business

publicity any non-paid message that communicates information about a company's merchandise, services, and activities

advertising a paid message that a business sends about its fashion products or ideas

Publicity

Publicity is a form of public relations. **Publicity** is any non-paid message that communicates information about a company's merchandise, services, and activities. From designers promoting their latest lines to retailers announcing store openings, all fashion professionals use publicity to get their messages out to the public. One method involves *press releases,* which are written as news stories sent out to newspapers and magazines. People tend to believe news stories more than advertisements, because they seem more credible. Fashion businesses, however, do not have control over the publicity they receive.

Advertising

As part of the promotional mix, **advertising** is a paid message that a business sends about its fashion products or ideas. It is the most widely visible and well-recognized element of the promotional mix and represents the largest part of a fashion business's promotional budget. The purpose of advertising is to inform, remind, and persuade. The acronym AIDA is used to describe advertising—attention, interest, desire, and action. An advertisement is designed to attract attention, develop interest, create desire, and produce action. Retailers generally advertise specific styles. Designers and manufacturers might promote their overall image instead of a special style because styles change so quickly.

Promotional and Institutional Advertising

There are two main categories of advertising—promotional and institutional. *Promotional advertising* in the fashion industry is designed to increase sales, introduce new products, explain product features and benefits, and support selling efforts. *Institutional advertising* is designed to create a favorable impression and goodwill for a fashion business. This type of advertising focuses on the image of a fashion business rather than a specific fashion product.

Types of Advertising Media

Advertising media include different types of media by which the message gets to the consumer. Media can be grouped into four categories:

- Print media

- Broadcast media

- Online media

- Specialty media

PRINT MEDIA *Print media* include in-home media such as magazines, newspapers, direct mail (newsletters, letters, brochures, catalogs, circulars, and invitations to events), directory advertising (telephone books and association publications). Out-of-home print media include outdoor advertising (billboards) and transit advertising (ads placed in buses, bus stations, train stations, airports).

- **Magazines**—Fashion magazines are targeted to specific target markets. Because of their high cost, they are used by large retailers and manufacturers with a national or global presence. Magazines are a good choice for many fashion businesses because of the beautiful color, detail, and creative possibilities. They have a long shelf life because most magazines are published monthly, and information does not go out of date immediately. They have high *pass-along readership,* which means the magazines are read for longer periods of time and are shared with several readers. However, magazines involve extensive preparation and have long lead times, meaning they must be prepared well in advance of the publication date.

- **Newspapers**—The newspaper print medium is the most common advertising vehicle for local retailers. The ad cost is lower than the cost for magazines, and the lead time is shorter. The response rate is easy to monitor because retailers can assess sales earned for the day or week when ads run. Newspapers are not as well targeted as magazines. Also, they do not use the same high-quality color reproduction techniques.

- **Directory advertising**—Another form of print advertising is directory advertising. For example, fashion businesses post advertisements in telephone directories such as the *Yellow Pages*. Retail businesses also list store names and addresses in the white pages. In addition, advertisements are placed in trade association directories, which are published annually. Fashion manufacturers, textile companies, designers, retailers, and other related businesses advertise and list contact information in these directories that are distributed within the fashion industry.

- **Direct mail**—Direct mail includes catalogs, newsletters, mailers, and bill enclosures mailed directly to customers' homes. Mailing lists may be comprised of current customers, such as those with a store's credit card. Retailers can also buy or develop lists based on the desired characteristics of potential customers. Direct mail is an effective way to reach a specific segment of the population.

THE Electronic CHANNEL

On the Wire

A wire service is a news organization that provides breaking news. These days wire services have gone online to provide instant breaking-news headlines around the world. The same current information about news and events in the fashion world is also online. Celebrity and designer news are broadcast from fashion centers around the globe. Highlights of international fashion shows and fashion events are sent instantaneously to newsrooms and broadcasters.

➡ Visit online fashion wire services and list some fashion stories and headlines posted through **marketingseries.glencoe.com**.

ADVERTISING COSTS

The Beauty Bar Salon spends 4 percent of its net profit on advertising. Net profit is $56,000. What is its advertising cost?

➡ For tips on finding the solution, go to **marketingseries.glencoe.com**.

OPENING DOORS TO DESIGN

Ian Gerard
Founder
GenArt

In 1994, with help from his brother Stefan, Ian Gerard founded GenArt. A nonprofit arts organization, Genart's goal is to promote new talent in the fields of art, film, and fashion. Ian Gerard has showcased approximately 1,000 artists, including 300 fashion designers.

What kind of training did he have?

Gerard graduated from New York University School of Law. He started GenArt while still at school, running the company out of his dorm room. He says that the venture was created to serve many emerging artists and designers who were struggling to find venues for their work: "In 1993, there was a big economic recession, and art galleries were not taking risks with young artists." Gerard started by holding gallery showings and eventually expanded into film and fashion showcases as corporate sponsorship increased. GenArt hosted the Fresh Faces of Fashion show during New York Fashion Week.

What is his key to success?

According to Gerard, GenArt's success was built on showing the average person that great art and design are accessible to those who are willing to buy from emerging artists. He says of his customers, "They were interested in art, but they would just go to the poster store and buy the same thing that everyone else had. They never understood that art by young artists, who were unknown, was not that much more expensive." He founded the company to bring artists, designers, collectors, and business people together.

How do companies such as GenArt help promote young fashion designers and their work?

Career Data: Fashion Promotor/ PR Agent

Education and Training
Bachelor's degree or master's degree in liberal arts, journalism, or communications

Skills and Abilities
Organizational, written, verbal, creative-thinking, and customer-service skills

Career Outlook Faster than average growth through 2012

Career Path Intern, account assistant, account manager to account executive

---

QUESTION

What are different types of print media used by the fashion industry?

- **Outdoor Advertising**—Billboards, transit ads, free-standing signs, and posters comprise outdoor advertising. The advertising messages run for a certain length of time. The location and content of these messages is very important. The advertisement must be placed in a location where it will be viewed by the target audience and be brief so it can be understood quickly.

BROADCAST MEDIA Television and radio advertising are forms of *broadcast media*. This type of media can be used to target specific audiences according to programming.

- **Television**—Television advertising uses a powerful combination of sound, color, and live-action effects to present a message. Although expensive, television advertising for fashion products can be effective. Television ads can target potential customers by TV viewing habits and preferences. For example, advertisers for teen clothes, makeup, or accessories may run commercials on television shows such as *Smallville* or on MTV shows.

- **Radio**—Radio broadcasts reach about 96 percent of people who are 12 years old and over. But advertising fashion products on the radio may not always be effective. It is difficult to present a fashion message without visuals. However, the ability of radio to reach a wide audience is very effective. Fashion marketers can select a specific radio station that matches their target market's listening habits and advertise items such as well-known clothing and fashion products. Radio advertising usually promotes sales and special events, such as fashion shows, contests, or celebrity appearances.

ONLINE MEDIA *Online media* advertising places advertising on the Internet. Popup ads and banner ads are two types of online ads. E-mail advertisement to potential and current customers is also a form of Internet advertising. Fashion companies use their own Web sites to promote the goods and services they provide. These businesses may also advertise on the Internet Web sites of other businesses or on home pages of Internet providers, such as AOL and Yahoo!. Subscribers see the ads when they log on to use the service.

SPECIALTY MEDIA *Specialty media* include special products such as magnets, calendars, and pens, which are imprinted with a company's name, address, or message. These items are usually given away at no charge to individuals or businesses within the trade. For example, in the fashion industry, manufacturers use these promotional items more often than do retailers. Fashion businesses and marketers include special media and other media for advertisement in fashion promotional plans and budgets.

Case Study — PART 2

BROADCAST STYLE

Continued from Part 1 on page 241

In 2003, Style Network transformed its brand and programming with a new line-up of programs that appealed to all tastes in style and fashion. E! Entertainment marketing and brand director Gavin Harvey noted, "People here understand the importance of establishing a brand. With Style, we want to tap into the vast audience that is fueling the industry of style, including fashion, beauty, and home entertainment." According to programming executive Stephen Schwartz, the goal of the reinvention was to create "a new generation of programming with real information that is practical, accessible, vibrant, and fun; programming that relates to the passion people have for their own sense of style." E! Executive Mark Sonneberg added, "Everyone has his or her own sense of style—and looks for help to create it."

The changes helped Style Network connect with viewers. The channel started out with only 7 million subscribers, but by the end of 2004, its roster included 45 million households that were following fashion.

ANALYZE AND WRITE

1. Why has Style Network's broader presentation of fashion and style attracted viewers? Write a paragraph explaining your answer.
2. In what ways can a TV channel devoted to fashion help promote individual fashion businesses? Write a paragraph explaining your answer.

Planning Fashion Promotion

fashion promotion plan
the detailed, written guide a business develops that states which promotional components will be used to reach specific goals in a designated period of time

A fashion business must plan carefully to effectively promote its product and image to customers. A **fashion promotion plan** is the detailed, written guide a business develops that states which promotional components will be used to reach specific goals in a designated period of time. The promotion plan outlines the organization, budget, preparation, and details of a promotional event. **Figure 12.2** highlights the key components of a fashion promotion plan and gives an example of each component.

Planning Schedules

Retail fashion marketers usually develop their promotional plans in six-month increments. These time periods are February through July and August through January. These periods coordinate with the merchandise buying plan schedules.

Figure 12.2

Fashion Promotion Plan

MAKING PLANS Most successful fashion businesses plan effective promotional strategies to sell their products. *Why would a business need to consider the section labeled "Evaluation and follow-up"?*

Plan Component	Example
1. Promotional goals and objectives	To promote junior sportswear during August and September to meet company sales goals
2. Message or theme	Back-to-School
3. Specific activities and timeline for when these should take place	Contest with a free $500 back-to-school wardrobe prize (August)
	In-store, back-to-school fashion show narrated by a popular radio DJ (September)
	Visual merchandising, with displays (August–September)
4. Type of media to be used	Newspaper advertising in local paper
	Free publicity on radio, due to station's involvement with the fashion show
5. Individual responsibilities	Buyer to coordinate with store and fashion merchandisers
6. Spending budget	Costs of contest, fashion show, advertising, display materials, and additional personnel
7. Evaluation and follow-up	Will measure sales of junior sportswear during promotional period

Licensed to Sell

How does a brand go from a million-dollar company to a billion-dollar company? It gets licensed through Cherokee®. The fashion company Cherokee opened its doors in 1973 as a manufacturer of women's shoes. The shoe business prospered, and Cherokee became a nationwide brand. Robert Margolis took over the company in 1981 and expanded the company to include apparel and accessories.

Then in 1996, the company radically changed directions. At that time, increasing numbers of companies, such as Gap, manufactured and sold their own clothes, eliminating the need for whole-sale manufacturers. Cherokee recognized this shift as a threat to its continuing business and turned to a new business model. The company closed its costly manufacturing and distribution units. Then they focused on licensing their brand to large retailers who would do the manufacturing and promotion for them.

NAME-BRAND SUCCESS

Since the switch, Cherokee has surged forward. Sales skyrocketed from $150 million to $2 billion in under four years. The company also acquired other brands, including Side Out and Carol Little, which are licensed alongside Cherokee. The company has successfully placed these brands with leading companies in Canada, Europe, and Japan.

In addition to licensing its own brands, Cherokee has profited from helping others. In 2000, the company brokered a billion-dollar deal for the Mossimo brand to be licensed to Target stores. Cherokee received 15 percent of Mossimo's revenues from Target stores, while Mossimo expanded its customer base. Both companies benefited from the wide reach and generous advertising budget that Target could provide. In turn, Target benefited by having designer labels that would attract young, brand-conscious shoppers.

1. How has a large retailer such as Target helped promote fashion brands such as Cherokee?
2. What well-known fashion brands do you think would sell at Target? Why?

Promotional Budgets

Advertising and promotional activities cost money. To pay for those promotional activities, fashion businesses set aside a portion of their business budgets for promotion. The promotional budget can be a percentage of the business's net sales. That percentage is usually between 5 and 10 percent. If there are more net sales, then there is more money for promotion.

Fashion Branding and Licensing

A consistent promotional message must be used to develop a brand image. A **brand** is a name, design, or symbol (or combination of them) that identifies a business or organization and its products. In fashion, *brand building* refers to the creation of an identity or image for a fashion product. For example, retailers carry name-brand merchandise because of its quality, availability, and potential for profit.

brand a name, design, or symbol (or combination of them) that identifies a business or organization and its products

Private-Label Brands

Private-label merchandise is merchandise that is produced to the exact specifications of a retailer and includes the store's own trademark or brand name. The store has control over the manufacturing and the retailing functions, and often becomes known for that brand. The Arizona line of clothing is a private label sold by J.C. Penney.

Licensing

licensing a legal agreement that gives manufacturers the exclusive right to produce and promote fashion products that display the name of a designer

At some point, a designer or manufacturer may decide to let others use its brand name. This is known as a *licensing* agreement. **Licensing** is a legal agreement that gives manufacturers the exclusive right to produce and promote fashion products that display the name of a designer. The designer receives royalties, or a percentage dollar amount of wholesale sales. Licensing allows designers to promote their names with limited risk. Designers of apparel and other fashion products license their names or logos to various manufacturers for a wide range of products, including home furnishings, perfume, eyeglasses, and footwear.

Promotion and Fashion Marketing

Fashion marketers choose the promotional mix that will be most effective in persuading potential customers to purchase a company's fashion products. Tools such as fashion promotion plans help define promotional goals and the strategies to achieve them.

Quick Check ✓

RESPOND to what you've read by answering these questions.

1. What are four types of advertising media? _____

_____

_____

_____

2. What is publicity? _____

_____

_____

_____

3. What is the difference between trade and consumer promotion? _____

_____

_____

_____

Worksheet 12.1

Observing Visual Merchandising

Visit three different types of fashion stores in your community. What attracts or bothers you about the visual merchandising in the store? Write your comments below.

Store #1:

Name of store:

_____

What attracts me about the visual merchandising?

_____

_____

What bothers me about the visual merchandising?

_____

_____

Store #2:

Name of store:

_____

What attracts me about the visual merchandising?

_____

_____

What bothers me about the visual merchandising?

_____

_____

Store #3:

Name of store:

_____

What attracts me about the visual merchandising?

_____

_____

What bothers me about the visual merchandising?

_____

_____

Worksheet 12.2

Observing the Promotional Mix

Choose a favorite fashion apparel store. Visit the store at least twice to learn about in-store promotions and personal selling. Over the next week, collect information about the different forms of promotion this store uses, such as:

- Newspaper and magazine ads
- Articles about the store or its personnel
- Television and radio ads
- Fashion shows
- Direct mailings
- Other types of publicity, promotions, and advertisements

Record your findings below.

Types of Promotion:

_____

_____

_____

_____

_____

_____

_____

_____

_____

_____

_____

_____

_____

_____

_____

_____

_____

Attach this page to an envelope filled with the promotional materials that you collect.

Portfolio Works

YOUR PROMOTIONAL PLAN

You are in charge of marketing a line of beachwear for high school and college students. Use the space below to write your promotional plan. Use the plan on page 254 as a model.

1. Promotional goals and objectives	
2. Message or theme	
3. Specific activities and timeline for when these should take place	
4. Type of media to be used	
5. Individual responsibilities	
6. Spending budget	
7. Evaluation and follow-up	

Add this page to your career portfolio.

CHAPTER SUMMARY

Section 12.1 Visual Merchandising and Display

visual merchandising
(p. 242)
display (p. 242)
fixtures (p. 246)

- Visual merchandising is the integrated look of an entire store. Effective visual merchandising sells fashion goods through promoting the store image and creating a positive experience for customers.

- The display areas of a store include the storefront, store layout, store interior, and interior displays.

- Good displays use various design elements: color, lighting, and harmony.

Section 12.2 Fashion Advertising and Promotion

promotion (p. 248)
promotional mix
(p. 248)
sales promotion (p. 248)
fashion shows (p. 249)
public relations (p. 249)
publicity (p. 250)
advertising (p. 250)
fashion promotion plan
(p. 254)
brand (p. 255)
licensing (p. 256)

- The four components of the promotional mix used by fashion marketers are: sales promotion, public relations and publicity, advertising, and personal selling.

- A fashion promotion plan is a detailed, written guide that a business develops. The plan states which promotional components will be used to reach specific goals in a designated period of time.

- Designers and manufacturers use branding to identify their particular business and products, creating an image for a line of apparel. Designers and manufacturers license their names and logos to promote their names and receive royalties.

CHECKING CONCEPTS

1. **Identify** one reason that stores use visual merchandising.
2. **Explain** the goal of visual merchandising.
3. **Identify** the visual merchandising features of a storefront.
4. **Describe** types of store layouts.
5. **List** the key design elements of displays.
6. **Identify** the four components of the promotional mix.
7. **Define** a fashion promotion plan.

Critical Thinking

8. **Discuss** the concept and importance of brand building for fashion businesses.

CROSS-CURRICULUM SKILLS

Work-Based Learning

Thinking Skills—Knowing How to Learn

9. With another student, make an outline of the information in this chapter. Exchange your outline with another pair of students. Make notes on each other's outline and return outlines.

Information—Organizing and Maintaining Information

10. Contact the local newspaper and radio and television stations to find out their ad costs. As a class, make a wall chart of pros and cons of different media advertising and their costs.

School-Based Learning

Arts

11. Use poster board and art supplies to design the front area of an apparel store. Display the designs in class.

Social Studies

12. Use the Internet or library to research and list three themes of other countries that can be used for visual merchandising.

Role Play: Promotions Manager

SITUATION You are to assume the role of promotions manager in the sales office of a quality clothing manufacturer. You are training an intern (judge) in your department. The intern (judge) has been working on advertisements for a fashion magazine and a trade newspaper. The intern (judge) wants to know why the company needs to advertise when it has a fine reputation and growing sales figures.

ACTIVITY You are to explain to the intern (judge) the uses and value of advertising in publications targeted at the public and publications targeted at industry professionals.

EVALUATION You will be evaluated on how well you meet the following performance indicators:

- Explain the types of promotion.
- Develop strategies to position product/business.
- Explain fashion brand images.
- Explain the types of advertising media.
- Orient new employees.

Some visual-merchandising designers work for national retail stores around the country. Use the Internet to access the Web site for Federated Department Stores.

- Click Store Locator.
- Check All Stores, and then click Find Stores.
- Choose a state under Select a State, and then click Go.
- List the Federated Department Stores located in this state.

➡ For a link to a Web site to help you do this activity, go to **marketingseries.glencoe.com**.

BusinessWeek News

YES, WE HAVE A NEW BANANA

For Marka Hansen, last year's holiday season was a test of her mettle as a fashion prophet. The president of Banana Republic had bet that blue would be the top-selling color in stretch merino-wool sweaters. She was wrong. "The number-one seller was moss green," says Hansen. "We didn't have enough."

Hansen is about to face more risky decisions as she transforms the 435-store Banana Republic, a unit of Gap Inc., into a more fashion-conscious retailer. Not long ago, Banana was purveyor of chic basics—casual office wear in black or beige. But take a look around the chain these days, and you'll find strapless dresses with pink and green flowers and black tops with ruffles. For men, Banana offers shirts made of Italian fabrics. Banana hopes the offerings will distinguish it from sister store Gap.

So far, Hansen seems to be getting more right than wrong. Last year, Banana accounted for 13 percent of Gap Inc.'s sales. Banana's same-store sales jumped 21 percent. Banana is renewing itself. Cynthia R. Cohen of Strategic Mindshare [says,] "It could attract new customers and get old customers to come in more often."

Why go to the trouble of reinventing a store that wasn't really broken? Gap Inc. headed into a three-year downturn in late 1999, partly because overlap between the two other chains [Old Navy and Banana Republic] led Gap shoppers to head for lower-priced Old Navy. Gap stores got back on track by returning to basics such as jeans and khakis. That created a new problem. Now it looked like Banana Republic. The solution: Shift Banana away from staples and toward trends.

Cut the Vogueing

Banana is joining a segment of the apparel business that's already crowded with brands ranging from Polo Ralph Lauren and Calvin Klein to Ann Taylor. It is trying to build a name in fashion and design circles, hiring new talent, including a men's designer from Nautica Enterprises, Inc. Banana has moved its shows out of the showroom and presented its fall line at New York's Chelsea Art Museum. *Vogue* and *Elle* have photographed Banana's clothes—and last fall, George Clooney appeared in *Vanity Fair* sporting Banana's blue-linen shirt.

In the past, Banana didn't have to worry about making the wrong fashion call since it sold mostly basics. "Now, we have to be on trend at the same time as the rest of the fashion business," says Hansen.

By Louise Lee

▶ CREATIVE JOURNAL

In your journal, write your responses:

CRITICAL THINKING

1. How does the situation regarding Gap Inc. and Banana Republic stores demonstrate the importance of having the right selection of merchandise that targets the right customer?

APPLICATION

2. What steps has Banana Republic taken to promote its new image? Write a 30-second commercial to advertise its style and some of its merchandise.

 Go to **businessweek.com** for current *BusinessWeek* Online articles.

UNIT LAB

House of Style

You've just entered the real world of fashion. The House of Style assists fashion businesses and individuals to conceive, plan, produce, and sell the latest and most popular fashion products. Acting as the owner, manager, or employee of the House of Style, you will have the opportunity to work on different projects to promote the success of this fashion business.

Visual Merchandising—Design a Store

SITUATION You are assisting the owner of a fashionable clothing store called Active Woman. The store sells women's casual clothing and active wear. The active wear includes golf, tennis, and exercise clothing. The store's owner also owns the store next door. That store sells women's shoes and accessory items. Each store has its own entrance from the mall. A doorway between the stores allows customers to flow between the two stores and shop for items from each. The two stores share a cash stand, which is located in between the stores. The two stores have very different looks and atmospheres. Until now, the stores have been managed separately. The owner wants to create a unified look to reflect the combined management.

ASSIGNMENT Complete these tasks:
- Plan the basic design of the stores, including all the elements of visual merchandising that should be in your plan.
- Estimate the costs of the components of your visual-merchandising plan.
- Create a final report.

TOOLS AND RESOURCES To complete the assignment, you will need to:
- Conduct research on the Internet, at the library, or by phone.
- Ask retailers about their experiences with effective visual merchandising.
- Have word-processing, spreadsheet, and presentation software.

RESEARCH Do your research:
- Determine the most important components of visual merchandising in these stores.
- Visit similar businesses and assess the visual merchandising of each store.
- Get cost estimates for the fixtures, equipment, and other items for your plan.

REPORT Prepare a written report using the following tools:
- *Word-processing program:* Prepare a written report about your visual-merchandising plan. List the fixtures, equipment, and other elements of your plan.
- *Spreadsheet program:* Prepare a chart comparing prices of the fixtures and equipment. Prepare a budget for your plan.
- *Presentation program:* Prepare a ten-slide visual presentation with key elements of your plan. Include key points, photos, other visuals, and key text.

PRESENTATION AND EVALUATION You will present your report to the owner and the bank that may finance your plan. You will be evaluated on the basis of:
- Knowledge of visual merchandising and its components
- Continuity of presentation
- Voice quality
- Eye contact

PORTFOLIO
Add this report to your career portfolio.

EXPLORING CAREERS IN FASHION MARKETING

> **❝** I am always doing that which I cannot do, in order that I may learn how to do it. **❞**
>
> —**Pablo Picasso**
> **Artist**

A career in the fashion industry is challenging and rewarding. A variety of opportunities exist, ranging from jobs in science to sales. Unit 4 will give you information about fashion careers as well as the process of researching, finding, getting, and keeping a job.

Chapter 13 explores the personal traits and skills necessary to work in the industry, the different careers that are available, the numerous opportunities for education and training, and the specifics of the job application process. In Chapter 14, you will learn about starting a new job or a new business as well as the skills that can help you achieve success on the job.

UNIT LAB Preview

House of Style

Think about all the different types of jobs in the fashion industry. How would you explore the careers in a specific area of the fashion industry?

Functions of Marketing

- Marketing-Information Management
- Financing
- Selling
- Pricing
- Distribution
- Promotion
- Product/Service Management

Foundations
- Professional Development
- Economics
- Business, Management, Entrepreneurship
- Communication, Interpersonal Skills

Academic Concepts • Technology • Academic Concepts • Technology

These functions are highlighted in this unit:
- Marketing-Information Management
- Product/Service Management
- Promotion

Preparing for Fashion Careers

Chapter Objectives

- Identify the personal traits valued by employers.
- Identify the personal skills valued by employers.
- Describe four areas of employment in the fashion industry.
- Discuss the education options for fashion careers.
- Describe ways to gain experience in the fashion industry prior to employment.

MAGAZINE MAKEUP

The tween and teen grooming market is estimated to be worth $6.9 billion and is expected to grow to $8 billion by 2008. Tweens are ages 8 to 14, and teens are ages 15 to 19. Many have disposable income in the form of allowances or earnings from part-time jobs. The grooming market includes consumers who use and buy haircare products and cosmetics. Competition among cosmetics manufacturers for access to this market is fierce. Well-established companies such as CoverGirl® and Maybelline® dominate.

In 2004, the fashion magazine *CosmoGIRL!* launched a new line of cosmetics targeted at teen girls ages 15 and up. In such a highly competitive market, how was *CosmoGIRL!* going to attract a market share from established cosmetics companies, such as CoverGirl and Maybelline, for their new line of makeup? What could they do as newcomers to stand out from the crowd?

ANALYZE AND WRITE

1. What jobs or careers do you think would be involved in promoting teen cosmetics?
2. Write three promotional ideas for teen makeup.

Case Study Part 2 on page 279

POWER READ

Be an active reader and use these reading strategies:

PREDICT what the section will be about.

CONNECT what you read with your life.

QUESTION as you read to make sure you understand the content.

RESPOND to what you've read.

Career Options

YOU WILL LEARN

- To identify the personal traits valued by employers.
- To identify the personal skills valued by employers.
- To describe four areas of employment in the fashion industry.

WHY IT'S IMPORTANT

Understanding the variety of jobs in the fashion industry will help you match your personal traits and skills with a future career.

KEY TERMS

- trait
- skill
- interpersonal skills
- communication
- team
- leadership

PREDICT

What are some interpersonal skills?

trait a distinguishing feature or characteristic of a personality

Career Foundations

Careers in fashion are challenging, exciting, and rewarding. The wide variety of opportunities in the industry attracts people with many different interests, goals, and abilities. Some jobs require a high degree of artistic creativity and originality, while others require business know-how and management skills. Knowledge of the basics of marketing is important for all jobs in the fashion industry. An interest in people and a willingness to work and learn are the foundations of success in the world of fashion.

Personal Traits

The fashion world is an extremely diverse environment. Having the right personal traits can make the difference between not getting a job or getting a job—and keeping it. A **trait** is a distinguishing feature or characteristic of a personality. Many employers value an employee's personal traits as much as his or her knowledge and training. Excellent skills are important, but good personality traits allow an employee to adapt to a job and fit in with other employees. Employers look for these ten personality traits in prospective employees:

1. **Enthusiasm**—a positive outlook toward the job and other employees
2. **Maturity**—the ability to act appropriately in the workplace
3. **Self-discipline**—the ability to control conduct, feelings, and actions in a positive manner
4. **Dependability**—the ability to complete an assigned task
5. **Initiative**—the ability to seek out new assignments and assume additional duties when necessary
6. **Positive Attitude**—having a positive outlook toward the job and other employees
7. **Productivity**—the ability to set priorities, manage time wisely, and display an acceptable level of production and quality control
8. **Reliability**—the extent to which an employee can be relied upon regarding task completion and follow-up
9. **Punctuality**—being punctual with an acceptable overall attendance record
10. **Independence**—the ability to demonstrate acceptable work habits and conduct as defined by company policy

Employers also look for people who can think critically, make decisions, and solve problems.

Personal Skills

A skill is the ability to competently perform a specific task. Personal skills can be learned and developed with education and training. Employers are especially interested in potential employees who may have interpersonal, communication, team-building, and leadership skills.

Interpersonal Skills

Interpersonal skills are skills involving the ability to identify and understand the personal traits of others, including values, ethics, and attitudes. These personal skills include the ability to work with others and to be responsible, trustworthy, honest, and loyal. Good interpersonal relationships involve demonstrating behavior that supports others and shows respect and empathy, which are important aspects of human relations. Understanding these personal traits and reasons for behavior can help you develop good working relationships in a team situation or customer-service situation. You can learn to be more aware of others and to react appropriately.

Communication Skills

Many employers consider interpersonal skills essential, but there are other personal skills that are equally important. Good communication skills are essential in the fashion industry. **Communication** is the process of giving and exchanging information, ideas, and feelings. It is a critical aspect of interpersonal relations and successful business activities. People spend about 70 percent of their waking hours communicating. Key areas of communication include reading, writing, listening, and speaking. These skills can be developed and practiced.

WRITING AND SPEAKING Being a good communicator and developing writing and public-speaking skills may help you get your first fashion job. Such skills will also allow you to give quality presentations of your work. It is important to develop good telephone skills as well as the ability to write effective business letters, memos, and e-mails.

TECHNOLOGY AND COMMUNICATION New technologies provide more opportunities for effective communication. Cell phones, e-mail, videoconferencing, and the Internet are all tools used by the fashion industry. These tools make it easier to communicate.

Team-Building Skills

Most work in the fashion industry is done in team situations. A **team** is a group of people who work together to achieve a common goal. *Teamwork* is the process they use to achieve that goal. For example, the textile segment of the fashion industry communicates with the garment production segment to develop new fabrics. In turn, garment producers work with retailers to provide the latest fashions for the consumer. This interaction between segments of the fashion industry demonstrates the necessity of teamwork. Team-building skills result in better ideas and more effective work.

skill the ability to competently perform a specific task

interpersonal skills skills involving the ability to identify and understand the personal traits of others, including values, ethics, and attitudes

CONNECT

How much time do you spend on communicating during the day?

communication the process of giving and exchanging information, ideas, and feelings

team a group of people who work together to achieve a common goal

Style Point

PAINT IT WITH WORDS If you enjoy talking about designs, but find it difficult to create them, you may find a career in fashion communications and marketing. A variety of jobs blend verbal skills with artful fashion. Examples of jobs include fashion writer, Web-site designer, fashion teacher, fashion editor, advertising writer, and sales representative.

PR POWER

Edwin Filipowski
Co-owner
Keeble, Cavaco & Duka Public
Relations

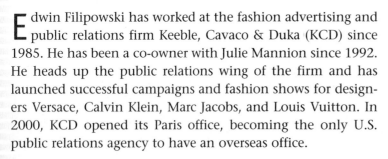

E dwin Filipowski has worked at the fashion advertising and public relations firm Keeble, Cavaco & Duka (KCD) since 1985. He has been a co-owner with Julie Mannion since 1992. He heads up the public relations wing of the firm and has launched successful campaigns and fashion shows for designers Versace, Calvin Klein, Marc Jacobs, and Louis Vuitton. In 2000, KCD opened its Paris office, becoming the only U.S. public relations agency to have an overseas office.

What kind of training did he have?

Filipowski attended Northwestern University and majored in journalism. He developed a fashion section in the school paper. He also won journalism internships at *Seventeen* magazine. He says, "By my senior year, I knew I didn't want to be a journalist. I skipped commencement and moved to New York with $200 in my pocket." In New York, he worked in public relations (PR) for an advertising firm. But he had his eye on the high-profile fashion publicity firm KCD. "In 1985, I read that Keeble, Cavaco & Duka had just landed a big account. I looked up the name of the best florist in Manhattan and sent Kezia (Keeble) flowers. I congratulated her on the new account and asked if she was looking for someone to work for her. I didn't realize it at the time, but I had sent her favorite flowers, freesias. I went in the next day for a three-hour interview, and she hired me."

What is his key to success?

"Truth and honesty are the best approach to PR. We are a service industry, working between designers and journalists. We should not be in the forefront ourselves."

Describe the traits and skills needed by a PR agent.

Career Data: Public Relations Agent

Education and Training
Bachelor's degree or master's degree in journalism or communications

Skills and Abilities
Organizational, written, verbal communications, creative-thinking, and customer-service skills

Career Outlook Faster than average growth through 2012

Career Path Intern, account assistant, account manager to account executive

Leadership Skills

leadership the process of motivating and guiding one or more individuals, a group, a business, or an organization to reach objectives

Leadership is the process of motivating and guiding one or more individuals, a group, a business, or an organization to reach objectives. A leader is a person who inspires, motivates, and influences others. A strong leader helps his or her team create a vision, and then helps the team accomplish it. Fashion marketers depend on industry leaders to develop new ideas for textiles, fabrics, and designs as well as new strategies for marketing.

PROMOTING CAREERS
Fashion photographers are part of the fashion promotion segment of the fashion industry. Photographers must be skilled with lighting, composition, and using camera equipment. *List some interpersonal skills that fashion photographers should have.*

QUESTION
What are four categories of fashion careers?

Fashion Monster
The first place job seekers look for job openings is usually not the classified ads in newspapers, but online at job Web sites. Sites such as Monster, Yahoo! HotJobs, and Craigslist allow job seekers to sift through opportunities. In 2004, Monster led the online job industry by offering postings in 27 U.S. markets.

➥Visit general job-search sites and fashion specialty sites, and note which listings best represent fashion employers through **marketingseries.glencoe.com**.

DEVELOPING LEADERSHIP Learning to be a leader can begin before getting a job. You can develop and practice your leadership skills through involvement in school activities and clubs, sports teams, religious groups, and/or volunteer organizations.

Types of Jobs in Fashion

The fashion industry encompasses more than design and buying careers. Career opportunities exist in each of the four segments of the fashion industry—textiles, fashion promotion, design and manufacturing, and retailing. (See **Figure 13.1** on pages 272–273.) Jobs in fashion range from creative jobs in design to technically skilled jobs in production and manufacturing. Numerous jobs exist in retail clothing stores, ranging from sales associate to store manager. On the business side, jobs involve buying, distribution, marketing, public relations, importing, and exporting. Media-related careers include fashion modeling, fashion journalism, illustration, and photography. For all of these jobs, fashion marketing knowledge is beneficial and essential.

Figure 13.1

Fashion Career Opportunities

WIDE WORLD OF FASHION The fashion industry is one of the largest employers in the United States with many diverse careers. All careers are touched by some aspect of marketing. *Which fashion industry jobs in this chart are most directly related to fashion marketing?*

Textiles	
Research Scientist	Develops new synthetic fibers
Laboratory Technician	Helps conduct research
Textile Designer/Artist	Creates new patterns and designs that are used in making fabrics
Textile Colorist	Decides which colors consumers will buy
Textile Stylist	Responsible for the final look of the fabric
Converter	Responsible for how the finished fabric will look
Production Supervisor	Coordinates the various departments of the mill
Machine Operator and Technician	Runs and maintains the production machinery
Quality-Control Inspector	Inspects and analyzes the quality of the product
Plant Engineer	Maintains the work-environment systems
Industrial Engineer	Oversees the methods and efficiency of the operations
Marketing Analyst	Conducts marketing research and evaluates information
Sales Representative	Presents the company's products and services

Fashion Promotion	
Art Director (Designer)	Develops advertising that will be placed in all forms of media
Graphic Designer	Produces the advertisements based on direction from the art designers
Advertising Director	Works for retail stores and publications and oversees the advertising activities
Fashion Copywriter	Works for advertising agencies, designers, or independently and writes advertising material for fashion-industry clients
Display Designer	Creates displays and is usually involved with special events and promotional activities
Display Manager	Responsible for visual-merchandising presentations in retail stores
Fashion Illustrator	Draws own garments or garments designed and produced by someone else
Fashion Model	Models clothing on the catwalk for ads or for mail-order catalogs
Fashion Photographer	Photographs models, fashion apparel, and accessories
Fashion Writer	Works mainly for newspapers and magazines, writing about the textile and apparel industry
Public Relations Agent	Represents and promotes businesses and products within the fashion industry

Design and Manufacturing	
Designer	Designs clothing, shoes, textiles or carpets, taking into account cost and demand
Sample Maker	Sews the designer's sample
Patternmaker	Makes the design into pattern pieces that can be used to produce garments
Pattern Grader	Cuts patterns into the various sizes that will be produced
Cutter	Operates the machinery that cuts around the pattern pieces
Sewing Machine Operator	Constructs and sews the apparel
Production Manager	Oversees the design, manufacture, selling, and delivery of a fashion line
Piece-Goods Buyer	Purchases the fabrics and trims
Supply-Chain Manager	Ensures that the right product is available when required, in the right quantity and at the right place
Engineers	*Machine:* Services and maintains machines and offers technical advice *Industrial:* Oversees the operations and selects the most efficient method and machinery *Costing:* Determines the price of the product by evaluating the cost to produce it *Quality control:* Develops specifications and oversees production from a standards viewpoint
Sales	Sells products and provides service to retail buyers
Market-Research Analyst	Studies consumer habits
Division Director	Oversees the product managers, plant managers, and sales managers
Retail	
Buyer	Buys clothes and accessories for a store or department to sell
Associate Buyer	Assists buyer in presenting merchandise to staff, tracking shipments, and calculating markdowns
Merchandise Planner/Allocator	Plans budgets, sales, stock levels, and coordinates distribution activities
Merchandising Coordinator	Makes sure retail stores are fully stocked
Trend Researcher	Analyzes and forecasts trends, using computer systems; makes purchase recommendations
Human Resources Manager	Analyzes staff needs; recruits, screens, and hires employees; oversees employer/employee relations and benefits
Store Manager	Oversees all aspects of the store's operation
Sales Associate	Sells fashion apparel and accessories in a retail store

Hot Property

Dress for Success

In a world where dressing for a job interview counts, Dress for Success helps low-income women by providing them with business suits for job interviews—and more suits when they begin a new job. Nancy Lublin founded Dress for Success in 1996 with a $5,000 inheritance from her grandfather. As a not-for-profit organization, the group relies on volunteers and donations from individuals, companies, and apparel manufacturers. More than 45,000 women in over 70 cities have been helped in the United States and other countries.

BUILDING CONFIDENCE

Women are referred to Dress for Success by not-for-profit and government organizations. These groups are dedicated to helping women who live in homeless or domestic-violence shelters, women in job-training programs, and women who are new to the country.

The first time a woman comes to Dress for Success, a personal shopper helps her choose a suit. The second time, she receives up to a week's worth of outfits. But the assistance does not stop with the clothing. The Dress for Success Professional Women's Group program provides ongoing support to help women build successful careers.

1. What personality traits would be helpful for someone working for Dress for Success?
2. What type of experience would be helpful for someone working for Dress of Success?

Other Fashion Careers

The positions listed in Figure 13.1 are some of the skill-specific jobs in the fashion industry. However, there are many other opportunities within the industry including accountants, administrative assistants, distribution personnel, human resource specialists, and office managers. Other jobs associated with the industry include jobs in fashion education. Some individuals can combine their interests in history and apparel and work as costume curators in museums or as costume designers. Entrepreneurial-minded people have started their own businesses as store owners, consultants, tailors and dressmakers, or import/export specialists. The opportunities are unlimited for individuals who develop skills through education and training.

Quick Check

RESPOND to what you've read by answering these questions.

1. What are at least three personal traits valued by employers?_____

_____

2. What are four types of personal skills employers seek in potential employees?_____

_____

3. What are the four key areas of communication?_____

_____

Section 13.2

Education and Training

Sources of Skills and Knowledge

You can discover your career direction by determining your skills and interests, but education and training will give you the advantage in fashion. Employers seek well-prepared employees in all areas of the fashion industry, from production to technical to management fields. In the past, entry-level employees received training as apprentices from professionals in the industry. Fashion education programs were not common. However, over the years, educational systems have been developed to address industry needs for skilled workers. Today there are a variety of educational resources available. Fashion marketers emphasize the benefits of gaining a solid sense of business and marketing through coursework and/or work experience. For example, a degree in fashion merchandising can lead to work in the retail or production segments of the fashion industry.

Technology Skills

Computer-related training is important when working in any of the fashion industry segments. Technical expertise is necessary in many of the fashion fields. Technical skills are essential for jobs that involve creating spreadsheets with Microsoft® Excel or editing illustrations using software programs such as Adobe® Photoshop or Illustrator. Hands-on creative work, which is integral to the fashion design process, requires specialized technical skills in painting, drawing, or photography.

Education

There is no other industry in which the fields of art, engineering, science, business, and technology are so integrated. Fashion is a fusion of art, history, current events, politics, and technology. For example, fashion designers combine skills in art, business, and technology. Textile producers must have an understanding of technology, engineering, and science. Meeting the needs of the fashion industry of tomorrow will require employees with skills and knowledge. With preparation, you will be ready to enter the fabulous world of fashion. Students can acquire skills and knowledge through:

- High school programs
- Community colleges
- Specialized and trade colleges
- Universities

AS YOU READ ...

YOU WILL LEARN
- To discuss the education options for fashion careers.
- To describe ways to gain experience in the fashion industry prior to employment.

WHY IT'S IMPORTANT
Understanding the opportunities for education and training will help you prepare for a successful career in the fashion industry.

KEY TERMS
- associate degree
- bachelor's degree
- internship
- job shadowing

PREDICT
What is an internship and how might it help someone interested in fashion marketing?

TECH NOTES

Majoring in Multimedia

To meet the fashion and entertainment industries' need for employees with graphic design and technical skills, the Fashion Institute of Design and Merchandising developed a two-year program leading to an associate degree in interactive multimedia. Students majoring in interactive multimedia learn to use state-of-the-art software for 3D modeling and animation, DVD authoring, and Web design. Students create their own DVD portfolios, which can be used to present their work to employers.

List careers you could pursue after getting a degree in interactive multimedia after reading information through marketingseries.glencoe.com.

Math Check

TUITION COSTS

Tuition for fashion merchandising school at Glendale Community College costs $13 per unit. The registration fee is $27 per quarter. How much does a four-unit course cost?

For tips on finding the solution, go to marketingseries.glencoe.com.

Non-Traditional Sources of Education

Fashion professionals agree that non-traditional forms of education can supplement fashion education. For example, read articles in your favorite fashion magazines to learn about the industry and current designers. Take art classes to develop a sense of color and proportion. Go to museums, travel, learn another language, and talk to people who are involved with fashion to learn about the industry.

High School Education

Pursuing a career in the fashion industry can begin in high school. Academic courses are essential for all fashion careers. You can develop your written and verbal skills through language arts, learn problem-solving techniques through math, and practice analytical skills in science. Computer experience is valuable in any fashion career. Marketing courses help prepare students who have a business-related curriculum. Specialized courses, such as retailing or fashion marketing, are part of marketing and business programs and can be beneficial for design students as well.

EXTRACURRICULAR EDUCATION School activities can help define your interests and develop your talents. Many academic and trade organizations foster public-speaking, leadership, and teamwork skills. For the budding fashion photographer, a position as a staff photographer for the school newspaper may help develop skills. For real-world experience, many high school career and technical-education programs also provide work-based experience.

ADVANCED PLACEMENT COURSES Many high school counselors suggest earning college credit by taking advanced courses. At community colleges, these classes may be inexpensive or free. If you live in a state that offers tech-prep programs, taking advanced courses might be a good option. This type of program is a partnership between high schools and community colleges that incorporates businesses and industry. The specially developed coursework allows students to transition from high school to college to exciting careers.

Post-Secondary Education

Whether your choice is a community college, a specialized or trade college, or a four-year college or university, there are many options for educational training in the fashion industry. Many schools offer degree programs that specialize in fashion merchandising and design.

ASSOCIATE DEGREES An **associate degree** is a college degree recognizing two years of coursework at a community college, specialized college, or trade school. Majors and courses may concentrate on fashion. This generally requires four to five semesters of college work to complete. This option is popular with many students because it allows quicker entry into the industry. Associate degrees are available in areas such as fashion merchandising, visual communications, and fashion design. Community college tuition is usually less expensive than tuition at state or private colleges.

CERTIFICATE PROGRAMS Another option at a community college, university extension program, or trade school is a certificate program, which requires about three semesters of classes. For example, an individual working in a computer-related area might obtain a certificate in a particular design program.

BACHELOR'S DEGREES To earn a bachelor's degree, many colleges or universities require that students take academic courses, such as math, literature, and social studies, in addition to the degree-related courses. The **bachelor's degree** is a college degree recognizing four or more years of undergraduate coursework at a college or university. A bachelor's degree is also referred to as a four-year degree. This expanded education might result in a Bachelor of Arts (B.A.) or Bachelor of Science (B.S.) degree for a specific discipline or major. A *major* is a specific field of study, such as fashion merchandising, business administration, or communications. Tuition at state-operated colleges and universities is generally less expensive than tuition at private institutions.

TRANSFER ADMISSIONS Some community colleges offer dual admissions agreements with four-year universities. That means that students can complete their freshman and sophomore college courses at a community college, and then transfer course credits to the partner university. This allows students to earn the four-year degree at a reduced cost.

associate degree a college degree recognizing two years of coursework at a community college, specialized college, or trade school

bachelor's degree a college degree recognizing four or more years of undergraduate coursework at a college or university

CONNECT

What types of degree or education would be most beneficial for you? Why?

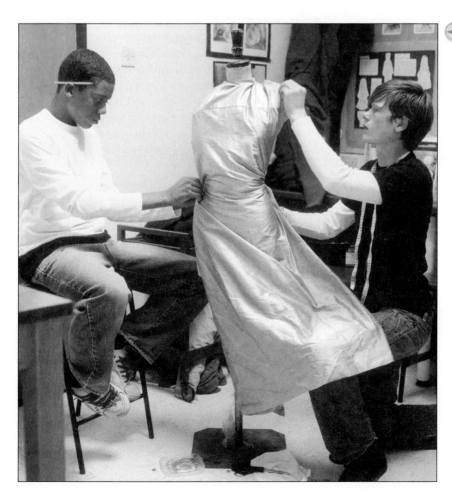

DESIGNING YOUR EDUCATION Matching the right educational program with your interests and aptitudes puts you on the right path toward a career in fashion. *Describe the types of degrees and credentials you might need for the particular career of your choice.*

Choosing Your Education

No matter what educational path you choose, it is important to consider these questions when selecting a program:

- What schools offer a program for the career you have chosen?

- How long does the program last?

- What is the cost and is financial assistance available?

To help answer these questions, most schools have Web sites that provide detailed information. If you search the Internet with key words such as *fashion, schools,* and *colleges,* you will find Web sites that offer compiled listings of schools with descriptions and contact information. Once you have narrowed your search, you can contact the school directly to get brochures, catalogs, and applications.

Figure 13.2

Career Planning Steps

STEP-BY-STEP CAREER PLAN By taking an organized approach to developing your chosen career, you will succeed in achieving your goal of working at a job that interests you. *Which step in this process do you need to develop the most? Which step might be easiest for you to do?*

8. Stay Informed
Maintain awareness about the fashion industry and current job opportunities.

1. Evaluate
Assess your aptitudes, traits, skills, and interests as well as your career and personal expectations.

2. Research
Investigate and research information about various fashion careers and their required education, salary levels, job outlooks, and locations to select a job that suits you.

7. Present Yourself
Equip yourself with a good résumé, cover letter, interviewing skills, and portfolio (if required) to sell yourself to employers.

CAREER PLANNING STEPS

3. Choose
Focus your efforts on one career area that interests you.

6. Network
Build a network of contacts, such as friends, family, or work associates, and communicate your availability and qualifications.

4. Educate and Train
Get the needed education and training to develop and improve your skills and to acquire the proper credentials.

5. Experience
Develop your skills through work experience during your school years and/or get involved in fashion-related extracurricular activities, volunteer work, professional associations, and training seminars.

Gaining Experience

Working in the fashion industry while still in high school or college can be a valuable learning experience. It allows people who are interested in fashion to see if they really like the business. Fashion careers can be demanding and require perseverance and planning to be successful. (See **Figure 13.2**.) Students can gain experience in fashion careers through part-time employment, internships, job shadowing, and work-study programs.

Part-Time Employment

Part-time work experience teaches you about a career first-hand while you earn money. It is a great opportunity to investigate a future career. Many high school students are able to find employment in the retail segment of the industry at clothing stores. Employers are usually willing to teach you if they know you are interested in the fashion industry. You will be able to determine if the industry is a good career option before you invest a lot of time and money in specialized training and education.

Internships

Supervised work experience can be acquired through an **internship**, which is a temporary paid or unpaid position giving students direct work experience and exposure to various aspects of a career. Internships should be related to a student's academic and career goals. Internships are an exceptionally important component of many college fashion programs. While part-time work might give you limited exposure to the industry, an internship may offer a broader experience.

INTERNSHIP ADVANTAGES Industry experts stress the importance and value of internships for acquiring the necessary skills to prepare for fashion-related jobs. Fashion internships can enhance classroom learning through access to the resources in the industry. Internship experience allows students to:

- Learn about the industry in which they are interested.

- Learn about various career options and/or specific jobs.

- Acquire experience in the working world.

- Network to gain contacts.

Case Study — PART 2

MAGAZINE MAKEUP

Continued from Part 1 on page 267

In 2004, to promote its line of branded cosmetics, *CosmoGIRL!* teamed up with Rite Aid, a national chain of drug stores, to launch their "Makeover Mania" promotion. The aim was to boost sales for both Rite Aid and CosmoGIRL! makeup, while building brand recognition for the product line.

The promotion was aimed at teen girls and offered a free gift redeemable with a mail-in Rite Aid proof of purchase for any CosmoGIRL! brand cosmetic. The gift was a pink-and-black, tiger-striped mirror featuring the CosmoGIRL! logo in the corner. The plastic magnetic mirror was designed for school lockers so that the CosmoGIRL! logo would be on display to the target demographic group.

Rite Aid promoted the give-away in stores by directing shoppers to check out *CosmoGIRL!* makeover ideas. The store also publicized a list of six must-have CosmoGIRL! makeup products. Over 5,000 mirrors have been redeemed. Bob Stepanian, the consultant who created the promotion, thinks that they succeeded because the mirror promotion was just right. It captured a look and style that appealed to their target audience.

ANALYZE AND WRITE

1. How did Rite Aid help promote the give-away and how did they benefit from the promotion? Write a paragraph explaining your answer.
2. Write a paragraph about the type of education and skills that marketers might need to work on a campaign for teen cosmetics.

internship a temporary paid or unpaid position giving students direct work experience and exposure to various aspects of a career

On the Runway in Africa

Seeking world attention as a fashion center, the country of Ethiopia in Africa held its first Fashion Week in Addis Ababa in 2004. "Now Ethiopia can take on the rest of the world and show them what talented designers we have," said a spokesperson before the big event. That's exactly what the country did. Local Ethiopian and other African designers mixed with designers from such fashion-conscious countries as Italy, Sweden, Denmark, England, and the United States.

Miss Universe Ethiopia was the catalyst who launched the Ethiopian fashion empire. As she traveled the world, she became a Fashion Ambassador for Ethiopia. The fine textiles and colorful fashions of Ethiopia were seen at the international beauty contest, at fashion shows, and on the runway at Fashion Week in Addis Ababa, Ethiopia.

Do you think the experience that Miss Universe Ethiopia gained as a fashion ambassador qualifies as training in the world of fashion? Explain your response.

QUESTION

What are at least three advantages of internships that would appeal to you?

job shadowing an activity in which a person follows a worker on the job to learn about the job and workplace

PAID/NON-PAID INTERNSHIPS Paid-internship programs offered by fashion businesses can be competitive. Another alternative is to arrange for a non-paid internship by approaching creative agencies, stylists, fashion editors, or fashion producers. Although you may not earn a wage, you will definitely gain experience and exposure to the industry. In addition, some states require employers to grant school credit for non-paid internships.

Job Shadowing

Some high school career and technical education programs offer the opportunity to "shadow" an employee for a day. **Job shadowing** is an activity in which a person follows a worker on the job to learn about the job and workplace. Students can spend a day at a company "shadowing" an employee by observing and asking questions of individual workers. This is a great way to observe jobs in the textile or design fields where there are few part-time or internship positions for high school students. Job shadowing can provide valuable resources and contacts for your job search. Ask your teacher or counselor to help arrange a job shadow day. You can also take advantage of the many national job-shadowing programs. Many companies participate in national Groundhog Job Shadow Day each year in February.

COWORKERS AS RESOURCES Remember that in any learning environment, coworkers are a great resource for real-life job information. Inquire about what a day on the job is like and the skills and training required.

Work-Study Programs

While offering fashion-related courses, many schools also provide work-study programs. High schools, specialized colleges, and other colleges often partner with employers to help students get on-the-job training for future careers. Sometimes these programs are called cooperative (co-op) programs for high school students. Internships may be part of a work-study program for college-level students. In a work-study program, students go to class part-time, studying career courses, and then work at related jobs part-time. A teacher, counselor, or professor may supervise the program.

WORK-STUDY ADVANTAGES Many employers are anxious to hire students as entry-level, part-time employees. These students may be trained and may eventually become full-time employees of a company. Students gain experience and are compensated with part-time pay and course credit toward graduation. As with internships, students can get a good picture of the fashion industry by working on the inside. Students gain an understanding of how the different jobs within the industry are interrelated and function to make a business successful. An entry-level employee on a work-study program may also become eligible for an apprenticeship or other training program at the particular company. No matter what direction a student takes, he or she will gain valuable on-the-job experience working in the real world of fashion. (See **Figure 13.3**.)

ETHICS & ISSUES

Unpaid Internships

Internships are an effective way for students to get started in the fashion world. However, most internships are unpaid, and in some cases, students do not receive college credit for the experience. According to *USA Today*, 60 percent of unpaid college interns come from households with an income above $100,000 per year. For students without financial support who need to work for income during summers and part-time during the school year, unpaid internships are not an option. *Do unpaid internships exclude lower-income students from career opportunities?*

Figure 13.3

Experience Counts

Work-Study Advantages
• Acquire career skills and knowledge.
• Apply your course knowledge to a job.
• Assess your interest and form realistic career goals.
• Gain valuable work experience for your résumé.
• Learn what employers expect of employees on the job.
• Learn to communicate and work with customers, coworkers, vendors, and others.
• Earn money.
• Earn school credit toward graduation.
• Expand your network as you meet contacts for your future career.
• Transition from school to the world of work.

WORK-EXPERIENCE BENEFITS
Work-study programs in high school and in college provide an edge for students pursuing careers in fashion. *Do you think real-world work experience could be even more valuable than classroom experience? Why?*

DECA PREPARATION By participating in competitive events sponsored by DECA, students gain real-world skills. *What other advantage do students have by participating in organizations such as DECA?*

Trade and Student Organizations

Trade associations serve the business community, and student associations such as DECA can offer a multitude of opportunities. DECA helps students build and utilize leadership and teamwork skills though chapter activities that serve the members, school, and community. Through these activities, students develop social and interpersonal skills, which are valuable in the workplace. They can explore career opportunities because the studies are co-curricular. In addition to classroom studies, students have the opportunity to become involved in local, state, regional, and national competitive events. These events enable students to demonstrate their abilities through role-play or written events. The business representatives who are involved with these student conferences have the chance to screen students before they enter the workforce. With the combination of education, training, practice, experience, and interest, students can look forward to rewarding and successful careers in fashion.

Quick Check

RESPOND to what you've read by answering these questions.

1. What are three ways students can gain experience in the fashion industry? _____

_____

_____

2. What are the benefits of an internship? _____

_____

_____

3. How can student organizations such as DECA help students prepare for a career? _____

_____

_____

Worksheet 13.1

Traits and Skills

Complete the graphic organizer below with the traits and skills that you have to be successful in a fashion-marketing career. Add a title for each circle.

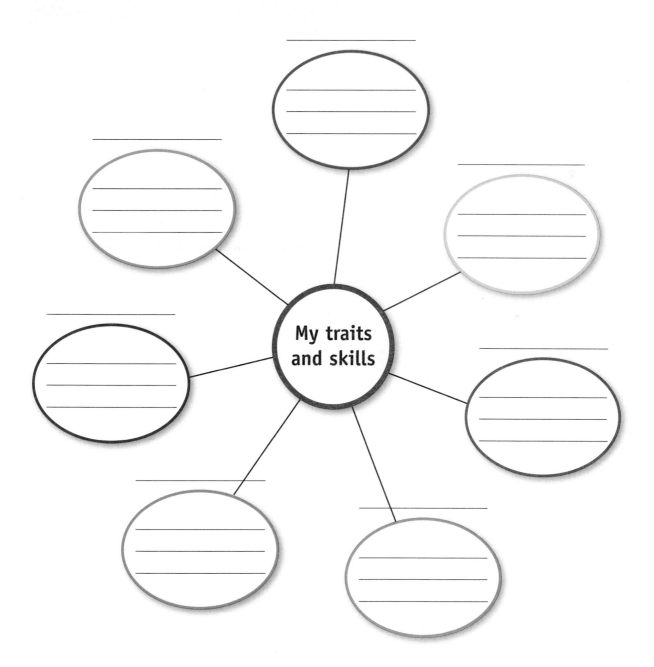

Worksheet 13.2

Education and Training

Think about two possible careers. Fill in the graphic organizer below with information about the education you will need to reach your goals.

Career	Type of Education Needed

Portfolio Works

WRITE A LETTER

Choose a specific job in the fashion industry. Imagine that you have a special talent, education, and/or business experience related to this job. You are applying for that particular job and must write a cover letter to a human resources representative. Write a one-page letter, highlighting your talent, education, or experience.

Dear Human Resources Representative:

_____

_____

_____

_____

_____

_____

_____

_____

_____

_____

_____

_____

_____

_____

_____

_____

_____

_____

Sincerely,

(Sign your name.)

Add this page to your career portfolio.

CHAPTER SUMMARY

Section 13.1 Career Options

trait (p. 268)
skill (p. 269)
interpersonal skills
(p. 269)
communication (p. 269)
team (p. 269)
leadership (p. 270)

- Employers value various personal traits in employees, including enthusiasm, maturity, self-discipline, dependability, initiative, positive attitude, productivity, reliability, punctuality, and independence.

- Employers also value personal skills, such as interpersonal, communication, team-building, and leadership skills.

- Four areas of employment in the fashion industry include textiles, design and manufacturing, fashion promotion, and retailing.

Section 13.2 Education and Training

associate degree (p. 276)
bachelor's degree (p. 277)
internship (p. 279)
job shadowing (p. 280)

- A variety of education options are available for people who are interested in training for fashion careers. They include non-traditional sources of education, such as reading magazines, art classes, museums, travel, learning language, and talking to professionals. Traditional educational programs are offered at high schools and community, specialized, and trade colleges as well as four-year colleges and universities.

- Students can acquire experience in the fashion industry before getting a job through part-time employment, internships, job shadowing, and work-study programs.

CHECKING CONCEPTS

1. **Define** the term *trait*.
2. **Identify** personal traits valued by employers.
3. **Differentiate** between a personal trait and a skill.
4. **Name** traits valued by employers.
5. **Describe** leadership skills.
6. **Identify** four areas of careers in the fashion industry.
7. **List** the education options available to train for a fashion career.

Critical Thinking

8. **Describe** a fashion career plan for a job of your choice that includes ways to gain experience before getting a job.

CROSS-CURRICULUM SKILLS

Work-Based Learning

Interpersonal Skills—Participating as a Team Member

9. Form four groups: textile developers, designers, garment producers, and store owners. Each group must create a design or plan related to its segment for hi-tech skiwear.

Thinking Skills—Knowing How to Learn

10. Make a list of the major section headings in this chapter. Write a summary of what you learned from each section.

School-Based Learning

Language Arts

11. Research and write an essay on a fashion career that interests you.

Computer Technology

12. Use the Internet to research schools that offer programs for fashion marketing. Summarize information on three schools.

 CONNECTION

Role Play: Fashion Marketing Student

SITUATION You are to assume the role of a second-year fashion marketing student. You are very interested in pursuing a career in the fashion industry and have conducted extensive research about careers in fashion and the education and training needed in that industry. Your teacher (judge) has asked you to speak at a marketing careers day about fashion-industry careers. You are to address the personal traits and skills necessary to succeed in the fashion industry.

ACTIVITY You are to review the outline of your presentation with your marketing teacher (judge).

EVALUATION You will be evaluated on how well you meet the following performance indicators:

- Discuss career opportunities in the field of apparel and accessories.
- Assess personal interests and skills for success in business.
- Identify sources of career information.
- Explain the need for ongoing education as a worker.
- Identify skills needed to enhance career progression.

 INTERNET ACTIVITY

Use the Internet to access the DECA Web site for information, and then answer the following questions:

- What is the purpose of DECA?
- What are three benefits of being a DECA member?
- E-mail the benefits to a classmate.
- Have the classmate bring your list to class.

➡ For a link to the DECA Web site to help you do this activity, go to **marketingseries.glencoe.com**.

Chapter 14

Working in Fashion

Section 14.1

Finding and Getting a Job

Section 14.2

Starting a Job or Business

Chapter Objectives

- Describe sources for researching fashion careers.
- Identify job sources in the fashion industry.
- Explain career networking.
- Discuss the components of the job-application process.
- Summarize the steps of the job-search process.
- Identify important strategies for success on the job.
- Identify the traits of successful entrepreneurs.

SURF'S UP

When Australian entrepreneurs Alan Green and John Law formed the surfwear company Quiksilver® in 1973, they said, "At the time, it was a good idea to make some money and still go surfing." The company's first product was a pair of boardshorts (swimming trunks). Before Quiksilver, surfers wore uncomfortable canvas lace-up trunks with long legs. As expert surfers, Green and Law knew what their friends and future customers wanted. So, they created durable, lightweight, quick-drying boardshorts that allowed free movement.

Then the two "dudes" met Jeff Hakman, a surfer from the United States who became the Quiksilver distributor in the U.S. By the mid-1970s, Hakman and another surfer Bob McKnight, who had a business degree, started with a small office/warehouse/distribution center in Newport Beach, California. Quiksilver's biggest challenge was offering a new product category, *surfwear,* unrecognized by most retailers. With only a few surf shops as outlets, how could the "stoked" entrepreneurs expand Quiksilver?

ANALYZE AND WRITE

1. Write two sentences about why Green and Law became entrepreneurs.
2. Write two sentences about how Hakman and McKnight started the U.S. business.

Case Study Part 2 on page 293

POWER READ

Be an active reader and use these reading strategies:

PREDICT what the section will be about.

CONNECT what you read with your life.

QUESTION as you read to make sure you understand the content.

RESPOND to what you've read.

Finding and Getting a Job

AS YOU READ ...

YOU WILL LEARN

- To describe sources for researching fashion careers.
- To identify job sources in the fashion industry.
- To explain career networking.
- To discuss the components of the job-application process.
- To summarize the steps of the job-search process.

WHY IT'S IMPORTANT

You need to determine what career information you need and where to find it to make wise career decisions. Preparation and research are keys to a successful job search.

KEY TERMS

- aptitude
- interest
- interest survey
- networking
- résumé
- cover letter
- job interview
- reference

PREDICT

What might be the difference between an aptitude and an interest?

aptitude a natural talent or ability for a particular skill

Researching Your Job

Now that you have decided to enter the fashion world, how do you decide which job is right for you? The choices in the fashion industry are almost unlimited. The next step is to research the job that interests you. The more career information you have, the better equipped you will be to make decisions about your future. It is important to choose a career that is compatible with your work values, personal goals, and lifestyle. You should also determine if your desired career matches your knowledge and skills, and if you need additional training and education.

Aptitudes and Interests

The first step to take before beginning your research is to identify your aptitudes, skills, and interests. An **aptitude** is a natural talent or ability for a particular skill. The ability to sew might lead to a designing or manufacturing position. An **interest** is an activity or concept that is enjoyable. Do you enjoy interacting with others? This interest may lead to a sales or marketing career.

Interest Surveys

An **interest survey** is a questionnaire designed to identify interests through responses to carefully focused questions. Surveys are often administered and interpreted through your high school counseling office. Many are also available as interactive computer software. Although interest surveys cannot pinpoint the exact career for you, they will give you a better idea of your interests and abilities.

Sources for Career Research

Once you have identified your career interests, you can begin researching specific career areas. There are numerous sources for information, including career guides, company directories, company Web sites, and information interviews.

Career Guides

Your school or public library is a good source of career information. You can access many career resource guides, which provide information on job descriptions, pay rates, and locations. These guides are also available online. The *Dictionary of Occupational Titles (DOT)* covers 20,000 jobs and their relationships with data, people, and things.

The *Occupational Outlook Handbook (OOH)* describes hundreds of occupations and gives information regarding working conditions, pay rates, the nature of the work, and where the best job opportunities may be found. In addition, you can learn what training or education and qualifications are required for specific jobs. The *Guide for Occupational Exploration (GOE)* organizes careers into 12 interest areas and provides information on the nature of the work, necessary skills, and required preparation.

Company Directories

Other resources include company directories. Ask the library staff to help find the best directory for you or check the *Guide to American Directories*. You can also access technical reports and annual reports of publicly traded corporations for detailed corporate information.

Company Web Sites

You can also explore specific companies in the areas that interest you. Many companies have Web sites that provide information concerning their products and basic information about the particular company. Employment opportunities may also be listed online.

interest an activity or concept that is enjoyable

interest survey a questionnaire designed to identify interests through responses to carefully focused questions

Hot Property

Original Rags

Advertised as "fiercely original American clothes for fiercely original American kids," American Rag designs clothes for "free-spirited 15- to 24-year olds who like to think and dress their own way."

CALIFORNIA ORIGINS

Founded in San Francisco, California, by Mark Werts, American Rag Companies opened its first store in 1984. The next store to open was American Rag's signature store on La Brea Avenue in Los Angeles, California. It quickly became a favorite shop for musicians, actors, designers, and other creative people looking to create their own individual style. Today American Rag is considered one of the most innovative, trend-setting retailers in the country.

ORIGINAL CASUAL

Casual styles with a distinctive look for guys include Phoenix-washed jean shorts, classic premium sun-bleached jeans, and color-blocked jackets. Cool styles for girls include racer-back polo shirts in red sequoia, snap-pocket miniskirts, parachute jackets, and draw-cord island pants.

NATIONAL BRAND

In 2003, the name was licensed to Tarrant Apparel Group, and an exclusive distribution agreement was signed with Federated Department Stores. So, American Rag Cie is now carried exclusively at one of the country's foremost retailers. American Rag Cie clothing is in Macy's stores in 22 states and in Guam and Puerto Rico.

1. Are you a good candidate to work for Macy's in American Rag? Explain your answer.
2. Would you prefer to work in one of the two American Rag Company stores or to work for a large department store, such as Macy's? Explain your answer.

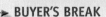
Informational Interviews

Whenever possible, speak directly with employees to learn all you can about a company's policies, products, and marketing procedures. An *informational interview* gives you the opportunity to meet personally with someone employed in your area of interest. Unlike an employment interview, an informational interview is not conducted with the end goal of getting a job. Instead, the objective is to obtain information only. You are able to ask specific questions and find out about the day-to-day demands of the job.

Research Questions

Before applying for a job, do research and find out all you can about the company before you interview for a position. The following questions are a useful guide for your company research:

1. How long has the company been in business?
2. How many people are employed?
3. What are the company's main fashion products and services?
4. Does the company have a good record of growth and expansion?
5. Do employees have an opportunity for advancement from within?

Swiss Movements

In a land known for its fine watchmaking, one watchmaker stands out—Patek Philippe. The crème de la crème of timepieces, the Patek Philippe holds the world record for the most expensive watch—an 18-carat gold pocket watch that was sold at auction for $11 million in 1999. Of the 100 most expensive wristwatches in the world, 80 are made by Patek Philippe.

Compare annual production of the Swiss watchmakers, and you will not see Patek Philippe on the top of the list. During 160 years of production, the company has manufactured less than one percent of the total annual production of the entire Swiss watch industry. Currently it produces only about 30,000 watches annually.

Patek Philippe timepieces are for discerning shoppers who shop in finer stores around the world. Own a Patek Philippe and receive the *Patek Philippe Magazine,* reserved for owners of the fine timepieces. The company even has its own museum in Geneva, where more than four centuries of watchmaking is displayed.

What type of skills might you need to work in a store that sells Patek Philippe watches?

Job Sources

There are many places to find jobs. Sources could be as close as someone in your own community or as far away as Paris! There are good jobs out there, but it requires effort and ingenuity to get them. Local fashion businesses, trade publications, and the Internet are all excellent places to start when looking for a job in fashion.

Local Fashion Businesses

Many large companies offer entry-level training programs, and smaller firms offer a wide variety of entry-level positions. Typical entry-level positions include executive trainee, buyer's assistant, and department manager.

Some of the best opportunities may be in the community where you live. While not every city has design or market centers, there are usually fashion apparel retailers who hire employees. A retail store is an excellent environment for an introduction to the world of fashion. Working at a store can provide the opportunity to interact with customers and to learn how fashion products move through the retail segment. You can also get exposure to visual merchandising and retail operations. You might also observe vendor presentations or participate in special events such as fashion shows or other promotional events.

Trade Publications

Trade publications, such as trade magazines, newspapers, journals, and newsletters, provide information targeted to those who work in the fashion industry. These publications are great sources for conducting research. Look in your school and local libraries for trade publications that are directly related to your career interests. The articles may focus on careers in the fashion industry. Check the classified sections of these publications and make a list of specific jobs that interest you.

Career Web Sites

The Internet makes career information available to you at the click of a button. Web sites such as Monster and CareerBuilder list job openings and offer helpful hints on conducting a job search. The U.S. Department of Labor's Web site is also a good tool and provides an online edition of the *Occupational Outlook Handbook*.

Case Study — PART 2

SURF'S UP
Continued from Part 1 on page 289

In the mid-1970s, Jeff Hakman and Bob McKnight opened a small warehouse in Newport Beach, California, and became Quiksilver distributors. With only a few surf shops interested in buying the original surfwear, the partners began to build business on word of mouth, quality, extreme service—and a vast surfing network.

By the 1980s and 1990s, Quiksilver continued to design and make novel apparel for surfers—and expanded their lines to include fashions for skateboarders and other outdoor athletes. Sales were boosted by Quiksilver sponsorship of legendary athletes such as surfer Kelly Slater and skateboarder Tony Hawk. Big Wave surfing competitions in Hawaii and other boardsport events for men and women allowed Quiksilver's influence to spread.

Today stores all over the world carry an assortment of Quiksilver apparel and accessories. Their 18 labels include popular brands such as Roxy, Raisin, and other brands. Quiksilver's original commitment to surfing and outdoor sports established its "street cred" and helped to inspire innovative fashions for decades.

ANALYZE AND WRITE
1. List the strategies that Hakman and McKnight used to develop business.
2. Write a list of sources that might provide information on jobs at Quiksilver.

CONNECT
At what fashion company would you like to work?

The U.S. Department of the Census provides forecasts about growth and decline for U.S. industries. You can find links to these and other valuable Web sites through the **marketingseries.glencoe.com** Web site.

Web sites specific to the fashion industry, such as the Fashion Center Web site, may help you in the career-search process. These sites allow you to fine-tune your research and identify jobs that correspond to your skills, experience, and training.

Other Sources

Another source for finding jobs is through an employment agency, which is a business that helps people find jobs. Several agencies even specialize in the fashion industry.

Career or job fairs that are hosted by colleges and universities are a good resource when looking for a position. These interactive functions give you the opportunity to meet employers face to face, find out more about the industry and specific companies and ask questions. You might be able to set up an interview.

Classified ads in newspapers can be valuable tools for researching openings in your area. You do not need to wait for a job opening to contact an employer.

However, remember that traditional job-search methods do not uncover most jobs. Most jobs are not advertised. You may find jobs through your network, or people you know. You need to be creative and use a variety of techniques in your search to find the perfect job.

The Importance of Networking

Most industry experts agree that finding a job is often linked to "knowing someone." There are ways to expand your contacts even when you think your opportunities for meeting people are limited. This is where networking comes into play. **Networking** is the process of finding contacts among people you know, such as family, friends, employers, and professionals who know you. Through networking, you can build professional relationships that are mutually rewarding.

Just as your fashion education can begin as early as high school, so can your ability to develop your networking skills and contacts. Tell your family, friends, and teachers about your interest in a fashion career. Make sure your employer knows of your career interest. When you meet adults, ask them what they do for a living. You may meet someone who works in the fashion industry or has contacts in the industry. Some of your best job leads will come from people you know. Fashion professionals admit that having industry contacts can be as important as having talent.

networking the process of finding contacts among people you know, such as family, friends, employers, and professionals who know you

Using Career Information

Once you have conducted your research, compare the information to your goals and values. For example, does the job you are seeking require the amount of time and money that you are willing to invest to get the necessary education? Is the salary range acceptable for the lifestyle you envision? Are the required hours compatible with the amount of leisure time you want? Are you willing to relocate to another city? Many of the positions in the fashion industry are with businesses that are located in design or market centers. All factors are important to consider before interviewing for a position. The career that enables you to meet your goals and live a life according to your values is the most rewarding.

Getting the Job

You have done your research. Now it is time to get the job. The job application, résumé, and cover letter are part of the job-application process and are used to secure a job interview. You have learned about companies that might be a good match for you. This is an opportunity for them to learn more about you.

Job Applications

The process of getting a job sometimes begins with a job application. However, many businesses ask for a job application when a prospective employee comes in for an interview. Most businesses have standard application forms, requiring basic personal information, such as your name, address, telephone number, a brief work history, education, and references. Remember to take identification, reference information, and a pen, and to write neatly and legibly on the application. Employers may make assumptions about the quality of your work based on the appearance of your application.

ETHICS & ISSUES

Résumé Building

Writing your résumé can be a challenging task. Trying to fit too much experience into a one-page document is as difficult as making too little experience fill a one-page document. In the world of fashion, interns, assistants, and photographers' assistants all build experience by multitasking and learning from established professionals. Sometimes responsibilities overlap, and apprentices perform tasks that may fall under a different, more important job description. *Do you think it acceptable to give yourself a bigger title on your résumé than you actually had at your job?*

Online Portfolio

Fashion is a visual industry. From designers to models, people who want to build a career in the fashion world need to show their past work, not just talk about it, when they seek work. A portfolio is a good way to do this. For designers, photographers, stylists, and models, a cost-effective way to show their work to as many people as possible is to create online portfolios.

➡Check out portfolio services online. Search for a model, a makeup artist, or a fashion photographer, and print your favorites through **marketingseries.glencoe.com**.

QUESTION

What document should you take to a job interview?

résumé a document that provides a brief summary of personal information, skills, work experience, education, activities, and honors

cover letter a brief one-page letter that introduces you to the employer, focuses on your skills, and explains why you are applying for the job

job interview a face-to-face meeting between a prospective employee and the person who makes hiring decisions for the company

Résumés

Most employers require a résumé from job applicants. A **résumé** is a document that provides a brief summary of personal information, skills, work experience, education, activities, and honors. (See **Figure 14.1** for a sample résumé.) Remember to include dates for everything listed. Your résumé should be brief: One page is sufficient, unless you have extensive work experience that is important to the job for which you are applying.

Cover Letter

When mailing a résumé to a prospective employer, always include a cover letter. A **cover letter** is a brief, one-page letter that introduces you to the employer, focuses on your skills, and explains why you are applying for the job. It provides you with the opportunity to present information that is not listed on your résumé and to explain why you are a strong candidate for the position. You should conclude the letter by thanking the person for his or her time and requesting an interview. Even though you have included your contact information in the résumé, make sure to mention it in the cover letter. Remember to proofread all documents several times before you send them to a prospective employer.

Job Interview

The **job interview** is a face-to-face meeting between a prospective employee and the person who makes hiring decisions for the company. The employer seeks to find out more about the job applicant and if his or her skills match the needs of the company. The interview is your opportunity to sell yourself. Making a good first impression is important. It is also important to determine if the company is a good match for you. For most people, the job interview is the most difficult part of the job search. The following tips are designed to build confidence and make the interview process less stressful:

- Dress appropriately and be well-groomed.

- Anticipate questions.

- Be on time.

- Go alone.

- Do not chew gum or candy.

- Use a firm handshake.

- Be confident—and be yourself.

- Look at the interviewer.

- Listen carefully.

- Talk slowly and give complete answers, using standard English.

- Be ready to explain why you want the job.

- When you are finished, thank the interviewer.

Figure 14.1

Résumé Sample

CAREER FACT SHEET Your résumé is a summary that highlights your skills and career experience. This sample format focuses on skills. It is useful for job hunters without much experience. *If you had extensive experience in the world of fashion, which section of your résumé would be highlighted?*

Name Address Phone number	
Job Objective	To obtain an entry-level position in the area of clothing retailing.

SKILLS

Computer Skills
· Proven ability to learn new software systems quickly
· Trained teachers and staff in computer and word-processing skills

Communication Skills
· Excellent communication with customers, teachers, staff, and parents
· Created a newsletter for parents and staff
· Drafted effective business correspondence

Hardworking
· Worked outside of school since age 16
· Worked 20 hours a week

Organizational Skills
· Demonstrated ability to organize office-information systems
· Accurate and detailed bookkeeping inventory
· Organized fundraiser for American Cancer Society

WORK EXPERIENCE

2005–2006	Sales associate Johnson's Men's Store, Amber, Ohio · Assisted customers, answered phones · Assisted buyer
2003	Intern sales associate X-Sports Shack, Amber, Ohio · Assisted customers, answered phones · Installed software package to improve efficiency of cashier

EDUCATION

2006	Freshman, Ohio State University Major: Marketing
2005	High School Diploma, Jackson Tate High School Amber, Ohio

AWARDS AND ACTIVITIES

2005	President, Marketing Club
2003	Outstanding Business Student Award
2003	United Way volunteer

TECH NOTES

Finding Jobs Online

Job seekers interested in fashion marketing careers can find a wide selection of resources online. Many Web sites list current job openings and internship opportunities. Some offer additional features, such as tips on résumé writing and interviewing. These online tools allow job seekers to discover new opportunities locally and nationally.

➡️ What type of fashion marketing job do you want? Find three job openings in your area, and then create your résumé based on your career goals, using the information at **marketingseries.glencoe.com.**

reference an individual who knows you and can provide information about your work skills and habits, responsibility level, leadership abilities, and character

References

A **reference** is an individual who knows you and can provide information about your work skills and habits, responsibility level, leadership abilities, and character. A former employer who can verify that you are a prompt and conscientious worker and/or a teacher who can attest to your leadership skills would be excellent references to include. Adult family friends can be references, but do not include family members. Employers typically ask for three references. Prepare this list on a separate page from the résumé and bring it to the interview.

Follow-Up

Following the interview, send a letter to the interviewer thanking him or her for the interview. This is also a good time to mention anything that you may have forgotten to say in the interview.

A Successful Search

The key to a successful job search can be summarized in six steps:

1. Identify your skills and define a career objective.
2. Research the market and develop a search strategy.
3. Network and use contacts productively.
4. Write a résumé that employers can read in 30 seconds.
5. Master effective interviewing techniques.
6. Be proactive and conscientious in your search.

Preparation, practice, and a positive attitude are the keys to a successful job search.

Quick Check

RESPOND to what you've read by answering these questions.

1. What is an informational interview? _____

_____

_____

2. What are the purposes of a cover letter and a list of references? _____

_____

_____

3. What are the six steps to a successful job search? _____

_____

_____

_____

Starting a Job or Business

Starting Your Job

The right personal traits and skills, combined with education and training, can help get your foot in the fashion door. Starting your first job in fashion is an exciting time in your career. You want to fit in with the company, enjoy the work you do, and make your employer happy. (See **Figure 14.2** on page 300.) Applying career strategies on the job will ensure that the door remains open. The following strategies can help make your new job a positive experience for you and for your employer:

1. Begin the job with confidence:
- Be confident. Regard yourself as a professional, though you may have entry-level status.
- Learn and follow office policies.
- Expect that problems will occur. Perseverance, patience, and a pleasant personality will help you overcome or cope with difficulties.
- If you do not understand how to do something, ask questions to get a clear understanding of what you are expected to do.

2. Integrate into a new environment:
- Allow others to tell you what forms of address are appropriate. For example, your boss may prefer being called Ms. Smith, or she may prefer to be called by her first name.
- Observe and learn to appreciate the routine functions of the business. They can make or break the success of the company's primary mission.
- Take responsibility if you make a mistake. Learn from your mistakes so you will not repeat them.

3. Develop rapport:
- Establish a good working relationship with your supervisor.
- Assure your supervisor that you want to learn.
- If you need more guidance, discuss it with your supervisor. However, respect the supervisor's other responsibilities and work schedule. Find the appropriate time and place to ask for help.
- Be positive and monitor your own progress.
- Make your relationships with coworkers and other departments as pleasant, productive, and efficient as possible.

4. Continue to succeed:

- Follow through with your work. Deadlines are important—adhere to them.
- Work diligently, seriously, and effectively.
- Take advantage of opportunities to network and cultivate professional relationships. Remember the fashion industry is a small world!

Success on the Job

Although your first position may not be the job of your dreams, it is an important step in your fashion career. Regardless of where you start, your responsibilities may increase as a result of your hard work and enthusiasm. Every position you hold offers something of value. You can also learn something from everyone with whom you work.

Advancement in the fashion industry is possible for those who display the necessary abilities. Opportunities may come from within a company. You never know when your work performance could lead to another position or a promotion. Therefore, it is important to do your best at all times. People are interconnected and have contacts throughout the fashion industry. News of a particularly good employee will travel quickly, but news of a poor employee will spread like wildfire. Your best recommendation in the future is the reputation you establish for yourself now.

Figure 14.2

Relating to Your Boss

POSITIVE RAPPORT Because your boss can affect your career path, it is important to build a good relationship with him or her. *What strategy might be the most challenging to apply? Why?*

- Set mutual goals and clarify expectations.
- Keep your boss informed.
- Understand your and your boss's duties, concerns, projects, and goals.
- Assess your and your boss's strengths and weaknesses. How can you support your supervisor?
- Understand and respect your boss's personal style.
- Maintain clear, direct, and honest communication. Ask for feedback.
- Acknowledge and praise good work accomplished by your supervisor and coworkers.
- Understand the performance-review system and evaluate yourself.
- Keep an accurate record of meetings and the dates that projects are due and submitted.
- Keep a file of memos sent, performance evaluations, list of achievements, and letters of appreciation.

Starting a Business

After you have worked in the industry and gained experience and training, you may decide to start your own business. **Entrepreneurship** is the process of starting and managing your own business. There is enormous potential for people who are willing to risk time and money to run a fashion business. The fashion industry offers many entrepreneurial opportunities, from running a design company to opening a fashion boutique.

Small Business Risks

According to the U.S. Small Business Administration, over 50 percent of all small businesses fail in the first year of doing business, and 95 percent fail within the first five years. Business risks fall into three categories: economic, natural, and human risks. Lack of experience, insufficient funds, and poor location are the most common causes of failure. The top-ten reasons for failures include:

1. Lack of experience
2. Insufficient funds (money)
3. Poor location
4. Poor inventory management
5. Over-investment in fixed assets
6. Poor credit arrangements
7. Personal use of business funds
8. Unexpected growth
9. Competition
10. Low sales

CONNECT
What type of fashion business would you like to own?

entrepreneurship the process of starting and managing your own business

QUESTION
What business risks relate to finances?

NEW BEGINNINGS **A great deal of effort and time go into planning, preparing, and opening a new clothing store as a small business.** *Why do you think most small businessowners are willing to work many more hours than most employees who work at large companies?*

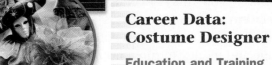

ENTERTAINING DESIGNS

Susan Soetaert
Freelance Costume Designer

What is your job?

"I am a freelance costume designer for theater, dance, television, and film."

What do you do in your job?

"My job involves working with a director and a script to come up with a costuming theme that fits a piece. I do this by researching the time period of a play or film, analyzing the themes of the work, and learning about the characters. I then create designs that simplify or exaggerate the themes and styles. I build, buy, or do both, to create the costumes. I've designed costumes for Broadway plays."

What kind of training did you have?

"I started out as an actress. I got my undergraduate degree in theater, and that's how I was introduced to costuming. I taught myself by working backstage in the costume shop. Eventually I decided to get a master's degree in costume design at New York University. I then started working in large costume houses for film, television, and theater. I was the costume shop manager at Eaves-Brooks and the purchasing manager at Barbara Matera costumes."

What advice would you give students?

"Learn about the historical significance of fashions and clothing trends as well as technical skills such as cutting and draping. Designers can draw on these influences to make a statement with their designs and about the characters. Internship and apprentice programs are the best way to learn skills while gaining professional experience."

What is your key to success?

"Get in the door through education and an internship program—and start working. Build up your experience and keep learning."

What business risks might relate to a freelance costume-design business?

Career Data: Costume Designer

Education and Training Associate degree, bachelor's degree, or master's degree, and apprenticeship

Skills and Abilities Design, construction, and management skills

Career Outlook Average growth through 2012

Career Path Internship, apprentice, shop assistant, shop manager, assistant designer, to designer

Skills for Entrepreneurship

Successful entrepreneurship turns ideas into action, and dreams into reality. Entrepreneurs require knowledge and skills in a wide variety of areas. Typically, successful entrepreneurs are leaders, goal-setters, and risk-takers who are:

- Achievement oriented
- Hardworking
- Non-conforming
- Self-confident
- Flexible
- Enthusiastic
- Optimistic
- Resourceful
- Independent

Self-Assessment

By evaluating your own strengths and weaknesses, you will be better prepared to make decisions about whether entrepreneurship is right for you. The following questions will help you determine if you want to start your own fashion business.

Are you a self-starter?
Entrepreneurs must be able to "pull up their socks" and make things happen. The saying, "If it is going to be, it is up to me," applies to the entrepreneur.

Are you able to get along with different personalities?
Businessowners work with a variety of people. Do you have the ability to deal with a difficult customer, an unreliable employee, or an inflexible vendor if necessary?

Are you good at making decisions?
Entrepreneurs may make frequent decisions with little time or help.

Are you physically and emotionally prepared to run a business?
Businessowners handle a variety of stressful situations every day. Can you watch out for your business while taking care of your health?

How well do you plan and organize?
Poor planning is a frequent cause of business failures. Many problems can be avoided by preparing a business plan and a marketing plan.

The Business Plan

A **business plan** is a proposal that describes a new business to potential investors and lenders. It outlines goals, a description of the business, and information about marketing, finances, and management. **Figure 14.3** on page 304 outlines the components of a typical business plan. The plan focuses on important issues and allows owners to make sound business decisions. It is a valuable tool for raising money to establish the business—and it provides a way to measure success.

business plan a proposal that describes a new business to potential investors and lenders

Figure 14.3

The Business Plan

PLANNING TO SUCCEED By considering all the necessary elements of running a business and providing an organized plan for yourself and investors, you can achieve your dreams of opening a fashion business. *What element of the business plan would interest a lender?*

I. Executive Summary

A brief introductory outline that highlights the key ideas of the business plan
(Investors can quickly read this "attention grabber" to understand the plan before getting into the specifics.)

II. Mission Statement

An outline of the business's purpose and the products and services it will offer
(The marketing team explains its business idea to the investor.)

III. Industry Overview

An analysis of the industry and markets in which a business will compete, and the factors affecting the business
(The marketing team demonstrates its knowledge of the industry. It is similar to a market overview, but it gives a macro view, or the big picture or overview.)

IV. Competitive Analysis

An analysis of the direct competitor's market position and its strengths and weaknesses
(The marketing team plans how it will carve out a place for the business in a competitive market.)

V. Marketing Plan

A detailed outline including a market overview and an outline of the business's market strategy
(The marketing team maps out its marketing objectives and explains how it will position, price, distribute, and promote its product or service.)

VI. Organization Plan

An organizational plan that details the business's key managerial roles and legal structure
(The marketing team explains the business structure.)

VII. Operating Plan

An operational plan that details a business's location, facilities, equipment, supplies and suppliers, and staffing requirements
(The marketing team outlines what it will need for the business to operate.)

VIII. Financial Plan

An outline of the business's profit and loss projections, cash flow, operating costs, funding needs, and how funds will be used to run the business
(The marketing team estimates the amount of money it needs to run the business, and how it will be spent.)

IX. Appendices and Exhibits

Any additional information that will help to prove the feasibility of the business plan, such as market studies, key players' résumés, credit reports, and tax statements
(The marketing team provides information that demonstrates it is qualified to create a business plan and that the business plan is feasible.)

The Marketing Plan

A **marketing plan** is a written document that provides direction for the marketing activities of a company for a specific period of time. It is part of a business plan. (See item V. in **Figure 14.3**.) It communicates the marketing goals, objectives, and strategies of a company. The specifics in the plan inform employees about their responsibilities, timelines for completion, and resources to be allocated. A marketing plan also helps a company monitor its performance. The type of business determines the complexity of the plan and the period of time covered by the plan. For example, a small clothing boutique may develop a simple marketing plan for a year. However, a large sportswear manufacturer might prepare a marketing plan for five years.

marketing plan a written document that provides direction for the marketing activities of a company for a specific period of time

ELEMENTS OF A MARKETING PLAN Marketing plans may differ from company to company. However, there are some basic elements, or sections, found in all marketing plans:

- Executive summary
- Situation analysis
- Marketing goals/objectives
- Marketing strategies
- Implementation
- Evaluation and control

1. **Executive Summary**—An executive summary is an overview of the entire marketing plan. It briefly addresses each topic in the plan. It also provides an explanation of the costs involved in the plan. The executive summary may also provide information to people who may be investing in the company.

2. **Situation Analysis**—A situation analysis is a study of the internal and external factors that impact a marketing plan. A SWOT analysis is a study of four factors:

- **S**trengths
- **W**eaknesses
- **O**pportunities
- **T**hreats

3. **Objective**—Objectives inform everyone about what should be accomplished by the marketing plan. These objectives are used to evaluate the marketing plan. Objectives should be simple, single-minded, specific, reasonable, measurable, and have a time frame.

4. **Marketing Strategies**—A marketing strategy is a method that identifies target markets and lists marketing-mix strategies that focus on those target markets. As part of the marketing strategy, the marketing plan must possess a *point of difference* in comparison to its competitors.

5. **Implementation**—Implementation involves putting the marketing plan into action. This section identifies who is responsible for each phase of the plan, the cost of each activity, and the time frame for executing each part of the plan.

6. **Evaluation and Control**—In the *evaluation* phase, the company reviews sales data, market share, brand-name recall, or any aspect of the marketing plan objectives. Information is compared with the objectives to see if the objectives were met. In the *control* phase, the company takes action to improve performance.

Math Check

RETAIL RENT

You have found a retail space on Main Street to rent for $725 per month. The landlord requires the first and last month's rent plus a $500 security deposit. What is the total amount you must pay the landlord to move into your new store?

➡️For tips on finding the solution, go to **marketingseries.glencoe.com.**

Financing

Lack of experience is the number-one reason businesses fail, but lack of proper financing is the number-two reason. Having the money available to start and operate a business is essential. However, an entrepreneur must also have the ability to spend funds appropriately.

Training

The Small Business Administration (SBA) has numerous online resources and courses to help you start your business. Investigate courses that are offered to help you strengthen your weak areas. The key to successful entrepreneurship is to discover what you enjoy doing the most, and then to find a business opportunity to suit your skills and interests.

Focus on the Future

Your career in fashion will provide many exciting experiences and allow you to develop new skills and broaden your talents. Working in the fashion industry can be very demanding. It is important to stay focused while also maintaining balance in your personal life.

Throughout the text, we have discussed information, strategies, and the steps you can take to succeed on the job and become a professional in the fashion industry. By developing and demonstrating your aptitudes and skills, personal qualities, and high standards of ethics, you will experience success personally and on the job. The most important strategies are to plan ahead, set clear goals, and work toward what you want to accomplish. You hold the key to your own future. Now is the time to use what you have learned to reach your goals!

Quick Check ✓

RESPOND to what you've read by answering these questions.

1. What are five strategies to help develop rapport with a supervisor?_____

_____

_____

_____

2. What are five self-assessment questions?_____

_____

_____

3. What are the three most common causes of failure for small businesses?_____

_____

_____

Worksheet 14.1

Fashion Trade Publications and Jobs

Use the library at school or in your community or bookstores and magazine stands to find fashion trade publications. Study the classified ad sections in the magazines to find four jobs that interest you. Make copies of those jobs ads, or clip them, and paste them below. Write one or two sentences about why you find the particular fashion job interesting.

Job #1

This job is interesting because

_____

_____

_____

_____

Job #2

This job is interesting because

_____

_____

_____

_____

Job #3

This job is interesting because

_____

_____

_____

_____

Job #4

This job is interesting because

_____

_____

_____

_____

Worksheet 14.2

Fashion People in the News

Search the Internet and newspapers and magazines for articles about two people in the fashion industry. Summarize an article about each person. Trade your summaries with another student's summaries, and then edit each other's summaries. Post the summaries on a board in the classroom.

Summary #1

Title of Article: _____

_____

_____

_____

_____

_____

_____

_____

_____

_____

Summary #2

Title of Article: _____

_____

_____

_____

_____

_____

_____

_____

_____

_____

_____

Portfolio Works

RESEARCHING COMPANIES

Make a list of five questions to answer when researching companies as potential places to work. Use the Internet to research two companies that interest you. Then answer your list of questions.

Questions:

1. _____
2. _____
3. _____
4. _____
5. _____

Company #1—Answers:

1. _____
2. _____
3. _____
4. _____
5. _____

Company #2—Answers:

1. _____
2. _____
3. _____
4. _____
5. _____

For which company would you like to work? Why?

_____

_____

_____

Add this page to your career portfolio.

CHAPTER SUMMARY

Section 14.1 Finding and Getting a Job

aptitude (p. 290)
interest (p. 290)
interest survey (p. 290)
networking (p. 295)
résumé (p. 296)
cover letter (p. 296)
job interview (p. 296)
reference (p. 298)

- Some sources for researching fashion careers are career guides, such as the *Occupational Outlook Handbook,* company directories, company Web sites, and informational interviews.

- Job sources in the fashion industry include local fashion businesses, trade publications, career Web sites, employment agencies, career or job fairs, classified ads in newspapers, or your network.

- Career networking is the process of finding contacts among people you know, such as family, friends, employers, and professionals who know you.

- Components of the job-application process include an application, résumé, cover letter, references, job interview, and follow-up.

- The steps of the job-search process are: 1) Identify your skills and define a career objective. 2) Research the market and develop a search strategy. 3) Network and use contacts productively. 4) Write a résumé that an employer can read in 30 seconds. 5) Master effective interviewing techniques. 6) Be proactive and conscientious in your search.

Section 14.2 Starting a Job or Business

entrepreneurship
    (p. 301)
business plan (p. 303)
marketing plan (p. 305)

- Some strategies for success on the job include: Begin the job with confidence; integrate into a new environment; develop rapport; and continue to succeed.

- Successful entrepreneurs are typically leaders, goal-setters, and risk-takers who are achievement-oriented, hardworking, nonconforming, self-confident, flexible, enthusiastic, optimistic, resourceful, and independent.

CHECKING CONCEPTS

1. **Identify** two publications that are good career guides.
2. **Identify** sources for jobs in the fashion industry.
3. **List** the people in a career network.
4. **Describe** the information needed to complete a job application.
5. **Explain** the step in the job-search process that requires writing.
6. **Identify** two strategies for success on the job.
7. **Describe** a business plan.

Critical Thinking

8. **Explain** the importance of financing in entrepreneurship.

CROSS-CURRICULUM SKILLS

Work-Based Learning

Basic Skills—Writing

9. Write a statement that describes your career goal in fashion marketing. Then make a list of skills you will need.

Interpersonal Skills—Teaching Others

10. Work with a partner. One of you is the job seeker, and the other one is the employer. Role-play an informal job interview. Then switch roles. Critique each other's interview.

School-Based Learning

Social Studies

11. Choose a country and research its fashion industry. Write a two-page essay explaining why you would or would not want to live and work there.

Arts

12. With a classmate, create a poster that summarizes strategies for success on the job. Display your posters in the classroom.

Role Play: Owner, Accessories Business

SITUATION You are to assume the role of owner of a fashion accessories business located in a midsized town. Your experience includes working for a clothing manufacturer and being a buyer and manager of a fashion accessories store. The marketing teacher at a local high school has asked you to speak to the fashion marketing class about owning a fashion business.

ACTIVITY You will review the topics in your presentation with your assistant manager (judge).

EVALUATION You will be evaluated on how well you meet the following performance indicators:

- Discuss career opportunities in the field of apparel and accessories.
- Identify desirable personality traits important to business.
- Explain the types of business ownership.
- Demonstrate a customer-service mindset.
- Explain types of retailers.

INTERNET ACTIVITY

Use the Internet to access the Small Business Administration Web site for information.

- Click Starting Your Business.
- Click Are you ready?
- Write an answer to the question and cite information from this article.
- E-mail the paper to your teacher.

➡ For a link to the Small Business Administration Web site to help you do this activity, go to **marketingseries.glencoe.com**.

LA-Z-BOY: UP FROM NAUGAHYDE

There's an old joke about motor scooters: They're fun until your friends see you on one. The same can be said about reclining chairs. Who wouldn't want to kick back in a La-Z-Boy Power Rocker with ten-speed heated massage? Then again, would you want your friends to see you in one?

That dilemma creates a big problem for La-Z-Boy, Inc. That company has one of the most recognizable brand names in the nation. Yet the 76-year-old Michigan-based company just isn't cool. That's why La-Z-Boy turned to someone who is: former fashion designer Todd Oldham, who created a new line of furniture and accessories for the easy-chair king. "I got lots of laughs," Oldham admits, when he first told his *fashionista* friends he was designing for La-Z-Boy.

The Next Generation

Laz-Z-Boy started moving beyond recliners in the early 1980s, but it hasn't done a great job of getting that message out. Its stodgy armchair image could become more of a problem as the new style-conscious 20-somethings roll in. Enter Oldham. La-Z-Boy hired him to design the new line, which includes furniture, lamps, picture frames, vases, and candles. The goal: to make younger buyers forget their reservations about the brand. Oldham put together a collection of stylish, retro furniture with simple lines. If the style doesn't wow younger shoppers, the prices might. The line is priced slightly below La-Z-Boy's regular lineup. And the size of the furniture has been scaled to fit apartments or starter homes. The arms, legs, and backs on Oldham's Snap sofa come off so it can become a daybed or squeezed up a narrow staircase.

La-Z-Boy is tweaking its marketing, too. The company is targeting hipper channels, such as *InStyle* magazine and MTV, with ads featuring the boyish-looking Oldham.

Despite the early praise, success is anything but assured for Oldham. His career as an upscale clothing designer fizzled in the late 1990s when he failed to build a following for his high-contrast colors and patterns. But La-Z-Boy dealers love him. If that excitement turns into sales, La-Z-Boy and Oldham both will be able to put their feet up for a while.

By Christopher Palmeri

CREATIVE JOURNAL

In your journal, write your responses:

CRITICAL THINKING

1. How did Todd Oldham apply his design experience to expand his career opportunities?

APPLICATION

2. Consider the fashion job that interests you most. Imagine you have taken courses and gained experience for that job, but you cannot find an available job. Use the Internet and newspapers to research three related fashion jobs to which you could apply your skills and experience. Write a one-page paper discussing your options.

 Go to **businessweek.com** for current *BusinessWeek* Online articles.

UNIT LAB

House of Style

You've just entered the real world of fashion. The House of Style assists fashion businesses and individuals to conceive, plan, produce, and sell the latest and most popular fashion products. Acting as the owner, manager, or employee of the House of Style, you will have the opportunity to work on different projects to promote the success of this fashion business.

Working With Textiles—Recruit New Employees

SITUATION You are assisting the human resource department of the Mills Fabric Company, a textile fabric manufacturer. The company engages in each step of fabric production, from design to the production of the completed product. Mills Fabrics employs many people in a variety of jobs, from textile designer to truck driver. Mills Fabrics is planning to open a retail fabric store at its plant. The company has a policy of promoting from within the company and spends a lot of money on employee training and retention. You are to create a plan for recruiting employees for the store and for Mills Fabrics in general. You are to present your plan to the head of the human resource department.

ASSIGNMENT Complete these tasks:
- Plan your new employee-recruitment plan using various media to get your message to potential employees.
- Estimate the costs of your new employee-recruitment plan.
- Create career ladders for the positions.
- Create a final report.

TOOLS AND RESOURCES To complete the assignment, you will need to:
- Conduct research about the jobs and career positions available at Mills Fabrics. Use the library, the Internet, and the telephone.
- Ask other fashion industry businessowners about their employee-recruitment plans.
- Have word-processing, spreadsheet, and presentation software.

RESEARCH Do your research:
- Find the best media to spread the word about the employment needs.
- Study the recruitment plans of other businesses and determine which are most effective.
- Get cost estimates for creating and implementing your plan.

REPORT Prepare a written report using the following tools:
- *Word-processing program:* Prepare a written report that includes an outline of your employee-recruitment plan, media, and number of employees needed.
- *Spreadsheet program:* Prepare a budget chart for your recruitment plan. Prepare a chart of the career ladders you determine.
- *Presentation program:* Prepare a ten-slide visual presentation with key points, some visuals, and some text.

PRESENTATION AND EVALUATION You will present your report to the Mills Fabrics human resource department. You will be evaluated on the basis of:
- Knowledge of retail careers and career recruitment
- Continuity of presentation
- Voice quality
- Eye contact

PORTFOLIO
Add this report to your career portfolio.

Famous Designers

The fashion industry is powered by creative designers from around the world. There are thousands of men and women who design and create apparel and accessories, but only a few are household names. Today's designers develop a niche for themselves in one market and then expand their offerings to attract more customers. A ready-to-wear (RTW) designer may create haute-couture lines for upscale clients in the same season that he or she designs lines of clothing for a discount superstore. Some designers work exclusively for a fashion house, while others freelance or branch out on their own. It is also not unusual for a designer to work under several top fashion firms before creating his or her own label.

Listed below are many famous and influential designers and design companies of the last 100 years. Keep in mind that this is only a sampling since there are thousands of fashion designers all over the globe.

Joseph Abboud Based in New York, he is an American designer of classic men's and women's RTW clothing.

Haider Ackermann Colombian-born, trained in Antwerp and now working in Paris, he is known for designs with an elegant edge. His styles are sophisticated and urban.

Adolfo Born in Cuba, he came to New York and made a name for himself making hats. In the late 1960s, this designer added separates for men and women.

Gilbert Adrian From 1923 to 1939, he was a top designer for MGM, where he dressed movies stars such as Greta Garbo and Katherine Hepburn.

Agnes b A French freelance designer since the 1960s, she established her own label of simple and chic collections in the early 1980s. Her collections include men's and women's apparel, maternity clothes, skincare products, and cosmetics.

Agua de Coco This group includes Brazilian designers of beachwear, sportswear, and accessories, which debuted on the Sao Paulo runway in 2002.

Agua Doce Founded in 1999, this design group is dedicated to swimwear and beach accessories. Based in Brazil, the company offers laid-back, simple styles.

Akris A Parisian designer of easy and classic ensembles for women, his Spring 2005 collection featured flowing, sensual gowns, white linen, tailored jackets, and unconstructed pants.

Azzedine Alaia Born in Tunisia, and based in Paris, this designer creates body-conscious RTW clothing.

Walter Albini He was among the first Italian designers of RTW.

Alfani Petite This company creates stylish men's and women's wear for petite consumers. The fashions are sophisticated and fashion forward.

Victor Alfaro Born in Mexico, he is known for U.S. women's wear.

Alice and Olivia Named after the designers' mothers, this fashion company creates pants. Designers are Americans Stacey Bendet and Rebecca Winn. Hand-painted fabrics, stripes, and colors are their signatures.

Linda Allard This American designer of career clothes and RTW heads up the Ellen Tracy label.

All Saints Designers Stuart Trevor and Lait Bolangaro teamed up to create edgy street wear for men and women. The company is based in London.

Alphadi Born in Timbuktu, he balances his native desert styles with western styles. His inspiration comes from the diversity of African culture. He got his start in the fashion world in 1983.

Alphorria Since 1985, this Brazilian designer has created elegant and sensual clothes.

Hardy Amies Amies is a British designer known for tailored suits, coats, and eveningwear.

Adeline André André is a contemporary high-fashion designer from Paris whose style focuses on basics. Fashions are elegant yet simple.

Giorgio Armani This Italian designer is known for finely tailored suits and upscale, casual RTW for men and women. He has been a major force in the fashion world since the 1990s.

Amaya Arzuaga This Spanish designer began her company in 1994 and debuted at London's Fashion Week in 1997.

Laura Ashley She is a London-based designer of Victorian-styled clothing. Romantic and pretty dresses, clothing, and home furnishings are available worldwide.

Badgley Mischka New York designers Mark Badgley and James Mischka create baroque-styled, colorful, ornate collections.

Cristobal Balenciaga This Spaniard was a major force in the fashion world from the 1940s until his retirement in 1968. He is known for many innovations in fashion design, including the cocoon coat, balloon skirt, pillbox hat, and patterned hosiery.

Bally This is a Swiss design company with successful lines of shoes, handbags, and other leather goods.

Pierre Balmain This Parisian designer began in the mid-1940s with classic daytime clothes and lavish eveningwear.

Patrick de Barentzen A daring Italian couture designer of the 1960s, he is known for playful apparel such as his *Infanta* skirt (an enormous skirt).

Jhane Barnes This American designer is known for upscale men's clothing.

Jean Barthet This influential hat maker in the 1950s and 1960s designed for Princess Grace, Sophia Loren, and other celebrities.

John Bartlett From Ohio, he founded his own label in 1992. Although he has much experience with women's wear, his men's line creates a stir each year.

BCBG Maxazria Max Azria created this company in the late 1980s. The BCBG stands for *Bon Chic Bon Genre,* or "good style, good attitude." The label is known for combining chic and sophisticated European styling with an American spirit.

Geoffrey Beene This American designer is an award-winning legend who creates beautiful, couture-quality and casual clothes. He also offers shoes, eyeglasses, gloves, hosiery, home furnishings, and more.

Alicia Bell From Chicago, she was an assistant at Vivienne Westwood before starting her own label in the early 2000s. She is known for her tailoring and details as well as a romantic, feminine look.

Benetton This family-run clothing company from Italy is known for fun and classic everyday wear. The sweaters and coats are very popular.

Antonio Berardi An Italian-English designer, he creates street-inspired clothing as well as high-end fashion.

Manolo Blahnik A popular high-fashion shoe designer from Spain, he is now based in London.

Bill Blass This American designer of classic, casual, RTW, and elegant fashions for men and women also designs everything from automobiles to candy.

Blumarine This label offers contemporary, flirty sportswear made with comfortable, stretchy fabrics.

Bottega Veneta This company is known for extraordinary leather goods, such as handbags and shoes.

Marc Bohan From the 1960s until 1989, he was a popular designer at Dior.

Nicolas Bosch From Spain, he is an award-winning fabric designer.

Hugo Boss This German clothier founded his company in 1923 and remained a leader in fashion, who is known for high-end suits, and classic women's wear.

Véronique Branquinho From Belgium, this contemporary designer is known for monochrome romanticism and detail in designs for men and women.

Donald Brooke A designer in the 1960s, his work was used frequently on the Broadway stages.

Marilyn Brooks A Canadian designer, she was popular in the 1970s with her funky, trendy fashions.

Dana Buchman Buchman designs bridge lines for the Liz Claiborne company. Fashions include casual, evening, and more.

Burberry For over 100 years, this company has been known for its trademark plaid. In recent years, the company emerged on the high-fashion scene.

Stephen Burrows This designer is known for colorful, body-conscious fashions such as draped jerseys.

Byblos Known for non-conformist styles, this Italian-based fashion firm is trendy and stylish.

Cacharel Jean Cacharel launched his line in Paris in 1964 with RTW collections for men, and then women. The designer's previous experience at a men's tailoring shop taught him to design comfortable, easy-to-wear fashions. In the 1960s, his women's shirts were a must-have item. In 2000, the husband-and-wife team of Clements-Ribiero was hired as head designers.

Callet Soeurs Three sisters in France ran this popular fashion house in the early 1900s. It was considered one of the best dressmaking houses of the era and was famous for the use of lace, chiffon, and embroidered patterns.

Robert Capucci An Italian designer, his designs were popular in the 1950s. Styles included draped and imaginative cuts.

Pierre Cardin Although he was born in Italy, this very famous French designer worked for Dior before opening his own couturier house in 1950. He is known for being the first Parisian couturier to sell his own RTW and license his name for other products.

Hattie Carnegie Carnegie began as a hat maker and expanded to custom designs and RTW. She was popular in the 1930s and 1940s.

Bonnie Cashin This American designer is known for being among the first to create comfortable country clothes, such as hooded jersey dresses and ponchos.

Oleg Cassini Based in New York, he is known for classic women's wear—and also licenses many products.

Jean-Charles de Castelbajac Based in Paris, he is known for rugged-looking apparel for men and women. He uses canvas, plaids, and quilted cottons.

Antonio Del Castillo He designed for Lanvin in the 1950s and 1960s, and later opened his own house of design.

John Cavanaugh In the 1950s, he was among the leading designers in England and was known for the nip-waisted, full-skirted look.

Céline Founded in Paris in 1947 as a shoe store for kids, the company expanded its line to include leather goods, accessories, and women's RTW. Today its product lines include fragrances and men's RTW.

Nino Cerruti This Italian designer created RTW knits, women's wear, and other licensed products.

Hussein Chalayan A top designer in England at the turn of the century, his designs had strong technical quality.

Gabrielle "Coco" Chanel This famous French couturier is known for introducing many things: slacks for women, the little black dress, boxy, collarless suits, legendary fragrances, and more. Though she died in 1971, her design house remains among the top fashion houses.

Chloé This Parisian fashion house first opened in 1952 with designers Jacques Lenoir and Gaby Aghion. Though its designers have changed through the years, Chloé's philosophy has not. It remains distinctive by offering modern, wearable clothes that are not necessarily the current fashion standard.

Lulu Cheung Based in Hong Kong, she designs elegant clothes for women.

David Chu From Taiwan, he is now based in New York and designs for Nautica, a classic sportswear firm.

Liz Claiborne An American designer, now retired, her company continues to generate coordinated sportswear, accessories, and more.

Ozzie Clark In the 1960s, this British designer was known for hot pants, maxi coats, and reviving 1940s fashions.

Cole Haan This contemporary American shoe designer creates casual and dressy styles.

Sean Combs Also known as P Diddy in the hip-hop world of music, this American men's wear designer began a line of clothing called Sean Jean to address urban contemporary fashion needs.

Comme des Garcons Led by designer Rei Kawakubo, this clothing company was the vanguard of New Wave fashions from Japan in the 1980s.

Sybil Connolly Connolly is a popular and influential Irish designer.

Jasper Conran Based in England, he designs bright, youthful fashions.

Andres Courrèges Known as the Basque tailor, he was very hot in the 1960s with tough chic, white clothing, and suits with roomy coats.

Costume National An Italian company led by designer Ennio Capasa and his brother Carlo, it is devoted to elegant, contemporary styles. Since 1986, they have blended cultural influences from around the globe.

Angela Cummings This designer is an inventive, tasteful jewelry designer at Tiffany's.

Lilly Dache From the 1930s to the 1950s, this American hat maker created popular draped turbans, snoods, and brimmed hats.

David Dart Award-winning American designer of 1990s, he designs contemporary California-style fashions.

Daryl K This Los Angeles-based designer is known for bright, colorful sportswear.

Donald Davies Dublin-based shirt designer of lightweight Irish tweed, he began making shirtdresses in the 1960s.

Xavier Delcour This young Belgian designer is known for hard-hitting fashions that use street funk and urban stylings. Based in Paris, his designs are popular among the young, rebellious fashion market.

Alessandro Dell'Acqua Modern and contemporary, this Italian designer offers chic RTW for men and women. Previously with Costume National and Helmut Lang, he launched a label in 1996.

Louis Dell'Olio Based in New York, he used to design for Anne Klein but now has his own company.

Ann Demeulemeester A Belgian-born designer, she emerged in the 1980s with avant-garde, cutting-edge, versatile, often all-black fashions.

Diesel This company is an Italian brand of hip, trendy sportswear that utilizes creative stylings and irreverent advertising. Designer Renzo Rosso founded the company and introduces new ideas to the fashion world. Known for innovative clothing and accessories, its designs are expanding into home furnishings.

Colette Dinnigan This Australian designer creates lingerie-inspired dresses.

Christian Dior In 1947, this French designer launched The New Look with closely fitted blouses and long, full skirts. Dior remains a top name in the fashion world, offering everything from cosmetics to haute couture to sunglasses.

David Dixon This Canadian designer is known for fine tailoring in men's and women's clothing.

Dolce & Gabbana Two Italian designers who teamed up in 1982 to become one of the hottest fashion duos in history, they are known for modern, romantic styles and high-end casual styles for men and women.

Jean Dresses This French couturier from 1925 to 1965 was among the first to start mass producing lower-priced goods for Americans.

Dsquared2 Twin brothers Dean and Dan Caten of Italy are fashion-forward designers who set trends in fashion and create a sensation in the pop-iconic world. Started in 1994, the team creates fashions for men and women, favoring lean, tailored jackets, tight T-shirts, and low-cut pants. Clientele include Madonna and Nicholas Cage.

Randolph Duke This American designer creates bold, striking clothing.

Escada This upscale German fashion label specializes in elegant, tailored sportswear.

Alber Elbaz With past experience at YSL and Krizia, Elbaz has been the creative director of Lanvin since 2001. He creates women's RTW from superb fabrics.

Perry Ellis One of the best-known American designers, he was popular for youthful, adventurous clothes of natural fibers and earth-tone colors. Since his death in 1986, the company has remained a top seller of casual sportswear.

Etro This popular contemporary designer uses colorful patterns, such as paisley. Etro is also known for incorporating intricate detail into each item.

Alberto Fabiani In the 1950s, he was one of the top Italian couturiers and was a master suit tailor. He designed fine, conservative apparel.

Jacques Fath He ran his own fashion house in Paris from 1937 to 1954. He specialized in plunging necklines and shaped clothing for women.

Fendi This Italian fashion standard is a family-owned business known for upscale RTW, furs, and handbags. Items are very well constructed and fashionable.

Louis Féraud Designing glamorous dresses and luxurious fashions put this French designer on the map in the 1980s. He made a name by creating dresses, gowns, and suits for two popular TV shows, *Dallas* and *Dynasty*. He died in 1999, but his company remains a force in the fashion world.

Salvatore Ferragamo Internationally known shoemaker and RTW designer from Italy, he pioneered wedge heels and platform soles for shoes.

Gianfranco Ferré This Italian designer heads Dior. He is famous for creating clean lines and complex, structured clothing.

Alberta Ferretti She is a master of soft, sheer, pretty, and breezy styles. Based in Milan, she has her own label and creates for the label Philosophy.

Andrew Fezza American RTW designer, he is known for his clean, relaxed, casually elegant fashions.

Katia Filippova Filippova is a Russian avant-garde designer of Western "pop" styles in Moscow.

Anne Fogarty She is known for revolutionizing junior sizes and apparel in the 1950s.

Fontana Sisters Family owned since 1907, this was a leading couture house in Italy in the 1950s.

Tom Ford This American designer made a name for himself at Gucci and YSL. He is a top couture designer known for classic, innovative design.

Federico Forquet A 1960s icon in Rome, he was known for coats and suits that were blocky with bold colors.

Mariano Fortuny An Italian designer of the early 20th century, he was known for long, delicate, pleated gowns, reminiscent of ancient Greek styles.

James Galanos An American designer of elegant fashions, his couture designs include gowns and dresses.

Irene Galitzine She started the palazzo-pajama craze of the 1960s and later designed furs, linens, and cosmetics.

John Galliano Specializing in bias-cut evening clothes and eccentric RTW, he has designed at Givenchy and Dior.

Jean-Paul Gaultier A French designer of controversial and unusual RTW, his lines are high-end and inspired by the street look. Unisex styling is his trademark.

Genny This is an Italian label that specializes in eveningwear and fine women's wear.

Rudi Gernreich American designer of daring clothes in the 1960s, he created see-through blouses, tight mini-dresses, and topless swimsuits.

Ghost Soft fabrics and feminine stylings highlight this popular British label.

Romeo Gigli This Italian designer is known for unusual colors and muted styles.

Marithé and François Girbaud They are contemporary designers of hip and trendy sportswear. Their denim and sportswear label began in the late 1960s and is still based in Paris. They have been devoted to youth culture and fashion-forward styles, staying ahead of the niche market.

Hubert de Givenchy A popular French designer of elegant designs since opening his house of fashion in 1952, he has many licensing agreements for everything from perfume and hosiery to sportswear and home furnishings.

Andrew Gn This designer from Paris creates simple, elegant, glamorous styles for the modern woman.

Gottex This is an Israeli design company that makes foundations such as lingerie, bathing suits, and beach cover-ups.

Alix Gres Wanting to be a sculptor, this French designer became popular creating draped and molded jersey dresses. He worked pre-WWII, but then closed business during the war. He reopened after the war and designed through the mid-1980s.

Aldo Gucci Based in Florence, Italy, his is one of the major design houses. The family-run business makes everything from fashionable apparel to leathers, luggage, and eyewear. Gucci owns design firms YSL and Alexander McQueen.

Halston One of America's top designers in the 1970s, he created ultra-suede dresses and suits, simple classics, lovely gowns, and RTW. He was popular among many celebrities until his death in 1990. His brand name is still licensed.

Norman Hartnell Owner of one of the biggest couture houses in London in the 1930s, he made gowns for Queen Elizabeth.

Edith Head This design icon was the leading American costume designer in the Hollywood film industry. She died in 1981.

Jacques Heim Parisian couturier from 1920s to 1960s, he designed the first bikini bathing suit.

Alexander Herchcovitch This designer of men's and women's fashions uses skull patterns and latex, which made him famous in the mid-1990s. He designs jeans, shoes, linens, and bath accessories.

Stan Herman Since the 1960s, he has designed uniforms and inexpensive fashions. He revived chenille as a fashion fabric and owned the Mr. Mort clothing line in the 1960s and 1970s.

Hermés Designer of fine French scarves, leather goods, ties, apparel, fragrances and gifts, Hermés creates very exclusive merchandise.

Caroline Herrera Born in Venezuela, this designer has made a name for herself in America with dresses, wedding and ball gowns, RTW, jewelry, fragrances, and made-to-order clothes.

Tommy Hilfiger A young, hip American designer who is popular with fashion fans of all ages. Hilfiger is known for an all-American, casual look. He designs everything from clothes to accessories to home furnishings.

Alannah Hill After growing up in Tasmania, this designer of very feminine fashions established her own label in the late 1990s.

Barbara Hulanicki She was known in the 1960s for the mod look, coordinating color in clothing, cosmetics, and stockings.

Iceberg This design company is popular with 20-something consumers interested in upscale, fashionable trends.

Irene A favorite among movie stars for many years, this designer also sold RTW in the 1960s.

Isani A Korean brother-and-sister team, Isani is known for youthful shirtdresses and Chanel-inspired suits.

Akira Isogawa An Australian boutique owner since 1993, who launched a first collection in 1996, Isogawa creates a wide range of sportswear and couture as well as costumes for the Sydney Dance Company.

Marc Jacobs An influential American designer of the 1990s and 2000s, his style is relaxed, grungy-hobo chic meets sophisticated style. Designs include stylish coats and cargo skirts and pants of textured fabrics. Lines include men's and women's RTW.

Charles James An American couturier from Chicago who operated dressmaking salons in London and Paris, he created eccentric and very innovative designs. James died in 1978.

Betsey Johnson Funky, youthful dresses and sportswear with a sense of humor are this American designer's trademarks.

Anand Jon From South India, he moved to New York to study design. He started in jewelry and moved to designing exquisite, elaborate Indo-chic fashions.

Stephen Jones One of London's top hat makers, he designed for Princess Diana.

Wolfgang Joop Joop is a German designer known for men's and women's clothing and has technical knowledge of fabric, using it in his designs.

Alexander Julian Men's wear designer based in New York, he uses interesting colors.

Gemma Kahng This designer is Korean and is known for creating classic suits in bright colors.

Norma Kamali An American designer known for creating body-conscious fashions, her styles are adventurous. She uses unique fabrics, including sweatshirt material with unexpected designs.

Jacques Kaplan This New York furrier is known for fun and unique designs.

Donna Karan This top American designer is a leader in simple, well-made sportswear. She popularized the bodysuit and has several licensed products including shoes, jewelry, hosiery, and eyewear.

Kasper Well-known in the United States, this American designer makes classic suits and separates for the professional.

Rei Kawakubo Japanese designer who made a name for himself creating French RTW, his clothes are animated with texture and pattern. In the 1980s, he led the company Comme des Garcons.

Dice Kayek Based in Paris, this youth-oriented designer creates modern looks that are conservative enough for a country club. His 2004 collection was reminiscent of 1960s, Jackie Kennedy-era fashions.

Kenzo This Japanese designer, based in Paris since the 1960s, is known for fun fashions and RTW as well as for several popular fragrances.

Emmanuelle Khanh One of Paris's first RTW designers in the 1960s, Khanh is known for whimsical, youthful fashions.

Charles Kleibacker Known for using the bias-cut, he opened his own business in New York in the 1960s.

Anne Klein This American designer is known for classic sportswear and redesigning junior styles into a more mature look. Though the designer died in 1974, the brand continues to sell.

Calvin Klein He became famous in the 1970s with his jeans and followed up for decades with designing simple, sophisticated sportswear. Klein uses natural fabrics and clean-cut lines for men and women.

Jean-Paul Knott A Parisian designer, he creates edgy, modern clothes for men and women.

Michael Kors One of America's top sportswear designers, he creates individual pieces and combines them to create fashionable outfits. His style is spare, simple, and wearable.

Krizia This Italian design firm was started by a husband-and-wife team. They use unique fabrics and animal themes.

Ana Kuzmanic Born in Yugoslavia, this designer creates feminine styles.

Lacoste A sportswear and active-wear design firm that was very popular in the 1970s, Lacoste was founded in 1927 by René Lacoste. He was a true innovator who revolutionized men's tennis attire with a classic woven long-sleeved shirt. The company revived in the early 2000s.

Christian Lacroix French RTW designer since the 1980s, he is known for dresses with fitted tops and bubble skirts. He also designs costumes for theater and ballet.

Karl Lagerfeld Born in Germany and based in France, this avant-garde designer creates fashions for Fendi and Chanel. He also designs clothes under his own name and shoes for several top shoemakers.

Helmut Lang An Austrian designer who became popular in the 1990s, he uses unusual high-tech fabrics to create rumpled, layered fashions. Lang is considered very fashion forward and techno-hip.

Jeanne Lanvin Before and after the two World Wars, Lanvin was one of the top Parisian couturiers who was known for several perfumes.

Eddie Lau Lau is a popular designer based in Hong Kong.

Ralph Lauren Beginning as a tie designer, Lauren is now among the best-known and popular American designers. He is famous for classic men's and women's lines. Largely influenced by the American West, his company makes everything from home furnishings and accessories to cosmetics.

Alicia Lawhon Originally from Mexico, this designer works in Hollywood. Since 1996, she has established a celebrity following. The first garment she made was a pair of bondage pants.

Marc Le Bihan An experimentalist designer based in Paris, he is known for his own style of Gothic fashions.

Léonard Parisian designer of wearable, sensible fashions; he uses rich fabrics, furs, and cashmere. Some collections are designed by Véronique Leroy.

Véronique Leroy This French designer is inspired by retro looks from the 1960s and 1970s. She uses tweeds and wools in her winter collections.

Allyson Lewis With past experience at Old Navy, Macy's, and Fenn Wright and Manson, she launched her own *ta/nin* label in 2000. It represents updated bridge sportswear for young, fashion-forward women.

Alexandra Lind A native New Yorker who began making clothes for herself at age 16, she is known for structured and tailored, yet sexy clothes. She debuted in 1999.

Loewe The company began as a small leather factory in Madrid in 1846 and has been known for its handbags for over 100 years. In the 1970s, Loewe expanded its product line to include scarves, women's clothing, and perfume. Men's wear was introduced in the 1980s.

Christian Louboutin The designer is a popular Parisian designer of elegant, stylish shoes.

Jean Louis He was a Hollywood fashion designer who headed up his own couture firm.

Lutz Based in Paris, this alternative fashion designer mixes interesting fabrics and shapes to create a modern look.

Bob Mackie Well-known Californian designer to the stars, Mackie made glamorous gowns as well as daytime clothing and swimwear.

Mainbocher Known for quality, Mainbocher was one of the first custom design houses in Paris.

Catherine Malandrino She designs women's clothing, including fitted blouses and elegant apparel.

Isabel Marant A Parisian-based designer of bohemian, independent, and expressive fashions, she uses violets and purples with whites and beiges.

Marcel Marongiu Classic men's wear designer of formal attire and casual looks, his designs are rich in color and versatile. Marongiu is based in Paris.

Alviero Martini Martini is an Italian designer of clothing, shoes, watches, ties, and scarves for men and women.

Germana Marucelli A popular Milan-based couturier in the 1950s and 1960s, Marucelli designed avant-garde fashions.

Keita Maruyama Ruffles and feminine styles dominate this young designer's collections for women. From casual to dressy styles, this Parisian-based designer is very versatile.

Matsuda Inspired by traditional Japanese clothing, this company makes fashions for men and women.

Vera Maxwell She was one of the first American sportswear designers.

Claire McCardell In the 1940s and 1950s, she was considered among the top American designers. She specialized in practical clothes for the average woman and used sturdy fabrics such as denim and wool jersey.

Stella McCartney A top designer since the late 1990s, she uses luscious fabrics and stylish, hip designs. Her early work was done with Christian Lacroix and Chloé.

Pat McDonagh This is a fashion designer from Canada.

Mary McFadden An American designer of women's clothing known for luxurious fabrics, hand-painted tunics, exquisite detailing with pleats and braided trim, she started out as a maker of exotic jewelry in the 1970s.

Alexander McQueen Born in London, he has been working in fashion since age 16. He is a fashion innovator, known for using shocking effects at his shows. His creations combine exquisite tailoring with hard-edged street style.

Nicole Miller This American designer started out creating men's ties and boxer shorts. She then expanded her line to include clothing with unique prints for men and women.

Nolan Miller A designer of glamorous fashions for celebrities, his work has been seen on many TV shows, most notably *Dynasty* of the 1980s.

Yvan Mispelaere Formerly with Louis Feraud, this Parisian designer is inventive and exciting.

Missoni This design firm is run by an Italian husband-and-wife team. They create RTW in simple knits and abstract patterns. High-end sportswear and evening clothes are their specialty.

Issey Miyake This Japanese designer is among the top designers in Paris today. He uses exotic fabrics and avant-garde designs.

Isaac Mizrahi A young, American designer, he gained experience under Perry Ellis and Calvin Klein before branching out on his own. Known for inventive, fun clothes in unexpected colors and fabrics, he designs for high-end clients and also mass markets a line for Target stores.

Anna Molinari Italian designer of several lines, her designs focus on romantic, sensual, and cultural influences.

Capt. Edward Molyneux The rich and famous were drawn to this Parisian designer's salon from the 1920s through the 1960s. Designs are known for purity of line.

Mondi This German RTW company is known for graceful knits and a variety of accessories, from wallets to handbags.

Claude Montana A French designer, Montana is known for bold, well-defined clothes with broad, exaggerated shoulders. Leather fashions are a specialty.

Pedro Morago Morago is a Spanish designer of relaxed, loose men's wear.

Hanae Mori Based in Paris, this Japanese designer creates fine apparel in beautiful colors. Mori also uses elaborate and creative beading.

Digby Morton In 1930s, this designer opened a fashion house in London, specializing in tailored suits, cable knit sweaters, and tweeds.

Roland Mouret A French-born designer, he is known for blending ease and glamour in dresses and women's wear.

Mr. John In the 1940s and 1950s, he was one of America's leading hat makers.

Thierry Mugler This Paris-based designer creates high style and avant-garde clothes and accessories.

Jean Muir Muir began designing in the 1960s and is known for elegant, detailed, classic fashions.

Josie Natori Based in New York, this designer is from the Philippines and is a popular high-end, elegant lingerie maker.

Alexandra Nea An Australian designer, she specializes in cocktail/eveningwear as well as unique and distinctive daywear.

Norman Norrell This American designer was known for precise tailoring and timeless elegance.

Margarita Nuez A Spanish designer, Nuez creates apparel for professional, working women.

Todd Oldham A hip, trendy American designer, Oldham is somewhat of a celebrity himself. He is known for offbeat prints, trims, and simple designs. He has designed a line of home accessories for Target, high-end lines of sportswear, and furniture for La-Z-Boy.

Frank Olive Olive has been a sharp hat maker since the 1960s.

André Oliver He was associated with Pierre Cardin and created clothes for men and women during the 1950s.

Paquin In 1891, this couturier was among the first to open a fashion house in Paris. The designer remained popular until the 1950s.

Andrew Paluba He is a young, New York designer who targets sophisticated youth and older clientele. Designs focus on new takes on the classics.

Mollie Parnis She is a popular and successful women's wear designer.

Jean Patou She designed elegant fashions for women in the 1920s and 1930s.

Mme. Paulette She was a top American hat maker in the 1950s and 1960s.

Sylvia Pedlar Founder of Irish Lingerie, she is known for high-fashion loungewear.

Alex Perry Based in Australia, he is one of the country's most popular designers of glamorous gowns, RTW, and couture.

Alice Philips Known for wearable sculptures of raw wool and earth tones, Philips's designs include ceremonial vests and more.

Bruno Pieters This young, Belgian-born designer launched his first complete RTW collection in 2002, proving his penchant for technique and craftsmanship. Experimental fashions include deconstructed silk chiffon dresses and pleated miniskirts.

Manuel Pina He is an internationally known Spanish designer of elegant clothes for women.

Robert Piquet He ran a fashion house from 1933 to 1951 and influenced Dior and Givenchy.

Plein Sud This technologically edgy French label includes designs by Faycal Amore. The company has existed for almost 20 years. Amore's clothes are sold to A-listers and everyday consumers.

Paul Poiret A French designer of the early 1900s, Poiret was considered the father of the French fashion industry. He introduced many fresh ideas, such as a hobble skirt, turbans, and kimono tunics.

Thea Porter In the 1960s and 1970s, this designer of anti-establishment attire was based in London.

Zac Posen This New York-based designer spent his high school years interning at the Metropolitan Museum of Art's Costume Institute, designing clothes and handbags for Tocca and Nicole Miller. He studied in London and designed custom-made dresses for models and rock stars.

Anna Potok This designer was founder of the leading fur design company Maximilian.

Jesus de Pozo This Spanish designer creates colorful but simple women's apparel.

Miuccia Prada She is one of today's top designers of RTW and high-end clothing, accessories, and more. From an Italian family whose business produces high-quality leather goods, Prada's fashions are soft, comfortable, chic, and conservative. Lines include Prada and Miu Miu.

Emilio Pucci Once a member of Italy's Olympic ski team, he is credited for designing light-weight jersey dresses in bright, bold, geometric fabrics. He died in 1992.

Lilly Pulitzer Popular during the 1960s and 1970s, this designer made a comeback with brightly printed cottons and resort attire.

Mary Quant Among the top designers of her day in London, England, in the mid-1950s, she has been credited with creating the mod look. Some of her notable contributions include miniskirts, hip-hugger pants, and hot pants.

Paco Rabanne A Spanish-born, Romanian designer who presented his first couture collection in Paris in 1964, Rabanne caught attention with futuristic garments made of plastic and aluminum. His style was called "space age," and year after year, he created groundbreaking, often bizarre clothing.

Madeleine de Rauche In the 1930s, this designer made functional sports clothes for women.

Tracy Reese A young American designer, Reese is known for brightly colored, whimsical designs that incorporate modern technology with vintage flair.

Oscar de la Renta Born in the Dominican Republic and based in New York, he is one of America's top designers of men's and women's collections. Designs include elegant, feminine daywear and men's suits.

Zandra Rhodes This British-based designer is known for using rich fabrics, such as silk and chiffon, and for designing outrageous evening looks. Many of the designs are based on history and art.

Clements Ribeiro "Focused and eclectic" best describes this husband-and-wife team. Their ability to mix colors and textures and create strong, interesting fashions helped put them on the map. Also, they are art directors for Cacharel.

Jacqueline de Ribes This former socialite uses her love of couture in her RTW designs.

Nina Ricci A Parisian designer who opened a fashion house in 1932, her designs were geared toward mature, elegant women. Her fragrance L'Air du Temps is a perennial favorite.

John Rocha This British designer who spent time in Paris is known for using innovative fabrics and colors, experimenting with textures and layering.

Marcel Rochas In the 1930s and 1940s, this French couturier created elegant clothing and fragrances.

Narciso Rodriguez This American designer of Cuban heritage gained worldwide recognition after designing Carolyn Bessette Kennedy's wedding dress. His signature is to create a frame in which to fit a woman's personality.

Carolyne Roehm Once an assistant to Oscar de la Renta, this socialite designs women's fashions.

Alice Roi This New Yorker specializes in original vintage designs. Her clothes are modern, not high tech, but original.

Gilles Rosier A Parisian designer formerly with Jean Paul Gaultier, he branched out on his own in 1992. Later he designed for Kenzo. He concentrates on his own label of women's fashions.

Christian Roth Based in New York, this designer is known for bright, colorful clothing in simple shapes.

Cynthia Rowley Based in New York, she is known for her creative and fun fashions for women.

Sonia Rykiel A Parisian RTW designer, she is famous for sweater dressing and knits.

Yves Saint Laurent One of the most influential French designers, he headed House of Dior at age 21. Later he opened his own RTW boutiques called *Rive Gauche*. Products include apparel, cosmetics, eyewear, and more.

Jil Sander This German designer began as a fashion journalist. Her creations include simple, fluid, well-proportioned apparel. She runs boutiques around the globe.

Count Fernando Sarmi He was the chief designer at Elizabeth Arden from 1951 to 1959 and is known for beautiful evening clothes. In the 1960s, he had his own line.

Arnold Scaasi This is an American designer who made glittering evening gowns, fancy dresses, and cocktail outfits for TV stars.

Jean-Louis Scherrer After opening his own fashion house in Paris in 1962, he became known for soft, refined dresses.

Elsa Schiaparelli One of most creative couturiers of the 1930s and 1940s, this designer was known for unconventional fashions such as fitted sweaters with bows and collars and other details.

Mila Schoen In the 1960s and 1970s, this Italian designer was prominent in the fashion world.

Ken Scott Originally from Indiana, this fabric and dress designer began working in Milan in 1956. His influences included Art Nouveau styles.

Junko Shimada This Japanese designer is popular in Paris. Colorful, rich fabrics and designs highlighted her 2004 collections.

Appendix 1

Ronaldus Shmask A New York-based men's wear designer, he is known for creating simple shapes and offbeat, solid-color clothes.

Crystal Siemens This Canadian designer is known for use of texture and color.

Simonetta She was among the first Italian designers of haute couture. She was married to fellow designer Albert Fabiani.

Adele Simpson She began in the 1940s by creating conservative and tasteful fashions.

Dominique Sirop His haute-couture clothes evolve season by season and are elegant, subtle, and inspiring. Sirop is based in Paris.

Martine Sitbon Born in Casablanca, Martine launched her collection in 1985 and later designed for Chloé. Her creations are made of exotic fabrics with unique cuts.

Francesco Smalto Paris-based men's wear designer, Smalto is known for pencil-thin pants, elegant and sophisticated suits, and pure lines.

Paul Smith This versatile British designer began in men's wear with his own label in 1976. He expanded to women's clothes and accessories.

Willi Smith This popular American designer began his own firm at age 28, making stylish, youthful clothes for men and women. Since his death in 1987, his company continues in the same tradition.

Franck Sorbier One of the most respected names in couture today, this Parisian-based designer is known for elegant, custom-made looks.

Stephen Sprouse This popular, contemporary, creative designer is known for the use of bold colors and 1960s influences.

St. John Designer Marie Gray's specialties are classic sophisticates and knits, including high-end suits for women.

Anna Sui An American designer of Chinese descent, she is known for mod, unconventional, adventurous, bohemian-styled clothing.

Alfred Sung He is a Canadian designer and couturier whose fashions are highly regarded by his peers.

Sybilla Although born in the United States, this designer creates fun fashions for the youth market in Spain.

Gustave Tassell A designer of refined, no-nonsense clothing, he started his own business in Los Angeles in the late 1950s.

Atsuro Tayama Based in Paris, this designer's recent collections favor fur, lamé, and leather in modern tuxedo-styled outfits.

Zang Toi Based in New York, this Malaysian designer creates fresh looks using bright colors.

Yuki Torii This Japanese designer found a niche with work in Paris.

Torrente Led by a young, French designer named Julien Fournié, this fashion company creates haute couture that focuses on femininity, shape, and elegant style.

Ellen Tracy Designer Linda Allard creates several lines of women's RTW for this established fashion firm.

Pauline Trigère She was a pioneer among female designers in the 1940s.

Alan Truong Born in Vietnam and based in New York, this young designer began his career creating evening gowns. By 2001, he turned to men's wear and has made a name for himself with colorful, fashion-forward designs.

Richard Tyler Originally from Australia, this designer is known for well-tailored and sophisticated styles. Based in New York and Los Angeles, he is popular with celebrities.

Patricia Underwood This British hat designer works in the United States.

Emanuel Ungaro A Paris-based designer of Italian descent, his body-conscious clothing and designs are colorful with unique patterns.

Valentina In 1928, this Russian designer opened up shop in the United States. Known for dramatic clothes, she designed for Greta Garbo.

Valentino Gowns, haute couture, and RTW make this Rome-based designer a worldwide favorite. He is a top designer of suits for men.

Carmen Marc Valvo Valvo is a designer of mid-priced evening gowns and cocktail dresses.

AF Vandevorst Based in Antwerp, this design company makes contemporary, creative fashions.

Tom Van Lingen This Belgian designer, who shows in Paris, offers a young, fresh look with colorful, abstract fashions.

Dries Van Noten A Belgian designer who has been on the fashion scene for many years, Van Noten is known for playful, feminine fashions.

John Varvatos This New York-based designer has his own label and designs for the sportswear company Nautica.

Philippe Venet He was Givenchy's master tailor from 1953 to 1962, after which he started his own company, designing lean suits with round shoulders.

Donatella Versace Gianni Versace's younger sister, she took over the Italian Versace fashion house.

Gianni Versace He was a prominent Italian designer of men's wear and women's wear and haute couture. His sister took over the company after his death in 1997.

Sally Victor Victor was a top American hat maker from the 1930s to the 1960s.

Madeleine Vionnet Along with Chanel and Balenciaga, this French couturier is considered among the top three couturiers of the 20th century. She is known for bias-cut dresses, cowl necklines, and handkerchief hems.

Vitorio & Lucchino This team of two designers from Spain is known for colorful lines of feminine and ornate clothing for women. They use fringe and lace with color and texture in the designs.

Adrienne Vittadini This well-known Hungarian-American designer uses colorful knits, modern prints, patterns, and comfortable fabrics in her upscale sportswear and evening lines.

Diane Von Furstenberg This designer is known for her landmark wrap-dress of the 1970s. She remains on the forefront of American designers, making everything from jeans to dresses. She and her company are based in New York.

Louis Vuitton Louis Vuitton was born in Anchay, France, in 1821 and walked to Paris at the age of 14. He got his start designing luggage, which is a staple of the Vuitton company. Marc Jacobs has been designing men's and women's clothing lines for the company since the 1990s.

Karen Walker An Australian designer, she specializes in fun, youthful fashions for women.

Amanda Wakeley A British designer with celebrity clientele, she is known for understated elegance and simple ideas expressed strongly. Lines include casual wear to eveningwear.

Vera Wang An American designer who was a child champion figure skater, she designs expensive and elegant wedding gowns as well as lovely evening dresses. She opened a private salon in Barney's New York where clients can make an appointment to meet with her.

Sharon Wauchob Originally from Ireland, this cult designer of alternative fashion is based in Paris.

John Weitz This designer was popular in the 1950s and 1960s with women's sportswear and men's apparel. Later he focused only on men's wear.

Vivienne Westwood A contemporary designer from England, she gets inspiration from trends in pop culture.

Bernard Willhelm Postmodern, urban, active wear for men highlights this designer's 2004 collections. Headquartered in Paris, his clothes are fun and eccentric.

Charles Frederick Worth French couturier of the 1880s, he designed for many royal figures during that time. His perfume, *Je Reviens*, is still sold today.

B.H. Wragge Pioneering sportswear separates in the 1940s and 1950s, this company was owned by Sydney Wragge.

Yohji Yamamoto Based in Paris, this Japanese designer is known for using layered knits to conceal rather than reveal. The style is minimalist but sexy and elegant.

Gaspard Yurkievich This Parisian launched his solo collection in 1998. His men's wear lines are youthful and energetic, geared toward forward-thinking fashionistas.

Slava Zaitsev This Russian designer is known for designing a variety of women's apparel.

Zucca Designer Akira Onozuka creates fresh, youthful fashions for men and women. He makes casual clothing that is artsy and fun.

Ben Zuckerman Known as a master tailor, this designer has had a major impact on styles of American suits and coats.

Appendix 2

The Art of a Fashion Show

Fashion is style—or the prevailing style or custom, as in dress or behavior. Fashion can also refer to apparel that is currently popular. A fashion show can be a simple or elaborate multimedia production designed to display and present new and current styles of clothing, accessories, hair, and cosmetics. Several elements make up a fashion show:

- Fashion models
- Fashion merchandise
- Staging
- Staff
- Budget

Fashion Models

Fashion models are men and women hired to exhibit style. Designers hire or cast models who have the appropriate "look" to represent their creations, including apparel and other fashion products. Models may specialize in runway, or live, fashion shows, or print modeling. Many successful models do both.

Once a model is hired to do a fashion show, he or she may attend a fitting prior to the show. The model might also meet with hair and makeup specialists before the show to develop and plan the model's appearance in the fashion show.

A *model lineup* form keeps track of what the model will wear, from stockings to jewelry. (See page 325 for a sample form.) It also includes a description of any props to be used and special instructions that might apply. The first line on the lineup form notes the lineup number for the model. This number designates the order of each outfit in which the model will appear.

Another important form used at fashion shows is the *fitting sheet*. (See page 326 for a sample form.) Fitting sheets are prepared for each outfit and include detailed information about the clothes and accessories to be worn. Also included is information about alterations and miscellaneous notations about the ensemble.

Fashion Merchandise

A *merchandise loan record* keeps track of items loaned by a designer, boutique, or department store for use in a fashion show. (See page 327 for a sample form.) The name of the store, title of the show, and department from which clothes are borrowed are among the necessary details included on this form.

	Model Lineup				

Name of model:

Title of show:

Lineup #	Apparel	Hosiery & shoes	Jewelry	Props & accessories	Instructions

Appendix 2

Fitting Sheet

Model's name: _____ Lineup #: _____

Sizes: Dress_____ Pant _____ Blouse _____

Shoe _____ Hosiery _____ Hat _____

Description of Garment:	**Accessories:**
(name of designer, type of garment, color, size, fabric, etc.)	(itemized description of all accessories, including shoes, belts, purses, jewelry, hats, scarves, etc.)
Necessary Alterations:	**Other Information:**
(hems, cuffs, fitted waist, etc.)	(special notes regarding props, wardrobe, the model, designer's requests, trends, etc.)

Merchandise Loan Record

Title of show: _____ Date of show: _____

Merchandise loaned from: _____

Designer or store: _____ Department: _____

Issued to: _____ Loan date: _____

Qty.	Style #	Color	Size	Description	Price

Merchandise returned by _____ Date _____

Received back in stock by _____

Appendix 2

Staging a Fashion Show

The staging and physical layout of a fashion show are key factors to the event's success. Runways from Paris and London to New York and Los Angeles are designed so that the models and their outfits are clearly visible, and that the transition of one model to the next is smooth.

IMPORTANT ELEMENTS Important elements of staging include a runway and stage elevated between 18 and 36 inches, so that the entire audience can see the show. In the audience, there should be no obstacles, such as pillars or furniture, obstructing the view of the stage and runway.

Models generally enter from one side of the stage and exit on the other side to avoid collisions. Creative set design and special effects must compliment each article of clothing and not interfere with a model's walk. Backdrops, when used, are placed out of the way of the model's entrance and exit areas. Any props that remain on the stage must also be clear of each model's path.

Another important factor when planning a runway layout is its close proximity to the dressing and backstage areas. Models must change clothes, do hair, and apply makeup quickly, and then return to the stage for another turn. Each model should have his or her own backstage space. Full-length mirrors should be near the stage entrance.

A staging area should be set up near the entrance to the stage where a starter will cue up models to enter the stage and runway.

For more important elements for staging a fashion show and laying out a runway, see pages 329–331.

Runway Layout Elements

I. **Stage/Runway**
   - **Elevation**—high enough from the floor so audience can see models
   - **Length**—extends into audience between 32 and 40 feet for close viewing of outfits
   - **Width**—usually four-feet wide to accommodate two models in passing
   - **Model Entrance & Exit**—separated to minimize confusion
   - **Set Design**—must complement clothes, make an impression, and be easy to assemble
   - **Backdrop**—must be well-engineered to work with lighting and special effects
   - **On Stage Props**—used to decorate stage and complement fashions
   - **Music**—Genre chosen should set the mood for the show; tunes played by DJ
   - **Commentator**—host or speaker who comments on and introduces outfits, models, and designers

II. **Backstage Areas**
   - **Dressing Area**—must be close to staging area and large for stylists and models
   - **Merchandise Storage/Clothing Racks**—keeps clothes clean, neat, and organized
   - **Hair and Makeup Stations**—for stylists to work on models' hair and makeup
   - **Mirrors**—numerous mirrors needed for every fashion show
   - **Tables & Chairs**—for models and stylists to rest, and hold props, accessories, etc.
   - **Individual Model Space**—assigned space for each model with outfits marked and lined up

III. **Audience**
   - **Seating Chart**—number of chairs needed and placement around stage
   - **Ushers & Service Personnel**—ushers to seat guests and beverage or food servers
   - **Press Area**—comfortable place for members of the media to view show and meet with designers afterward
   - **Audio Friendly**—speakers well placed so audience can hear; music should not drown out commentator
   - **VIP Area**—cordoned-off area and assigned seating for celebrities and VIPs

IV. **The Show**
   - **Choreography**—planned movements by models to best exhibit clothes and accessories
   - **Lighting**—whether high-tech or simple spotlight, must be precisely designed and planned in advance of show
   - **Special Effects**—artificial smoke, holograms, lasers, etc.

Basic Runway Floor Plan
Staging area and throughway to backstage

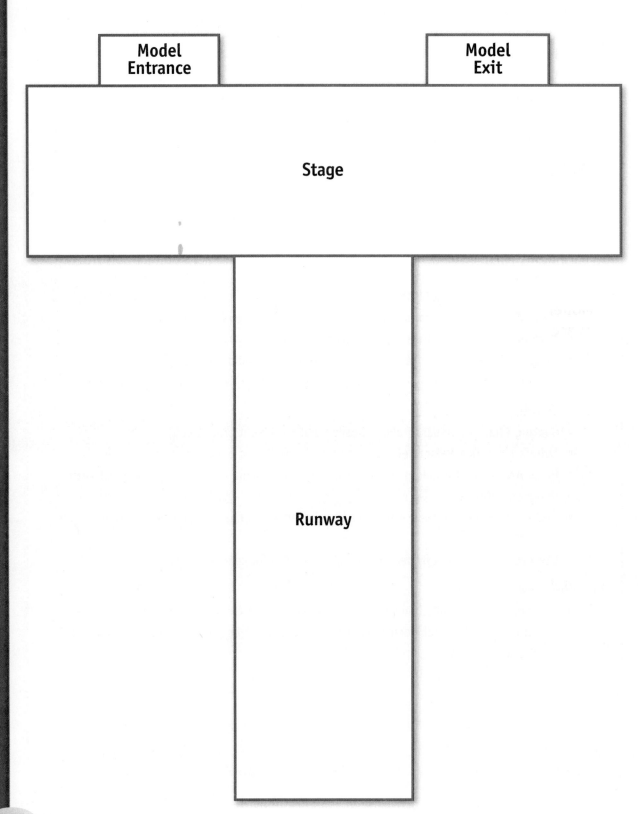

Backstage Area

Model
space

Model
space

Model
space

Clothes racks,
accessory tables, etc.

ENTRANCE TO STAGE AND RUNWAY AREA>

Model
space

Model
space

Hair and Makeup Station	Hair and Makeup Station	Hair and Makeup Station	Hair and Makeup Station	Hair and Makeup Station

Appendix 2

Fashion Show Staff

The number of people needed to develop, organize and put on a fashion show depends upon the size and scope of the show. Smaller shows need fewer models and fewer people to put those models together. Large-scale productions involve special effects, such as smoke and dramatic lighting, so more personnel are required.

When deciding upon the staff needed to put together a fashion show, think of *before*, *during*, and *after* the show. The *before* involves those who plan and organize the show. Personnel used *during* the show are the people working on and behind the stage as well as in the audience. *After* the show is over, people are needed to clean up, follow up, and return items used in the show.

See the list of *fashion show staff* on page 333 that breaks down various jobs needed to put on a fashion show and lists each staff member's duties. A *fashion show committee* breakdown is outlined below.

Fashion Show Committees

Merchandise:
Duties/jobs include selection and return of merchandise, pre-show fittings and alterations, dressing-room supervisor, dressers, lineup and cue managers, starters

Promotion:
Duties/jobs include publicity coordinator, advertising coordinator, photographer, invitations, ticket sales and distribution, editor of event program

Commentary:
Commentary writer, commentator, general announcer (if needed)

Models:
Model selection and training, model coordinator, choreographer, hair technician, makeup technician

Staging:
Set and runway design and construction, props manager, music director, musicians or recordings, backstage manager, sound technician, lighting technician, security, safety advisor, medic

Hospitality:
Site reservation, food/beverage coordinator, caterer, servers, room and table decorations, seating host and/or ushers, gifts and door prizes, insurance

---

Fashion Show Staff

1. **Planning a Fashion Show**
   - **Fashion show coordinator**—oversees all aspects and committees of show
   - **Budget preparers**—determine how much money will be needed in the various areas
   - **Location scouts**—find and secure the venue
   - **Production designers**—design the stage and seating areas
   - **Stage decorator(s)**—works with designers to decorate stage, choose backdrop, etc.
   - **Merchandise coordinators**—gather clothes and accessories to be shown at fashion show
   - **Caterer**—plans and prepares food and drinks to be served during the show
   - **Construction crew**—builds stage and runway; may assist with set up of venue
   - **Lighting crew**—designs and installs appropriate lighting equipment
   - **Publicist**—writes press releases and informs media about event
   - **Program editor**—designs, writes (or assigns writing), and has event programs printed
   - **Ticket/invitation coordinator**—designs invitations and/or sells tickets to the show
   - **Audio technician**—sets up public address system and assists with all aspects of sound

2. **During the Show**
   - **Models**—walk the runway wearing apparel and accessories featured in fashion show
   - **Dressers**—assist models with outfits and accessories
   - **Hair stylists**—style hair using latest trends and techniques
   - **Makeup artists**—apply makeup to models according to predetermined look
   - **Starters**—organize models right before they head onto runway and cue each start
   - **Commentator**—introduces and comments on outfits, models, and designers
   - **Transportation**—drivers used to transport merchandise, talent, and VIPs to and from the show
   - **Hosts/ushers**—greet guests, assist them to seats; available for general information
   - **Food and beverage servers**—serve food and drinks either at seats or at a centrally located bar and buffet station
   - **Special-effects operators**—operate lights, smoke machines, and any other special effects needed for the show
   - **DJ or band**—spins the tunes; a live band may be used instead of or in addition to a DJ
   - **Photographer**—shoots film and video of fashion show
   - **Security**—keeps onlookers away from models and staging areas, protects merchandise, secures audience, etc.

3. **Wrapping It Up**
   - **Striking Crew**—physically disassembles stage, set, and all equipment
   - **Accountant**—balances budget, pays bills, accounts for ticket sales, etc.

Appendix 2

Fashion Show Budget

Staying on budget is of utmost importance in a fashion show. Organizers develop a *fashion show budget* well in advance of the actual event. Because fashion shows vary in size and scope, budgets vary by categories, expenditure amounts, and personnel.

Fashion Show Budget
Title of show: _____
Designer (s): _____
Location: _____
Date: _____
Time: _____
Planned budget: $_____ Actual budget: $_____

	Budget (planned)	Actual
Revenues:		
Ticket sales (number sold x price)	_____	_____
Cooperative sponsorship money	_____	_____
Company promotion allocation	_____	_____
TOTAL REVENUES:	_____	_____
Expenditures:		
Physical Facility:		
Site rental	_____	_____
Stage backdrop and decorations	_____	_____
Props	_____	_____
Runway design and construction	_____	_____
Lighting design and installation	_____	_____
Chairs	_____	_____
Tables	_____	_____
Decorations, flowers, etc.	_____	_____

	Budget (planned)	Actual
Equipment and Technicians:		
Music		
PA system		
Photographer, videographer, and crew		
Hair stylist		
Makeup artist		
Publicity and Advertising:		
Press releases		
Photography		
Publicity distribution		
Advertisement production		
Media space and time		
Tickets and invitations		
Programs		
Show Personnel:		
Models		
Dressers		
Starters		
Commentator		
Transportation		
Hosts and ushers		
Merchandise:		
Damages, repairs, and losses		
Security		
Hospitality:		
Food and beverages		
Entertainment		
Gifts and prizes		
Gratuities		
VIP transportation and hotels		
Insurance		
Taxes		
Emergency reserve		
TOTAL EXPENDITURES:		

Glossary

accessories fashion items that are added to complete or enhance outfits (p. 94)

advertising a paid message that a business sends about its fashion products or ideas (p. 250)

apparel term used for clothing, as in personal attire or garments (p. 94)

aptitude a natural talent or ability for a particular skill (p. 290)

associate degree a college degree recognizing two years of coursework at a community college or trade school (p. 276)

bachelor's degree a college degree recognizing four or more years of undergraduate coursework at a college or university (p. 277)

balance of trade the relationship between a country's imports and exports (p. 56)

bar codes standardized symbols made up of dark vertical bars and white spaces that carry information such as vendor, style, size, and color (p. 233)

behavioristics statistics about consumers based on their knowledge, attitudes, use, or response to a product (p. 28)

better garments more reasonably priced garments that maintain high quality (p. 222)

boutique a type of specialty store that offers a more limited selection of merchandise and may focus on few-of-a-kind items (p. 204)

brand a name, design, or symbol (or combination of them) that identifies a business or organization and its products (p. 255)

bridge line a secondary line that is the most expensive category of ready-to-wear (p. 164)

budget lines the least expensive category of garments that are knockoffs or down-scaled duplications of designer styles, which are mass-marketed (p. 222)

business plan a proposal that describes a new business to potential investors and lenders (p. 303)

buying behavior the way consumers react to satisfying a need or want when making a purchase (p. 207)

buying center a central district in a city where fashion businesses sell products to retail buyers (p. 72)

channel of distribution the path a product takes from the producer to the consumer (p. 34)

collection a group of clothes designed and produced for a specific season (p. 138)

color a visual characteristic, representing hue and tone, that is one of the most important elements of fashion design (p. 139)

communication the process of giving and exchanging information, ideas, and feelings (p. 269)

computer-aided design (CAD) computer programs that perform many design functions to create fashion designs (p. 143)

computer-aided manufacturing (CAM) a system that automatically moves the garment parts through each phase of the cutting-and-sewing process (p. 148)

computer-integrated manufacturing (CIM) the production process that implements various technological systems: computer-aided design (CAD) and computer-aided manufacturing (CAM) (p. 229)

corporation a business that is chartered by a state and legally operates apart from the owner or owners (p. 51)

cost of product the cost of the merchandise from the manufacturer (p. 223)

couturiers professional fashion designers involved in designing, making, and selling high fashion (p. 68)

cover letter a brief one-page letter that introduces you to the employer, focuses on your skills, and explains why you are applying for the job (p. 296)

culture the system of shared beliefs, values, customs, behaviors, and artifacts attributed to members of a specific society (p. 80)

custom-made made specifically to the customer's measurements (p. 159)

dandyism during the 1800s, a style of dress for men and a lifestyle that celebrated elegance and refinement (p. 14)

demand the consumer's willingness and ability to buy and/or use products (p. 59)

demi-couture ready-to-wear designs produced by fashion houses but not mass-produced (p. 164)

demographics statistics that describe a population in terms of personal characteristics such as age, gender, income, ethnic background, education, religion, occupation, and lifestyle (p. 27)

denier a unit of measurement used to identify the thickness or diameter of a fiber (p. 125)

department store a retail operation that carries different kinds of merchandise and houses them in separate sections, or departments (p. 202)

design a particular or unique version of a style because of a specific arrangement of the basic design elements (p. 7)

design center a district in a city where fashion design and production firms are clustered together (p. 68)

designer store a designer-manufacturer retail operation that owns and operates the retail store and carries only its own lines (p. 204)

disco style of the 1970s, a fashion consisting of gold lamé, leopard print, stretch halter jumpsuits, and white clothing that glowed under ultraviolet lighting (p. 16)

discount store a retail operation that offers volume merchandise and limited service and sells goods below usual retail prices (p. 205)

display a presentation of merchandise to attract customers so they will examine it and buy it (p. 242)

entrepreneurship the process of starting and managing your own business (p. 301)

experimental method a research method whereby a researcher observes the results of changing one or more marketing variables while keeping other variables constant (p. 188)

exports goods that a country sends to a foreign source or goods that a country sells to other countries (p. 55)

extrusion a synthetic textile process in which solid raw materials are dissolved by chemicals or melted with heat to form a thick liquid that is extruded, or forced out, through the tiny holes of a device called a *spinneret* to create long fibers (p. 128)

fabrics long pieces of cloth (p. 114)

fad a fashion that is popular for a short period of time (p. 106)

fashion cycle the period of time or life span during which the fashion exists, moving through stages, from introduction through obsolescence (p. 101)

fashion leaders trendsetters, or individuals who are the first to wear new styles, after which the fashion is adopted by the public (p. 103)

fashion magazine a consumer magazine sold commercially, featuring articles, illustrations, and advertisements with an international emphasis (p. 183)

fashion merchandise goods that are popular at a particular time (p. 6)

fashion merchandising the planning, buying, and selling of fashion apparel and accessories to offer the right merchandise blend to meet consumer demand (p. 30)

fashion movement the ongoing motion of fashion moving through the fashion cycle (p. 103)

fashion promotion plan the detailed, written guide a business develops that states which promotional components will be used to reach specific goals in a designated period of time (p. 254)

fashion shows special events that are theatrical with live models presenting fashion apparel and accessories (p. 249)

fashion trend the direction of the movement of fashion that is accepted in the marketplace (p. 105)

fashion weeks periods of time during each year when fashion designers present new designs or collections (p. 68)

Glossary

Fédération Française de la Couture the French Fashion Federation, the organization that regulates the haute-couture industry (p. 158)

feminist movement of the 1970s, the organized effort to establish equal social, economic, and political rights and opportunities for women; influenced women's fashion with shorter hemlines and the pantsuit for the workplace (p. 16)

fibers thin, hairlike strands that are the basic units used to make fabrics and textile products (p. 114)

filament a very long, fine, continuous thread (p. 117)

finished fabric fabric that has gone through all the necessary finishing processes and is ready to be used in the manufacturing of garments (p. 128)

fixtures permanent or movable store furnishings that are used to hold or display merchandise (p. 246)

focus group a panel of six to ten consumers who discuss opinions about a topic under the guidance of a moderator (p. 188)

functions of marketing the activities that include product/service management, distribution, financing, pricing, marketing-information management, promotion, and selling (p. 35)

garment any article of wearing apparel, such as a dress, suit, coat, or sweater (p. 7)

geographics statistics about where people live (p. 28)

global sourcing the identifying and negotiating of supply chains in numerous world locations (p. 78)

globalization the increasing integration of the world economy (p. 55)

grading the technical process of increasing or decreasing the sizes of a pattern to correspond to a garment size (p. 147)

grunge a style started by the youth culture in the Pacific Northwest region of the United States in the early 1990s; it is messy, uncombed, and disheveled (p. 17)

hardlines lines of products that are non-textile, such as small and large appliances, home accessories, and items not made of fabric (p. 94)

haute couture French term for high fashion, which is expensive, trend-setting, custom-made apparel (p. 68)

hippie style of the 1960s, a fashion consisting of clothing from the Middle and Far East, bright colors, peasant embroidery, cheesecloth, and safari jackets (p. 16)

home furnishings the fashion product category that includes textiles used to furnish and decorate the home, such as towels, linens, and bedding (p. 96)

imports goods that come into a country from foreign sources or goods that a country buys from other countries (p. 55)

interest an activity or concept that is enjoyable (p. 290)

interest survey a questionnaire designed to identify interests through responses to carefully focused questions (p. 290)

internship a temporary paid or unpaid position giving students direct work experience and exposure to various aspects of a career (p. 279)

interpersonal skills skills involving the ability to identify and understand the personal traits of others, including values, ethics, and attitudes (p. 269)

inventory control the process used to track the buying and storing of products for sale as well as costs for ordering, shipping, handling, and storage (p. 234)

job interview a face-to-face meeting between a prospective employee and the person who makes hiring decisions for the company (p. 296)

job shadowing an activity in which a person follows a worker on the job to learn about the job and workplace (p. 280)

knits knitted fabrics made from only one set of yarns that runs in the same direction (p. 130)

leadership the process of motivating and guiding one or more individuals, a group, a business, or an organization to reach objectives (p. 270)

licensing a legal agreement that gives manufacturers the exclusive right to produce and promote fashion products that display the name of a designer (p. 256)

line a distinct elongated mark that directs the eye movement when viewing the garment (p. 140)

lines groups of styles and designs produced and sold as a set of related products for a given season (p. 94)

manufactured fibers fibers created by a manufacturing process of any substance that is not a fiber (p. 120)

market research the systematic gathering, recording, analyzing, and presentation of information related to marketing goods and services (p. 187)

market segmentation a way of analyzing a market by categorizing specific characteristics (p. 27)

market weeks the major times scheduled by fashion producers to show fashions to buyers (p. 72)

marketing the process of developing, promoting, and distributing products to satisfy customers' needs and wants (p. 26)

marketing concept the idea that businesses must satisfy customers' needs and wants in order to make a profit (p. 26)

marketing mix four basic marketing strategies, known as the four Ps of marketing—product, place, price, and promotion (p. 31)

marketing plan a written document that provides direction for the marketing activities of a company for a specific period of time (p. 305)

markup the difference between the cost of product and the retail price (p. 224)

mart a building that houses thousands of showrooms for a specific merchandise category (p. 73)

merchandise buying the process of purchasing merchandise for resale from manufacturers or vendors during buying trips (p. 202)

merchandise information system a system that produces, stores, and analyzes information that enables fashion marketers to make decisions about merchandise for sale (p. 191)

moderate lines medium-priced garments with well-known brand names, such as Levi Strauss, and private brands seen in department stores (p. 222)

natural fibers textile fibers made from plants or animals (p. 115)

networking the process of finding contacts among people you know, such as family, friends, employers, and professionals who know you (p. 295)

New Look a style of the 1940s and 1950s that featured long hemlines, narrow shoulders, and tightly fitted bodices, with long, full, or narrow skirts (p. 15)

nonpersonal selling the type of selling that does not involve interaction between people (p. 208)

observation method a research method that involves watching people and recording consumer behavior by cameras or individuals (p. 187)

operating expenses all costs associated with the actual business operations: cost of buildings or rents, salaries, and taxes (p. 223)

outlet a discount store that is owned by a manufacturer that sells its own merchandise in the store (p. 204)

partnership a business created through a legal agreement between two or more people who are jointly responsible for the success or failure of the business (p. 51)

Glossary

patternmaking the process of transforming the design into the appropriate pieces needed to produce an apparel item (p. 147)

personal selling the type of selling that involves direct interaction between sales associates and potential buyers by telephone or in person (p. 208)

prêt-à-porter French term for designer ready-to-wear clothing (p. 148)

primary market the industry segment that includes businesses that grow and produce the raw materials that become fashion apparel or accessories (p. 46)

principles of design the standards for creating good design that include proportion, balance, rhythm, emphasis, and harmony (p. 140)

product assortment the range of items or merchandise within categories that a company sells (p. 186)

product mix the total selection of goods and services that a company makes or sells (p. 185)

profit the money a business makes after all costs and expenses are paid (p. 60)

promotion any form of communication a business uses to inform, persuade, or remind people about its products or to enhance its image (p. 248)

promotional mix any combination of the four components of promotion: sales promotion, public relations and publicity, advertising, and personal selling (p. 248)

psychographics studies of consumers based on social and psychological characteristics, such as attitudes, interests, and opinions (p. 27)

public relations a promotional technique that uses any form of communication to create a positive image for the business (p. 249)

publicity any non-paid message that communicates information about a company's merchandise, services, and activities (p. 250)

punk fashion of the 1970s, a style featuring intentionally torn clothing worn by young people with limited income, such as students and the unemployed (p. 16)

rag trade the slang term meaning the garment industry (p. 180)

ready-to-wear (RTW) standard-sized garments made in advance and offered for sale to any purchaser (p. 164)

reference an individual who knows you and can provide information about your work skills and habits, responsibility level, leadership abilities, and character (p. 298)

résumé a document that provides a brief summary of personal information, skills, work experience, education, activities, and honors (p. 296)

retailing the selling of products to customers (p. 49)

risk the possibility that a loss can occur as the result of a business decision or activity (p. 52)

risk management a strategy to offset business risks (p. 52)

sales promotion a short-term incentive used to interest customers in buying products (p. 248)

secondary market the industry segment that includes businesses that transform raw materials into fashion in the merchandise production phase (p. 46)

selling price retail price, or the amount the consumer pays (p. 222)

silhouette the overall form, or outline, of a garment (p. 140)

sizing system a set of sizes based on common assumptions and methods of development (p. 149)

skill the ability to competently perform a specific task (p. 269)

softlines lines of products made from textiles that include apparel as well as household items made from textiles such as towels, table linens, and bedding (p. 94)

sole proprietorship a business owned and operated by one person (p. 49)

specialty store a retail operation that offers only one category or related categories of fashion merchandise (p. 203)

staple items basic merchandise items that customers purchase on a regular basis (p. 6)

steps of selling the basic selling process that includes seven steps: approach the customer, determine needs, present the product, overcome objections, close the sale, perform suggestion selling, and follow up (p. 208)

style a particular shape or type of apparel item identified by the distinct features that make it unique (p. 6)

supply the quantity of product offered for sale at all possible prices (p. 59)

survey method a research method that involves gathering information from people through surveys or questionnaires (p. 187)

target market the specific group of people that a business is trying to reach (p. 27)

team a group of people who work together to achieve a common goal (p. 269)

tertiary market the industry segment that includes retail businesses such as stores (p. 46)

texture a characteristic of the surface of a material in terms of how it feels and looks (p. 140)

trade association a nonprofit organization that provides services to specific groups who develop, make, and sell products within an industry (p. 181)

trade publication a magazine, newspaper, book, or journal offering a variety of information to a certain industry or a segment of an industry (p. 182)

trade quotas restrictions on the quantity of a particular good or service that a country is allowed to sell or trade (p. 60)

trait a distinguishing feature or characteristic of a personality (p. 268)

trickle-across theory a hypothesis stating that fashion acceptance begins among several socioeconomic classes at the same time (p. 106)

trickle-down theory a hypothesis that states the movement of fashion starts at the top with consumers of higher socio-economic status and moves down to the general public (p. 105)

trickle-up theory a hypothesis that states the movement of fashion starts with consumers on lower-income levels and then moves to consumers with higher incomes (p. 105)

vendeuse the haute-couture sales associate who works with a customer and is paid by commission on the clothes that customers purchase (p. 160)

visual merchandising the integrated look of an entire store (p. 242)

weaves woven fabrics that are composed of two sets of yarns with one set running the length and the other set running crosswise (p. 129)

wholesale the price that retail buyers pay for goods they purchase from manufacturers (p. 147)

yarns uninterrupted threads of textile fibers that are ready to be turned into fabrics (p. 114)

Index

Index

G

Index

Index

Retail segment, in soft-goods chain, 34
Retail Week, 183
Revlon, Inc., 249
Rhythm, as design principle, 142
Ricci, Nina, 163
Rise stage, of fashion cycle, 102
Risks
    business, 50, 52–54
    of entrepreneurship, 301
    of global sourcing, 78
    management of, 52
Rite Aid drugstores, 279
Rodriguez, Narciso, 161
Rome, Italy, 69
Rubber, 125
Russia, 210

S

Saatchi & Saatchi Advertising, 102
Sadsad, Cherylin, 141
Safety, clothing for, 11
Sales
    analysis of, 144, 146
    company division of, 146
    of haute couture, 160
    as marketing function, 37
    math and, 214
    to other salespeople, 226
    personal selling in, 33, 208
    selling steps in, 208–214
    training in, 202
Sales promotion, 32–33, 248–249
Samples, 143, 147
Satin weave, 130
Saturday Night Fever, 16
Scale, as design principle, 141–142
Scanning features, in CAD systems, 144
Schiaparelli, Elsa, 167
Schwartz, Stephen, 253
Seams, in clothing, 7
Search engines, 249
Sears, Inc., 146
Seasonal colors, 140
Secondary market, 46–49
Segmentation, market, 26–27, 189–191
Seibu Department Store (Japan), 202
Self-assessment, in job search, 303
Self-discipline, as personal trait, 268
Self-employed designers, 138
Selfridges (London), 223
Selling. *See* Sales
Selling floor, 208
Selling price, 222
Services, fashion, 35, 180
Seventeen magazine, 183, 208

Sewing garments, 148
Sewing machine, 165
Shape (silhouette), 7
Shareholders, of corporations, 51
Shoplifting, 52
Shortages, 59
Silhouette, 7, 14–15, 140
Silk, 28, 67, 117–118, 139
Simmons, Russell, 146
Singer, Isaac, 165
Situation analysis, in marketing plan, 305
Size classifications, 149–150
Sketch pads with electronic pens, in CAD systems, 143–144, 231
Small Business Administration (SBA), 301, 306, 311
Smart tags, 233
Smith, Brian, 8
Social needs, for clothing, 12
Soetaert, Susan, 302
Soft-goods chain, 34
Softlines, as style groups, 94
Software systems, 10
Sole proprietorships, 49–50, 52
Sole Technologies, Inc. (STI), 230
Sonneberg, Mark, 253
South Africa, 98
Spade, Kate, 137, 145
Spam, 208, 249
Spandex, 125
Speaking skills, 269
Special offer sales, 212
Specialty media, 253
Specialty stores, 203
Speculative risks, 53
Spinnerets (production), 128
Sportswear International, 183
St. Laurent, Yves, 68, 163
St. Petersburg, Russia, 210
Staple items, 6
Stetson hats, 18
Stocks, of corporations, 51
Stoned Cherrie clothing, 98
Storage, in information system, 37
Stores. *See* Promotion; Visual merchandising; *and specifically named stores*
STORES magazine, 183
Straight silhouette, 7
Strategic Mindshare, Inc., 262
"Street cred," 88, 293
Stuff by Hilary Duff, Inc., 45, 59
Style, 6, 16, 18, 81, 105
Style Network, 241, 253
Suede, 119
Suggestion selling, 212
Sunglasses, 95
Sun Tech line, Nike, Inc., 88

Supply and demand, 59–60
Support industries, 49
Surf Zone brand, 172
Surplus, 59
Surplus, trade, 56
Survey research, 187
Sweatshop conditions, 60
Switzerland, 292
SWOT analysis (strengths, weaknesses, opportunities, threats), 305
Symmetrical balance, 142
Synthetic textiles, 120–127
    acetate, 121
    acrylic, 122
    leather blended with, 119
    lyocell, 126
    microfibers, 125–126
    nylon, 121–122
    polyester, 123–124
    production of, 128
    rayon, 120
    spandex, 125

T

T. J. Maxx, 221, 227
Tailoring, digital, 33
Target marketing, 26–29, 189, 204
Target Stores, Inc., 179, 191, 205, 222, 234
Tattoos, 81
Taxes, 50–51
Teambuilding skills, 269
Technology, 229–235
    careers and, 269
    communications, 229
    design and, 230–231
    education in, 275
    manufacturing and, 232
    retailers and, 232–234
    textiles and, 229–230
    trade shows and, 232
Tech Notes
    body scanning, 33
    futuristic fabrics, 115
    multimedia, 276
    online auctions, 160
    patternmaking software, 148
    smart tags, 233
    tech-cessories, 97
    trend spotting, 192
    virtual dressing room, 202
Teen Glamour magazine, 183
"Teentailers," 174
Teen Vogue magazine, 183
Television, 69, 82, 207, 253
Tencel fabric, 126
Tertiary market, 46, 49
Texas, 72, 75–76

Credits